Kultura Essays

KULTURA ESSAYS

Leopold Tyrmand, Editor

THE FREE PRESS, NEW YORK

in cooperation with

THE STATE UNIVERSITY OF NEW YORK AT ALBANY

COLLIER-MACMILLAN LIMITED, LONDON

The Free Press
A Division of The Macmillan Company
866 Third Avenue, New York 10022

Collier-Macmillan Canada Ltd., Toronto, Ontario

Library of Congress Catalog Card Number: 70–99732

printing number
1 2 3 4 5 6 7 8 9 10

Contents

Foreword

Iₙ winter, 1968, I watched as Leopold Tyrmand began what seemed at that time the Herculean task of extracting a sample of articles from twenty-two years of *Kultura*. The result of his efforts, gathered in the two companion anthologies, *Kultura Essays* and *Explorations in Freedom: Prose, Narrative, and Poetry from Kultura*, testify to the journal's scope and vitality. *Kultura's raison d'être* is made explicit in several places, but the simple answer I came to give my colleagues who asked "What is *Kultura?*"—that it was "a Polish émigré journal"—is neither sufficient nor, indeed, correct.

The phenomenon that is *Kultura* must be viewed in some larger context to grasp fully the implications of these volumes that reflect its quarter-century of growth. As a sociologist, I find it useful to consider *Kultura* as a *social movement*. I am convinced that, looked at under this rubric, those characteristics that make it much more than just another "émigré journal" come sharply into focus. Further, delineating *Kultura* in this sense may make some contribution to an understanding of modern social movements in general.

Cameron, in *Modern Social Movements*,[1] presents a short, useful definition which I shall adopt here.

> A social movement occurs when a fairly large number of people band together in order to alter or supplant some portion of the existing culture or social order.[2]

Cameron is quick to point out ambiguities in several of the terms he uses, but stresses that the main characteristic of a

1 Cameron, William Bruce, *Modern Social Movements: A Sociological Outline*, Random House, New York, 1966.
2 Cameron, p. 7.

social movement is its emphasis on changing the culture or the social structure, or redistributing power within a society. Certainly it is to this end that *Kultura* came into being and continues to exist.

This is not to say that *Kultura* serves no other purpose. For the Eastern European specialist, the journal may be no more than a source of otherwise unavailable data; for the student of contemporary Polish literature, only a good resource; but many human institutions and associations have more than one function. To examine *Kultura* as a social movement I shall take a brief look at its *origins* and stated *purpose*, consider some of the characteristics of its *"leader"* and its *"followers,"* and attempt a description of its *structure* and *mode of action*. I shall not attempt to assess its significance. That task exceeds the scope of this paper, and must lie with others who are better qualified.

Emigré journals and papers have played an important part in helping displaced nationals (of whom the world has known many in the past century) to adjust to new life styles. Few have persisted for any length of time. Many have been "reactionary," in the sense that they were oriented to a restoration of old regimes, and others have frankly served as a medium for introducing readers to a new culture. Few have had clearly stated the long-range goal of altering the existing culture— with some notable exceptions.[3]

Kultura began with a man and an idea: The man was Jerzy Giedroyć, a Polish publisher and editor, and the idea was a revisionist approach to the problems of eastern Europe. Serving with the Polish Army in the Near East and Africa, he found himself, after Yalta, a man without a country—at least, without a country to which he could willingly return. He begins his "Manifesto" with the words:

La revue *Kultura* a été fondée en 1947, c'est-à-dire l'anné ou l'on faisait table rasé des derrières traces laissées par les accords de Yalta . . .[4]

3 For example, *The Bell*, a Russian émigré paper, edited by Hertzen and Ogarev. It lasted for ten years, and was designed to bring about social and political changes in eastern Europe. See Edward Carr's *The Romantic Exiles*, Beacon Press, Boston, 1961, for a good account of exiles in mid-nineteenth-century Europe.

4 The "Manifesto" is a long statement of *Kultura*'s rationale, circulated by Giedroyć after the Hungarian Revolt in 1956. For a formal analysis of *Kultura*, see Mieroszewski's article (in this volume) "The Political Thought of Kultura."

and goes on to argue that it is not sufficient that exiles only stand and wait; they must, he insists, make their presence and their positions known. Their positions must begin by a realistic appraisal of what exists and a clear analysis of the factors needed to bring about change. He maintained that the most potent force for change in Eastern Europe was *l'intelligentsia*, and from this group he sought both his writers and his audience.

Beginning in Rome, but moving soon to Paris, he established the *Institut Littéraire* (a publishing house) and the journal *Kultura*. In this venture he was joined by a few collaborators: Zofia and Zygmunt Hertz, and later by Juliusz Mieroszewski, Józef Czapski, Gustaw Herling-Grudziński, and by his younger brother Henryk Giedroyć. All of them served with Polish forces in the Near East and Africa. These composed *Kultura*'s "inner circle."

Giedroyć was a man obsessed with a feeling of "mission." Penniless, in exile, at a time when war had shattered the Europe he knew, he held to a faith that through *Kultura* Poland—and the world—could be saved.[5] Giedroyć had a love of independence from reliance on others (which is beautifully illustrated in *Kultura*'s independent and individualistic stance). He believed *Kultura* could succeed only if it were supported entirely by its readers. The first issues appeared thanks to loans accorded to him and repaid scrupulously (and through subsidies provided by old friends). The first issue ran to 1,000 copies and was mailed all over the world as a sample. With time the number of subscribers grew and permitted the regular publication of the review. Its circulation continued to grow every year.

Giedroyć rapidly developed a structure composed of "contributing editors" around the world: mostly Polish exiles who both contributed and solicited articles. He persuaded a number of "stars" to write for *Kultura*, drawing on many of the best minds in Europe. Believing that *Kultura* should create opinions and shake up existing views, he enlisted a variety of talents, literary, political, economic, and philosophical, and offered a spectrum of ideas—all, however, subject to his personal editorial rule.

A second circle of *Kultura* supporters thus grew: both

5 I am indebted to my colleague, Alicja Iwańska, and to other American contributors to *Kultura* for sharing their personal knowledge of Giedroyć and the "Inner Circle." The interpretation is mine. Compare with Tyrmand's "Preface" in this volume.

writers and faithful readers, mostly Polish, many living in
Poland, but other eastern European exiles in both Europe and
America were included.

Many of this group are frequent visitors to Maison Laffitte,
the house outside of Paris where *Kultura* is put together.
Here, the editor, his staff, and visitors gather around the
table and talk. Ideas are exchanged, argued, fought; and
routine business transacted. A constant stream of letters and
articles pours in from all corners of the world. Giedroyć reads
all, and sends out long letters to each correspondent. These
are the "believers" who support *Kultura* through their faith
and works.

The outermost circle is made up of *Kultura*'s readers: an
uncountable aggregate. Some of their characteristics can be
inferred from the nature of the journal itself: they can read
Polish, they have some special interest in or relationship with
the disciplines represented in *Kultura*'s articles, many are in
the academic world, some are Eastern European specialists in
universities or in government posts, some are language students, and others are perhaps reading *Kultura* as an assignment from their superiors. It is rumored, repeatedly, that
Kultura is required reading for certain levels of government
officials throughout Eastern Europe. Some support for this
comes from the official and public condemnation of *Kultura*
in Poland, where the government has denounced it as an
"opposition" journal!

Many young writers are represented in current issues, and
one suspects younger readers are being attracted for whom
the historical context out of which *Kultura* developed represents ancient times. This receptive attitude promotes, without
overt proselytizing, a source of continuing commitment to
Kultura's goals, and helps to prevent the isolation of an aging
group of early supporters.

From time to time an article in *Kultura* will explicitly re-
state its objectives, and thus its rationale is kept in constant
view. Also, as its influence is reaffirmed by other articles, both
in *Kultura* itself, or through references in other media, the
appeal and legitimacy of *Kultura* is reinforced. *Kultura* is
in every sense an ideological journal which, one might claim,
has come to be both the carrier for and the symbol of the
belief-systems of its readers.

The listing of *Kultura*'s editorial staff and its contributing
editors on its masthead makes at least the "inner" and part
of the "second circle" highly visible. This suggests, as

Cameron notes,[6] that public opinion exerts more control over it, as a social movement, than would be the case if it were less visible. Its healthy economic status tends to support this inference.

None of this implies that *Kultura* is a democratically organized institution in the conventional sense. It does not have voting members, or a formal set of by-laws, but its position is clear, without being rigid, and the charismatic quality of its leadership is so balanced by the rationality and consistency with which it deals with world problems that *Kultura* appears to be a truly "open-ended" movement, ever ready to adapt itself to changing conditions. And, in a way, this is a reflection of Giedroyć, the man who prefers "to remain in the shadows," to work through others, who strives to avoid becoming an "organization," but whose presence speaks on every page.[7]

Perhaps *Kultura*'s chief strength as a movement comes from its choice of nonviolent means to achieve its end: change. For intellectuals, whether truly so or self-defined, appeals based on reason still are cherished. *Kultura*'s long and open opposition to the use of force or violence is well documented. *Kultura*'s major premise, that change must be first affected in the minds of men, is testified to in its own pages.

All of these things that I have touched upon reinforce my own feeling that *Kultura* is indeed a social movement of some importance. Recent events in Eastern Europe (even tragic events) can be seen as supportive of *Kultura*'s position. Whether the association is coincidental doesn't really matter.

Because *Kultura* makes no claim for its unique role, and has no pretensions to organize itself more formally as an instrument to *control* power, but is content to let the power of ideas bring about change in a variety of ways, it may be the most effective social mechanism for promoting a *rapprochement* of East and West that we have yet tried. After twenty-two healthy years, it would appear that the ultimate measure of its success might be its disappearance as a distinct voice calling for "revision" of world policies. Paradoxically, one might wish it a speedy success, while at the same time foreseeing another quarter-century of vitality.

Paul F. Wheeler
Professor and Associate Dean, College of Arts and Sciences
The State University of New York at Albany

6 Cameron, p. 83.
7 See Note 5.

Preface

The companion anthologies, *Kultura Essays* and *Explorations in Freedom: Prose, Narrative, and Poetry from Kultura*, are the result of a cooperative effort which has been put forth by the State University of New York at Albany (SUNYA) and The Free Press. Early in 1967, SUNYA's College of Arts and Sciences began to take a special interest in the activity of the *Institut Littéraire*—a Polish émigré institute in Paris. For the past two decades, the *Institut Littéraire* has been publishing books by noteworthy authors. Its reputation, however, rests above all upon its monthly review *Kultura*, whose impact upon the Polish intelligentsia, at home and abroad, has been both striking and unique. It represents a rare case of political and cultural opposition originating in exile but influencing the ideological scene in the home country. Moreover, during the past ten years, the *Institut Littéraire* has expanded its range and, by defying the means of suppression at the disposal of a modern police state, has become a challenging outlet for all those from behind the Iron Curtain who either fled their countries, or remained there but found it impossible to publish except under a pseudonym and in the West, thereby pursuing the heroic path of clandestin opposition. The *Institut Littéraire* gained worldwide recognition by publishing some Russian manuscripts rescued from the hands of censors and the secret police, although their authors, above all Andrey Sinyavsky and Yuri Daniel, did not escape, unfortunately, the most cruel punishment meted out to those who want to be free in the Soviet Union.

The reader of these anthologies certainly will discover why

Russians, Ukrainians, Hungarians, and others have chosen the modest Polish émigré publishing house as the means of channeling to the free world their flaming protests and superb artistry.

Recognizing *Kultura*'s literary merits and its unusual position in the contemporary ideological struggle, the Dean of SUNYA's College, Dr. O. William Perlmutter, together with the Chairman of its Sociology Department, Prof. Paul F. Wheeler, and the Professor of Sociology and Anthropology, Dr. Alicja Iwańska, joined forces with The Free Press in a decision to publish two selections of writings from *Kultura* in English.

As editor, my principal task was to choose appropriate texts. My general approach was based on three premises:

• Eastern Europe, including Russia, today presents a boiling kettle of ideas. The shapelessness and immediacy of many of them, and their dialectical complexity, often molded on the spur of the moment by political situations, appear confusing to Western observers. From the lack of understanding and the routine superficiality of press reports, biased and fallacious conclusions are drawn. I have tried to permit the most competent, involved, and committed spokesmen to comment on ideas and facts which are so frequently misinterpreted. My hope remains that these anthologies, as conceived and completed, will clarify and create a truer image of issues and events in an area which, incontestably, bears a good deal of responsibility for mankind's future.

• *Kultura* is distinguished by a significant trait of ecumenism. It is difficult to subordinate narrow, national priorities to more general ends within a geographical heritage where ethnic diversities and animosities have made history. Yet, in keeping with the tradition of Polish universalism, *Kultura* has attempted to overcome the hardships of Eastern European particularism and build an awareness of a common destiny and vital interests. Its fundamental political postulate is a commonwealth of nations that have entered the road to socialism but must free themselves from the oppressive totalitarianism of the present Communist state. I consider it especially important to convey this.

• Finally, these anthologies should produce testimony of the Polish and Eastern European involvement in the crucial problems of our epoch. They should determine the notion of totalitarian communism and its trend toward the ruthless extinction of human and humanistic values, not only as an endemic Eastern European issue, but as a universal condition of our time. The literary part of the anthology should also reflect the artistic skills of several writers whose spirit of innovation is jeopardized both by their situation as exiles without a vast audience and by the language barrier.

It remains for readers, students, and critics to judge whether these aims have been satisfied. None could have been achieved, however, without help from the twenty-three competent translators, to whom I hereby extend my thanks for their efforts.

As the result of the preparatory work in Albany, SUNYA's library is now in possession of a collection of the *Institut Littéraire* publications, including a complete set of *Kultura*. Some of its early issues are presently collector's items. In the future, they may be able to reveal to scholars and researchers many aspects of our time that are commonly overlooked by contemporaries.

But the greatest credit has to be given to the person to whom *Kultura* owes its very existence. Undeniably, *Kultura*'s strength derives from the coalescence of gifted intellects and pens. Yet, despite its abundance of heterogeneous elements, it is essentially a one-man enterprise—the fruit of his individual talent, perseverance, intransigence, and untiring labor. That man is Jerzy Giedroyć.

Giedroyć was born in 1906 in Poland into an old family of mixed Polish-Russian-Lithuanian descent. He was educated in Moscow and Warsaw, and studied law and history at Warsaw University. He worked first with the official Polish news agency, and then in the ministries of agriculture, industry, and commerce. In 1929 he started publishing a biweekly, which later became a weekly, which under the title of *Polityka* succeeded in gathering together a number of outstanding young writers and intellectuals and aroused much interest in Warsaw at that time. That circle cradled many figures still influencing Polish political and intellectual life.

With the outbreak of World War II, Giedroyć worked in the Polish Embassy in Bucharest, then enlisted as a private and took part in 1941 in the battle of Tobruk during the Libyan campaign. Later he was transferred to the press bureau of the Polish Corps in Africa, then to the Ministry of Information in London.

After the war, when Communist rule over Eastern Europe became a grim reality, Jerzy Giedroyć decided to continue fighting on the ideological and political levels. He organized a publishing enterprise in Rome, and then transferred it to Paris, where he established the *Institut Littéraire*. In 1947 he began the publication of *Kultura* with the help of his brother Henryk Giedroyć and Zofia and Zygmunt Hertz, who have remained his most faithful collaborators over the past twenty years. In 1968, the prestigious French academic lexicon, *Dictionnaire des Littératures*, wrote in its *Kultura* entry:

> Kultura (Culture).—Revue mensuelle polonaise paraissant depuis 1947 à Paris. Elle groupe les écrivains émigrés qui suivent avec objectivité les transformations opérées en Pologne et publie dans une collection spéciale les œuvres marquantes des écrivains émigrés. A l'heure actuelle elle est une des meilleures revues européennes.

I hope that the pages of this anthology will serve as adequate evidence of Jerzy Giedroyć's intellectual and ideological pilgrimage and quest.

Leopold Tyrmand

POSTSCRIPT: Zbigniew A. Jordan's article, *Marxist Revisionism: Its Background, Sources, and Main Tendencies* (see p. 102), incorporates parts of its author's various contributions to *Kultura*. It appeared first in a German translation under the title, "Marxistischer Revisionismus in Polen: Hintergrund, Wurzeln und Hauptströmungen," in *Marxismusstudien*, Fünfte Fogle, pp. 85–129, published by J. C. B. Mohr (Paul Siebeck), Tübingen, 1968, whose permission to use the original English text is gratefully acknowledged.

ON READING THUCYDIDES

Paweł Hostowiec

> The great theater of the world has a small
> personnel. In historical costumes, with the
> language of various epochs in their mouths, the
> same figures keep appearing, playing in a few
> eternal conflicts.
>
> Ernst Jünger

HISTORIANS AND MEMORIALISTS

A S EARLY AS the Renaissance, historians came to be divided
into scholars and into memorialists who themselves took part in
events and described a section of history known to them, or who
dealt in reflections on historical themes.

For readers, the memorialists have always had a certain ascendancy over the scholars. The works of Thucydides, Julius Caesar,
Tacitus, Machiavelli, and Bolingbroke, copied and printed by
innumerable scribes and typographers, have been read over the
centuries with unflagging interest. The works of learned historians—
presenting the same events in a more universal and systematic
manner—do not enjoy the same success. They are usually read until
the bibliography at the end of the book is out-dated. Few appear
in more than one edition.

The reason for the preference for memorialists is not entirely
clear. Those who take part in events often have the advantage over
scholars, in that they possess the authority of historical figures—
celebrated monarchs, or warriors. This fact may have some significance as far as Caesar's military notes, the Testament of Charles V,
or *La Memorial de Ste.-Hélène* are concerned, but it does nothing to
explain the fame of Thucydides, Machiavelli, and Bolingbroke, the
most eminent writers of this group. Thucydides was a little-known

Athenian admiral, deprived of his rank and sentenced to exile, as a result of military failures, by a people's court. Machiavelli was a Florentine diplomat in retirement, while Bolingbroke was an English minister accused of high treason and removed in disgrace from political life. Their rank as historical figures is modest, and in no way explains their celebrity among readers.

It is also doubtful whether narratives by individuals who took part in the events described arouse more confidence in readers than do the works of scholars. The great fabrics of events do not fit into the recollections of an eye-witness. Moreover, there is an almost total want in Thucydides, Machiavelli, and Bolingbroke of what might be called "an eye-witness narrative." Personal experience finds a different kind of expression in their works.

The ascendancy of the memorialists seems to have its source in the structure of the fabric of their narratives.

A historian has before him a stream of accomplished facts, rigid and irreversible. His interests, methods, and vision of the past may vary, the nature of his documentation may be different—but the subject matter remains the same. Observing accomplished facts from a certain distance, in the past, a historian sees them arranged, as it were, in one direction and illuminated from one side.

The subject-matter of history, as narrated by those who took part in the events, has a different structure. These writers saw each of the historical facts they describe as it approached, occurred, and moved into the past. They saw them at the same time in conditional shape, before decisions and the executive capacities of their contemporaries gave them the form of irreversible and accomplished facts, later investigated by historians. Approaching facts that came into being appeared to them dependent upon a decision, upon the choice of a direction: Constantinople to the left, Rome to the left.

The variety of experience suggests that memorialists and historians connect facts differently. The memorialist writes down the protocol of experiment, the result of which did not entirely correspond to what was foreseen. The way in which he connects facts, the motives of individuals, and collective activity come into the foreground and are an important component part of the phenomena in his field of vision. For a historian, standing in the face of past, irreversibly accomplished events, the motives of activity lie on another level, and are rather the literary element of his narrative. Historical figures and collectives have been preserved for him in this or that manner, obviously incapable of being preserved otherwise; other possible decisions or methods of proceeding do not enter into his field of perception.

So a historian presents the past in its unrepeatable aspects, while the memorialist directs his attention to the motives of action primarily, and to the capacity for forseeing its results. Whenever we seek the correct statement of past facts, we turn to the world of learned historians. When we wish to know the mechanism of collective phenomena, when we seek material in the past for comparisons which can illuminate the phenomena of today—then we turn to the memorialists.

THE PELOPONNESIAN WAR

Thucydides is not read in schools today, and a knowledge of his works does not enter into what is called the field of general education. So we should mention that he wrote a history of the Peloponnesian war (431–404 B.C.). This war brought to an end the wealth and political significance of ancient Greece, later taken over by the Macedonians and Romans. Thucydides, as an Athenian citizen, at once evaluated the importance of the coming events, and immediately after the outbreak of the war, began recording its history. Condemned to exile in the eighth year of the war by an Athenian people's court, he spent twenty years in exile, writing the history of the war as it proceeded. After the final defeat of Athens, a general amnesty allowed him to return to his native city, where he soon afterward died or was murdered. His unfinished history covers the first 21 years of the war. Its most striking feature is Thucydides' aim to be impartial. In speeches put into the mouths of politicians and diplomats, Thucydides recapitulates the arguments of all sides.

In the very first chapters of Thucydides, we see a picture well known to us from later experience of the growing antagonism of two powerful states—today we would call them "powers"—each of which is surrounded by weaker allies and satellites. This antagonism develops on several parallel levels. On the tribal level (which today we would call "national"), the Ionian tribes are grouped around Athens, and the Doric around Sparta. On the political, or more precisely, the "ideological" level, Athens has a democratic system, and supports democracy throughout its sphere of influence. Sparta, on the other hand, is ruled by a numerically smaller level of "oligarchies," and supports governments of this type within the boundaries of its influence.

In addition, both states shared the goal of hegemony over the Greek world by the divergent development of technical and military means. Athens possessed a more powerful fleet, Sparta the more powerful land forces. The city and port of Athens are an impregnable fortress surrounded by "long walls," but the land forces of Athens do not suffice for the defence of the area surrounding the capital, which is laid waste annually at harvest time by the armies of Lacedaemonia, moving at will all over the country. But the Athenians rule the sea; they can land unexpectedly on their enemy's coastline, fortify the more easily defended points there, disturb him, and carry on an ideological war on his own territory. Almost all the islands belonging to the Spartan bloc fall into the hands of Athens sooner or later. However, Sparta and Athens cannot try for a fall with each other, nor can they wage a battle that will decide the war's outcome. To the very end, no one knows whether the possession of a stronger fleet or stronger land forces will lead to victory. Each defeat makes doubtful the value of a general strategic concept, each mistake or miscalculation mounts to the dimensions of high treason. The unfortunate commanders are sentenced to exile, or have to flee, from the people's wrath, to the enemy. Several times victory seems out of reach to both sides, and the supporters of co-existence gain the upper hand. Peace is signed, but a feeling of mutual threat persists, preparations for war continue, and the fighting soon begins again.

When the war breaks out, Greece is free of tyrants. All of her towns have a more or less democratic system. Decisions are reached by all free persons, or else by the ruling oligarchs. The Peloponnesian war has a democratic character, draws everyone into the whirlpool of events, places common responsibility, and deludes with the hope of victory and fear of defeat; no one is allowed to remain far from events. Hence its ruthless and uncompromising character.

In a few once famous books, the Italian historian Guglielmo Ferrero explained why modern popular wars, beginning with the French Revolution, have a ruthless and destructive nature, such as wars waged by absolute monarchs did not have. Ferrero's speculations often come to mind during a reading of Thucydides.

THE FATE OF ALLIES AND SATELLITES

Unable to measure themselves against their main opponents, the Athenians and Spartans waged war for a long time at the cost of their allies.

The role of a weaker ally is never enviable. In old treatises on the art of war, we find it laid down that if you are facing two allied opponents, the weaker must be attacked first, for the stronger can always find many reasons for not going to his aid. Machiavelli generally advises against an alliance with a stronger partner, for no matter what the outcome of the war, the weaker will always come off worst. In the case of defeat, the stronger partner will try to make peace at the cost of his weaker ally; in the case of victory, the latter will find himself alone with the victor, without any chance of maneuvering, and at his mercy. Ancient authors seem to owe this truth to reading Thucydides. Since Greek times, men have pondered what is to be gained by allying oneself with a stronger partner. We cannot refrain from wondering why such industrious readers of Machiavelli as Mussolini—and many others—did not observe lessons for themselves in the Florentine master.

Athens and Sparta waged war against the allies of their opponents in various ways: by force and terror, by destroying towns, and by murdering and enslaving their inhabitants, but also by ideological warfare. Even earlier, the Athenians who had brought from Delos a federal treasure enforced by taxation, or rather the contributions of their allies, began behaving unceremoniously toward the latter, not asking their views regarding the spending the common funds, nor in matters of general policy. The Spartans therefore adopt opposite tactics; they summon their allies to a council, at which war is voted by a majority. Henceforward they will wage war for the liberation of the Greek republics from the Athenian yoke. These tactics bring great success. On their side, the Athenians try to enflame a revolt of the Helots in Sparta, and with this purpose in mind, they occupy several points on the coast of Sparta. The Spartans respond to this by summoning part of the Helots to the army, and promising freedom to the defenders of the Fatherland. Later, the Romans followed this example, arming slaves and promising them their freedom during Hannibal's invasion. These undertakings give a measure of the social changes which popular wars bring with them. Like some monstrous factory, the Peloponnesian war was grinding on one side the thousand former republican elites, changing them into slaves, while on the other, it brought freedom to those who previously had not been able to acquire it by their own power.

Already in the year preceding the war, every manifestation of inner life in the smaller republics had been considered in Athens and Sparta from the point of view of their usefulness for the hegemonic plans of these states, which were ready for armed intervention in the event of a supposed infringement of the existing balance of power. General war began from one such intervention on the distant coast of present-day Albania. Corinth and Corcyra, republics belonging to the Doric group, were struggling there for influence in the town of Epidamnos. Corcyra was victorious in an armed conflict, after which Corinth began preparing for revenge. Alarmed by these preparations, the people of Corinth applied to Athens for aid. After hearing the envoys of Corcyra and Corinth, and having discussed the matter at two popular gatherings of the people, the Athenians decided to enter into an alliance with

Corcyra, and render her limited aid with the purpose of extending the conflict. Among the states belonging to the Lacedaemonian bloc, Corinth and Corcyra possessed the largest fleets, and the neutralizing of these two fleets in an extended conflict seemed useful to the Athenians.

In this first, still local, armed clash, a detail appears which is repeated henceforward until the end of the war: After winning a victory over the Corinthian fleet, the people of Corcyra murdered all the prisoners, apart from Corinthian citizens, whom they fettered in chains.

We should be very wrong to dismiss this detail as a manifestation of barbarity typical of the ancient world. The massacres of prisoners and citizens of captured towns were not an uncontrolled reaction, but most often a carefully thought-out undertaking, the result of Greek rationalism, which penetrated in the times of Pericles into the field of politics and strategy. In the *Discorso* of Machiavelli, an unparalleled guide to the somber abyss of rationalized balance of power, we find a short chapter on the most effective means for making peace impossible. To deprive a people or a prince of the desire to seek a compromise (writes the Florentine) there is no more certain method than that of offending the opposite side by some terrible cruelty or other. The master next quotes a few examples, explaining what motives can direct people taking recourse in such methods. One is especially instructive. Two Roman colonies— Velitrae and Circoei—rebelled, counting on the support of other peoples of Latium, but the defeat of the latter put an end to their plans. Some of the citizens decided to send envoys to Rome for peace talks. However, the leaders of the revolt, fearing that all the guilt would be placed on them and that they would not escape terrible punishment, decided to render the talks invalid by some act of cruelty in Roman territory.

The rivalry between Athens and Sparta maintained a state of latent or open civil war in the smaller republics. In each of them, representatives of democracy opposed one another, counting on the help of Athens, while the oligarchists counted on help from Sparta. The parties in authority, if they heedlessly started some external war, had to wage it to the bitter end, for admitting failure, an attempt to make peace, or any gesture which might weaken the psychic tension of the besieged city, threatened them with the coming to power of their internal opponents, with whom it was not possible to count upon treaties. The later fate of Corcyra bears witness to the fact that predictions of this kind were often correct. To an authority carrying out peace negotiations under such conditions, it sometimes seemed safer than continuing to wage war, and Machiavelli's formula for rendering peace impossible came to mind as the only logical conclusion in this state of affairs.

The massacres of free peoples and the terrible deeds that accompanied the Peloponnesian war also had other motives, which emerged just as logically from the position and strategy of Athens. Speaking at a popular assembly for declaring war against Sparta, Pericles envisaged in the following manner the situation of the republic which was then at the height of its power, and the strategy emerging from this position. Athens' power (he said) lies in her fleet; the Athenians can look calmly at the Spartans laying waste to the environs of the city, for that had no relevance to the outcome of the war. As long as the Athenians dominated the sea, they could keep their allies obedient, providing them with means for continuing to wage the war. However, any compromise with the Spartans, who claimed the right to a few towns occupied by the Athenians, could only lead to a weakening of the latter's authority over their allies, and the fall of the republic. Under such conditions, according to Pericles, Athens had no choice but war.

To a city besieged from the land, keeping obedient allies who provided money, food, and wood for ship-building seemed the alpha and omega, the key not only to victory, but to existence itself. Choosing war rather than the slightest curtailment of their authority over their allies, the Athenians—if they wanted to be consistent—could not tolerate any tendencies to independence in the latter. Their rule became increasingly hard, increasingly ruthless.

In a speech made after the first military defeats, Pericles appealed for more effort and sacrifices, and drew the attention of the Athenian people to the danger threatening them in the event of defeat by the hatred caused by the long wielding of authority; for the Athenian people possessed authority that placed them in the position of a tyrant: its execution may be unjust, but its abdication would certainly be dangerous.

Pericles' arguments, which are a model for so many speeches still ringing in our ears, allow us to recognize the stages of the dramatic development of relations between a great power and its small allies.

First Stage. To obtain hegemony, and even to maintain our position vis-à-vis a powerful rival, the possession of allies, satellites, and colonies is essential. We shall not part with them under any circumstances, or at any price; so we have nothing to discuss with them.

Second Stage. Our allies, satellites, and colonies have had enough of us; they hate us. If we let go of them, they will increase the ranks of our enemies; their intransigent hostility renders difficult any understanding with the latter; it lessens the possibilities of co-existence. We must therefore keep them obedient at any price, not drawing the line at any methods.

Third Stage. Our allies, satellites, and so on, have rebelled, they are putting up armed resistance. If they break down, the forces of the enemy will increase; but putting down their resistance will require a long struggle, and the engagement of part of our own forces. The best solution would be to murder them all.

Pericles envisaged the first two stages, but here is the third.

In the fourth year of the war, Mytilene and other towns of the island of Lesbos, previously allied with Athens, began preparing to secede. The Athenians had a certain number of supporters on the island, who informed them of these preparations. The towns of the island were not yet strong enough to maintain resistance for a longer time, so Mytilene sent envoys to Athens for a peaceable settlement of the matter. Fearing the failure of the negotiations, the citizens of Mytilene also sent envoys to Sparta, to ensure themselves possible aid from that side. A treaty was signed in the meantime with an Athenian admiral, according to which—until news was received from Athens—the admiral was to refrain from any repressive measures.

News of the attempt to secede by Mytilene evoked a storm of anger in Athens. After a public debate, the people resolved to put the envoys to death as well as all the citizens of Mytilene capable of bearing arms, while the women and children were to be sold as slaves. This order was immediately sent to the admiral awaiting it on the island. The next day, on the initiative of several respected citizens, the discussion was taken up anew. Various opinions were long weighed. The general execution of their allies still had numerous supporters. As their main argument, the opponents put forward the little profit the Athenians would gain from such a large massacre. By an insignificant majority of votes, the people recalled their previous resolution, ordering that only the most guilty be put to death. As a result, some one thousand death sentences were passed on the island.

The fate of the allies of Athens were no better, when as a result of military events they fell into the hands of the Lacedaemonians. The inhabitants of Plataea were the first to find themselves in this position, after a prolonged siege. At one moment the commander of the Spartan army saw that the citizens of Plataea, weakened by famine, could no longer put up resistance. However, his orders forbade him from taking the town by storm. For the Spartans foresaw that in peace talks they would have to return territorial gains; in order to bargain for Plataea they wished to have the support of the argument that the citizens of the town had surrendered it of their own free will. So the Spartan commander proposed surrender to the besieged town, promising that no one would be sentenced without trial. A few days later, a Spartan judge arrived in Plataea. Thucydides has preserved an extended summary of the speeches of the interested parties, namely the citizens of Plataea and the Thebans, who were also concerned in this case. With a laconicism appropriate to the Spartans, the judge asked the citizens of Plataea one question only: whether during the war they had rendered any services to Sparta, and after a negative reply, all without exception were sentenced to death. Women and children were sold as slaves.

Elsewhere we read that a Spartan admiral, while sailing along the coast of Ionia, at one point ordered that most of the prisoners taken during the expedition be killed. Envoys from the island of Samos drew his attention to the fact that in allegedly waging war for the liberation of Greece from the Athenian yoke, he ought not to take the lives of prisoners who had not even had the opportunity of fighting against Sparta. Recognizing the rightness of these arguments, the admiral ordered that those still alive be set free.

In towns which, with the help of Lacedaemonia, had seceded from Athens, there was for the most part freedom or self-government. But this idyll terminated with the first peace negotiations. The Spartans handed back to Athens the towns that had seceded from her during the war. In accordance with tribal custom, the right of inhabitants in some towns to leave with all their moveable goods was observed, but in others the entire population was handed over to the tender mercies of the Athenians.

MODELS OF AUTHORITY

The ancient world has handed down to later ages two models of authority: a town republic, and a happy autocrat—Alexander of Macedonia, Augustus, Antoninius Pius, and the like. Reading Thucydides, we have the impression that these models did not contradict each other in the eyes of the ancients, but rather complemented one another. Each of them found a contradiction in itself, in its extreme and caricatured forms. The opposite of the republic was a picture of the people running riot, the opposite of the happy autocrat was tyranny. The excesses of tyranny and democracy so preoccupied the imaginations of the ancients that the contrariety of democratic and absolute rules partly escaped their attention. A similar attitude toward various systems of government can be found in Machiavelli.

TREASON AS A SYSTEM

Greek history has left us striking examples of constancy, faithfulness, strength of character, and devotion. The most celebrated was the death of three hundred Spartans at Thermopylae "obedient to the laws of their fatherland." Attentive reading of Thucydides brings other examples. But far more frequently we read in his history of inconstancy, changes of front, reverses of allies, and treachery. These examples rarely refer to the main warring states, although here too they are not lacking. They refer mainly to the smaller republics. Every leader besieging a town had his allies and informers inside it, who often succeeded in opening the gates by stealth and letting the besiegers into the town.

The wide diffusion of treachery in the smaller republics obviously had its causes. Smaller states do not, generally, have the opportunity of making a free choice of allies, and they had still less during the Peloponnesian war. The republics within the range of the Athenian fleet were forced into the roles of Athenian satellites; the continental republics were dependent on Sparta. What is the value of alliances and obligations undertaken under force? These obligations were not associated with a sense of honor. Breaking an enforced alliance was often the secret aspiration of most citizens.

Generally, Athenian and Spartan prisoners were not killed, but were kept for later exchange. Neither of the great powers wanted to shut the door to peace. Prisoners from the lesser republics were put to death unceremoniously. After capturing a besieged town, the entire male population was massacred, the women sold. Only a traitor had any chance of surviving in such a system.

Treachery was all the easier in that it possessed organized forms already prepared in advance. The people governed everywhere in the allies of Athens, but supporters of oligarchy, awaiting the arrival of the Spartan armies, existed everywhere. Oligarchies prevailed in the area of Spartan influence, but at least part of the people were awaiting the arrival of the Athenians to overthrow the existing government and take power into their own hands. Treachery found support in the existing parties and opposing groups. Lesser republics had to tolerate this state of affairs. Unable to ensure security to their citizens, they left them to their own devices. The great majority of citizens, dependent on the shifting chances of war, increased the ranks of the Athenian or Lacedaemonian parties.

Readers of Thucydides did not appreciate this in the nineteenth century. Some took the Athenian historian as a misanthrope, having but little notion of the character of his contemporaries.

Others saw in the facts he described manifestations of the profound demoralization of the Hellenic world. These opinions seem erroneous. It is easier for a present-day reader to understand the situation of the smaller republic at that time. Europeans today do not choose their allies, and their own governments cannot ensure them against exile, if the worst comes to the worst, in Siberia. Everyone must find his own security. Under such conditions, the word "treason" takes on new meanings, unknown previously. Moreover, the very diffusion of the phenomenon creates an innumerable variety of degrees and shades in it, from "common or garden" treason to elegant treason as committed by Alcibiades himself.

THEORY OF THE BALANCE OF POWER

The theory of the balance of power is assuredly as old as the world, and no one can claim to have invented it. The version to be found in Thucydides is too well worded to be the first sketch, although we hear it from the lips of a man as resourceful as Alcibiades.

Toward the end of the war, after the defeat of the Athenian army and fleet in Sicily, the Spartans, who possessed a fleet equal to that of the Athenians, transferred the war to the coast of Ionia, where their oldest allies had begun to secede from Athens. On this occasion, the Spartans made an alliance with a representative of King Tisafernes of Persia, who undertook to bear part of the costs of maintaining the fleet. The political adviser of Tisafernes was at this time Alcibiades, the former Athenian commander, who had fled to Sparta and then to Persia. Here, in summary, is the advice he gave to the great king's representative:

Do not hasten to end the war, and avoid anything which might give ascendancy to one state in Greece on land or sea. On the contrary, it is necessary to take care that neither side has decisive ascendancy. As long as this state of affairs lasts, the Great King can set one Greek state against another, should any one of them begin to threaten his interests. If ascendancy on land and sea were to fall into the hands of one state, the King would not be able to find in Greece any ally, and would have to enter into a war himself, as costly as it would be perilous. But in maintaining a balance of power, the King has the possibility of weakening the Greeks by their own hands, without expending larger sums. On the basis of these premises, Alcibiades advised Tisafernes to weaken Athens first, and in the next stage to drive the Lacedaemonians from Ionia.

Though assuredly not new even then, the theory of the balance of power as uttered by Alcibiades has the freshness of volatile thought; sparkling, not yet worn-out, full of promise. However, it is difficult to judge whether Alcibiades himself took it seriously. Perhaps it was only a side product of his inexhaustible ingenuity, adapted to the tastes of his temporary protector.

Another theoretician of the balance of power, writing at the beginning of the eighteenth century, Lord Bolingbroke, took the theory seriously, for he risked his entire career for its sake and was forced, like Alcibiades before him, to flee to his enemies. But Bolingbroke knew the limits of his theory too, and he knew that to evaluate in a positive manner which side is the stronger, is only possible *ex eventu*, when it is already too late. The theory of the balance of power came to him in old age, the age of discretion, scepticism, and disillusion. Today the entire theory is a dusty relic, a dead concept, of interest only in historical perspective.

LITERARY MOTIFS

The description of the plague in Athens is one of the most celebrated passages in Thucydides. The author lived through the epidemic himself, and writes with an expert's knowledge of its manifestations and course, although it is hard to judge from what he writes which of the diseases known to us it was. He devotes a chapter to the anarchy and demoralization caused by the uncertainty of life during the epidemic. This chapter seems to have been a model for all later literary descriptions of the plague, from Boccaccio, Defoe, and others, down to Camus, who sought to see in the plague a possible source of virtues, by a kind of humility.

In Thucydides, however, the most striking pages are those showing the madness of the people, their blindness and lack of orientation when faced with the coldly calculated hysteria of the demagogues, who proposed ever more extreme decisions to them. The reader inquires why these descriptions have not found imitators, and why the motif of the madness of the people appears so rarely in literature. We must come to terms with the fact that a tyrant was always more "literary" material, and more easily found apologists and singers to extol him.

No matter how great his crimes, the figure of a tyrant is not without a certain glow, though a somber one. He stands alone against everyone. Even the Prefect of the Praetorians and the Magister of the Court left their weapons at the entry when going into Caesar's palace. The undertakings of a tyrant require what Machiavelli calls *virtu*. His solitariness means that he cannot burden other people with his crimes, thus favoring the hypothesis that those who endure his caprices were worthy of a better fate. The sight of peoples blinded with egoism, bound by a desire for carrying out acts of violence, gives no cause for such moderately pleasant hypotheses; only contempt and sorrow remain after them.

Translated by John David Welsh

PRESENT-DAY HUMANISTIC STUDIES

Paweł Hostowiec

Over the past twenty-five years, doctors have provided us with several systems of typology based on somatic traits, that is, on the structure of the body. Various devised tests or reactions to specific stimuli enable us to complement the classification by a number of sub-types.

This new typology, born in clinics and laboratories, where it indeed has its *raison d'être*, has come out into the street and provides a source of innocent merriment to many of our contemporaries. Waiting for a street-car, or idling in a café, we can while away the time by trying to identify the somatotypes of our chance companions—asthenic, pyknik, athletic, basedic, tetanic, and so on—drawing inferences about their behavior in various situations, their manner of speaking, their reactions to the Rorschach tables.

To anyone with a knowledge of history, typology of this kind, detached from a medical context, is somewhat reminiscent of the attempts made in classical antiquity to classify human beings according to Olympian models: Juno, Minerva, Diana, Vesta, Jove, Apollo, Mars, Vulcan, Mercury . . . Sculpture has preserved for us their somatic traits, and literature their spiritual traits. This point leads to another: by associating the characters of the gods and humans with the structure of the body, the Ancients reveal themselves as fatalists. Subservient to the influence of planets, they saw man's destiny as irrevocably involved with his horoscope.

The ease and rapidity with which new typologies based on somatic traits has spread among the profane allow us to draw certain conclusions about the temporary twilight of those concepts on which were based all attempts to educate and train man. We cannot change the structure of the human body. But if man's character is bound up with this, then attempts to educate him can hardly count on success. In their plans for remaking the world, the Germans drew radical conclusions from this premise, replacing pedagogy by zoo-technology, and massacring any types regarded as undesirable. Learned typologists tried their best to put the slaughter on the right track, and to create scientific premises for mass surgery of this kind. So, for the German scientist, they distinguished the particularly repulsive type "S," deserving extermination and easily recognizable by a special tendency to synesthesia, or the association of visual and audial impressions. A classical example of synesthesia is Rimbaud's well-known sonnet *Les Voyelles*: "a noir, e blanc, i rouge, u vert. . . ." To scientists, this is proof of an organic inferiority of mind, which tends to use symbols and allegory rather than logical concepts.

The preceding remarks are intended to characterize the ideas and interests of the present generations. The variety of classifications based on somatic features and the unexpected results of laboratory theories in the hands of barbarians who take up a book by the first professor to come along, and elevate it into an article of faith, have drawn attention away from a classification based on traits acquired in school and by training.

To be sure, such a classification exists in the form of specialized scientific institutions, but a classification based upon an academic diploma is not enough. It so happens that schools give their graduates something more than a diploma, which in any case says nothing about upbringing. After all, managers of offices and businesses consider not only the diploma when making an appointment, but its owner too.

In any chance conversation with a stranger, we try to answer the question: What is our interlocutor's background? Did he study the sciences, or the humanities? Has he worked in a laboratory, or in libraries and archives? As a rule, the answer is not far to seek, and a few minutes of conversation will give us the clue. This implies that acquired traits are just as obvious as inborn somatic features, which are sometimes so difficult to identify and interpret. During the past few decades, the abyss dividing various school backgrounds has undergone a marked deepening.

II

The nineteenth century was unaware of any great opposition between the humanistic and the natural sciences. There is no large divergence between Darwin and Claude Bernard on the one hand, and Hipolite Taine on the other. Both sides were linked by similar views of man, his past, and his inherent possibilities. The Darwinians saw man as the result of a long evolution of species, based on elimination and adaptation. Historians saw him in his historical environment, weighted down by his heritage from previous generations. To Sociologists, man was the worthy son of his social group. The economists submitted man's individual efforts to the laws of nature ruled by a free play of economic forces.

These views were not contradictory, but were rather interrelated, and they created premises for the liberalism of that time, which rejected force as useless and unable to affect biological evolution, or to reverse a past weighed down on present generations, or to undermine laws governed by economic phenomena.

As viewed from a laboratory or archives, man was being carried along by slow evolutionary processes. Not even a knowledge of the disasters that had engulfed states and races in the past, transforming their countries into deserts, aroused any doubt in the minds of nineteenth-century man.

The divergence between the two backgrounds became clearer as technology developed and gained ascendancy. Admittedly, the division of higher scientific institutions into separate fields of speciality dates from the Napoleonic era, even though the *universitas* defended its unity for a long time. But finally the utilitarian concept of knowledge gained the ascendancy. Scientific institutions were harnessed to the mechanism of the modern State, based on the morality of a besieged city. At that time there emerged a generation of technocrats, who saw no difficulties in the rational organization of nations on the model of termites, providing that all prejudices and traditions be thrown overboard.

Technology rapidly altered the landscape of much of the globe, covering it with the ruins of forests, networks of railroads and wires, thousands of chimney-pots, and heaps of slag. Technology changed the oldest of cities into ruins, or built cement hexagons in which the conditions of life proved to be fundamentally different from anything ever seen during the preceding thousands of years. Representatives of the people, parliaments and city councils, offered no resistance to these changes, but were drawn into what is called the dynamic vision of a world moving toward rapid and radical metamorphosis.

Humanists have been unable to keep up with this rapidly changing world-picture. Their knowledge of the past provided no key to understanding the altered and often threatening vision of the recent past. Humanistic studies are but poorly linked with the moral atmosphere of a besieged city that surrounds museums and libraries. Their relevance has decreased. Despite the gathering of increasingly rich materials, the number of persons devoting themselves to historical research continues to decrease. Not one of these people has the authority of the earlier humanists. The last celebrated historian was Guglielmo Ferrero, who died without pupils, surrounded only by a handful of chance listeners.

With the exception of economics, which has found its own way in the modern world, humanistic studies are in a state of obvious decline. Rejected by the young, barely tolerated by authorities (when the latter are still liberal), humanistic studies today have something outdated about them, smothered by dusty papers.

These circumstances make us wonder whether there still exists a humanistic background, and in what schools young people can obtain it?

III

By definition, humanistic studies have as their object man, the products of his hands and mind, but they are in reality terribly bookish, *livresque* in the worst sense. People who devote themselves to such studies are drowning in books, mostly (be it noted) of poor quality, far from any contact with living people. In order to obtain a basic humanistic education and the accompanying diplomas, the best formula under present circumstances seems to be a stay of several years in a monastery. Surrounded by books, texts, and dictionaries, wearing a comfortable dressing-gown, secluded from amusements, a young man would have the best conditions in which to master rapidly the main humanistic disciplines. Nor does reality differ fundamentally from this idealized view. A serious humanistic education always has something of library dust and the dressing-gown about it.

Books are very valuable objects, essential even for a humanist. But is the school bench and the monastery the best way to acquire an understanding of man, of his institutions, his traditions, and customs which he still cannot abandon, of his variety—including as it does Prospero, Ariel, and Caliban? Would it not be better if young people sought direct contact with living people and their institutions? The present writer would like briefly to offer a vision of experimental social education.

Suppose that the UNO commissioners now traveling through Israel, Greece, and the former Italian colonies were to take with them their sons between the ages of fourteen and eighteen. These youths would accompany them throughout their visits of inquiry, and would later be witnesses at the Lake Success meetings. Or let us imagine members of Parliament taking their adolescent sons on an electoral campaign. Or let us imagine parents sending their children for a course of education lasting several months in a Displaced Persons camp in Germany, or with smugglers along a frontier. Finally, let us imagine the gap dividing these young people on their return from their contemporaries, who spent the time playing football and pouring over textbooks.

One or two of these young travelers might go a little astray, might even abandon the conventional ways leading to an average career. But what is the "average" worth today? All my sympathies are on the side of a youth who goes astray at the sight of Caliban reigning over Prospero's island. I would like to meet him very much. If I never do, my old age will be appallingly lonely.

To return to reality: A humanistic background like those described above are also to be found in nature as the result of good fortune, of early initiation into the secrets of social life. We cannot overlook the extra-scholastic nature of these, nor the importance of the family and environment in a humanistic education.

But before moving on to other variants of present-day humanistic upbringing, we should like to describe an incident revelatory of extra-scholastic education.

Until recent times, there existed regions in the mountains of Eastern Europe, the valleys of the Balkans, and the Carpathians, where public education barely existed. Such schools as were there were little more than superficial, and were little frequented. Yet anyone who came into contact with the local young people was pleasantly surprised by their excellent upbringing, their civility, the correctness of their manners, their optimism, and their resourcefulness. How did poverty-stricken mountaineers manage to give their children such a model upbringing?

The answer is that young people there were initiated at an early age into the life of adults, into their social organizations, rites and traditions, crafts and amusements. Every year, early in November, young people make up small groups, preparing for the ancient rites connected with the *solstitium hibernium*. Helped by an elected master of ceremonies, they learn dances, songs, behavior, and make up couplets with references to contemporary social events. During the holiday, groups of young people are guests of all the householders, and will sing and dance in all the huts. What can be said to provoke merriment, yet without offending anyone? Young people of the mountains find this out at the age of fifteen or sixteen, and consequently they later feel much more at ease in society than any Ph.D.

During the period devoted to the patron saint of the village, the inhabitants form picturesque groups around the shrine. They stand in their colorful holiday costumes, with ribbons on their hats, hung with brass ornaments, pipes in their mouths, and embroidered tobacco pouches full of local tobacco on their chests. Supernatural powers walk on this day, floating above the heads of the assembly, as in a Greek tragedy. Faced by the *mysterium tremendum*, the community stands proud and exalted. On days such as these, the young people learn of man's dignity, which educated persons may—with a certain effort of the imagination—read of in Seneca.

Young people of the mountains apply themselves at an early age to work and crafts, at an age when youths at school still do not know how to draw independently. Their education is very close to what we know about education among the people of classical antiquity, so it belongs to the classical humanistic traditions.

Chance once brought me at dusk to an isolated mountain village, where a stranger was often not seen from one year to the next. Scarcely had I dismounted from my horse, on a nearby hill, than a group of boys surrounded me, playing with greak skill and art on the pipes, like the *pifferari* heard by Hector Berlioz when he held his stipendium at the École de Rome. The tunes of ritual and wedding dances followed one another. This concert and manifestations of friendship lasted by my campfire until late at night. Old people seemed absent that day.

Not until the next day, as I traveled on, did I realize that the boys had from the first recognized me as a friend, rightly estimating that they would not give me any greater pleasure than a *concert champêtre* in my honor. I learned the source of this penetration much later on. The village was populated by smugglers, who were out at work on that day. From a very youthful age, the boys took part in frontier expeditions, studying the terrain and giving warning of danger. Despite several meetings, always accompanied by concerts, not one of them betrayed that he had been abroad more than once, and knew all the customs and cunning of the frontier guards. Early initiation into the profession of a smuggler had taught them to estimate at once the intentions and character of an unknown traveler.

With their dark watchful eyes and small nimble hands, they were reminiscent of the children of good fairies rather than of man. I think of them with gratitude and sorrow. Their cordial, unconstrained, and merry attitude was sincere and genuine. Some years later, during the war and persecutions, they led many refugees across the frontier, just as disinterestedly and benevolently as when they played on their pipes for a stranger. Many of them perished in concentration camps, guarded by contemporaries who had been to school.

IV

During the inter-war period, the study of art seemed to have more powers of attraction for young people than philological and historical studies. In many countries, this brought with it an increase in the standards and numbers of institutions answering to these tastes. A part of the general education became broadened in them. There has also been a marked increase in the artistic public since the end of the nineteenth century. Artists are no longer a minute group isolated amidst the profane. Matters which interest them are now discussed by wide circles of the public. In contrast to technical schools and universities, schools of art do not open the way to any conventional and easy career to their graduates. Hence—especially in Eastern Europe—artistic studies attracted the most independent and enterprising groups of young people. Consequently, artistic upbringing deserves special attention today.

The study of art always went its own separate way, never mixing well with any general plan of education. For long periods of time, artists could only obtain an education privately. Schools claimed only to teach a trade, a technique required in any given branch of art. Until recently, most schools of art had the status of trade schools, refusing their graduates the rank and rights to which students of higher schools were entitled.

The position of these schools did not correspond to the role that art plays in the intellectual life of our time, nor to the ambitions and character of art, especially modernistic art, which is to a large degree non-technical, intellectual, and eschatological—that is to say, concerning itself with the ultimate problems of existence.

This divergence derived partly from the different aims of schools of art and universities. The latter are concerned with artistic phenomena only in a small area, teaching the analysis and classification of works of art. Even the study of writing is left to the middle grades. The time when students were required to write Latin verses is long past. On the other hand, schools of art claim primarily to teach the practical skills of technique. So universities produce only historians, critics, passive scholars, at most digesters of art, while schools of art produce creative and performing individuals.

The caution and distance with which the university world regards artistic phenomena has a deeper reason. The Positivist doctrine from which the contemporary university emerged does not know how to come to terms with the irrational and magical element that plays such an important part in artistic creativity.

To a person looking at a work of art from outside, his enjoyment is a decisive factor. From this it is possible to describe and explain the entire world of art more or less *ex naturalibus*, without using any vague or doubtful terminology. Relating it to genres, forms, and processes can provide a topic for many generations of scholars yet to come.

But the matter looks different from the point of view of an artist. If it were merely a question of providing the public with objects of artistic enjoyment, then there would assuredly be few prepared to undertake the task. Art has traditions which cannot be reduced to such a simple formula.

Essentially, art has not moved very far from its magical beginnings. Magic is a system of thought based on the omnipotence of the word. Correctedly uttered, a formula can bring good health or death, rain or drought; it can change a man into a donkey and vice-versa; it facilitates the summoning-up of spirits, seeing into the future, and gaining influence over supernatural powers. From these concepts there emerged the feeling of the form of a word as a decisive factor in its magical power. Despite centuries of rationalism, the word has not entirely lost these properties even today. An inappropriate verbal form may deprive an official of his post, a student of his diploma, while in dictatorial countries it may well lead to a prolonged stay in jail.

Lyrical poetry emerged largely from magical formulae. Opening any book of poetry, we find forms of hymns, invocations, incantations, and the like. As a rule, verses addressed to beautiful women take the form of words by which an attempt is made to propitiate or conciliate supernatural powers. These similarities are by no means accidental. Magic still has its practitioners in some mountain regions. Formulae are used for casting spells, getting rid of diseases, arousing or calming snakes, and they have verse forms, full of alliteration and assonances, well worth the notice of persons concerned with literary studies.

An artist of the word always has a certain awareness of the magic power of form. Without a touch of magic, a poet's word would be as modest and cautious as the words of the author of this essay, who has set himself on an investigatory task.

The work of an artist is the recollection of the all-powerful *fiat* by which the Creator summoned up the world out of chaos. A work of art is a fragment of a fictitious world created by an artist, arranged according to values other than those of the world known to us from experience. Various literary genres often preserve their own patterns; thus, melodrama divides characters into black or white, comedy into serious and absurd, and the action of tragedy takes place in a cosmos of small dimensions, in which the gods watch man's madness from close by.

One of the creators of Gestalt psychology, Wolfgang Kohler, writes in his book on the theory of values that no one who has not worked in a laboratory can imagine how clumsy it would be to make any value judgement there. The ability proper to works of art of arranging according to values of a fictitious world contained in them constitutes the frontier that divides art from the world of positivist thought.

In contemporary literature, we are especially struck by the awareness of the magical power of the word, which moves unseen links for those of us who think in the proper terminology, or who bustle with unperturbed optimism around material affairs. Suffice it to recall the poetic formulae of destruction and extermination which warned us for two generations before Europe, covered by ruins, reached its unclear parting of the ways.

V

The magical beginnings of the plastic arts are also known. The solemn rows of statues and temples bound the supernatural powers, making them accessible to sacrifices and prayers. What was left to the plastic arts of this period? As formerly with the world of the Olympians and demi-gods, so today a work of art links us to a fictitious world with a different hierarchy of values. In the old masters, with their many symbols, the order of this world was easier to decipher and describe. In later art, its outlines are more misty and individual.

Even in less ambitious objects of applied art, we also find this link with an invisible world of a different order. Suffice it to think of the context of a given object, or the environment appropriate to it. Some pieces of Mauretanian furniture, with their flamboyantly severe lines, painted gold and purple, can surely be placed only in Paradise, before the very throne of Allah. Their owners kept them in a half-light, for light would have required the erection of separate buildings for them, the shapes of which no builder had yet been able to conceive.

Young people leaving professional schools of art have hands which possess an irrational power of form-creativity. The power to create forms allows them to present concretely and to render accessible to themselves and to others the fictitious world existing in their imagination, which to the profane is only an elusive feeling, a continually fugitive and misty dream.

The possibility of closer contact with reality of a different hierarchy has always been a source of marvel and hope. In the stuffy atmosphere of a besieged city in which the peoples of the world shut themselves, an artistic education seems to be the most attractive variety of humanistic upbringing.

VI

The study of music stands still lower in the school hierarchy, and leaves much to be desired. In schools of music, art is treated on the level of a modest trade. The very knowledge of it is restricted to a small repertoire. The range and humanistic meaning of music remains bashfully concealed from the pupils.

The enlightened musical public constitutes a very small group of persons, drowning in the crowds who attend concerts. Listeners let themselves be drawn for only a short time into a flowing world of sounds which immediately afterward escapes them, leaving behind only vague recollections. In the crowd of the profane, the artist remains solitary. In him alone the flowing musical created thing possesses continuity and concreteness.

The world of the Olympians did not reveal itself easily, nor to the first comer. The approach to it required preparations, the rejection of a more sober vision of things, and a shift into a region of elevated, rare, and unusual feelings. The ability to move a listener into a region of feelings new to him was always attributed to music, and hence its role in religious rites. The learned mullah of St. Petersburg, Musa Begiyev, believed that music would assuredly be the language of future prophets, standing half-way between man and Allah.

From these beginnings, music has enriched her language and range of experiences enormously. The variety of impressions and experiences summoned up by music seem endless. And here too, form also has a decisive meaning.

Musical education is a complex phenomenon. It is composed of an almost magical form-creative power of hands and the knowledge of a varied scale of impressions and experiences such as musical literature possesses. Seen from this angle, a musical education consists of a still narrowly distributed and new, but particularly promising variety of the humanistic upbringing.

VII

The present state of literary and historical education, correctly regarded hitherto as the basis of a humanistic upbringing, provides much food for thought. We should like to dwell briefly on two aspects.

In the nineteenth century there existed a certain—if not unity, then at least a correspondence between the main concepts held by the natural scientists and the humanists. The natural sciences, being in a state of great development, radiated upon humanistic studies, bringing a number of their own ideas and tendencies to bear.

Today, in the present age of neo-Positivism, the link between the two seems to have been broken. In recent decades, the sciences have created a certain area of ideas and terms regarded as obligatory for proper understanding. But humanistic studies are not keeping up with the demands.

Let us take, for example, the word "causality," often used by humanists. Already forty years ago, Bertrand Russell recommended that the word be removed from the dictionary of philosophy on the grounds that it did not possess a sufficiently defined content. A German scholar told me of a conversation on this matter with Albert Einstein. The eminent mathematician adopted a more tolerant attitude. If the concept of causality is necessary to the lower disciplines of knowledge—botany or history—for their methodology, then it should be left to them, but the concept must not appear in the vocabulary of more demanding persons.

History never possessed a highly thought-out methodology, and to this very day uses concepts dating from the time of Thucydides. He it was who undertook to explain the entire Peloponnesian war *per causas*. An observant reader notices after a brief sampling that Thucydides wrote a book which is excellent in many respects, but which contains no explanation *per causas*. His failure did not deter any of his followers.

Until the humanistic disciplines can assimilate the main ideas and terms used today in the sciences and in colloquial speech, they will continue to give the impression of dubious and irrelevant knowledge, not keeping pace with the general level of the sciences. The modernization of humanistic methodology remains to be achieved. The drift of young people away from these disciplines renders the task difficult, and the gap between the humanistic and natural sciences seems to be constantly on the increase.

Attempts to modernize literary research are not giving satisfaction. The adoption of the methods and mannerisms of the laboratory in the field of literature is fraught with danger. Anyone who has frequented laboratories knows how greatly work there depends on instruments, and how much this dependence has mechanized research, so that very often even an average level of intelligence is not required. Attempts to adapt the attitude of a laboratory worker, who may not give voice to a value judgement, to literary research, can only lead to profound errors and disillusion. Literary studies have of late entered upon precisely this uncertain path. Not without disappointment does today's reader lay aside hundreds of volumes of fashionable technical literary analysis, modeled upon the expertise of laboratories.

It is difficult for the present writer, as a faithful son of Positivism, to put contemporary Positivism on trial. All the same, it is not possible to conceal that laboratory workers have recently provided us with painful disillusions. Living in fear of making a value judgement, they have not adopted a definite attitude toward the most important matters of our time. In their white tunics, they remain silent, obediently manufacturing atom bombs. The humanists have little cause to envy them. We await something different from a humanistic upbringing.

Translated by John David Welsh

NOTES ON IDEOLOGY
End or Crisis?

Aleksander Hertz

I

IT IS DOUBTFUL whether anyone would ever be able to attempt the task of cataloguing all the multifarious facts to which the terms "ideology" and "ideological movement" have been applied. The value of such work would in fact be very dubious. These terms have been used to describe all kinds of conceptions and organizational endeavors which have often quickly passed into oblivion.

However, so have numerous conceptions and organizational endeavors, the ideological character of which has been indisputable. Some—to mention only the suffragettes—had achieved their objectives, the state of affairs attained by them soon becoming something obvious and generally accepted. Others—like the Anti-Saloon League—while also achieving their objectives, had consequences that were highly negative and discreditable. If retained in human memory, such movements served as a warning against ill-considered or aberrant attempts at collective action.

The number of ideologies and ideological movements of all kinds has been legion. Some, like Social Democracy, have played an immense role in history. Others—albeit in certain periods highly influential and active—were transitory or ephemeral phenomena. Many left deep traces, even though their original ideological character had become considerably weakened or had disappeared altogether.

It will probably be no mistake to say that in the most recent times two groups of ideological systems and movements have played the greatest role and had the most decisive impact on the aspect of the age. The point of departure of one of the two groups has been the nation as the supreme value; that of the other has been social class. The former have been national ideologies, usually defined as *nationalism*; the latter have been class ideologies, the most momentous of which has turned out to be *communism*.

This division must not be treated too rigorously. In practice, it was quite common for the two values to be linked with each other. National ideologies have often had a strong class coloring, and—vice-versa—class ideologies, communism in the first place, have laid a major emphasis on national elements. National socialism did not occur only in the Nazi version, although even within Nazism itself there existed class elements. Tito has not been the sole inventor of national communism. National elements have been prominent in all the other Communist movements as well. In Chinese communism, they even have racial undertones. Stalinism was a nationalistic and chauvinistic communism, displaying visible features of national Messianism.

In all these cases what was important was the interpretation of the mutual relationship between nation and class. In the interpretations offered by nationalist ideologies, class elements—when recognized, which was not always the case—were deduced from the supreme value of the nation to which they were subordinated. In class ideologies, national elements were treated as derivatives of the class struggle and considered in terms of class. To what extent all these interpretations have been productive, and to what extent they have been in accord with collective emotions, is not of interest to us now.

We cannot engage in any detailed discussion of these problems. Taking as general a view of them as possible, let us state that nationalism and communism in all their diverse versions have together played in our own times the greatest historical role. In the years between the two world wars they did so above all in Europe. At the present moment, they do so above all in the countries of Asia, Africa and—to a considerable extent—Latin America. And certainly these two groups of ideologies, more often than not at loggerheads, have had a fundamental bearing on the history of the age we happen to live in. It is to these two ideological attitudes that we propose to limit our concluding remarks.

II

In the highly industrialized, non-Communist countries we are now witnessing a strong reaction against ideology. There are grounds to believe that this reaction is under way also in some Communist

countries where, however, it cannot—for understandable reasons—
come into the open. In the United States, France, West Germany,
Britain, and so on, a phalanx of authors and philosophers have
heralded the end of the age of ideology and affirmed its bankruptcy.

This reaction has, above all, its emotional justification. It is
understandable in view of what happened in the years between the
wars. It is understandable also in view of the aftermath of that
period—the war and its terrible sacrifices. The bestialities of Nazism
on the one hand and of Stalinism on the other necessarily gave rise
to feelings of repulsion and to condemnation of the ideological
exercises which had provided the motivation for the crimes. Several
centuries had to elapse before Spaniards displayed a similar
emotional reaction to the ideological follies of their ancestors. And
the events in Spain in the late fifteenth century had surely been
quite innocent and humanitarian when compared with the rule of
Hitler or Stalin.

The ideologies of these two regimes very soon became subject to
a process of practical verification. German nationalism produced
the country's military debacle and the annihilation of the entire
system. It had brought them about by way of a frightful war, the
ravages and atrocities of which have never been surpassed in modern
times. Khrushchev's famous speech, while formally and officially no
more than a statement of the fact of the verification of the ideology
of Stalinism, really amounted to a verification of communism as a
whole. In both cases the finale acted like a bombshell. In the
former case, it was the work of History itself; in the latter, its agent
was the leader of the entire movement.

In both cases the verification was violent and brutal. Nationalist
ideologies had made a jungle of human relationships; they had
failed to live up to their promises and brought appalling sufferings
to millions of human beings. Under their influence, masses of
people ran amuck, and the end result was catastrophe. Communism
was no less of a failure. Its promises remained unfulfilled. No
classless society of free and creative people had ever emerged. The
old social structure had been replaced by a new stratification.
Pareto's theory of the circulation of élites found another illustration
in Communist regimes. A system of oppression and exploitation
had been built up, with prisons and concentration camps the daily
fare of the masses. The old imperialism had been retained, embellished with new rationalizations and slogans. The Soviets' Communist tanks slaughtered workers in the streets of Budapest.

Emotionally, there was every reason for the anti-ideological
reactions of the many European and American intellectuals. And
the reasons were much more cogent than those adduced by Max

Stirner back in the mid-nineteenth century. It may be surmised that in the attitudes of people like Aron and Bell there was some unconscious Stirnerism, with much deeper and stronger roots than that of Stirner himself.

One might take this to be a case of emotional anti-ideologism. However, the distrust of ideology and ideological operations was not limited to intellectuals alone. In Europe and America, wide sections of the community displayed a marked aversion to whatever smacked of the traditional ideologies. The neo-Fascist and neo-Nazi groups in Italy and Germany became both anachronistic and unattractive to the public at large. In countries like France and Italy where mass Communist parties had survived, they had lost their revolutionary vigor and in practice became similar to all other political groupings. Their objective now became practical-minded reformism and action within the framework of the parliamentary system. In the Soviet Union and the other European Communist countries the de-ideologization of communism has been more and more evident. The Party has become institutionalized and has turned into a powerful bureaucratic machine, the ruling group's tool of government. The ideology itself has been transformed into a formula which is treated less and less seriously.

The downfall of the great colonial empires was accepted very calmly by public opinion in the home countries as an event that was both natural and inevitable. Neither in Britain nor in the Netherlands were there any protests or pronouncements that would hark back to the old nationalist or imperialist traditions. There were some attempts at resistance in France, where the links between Algeria and the metropolis had been much closer than in the case of the other colonialist countries, but even there such attempts had no deeper appeal to the community. General de Gaulle resolved the Algerian problem with the benevolent support of the majority of the country's public opinion.

De Gaulle is, of course, a French nationalist and patriot. Even so, he is far removed from the traditions of the *Action Française*. As a matter of fact, the carriers of these traditions were the generals who rebelled against him. The rebellion had calamitous consequences for them. And it does not seem either that "Gaullism" can be considered as an ideology or an ideological movement. It is rather a form of an authoritarian regime, but one deprived of the emotional and charismatic contents and the conceptions of absolute truth which were a feature of the great ideological movements of the preceding period.

One of the causes of Senator Goldwater's defeat in 1964 was the ideological coloring that the Republican candidate gave to his election campaign. Of course, this was in the United States where electors display an invariably hostile attitude to attempts to introduce ideology into the technique of the political game. However, the magnitude of Goldwater's defeat was certainly influenced by the specifically post-war aversion of the voting masses to anything that smacks of ideology or ideologization. Among the Senator's supporters the number of people who found his emphasis on ideology attractive was relatively insignificant.

The view may safely be ventured that the psychological climate among the present generation of Euro-Americans does not favor ideology. Emotionally, people deprecate ideologies, are disappointed with them, and do not trust them. And this must have affected that return to modified Stirnerism which has been noticeable among numerous intellectuals.

III

But, their argumentation has been based on non-emotional assumptions. They rely chiefly on rational assumptions, deriving from an analysis of the results of the practical verification of the traditional ideologies.

These have displayed a total discrepancy between their forecasts and the actual course of historical developments. Even worse: in many cases, what happened was in clear contradiction with what had been prophesied. At the same time, the transformations that had occurred within the ideologies and the movements dependent on them deviated glaringly from the conceptions of the creator-prophets and their commentators. History has been very severe to ideologies, a fact that cannot have escaped the notice of observers.

Stalinism was the most striking case. Could it really be reduced to the excesses of an individual or to accidental "errors and distortions"? Such interpretations, advanced by people who regarded themselves as Marxists, had a highly unconvincing ring. This was no Marxism, but some vulgarized version of Carlylism which reduced history to the part played in it by outstanding individuals. No Marxist ought to have subscribed to such an interpretation, just as no serious modern student of historical processes could. The Communist Marxists' use of it was the best evidence of the lamentable standard of modern Communist thought.

Stalinism could not have been a fortuitous development. It must have been somehow historically conditioned. Andrzej Stawar seems to have been absolutely right in perceiving the roots of Stalinism in the views and activities of none other than Lenin himself. The latter may well have distrusted and feared Stalin.

Even so, it was Lenin who had laid the foundations for the activities of his successor in the Communist movement. Of course, the entire tangled knot of historical circumstance—in and outside Russia—was of decisive importance in making it possible for the personality and role of Stalin to come to the fore. The age of Stalin was also that of Hitler.

However, Stalinism was but one of the many facts that impressed themselves on observers. Objectively, the most important were the historical transformations that had begun in the post-war period. Within the range of the civilization of most advanced industrialization they had created relationships which both diverged from the ideological forecasts and were a highly unfavorable circumstance for the emergence and development of ideologies and ideological movements.

Among the consequences of the great technological revolution was far-advanced *social stability*. This has been a situation quite different from that of the years between the wars. An age of *prosperity* ensued, one from which the widest masses of people were able to benefit. Unemployment either totally disappeared or was reduced to negligible proportions. More than that: in the highly industrialized countries a constant demand for workers has been felt. The living standard of the general public has reached a level previously enjoyed only by very well-off people. And it has also been rising markedly in the Soviet Union, even though the standard of living there still lags behind that in many of the so-called capitalist countries. Social contrasts have been considerably attenuated. In a country like the United States the differences in the way of life are relatively insignificant, and often hardly noticeable. A similar trend can be observed in the other highly-industrialized countries. The individual's sense of *economic security* has spread and become very much strengthened. The Welfare State sees to the individual's interests by protecting him against the effects of unemployment, looking after his health, and ensuring him a means of livelihood in old age. As a matter of fact, the prospect of a lack of job and a loss of the ability to earn money is now in most cases purely theoretical.

The picture is not, of course, one of unblemished brightness. None of the highly-industrialized countries is perfection personified. Nonetheless, a high degree of social stabilization has been attained. Nothing comparable in range or scale had ever existed before.

There have occurred very fundamental social restratifications. In the new industrial system the part played by the former individual proprietors has been gradually taken over by a class of

managers, specialists, technologists, and organizers. The proletariat, whose only qualification consisted of strong muscles, has
gradually been disappearing. Its place has been taken by technically
highly-skilled workers, capable of operating complex machinery,
and very well paid. In a country like the United States the worker
in the traditional meaning of the word has become an obsolete
concept. The number of white-collar workers already exceeds that
of blue-collar workers. In practice, the principal difference between
the two consists of the former being paid weekly or monthly and
the latter on the basis of the hours or days worked. But even this
difference becomes blurred as more and more American industrial
workers get their pay in weekly or monthly instalments. There is a
similar trend in the other highly-industrialized countries.

This leads to the emergence of *conservative* attitudes among the
masses. In fact, in the highly-industrialized countries political
differentiation is limited to various shades of conservatism. Social
Democratic parties differ only slightly from their "bourgeois"
opposite numbers. Sometimes they are even more cautious than
the latter and even less inclined to pursue policies involving some
degree of risk. This applies also to Communist parties in countries
where they have a mass following. Their radicalism is a matter of
form rather than substance. If workers still belong to them, this is
more for reasons of tradition and habit than because of any true
revolutionary aspirations. Very significantly, the membership of the
American Communist Party—a tiny and marginal grouping—
largely consists of the intelligentsia. The participation of workers is
insignificant.

This conservatism requires some explanation. The civilization of
which we are part is going through revolutionary transformations
which are both very extensive and far-reaching. We live in an age of
one of the greatest revolutions in the world's history. The conservative attitude of the human communities of our time has its
roots in their affirmative approach to changing reality. Man as
shaped by our civilization considers this reality as something
absolutely correct and concordant with his interests. He consents
to the changes which occur in it and in fact regards them as desirable. He sees them as part of a pattern of relationships which he
accepts as proper and of which he approves. Americans accept the
system termed "capitalism" as proper and concordant with their
needs; the citizens of the Soviet Union take a similar approach to
"socialism." And this reflects the conservatism of both of them.

This is not to say that either of them are satisfied with everything
that happens around them. They believe that quite a few things call
for basic improvement. But they want such improvement to be

effected within the framework of the system of which they generally approve. They demand reforms but reject violent revolutionary transformations. And they think of such reforms in terms of practical solutions to existing problems. This is a highly pragmatic and rational attitude.

It is also far from being ideological. Very significantly, all the attempts at an ideologically-tainted conservatism have failed to produce any major results. Goldwaterism was a disastrous fiasco. Groupings like the American Conservative Party and the John Birch Society and similar ventures in other countries have been marginal phenomena, their influence on public life taken as a whole being close to nil. The principal current of that life has displayed an unmistakable distrust of such ideological efforts.

Things have hardly been different in the case of ideological attempts on the extreme left. Communist radicalism, as inspired by the Chinese experience, has been a failure in the Euro-American part of the world. While pro-Chinese groupings have been set up here and there, so far they have all been ephemeral and have appealed to romantically-inclined young members of the intelligentsia rather than to the masses of the public. Even among the American Negroes—a community that would seem to be particularly prone to the ideological approach—phenomena like Black Power are, for all their aggressiveness, relatively insignificant in relation to the main trends of Black America.

A world of social stability and a sense of security, a world which affirms existing reality and, consequently, adopts an attitude of conservatism, hardly provides a fertile breeding-ground for ideologies and the development of ideological movements. Therein are rooted the basic arguments advanced by the champions of the claim about the end of the age of ideology.

One more factor merits attention. And this is the transformation under way among educated people or the intelligentsia, that basic instrument of ideology-making. Today's civilization has vastly increased the practical importance of education and highly specialized training in particular. Modern technology is unable to develop without an army of specialists of all descriptions. The growth of institutions of higher education has assumed tremendous proportions, their importance in public life becoming greater and greater.

Especially in the United States intellectuals have begun to play a role they never played before. And there has developed among them a sense of the importance of that role and of their own historical importance. There is less and less place among them for "Bohemianism" in the old sense. This has a marked influence on the intellectuals' activity in the wider arena of public life. These intellectuals rapidly undergo transformations that are peculiar to the present stage in the development of our civilization. They are integrated within the general organization of this civilization and occupy a major place in its social system. And they become as well a component of the general social stability of our times.

Even so, it is in the very nature of things that intellectuals should be a group that is much less conformist than other groups. They have a clearer view of the deficiencies of public life and are able both to define such deficiencies with greater clarity and to formulate methods of repairing them. However, their attitudes are pragmatic rather than ideology-producing. Let us bear in mind also that for intellectuals the verification of the traditional ideologies was an experience of particular emotional power. They perform the important function of protest, but on the whole accept the assumptions underlying the existing system. Actions on which they embark —against war, for equal rights for Negroes, against colonialism, and so on—have not so far led to ideological formulations; they have been an expression of protests and attempts to find a pragmatic solution to practical problems of public life.

People who—albeit not without reservations—accept existing reality and are on the whole satisfied with it do not provide a breeding-ground for the development of ideologies and ideological movements. Essentially they are conservatives, even when they belong to political groupings which are formally ideological and revolutionary. The conservatism of Social Democracy and the revisionism of communism are not a consequence of any "betrayal" on the part of their leaders, but a result of the attitudes of the masses. The most conservative sections of today's public include industrial workers—in other words, the social group that is still traditionally defined as the working class. In the United States, it is precisely industrial workers who display a strong resistance to the civil rights program. The motives have a class character: the migration of Negroes to White-inhabited districts will result in a drop in the market value of the worker-owned housing. This is hardly a "proletarian" frame of mind. And similar phenomena are observed outside the United States as well.

Thus, the arguments marshalled by Aron, Bell, and others have a solid foundation in socio-historic fact. But there is also another side to the picture which makes it imperative for us to be very cautious in talking about an end to the age of ideology.

IV

One must, above all, be always cautious with forecasts. The statement is fully justified that at the present juncture there exist in the Euro-American part of the world distinct *trends* which do not favor the emergence and development of ideologies and ideological movements. However, can we be quite sure that these trends are lasting? Can we be confident enough to assert that situations will not emerge, as yet unforeseen, which will create a favorable ground for ideology-making? We are by no means protected against situations of disaster, such as would disrupt the present state of equilibrium and security and result in an atmosphere of panic. All that is possible. Prudence would recommend at least some dose of pessimism.

It does seem obvious that the traditional ideologies are indeed suffering from a profound *crisis*. But, as indicated above, a crisis of an ideology sets in as soon as that ideology is subjected to verification, and verification can have tragic consequences for an ideology. It may, however, lead to a transformation of its substance and form, to its adjustment to changed conditions—in a word, to its modernization. This is the direction taken by the efforts of numerous Communist revisionists. If objective conditions are favorable, these efforts may be successful.

Undoubtedly the trend toward social stability and an increased sense of security is at present both very strong and general. But it has its limits as well. In our civilization there is no lack of environments that have a weak stability and from which a sense of security is missing. Suffice it to mention America's Negroes. What is more important, however, is that our civilization has opened up vast possibilities for the development of psychopathological states, for all kinds of emotional disturbances, and for the emergence of all kinds of collective phobias and neuroses. These things can very well go hand in hand with stabilization and economic security; they may in fact be conditioned by them. And this in turn may provide a good nourishment for ideology and mass ideological movements.

The crisis of the traditional ideological systems and movements is in itself conducive to such psycho-pathological sentiments. Ideologies have in a way been confessions of faith, compasses, sources of hope, and driving forces for action. In order to live, man must believe in something and must aspire to something. The destruction of the faith in the gods of old opens up a moral vacuum in his mind and stimulates a feeling of loneliness and loss. This vacuum is clearly discernible today and efforts are made somehow to fill it. It would be dangerous if it were otherwise.

It would seem that therein lay the essence of the Kennedy cult. The tragically deceased American President was not an ideologist and was very far from being the leader of a movement. His was not a charismatic personality. He was a pragmatist and a man of practical action. In his activity he aimed at very tangible achievements, at direct reforms—not guided by any vision of a perfect future. And in this he was a very modern man. As few others have, he fitted in with the aspirations of millions of present-day human beings. His personality and his activity served to fill the vacuum that resulted from the crisis of the traditional ideologies.

This was highly symptomatic. People feel a sense of vacuum, and they miss some compass—some philosophy of collective life.

One of the most revealing phenomena of our times has been the novel definition of the role of religious groups, the Catholic Church above all. The Second Vatican Council was an impressive attempt to modernize Catholicism, to adjust it to the exigences of present-day life. The ecumenical idea had the effect of turning the spotlight on the value and importance of every human individual, irrespective of his religious affiliation or the absence of such affiliation. Translated into terms of practical action, this was a concept of universalist humanism.

Another element was the association of the Church with social activity over an extraordinarily wide range of objectives. The altar was now turned to face not merely the faithful, but also all manifestations of public life.

It is becoming increasingly clear that the Second Vatican Council has had a major impact also on non-Catholic denominations, primarily Protestants and Jews. It gave them a stimulus for a re-thinking of things, for modernization, for finding for religion a new place in the living reality of the day.

Ecclesiastics of all denominations have taken a strikingly active part in present-day collective actions, including those with a pronounced ideological coloring. In the United States, Catholic, Protestant, and Jewish clergymen have been in the front ranks of the fighters for the emancipation of Black America. Many of them have committed themselves to pacifist, reformist, and other campaigns. For many centuries the clergy has not been involved in similar social activity or displayed such qualities of leadership.

This influences wider sections of the public, and especially young people. It is not an influence of a confessional nature. Christianity has in this case been treated primarily as a moral system and a basis for collective action. And this implies efforts to eliminate evil, to solve practical problems of everyday life, and to promote some juster principles of human intercourse.

It is impossible to foresee the future course of developments. But there is certainly a possibility of new ideological conceptions filling the present vacuum. These conceptions will probably differ widely from the traditional ideologies and ideological movements. They will be different in both their substance and their external form. They will constitute a great transformation, but they will not mean an end to the age of ideology. And it cannot at all be excluded that they will have no influence on the remnants of the traditional ideologies. What we have in mind here is primarily communism. One must not cherish illusions that a modernization of communism in its Western version could be an easy thing. Such modernization is, however, possible. And so is even that of East European communism.

Still, these are far-fetched speculations. What is important is that the present profound crisis of the traditional ideologies must not necessarily eliminate the possibility of new ideologies and ideological movements emerging. What kind of ideologies these will be and what directions will they take, whether the consequences of some of them may not again become man's curse—these are all questions which it would be premature to discuss.

V

What has been said above applies to the Euro-American part of the world and the civilization of highly advanced industrialization. However, that part is rather small in relation to the entire planet. Over wide areas of the world conditions are totally different. And they are highly conducive to all ideology-making.

The Russia of 1917 was an extremely backward country in relation to Western Europe. But the China of 1950 lagged behind that Russia of 1917 by several centuries. Extensive areas in Africa represent a civilization which corresponds to that of Europe in the age of the great migrations. The nations of Asia and Africa, and to a certain extent also of Latin America, are now expected to adopt a civilization which was elsewhere the product of long centuries. It is a fantastic jump from a distant past into the present.

And the question is not merely one of technological adaptation, which is in itself an enormous undertaking in the existing conditions. The question is rather that of a great social and cultural revolution, a revolution of manners, one extending to all spheres of private and public life. This revolution destroys traditional institutions, centuries-old forms and modes of existence, the entire pattern of hitherto strongly-rooted values. It creates a state of social flux, tears individuals away from their earlier way of life, and brings with it new forms of existence.

All this happens in conditions of as yet primitive technology, of economic backwardness, undernourishment, a high mortality rate, and a colossal birth rate. Modernization of the façade is not accompanied by economic or social modernization. The old forms are broken up; the emergence of new forms is only gradual and by no means easy.

We can hardly embark here on a discussion of these facts. They are common knowledge. They account for what has been said about an end or crisis of ideology not being at all applicable to vast areas of this globe. Excellent conditions exist there for the development of all kinds of ideology-making, including the traditional ideologies.

We encounter there a wealth of combinations of nationalism with a peculiar type of socialism and communism. There are prophets and charismatic leaders, such as Mao Tse-Tung, Castro, Sukarno, and Nkrumah, not to mention the lesser ones. The careers of some of them turned out to have been of rather short duration, but there is a standing chance of others emerging in their place. Mao Tse-Tung is a man of the calibre of a Hitler or Stalin. Ideologies are something very much alive there, and ideological movements show an extraordinary dynamics. The atmosphere is charged with revolution. Sanguinary and cruel ideological clashes are the order of the day. Nobody yet knows with any exactness the number of true or alleged Communists murdered in Indonesia, but the range and intensity of these atrocities were appalling. The "proletarian cultural revolution" in China seems like a true nightmare. General slaughter, tortures, the mass extermination of adversaries—all this has become the daily bread of people over wide expanses of our planet. It is not at all inferior to the follies of Hitlerism or Stalinism. And it is no less ideological in nature.

Thus, while in one part of the globe processes of a retreat from ideology seem to be visibly on the move, the other part is dominated by ideology and a great dynamics of ideological movements. And of special importance there is communism—alive, attractive, and full of substance. The great schism in world communism is not a matter of differences of interpretation; it is one of different civilizations and cultural systems.

A comparison springs to mind between the present rift in communism and that which half a century ago broke up the international Socialist movement. The analogies are striking in many respects. The meaning of the earlier rift was not always correctly understood at the time. It was being limited—especially among Socialists—to differences of interpretation and varying views on tactics. Hopes were even entertained that the breach would be a temporary one, and attempts were made to restore unity. On the Communist side, the responsibility was pinned on the Socialist leaders, who were said to have betrayed the workers and their interests. Lenin demagogically branded Kautsky as a renegade. The language that the Communists then used when referring to their Socialist adversaries did not differ much from that to which the Chinese Communists now resort when addressing the "modern revisionists."

In fact, then—as now—the issues at stake were of far greater import. Kautsky and other Socialist leaders of that time were not "betraying" the working masses, but were responding to the tendencies prevalent among them. The masses cherished revolutionary sentiments, but these did not extend to the whole of the working class and were—as it transpired later—rather superficial. The industrial workers of Western Europe took a much keener interest in practical attainments within the existing system than in any violent upheaval. Even then objective reality was very much different from what it was in Marx's time—which was still a fact of life in Russia.

Similarly, Khrushchev, Brezhnev, and Kosygin are no "traitors" to the interests of the Soviet Union's working people. They base their "revisionism" on the true attitudes, interests, and aspirations of the masses. They know that in present-day conditions Stalinism would not survive. Since the days of Lenin and the October Revolution the Soviet Union has traversed a very long stretch of road which has brought it more and more unmistakably to the type of civilization characteristic of highly industrialized countries. China has only just started on that road. With all her achievements, she is representative of a civilization which either has long ceased to exist (if it ever existed at all!) in the Euro-American part of the world or is in the closing stage of its disappearance.

Thus, we have entered an age of conflict between two different realities. On the one hand, we have a world where the consequences of the technological revolution have made their presence felt in every single sphere of collective life. This is a world that has reached a high degree of stability of relationships and economic security. At the same time, it is a world of a retreat from ideology, one in which ideology is being dislodged by a pragmatic approach to the problems of change.

On the other hand, we have a world where the technological revolution has not yet occurred or is only in its early embryonic stage. The rule there is a general lack of social stability and a general absence of economic security. However, already new collective aspirations are emerging there at the same time, coupled with a capacity to compare one's won condition with that of others and to draw practical conclusions therefrom. That world has already evolved its own leaderships, utterly convinced about their own mission. It is a world of dynamic and charismatic ideologies and ideological movements.

It may as well be conceded that—as all other things in human history—these are but transitory situations. Today's Soviet Union differs hugely from the Russia of the days of the October Revolution. The China of the future will surely be very different from the China of the age of Mao Tse-Tung. The changes that shape the present-day aspect of the Euro-American civilization will of necessity transform reality in the rest of the world as well. On condition, though, that they will have the chance of taking place— that is, that the entire globe does not fall victim to some gigantic holocaust that will annihilate its present possibilities and development trends. Given the ideological dynamics of a certain part of the world, and the revolutionary tension that prevails in it, the probability of such a holocaust occurring cannot be dismissed.

All this seems to be a very far cry from the "end of the age of ideology." Indisputably, we are living through a period of acute ideological crisis. The Euro-American civilization is clearly turning away from the traditional ideological systems, which are visibly on the wane and have lost their old emotional substance. As for new ideologies, either the need for them is not too distinctly felt or they are still *in statu nascendi*. In the rest of the world the accent is on ideological dynamics. The ideologies are in most cases very nebulous, appealing to feelings rather than to the capacity to rationalize. Hence the anxieties their possible practical consequences may give rise to are all the greater.

VI

We are nearing the end of our remarks. In summing up, let us restrict ourselves to just a few very general observations.

Ideologies do not emerge victorious from that supreme and inevitable test which consists in a confrontation of their promises with what historical developments actually bring. These are the processes of verification which throw doubt on the charisma of ideology and lead to its crisis. Such verifications are often very tragic and entangle people in situations of catastrophe.

The power of ideologies resides in the emotional substance that conditions them and is roused by them. When analyzed rationally by critical minds, ideologies disclose their inner contradictions, their discrepancy with the facts of experience, and the naïveté of their ambitions. Their errors become particularly apparent when ideologies are viewed from a distance of time, when—to put it differently—the processes of verification are already much advanced. However, when it comes to social consequences, the rational side of an ideology is of but little importance. What is decisive are emotional elements which condition the dynamics of ideologies and of the movements connected with them.

Ideologies very seldom—if ever—attain the goals they have set themselves. However, by putting human masses into a state of action, they may reach short-term objectives of very considerable historical importance. Social Democracy never achieved the goals set by Marx, but its own impact and that of its ideas on the history of the latter half of the nineteenth and the first half of the twentieth century has been prodigious. It has at the same time been very beneficial socially. Social Democracy contributed decisively to the introduction of a number of major reforms which have paved the way for the present social stability and the sense of economic security in the highly industrialized countries. Communism was a major driving force in the industrialization and modernization of the Soviet Union. Nationalist movements have contributed greatly to raising the national and social consciousness of the human masses and to awakening their cultural aspirations.

The immense part played in human history by ideologies of all kinds cannot be overlooked. Of course, the socio-historical conditioning of the emergence and development of these ideologies has always been the determining factor. No ideology has emerged or operated in isolation from the conditions of time and place, and they have all been historical phenomena. But ideology as such becomes a powerful stimulant for collective action and is in itself an extraordinarily important element of history.

Its charismatic and revolutionary nature, its claims to be the repository of absolute truth, its powerful emotionalism—all this has more than once led to catastrophic situations involving tragedy for man. The greatest crimes and the greatest atrocities have been perpetrated in the name of ideology and for the sake of giving effect to its preachings. From religious strife to the massacres in Indonesia runs the path of ideological showdowns.

Perhaps the most important driving force of history has been the rationalized folly of frightened man. An irrational creature, man makes constant use of rationalization. And this is extremely well reflected in his ideologies. Without ideology, man is at a loss; armed with one, he often commits the greatest of follies in its name.

Therein lies the tragic dilemma of man and his history. And regardless of the view we take of individual ideologies and of the part they have played in history, we must always bear in mind the contribution of that basic ingredient—human folly.

This ingredient is revealed whenever an ideology is subjected to practical verification. When looking back, people perceive the follies of their predecessors with horror and shame. Today's Spaniards are ashamed of the follies of their ancestors in the late fifteenth century. Young Germans are ashamed of the follies of their parents. And Soviet citizens are beginning to be ashamed of the follies of Stalinism. Doctor Zhivago's perennial question comes to mind as to the sense of that nonsense. But are those who feel shame immune to another eruption of human folly? The future course of history will give us an answer to that question. A great part of our globe now lives in a state of ideological folly. What guarantees are there that that folly will not explode elsewhere as well?

Translated by Marek Latynski

CZECHOSLOVAK OBSERVATIONS

Vlasta Šlikova

Today it is difficult, even absurd, to write any account of the events in Czechoslovakia, because of the immense changes that have taken place there recently. Attempting to evaluate specific moments in the post-January Czechoslovak Renaissance, it seems at times as though each of them had various causes and meanings, as though everything that happened was just then happening, penetrating us, changing us, and informing our national situation and private lives with a new meaning. Our judgments were not logical. Rather, we existed in an atmosphere of inspiration and doubt and we searched: we searched for a new way, a true, human way to an honorable and just future—and we searched for our own true face, which we had to conceal for so long beneath empty phrases that at times we doubted its very existence. But now there are foreign tanks in our country and the NKVD is waiting . . .

Before August 21, we grappled with the question: What does democratization really mean—the end of demoralization? We lived for too long in a world of fear, and in moments of anxiety and pessimism it seemed to us that fear had attached itself to us forever, that we had accustomed ourselves to fear as though to our personal moral collapse. A person who is afraid gradually ceases to be himself. He does not do what he says. He does not say what he thinks. And he stops thinking and acting. He operates under the impression that what is has nothing in common with him personally, that what takes place around him happens without him. The person who is afraid is alienated. He never finds any support to lean upon because he has no confidence in anyone. And that probably explains why he is frequently cruel. Before that fateful January even we had concentration camps; we were ashamed to admit that we were the citizens of a country in which people were tortured, yet we loved

43

that country and were unable to find a name for that sense of dread and accommodation. Frequently there was a desire not to think about it—not to know—to pretend instead that what we do not think about or know does not exist. This concerned, however, not just external concentration camps. Each of us lived in his personal prison of uncertainty and fear. Each of us had the impression that he was or could be persecuted, and there were those who believed that they could save themselves by persecuting others. And so, Catholics persecuted Catholics because of their religiousness, people of "bourgeois origin" persecuted their former friends of similar origin . . . Some thought that they could save themselves only by cruelty, by great cruelty which ended with sentences of death pronounced against innocent people, by petty cruelties which poisoned life and did not permit one to think freely or to freely create a human character and in general be a person. People were deprived of work because of their "social origin," because of their philosophical convictions (at times only on the basis of an unfounded suspicion that a given person might possess certain "unofficial" views), and finally very often because of personal conflicts with people who happened to be more powerful.

A certain stratum grew accustomed to what it regarded as its right to make decisions concerning other people, their fate, their work, their studies—and their thoughts. Even the most influential government functionaries were afraid, because the higher the position held, the more vulnerable one was. In order to ally their own fear, they grew intoxicated with their personal power. They thought: "I'm afraid, I'm wretched, but the person whom I'm persecuting is more wretched than I am because he is afraid of me."

People who were afraid felt a need to be feared in turn, finding in this at times a sort of perverse satisfaction. It was unbearable and had to end. It is hard to say how the change came about. In the period before January everything seemed hopeless. Yet in January everything gave the impression of a peaceful development which would bring certain "corrections," but which would end in the greatest likelihood like the "Polish thaw" (we still had no idea of the kind of "frosts" that can follow the "thaws"). The idea of a "thaw" was pleasant, but we had grown out of the habit of placing excessive confidence in anything that could be beautiful.

It is hard to say precisely when "the pebble caused the avalanche"—when there truly occurred that outburst of inspiration which changed our relationship to the world and to ourselves, which changed, or perhaps to a certain degree created us. But it is quite difficult to speak here still of "us" as about a unified mass. At certain moments we were truly unified, but that is something that developed only later, in those days of the August occupation. Before then we wanted everything to end well; later, however, we were afraid, but in a different way than we were previously. No longer were our private fates concerned; those who believed in the future had no sense of isolation. There were, of course, differences between us, and we ourselves were changing, as people who just then were gradually becoming themselves, who just then were searching for their own gestures and faces.

People began speaking without cessation. Before, we were a country of silence. People were afraid to relate political anecdotes, to talk with foreigners, even to speak openly with their own friends in empty streets—after all, who knew, perhaps someone hiding in the shadows might overhear something ... Moreover, people almost had no friends; a person could hardly bring himself to place complete trust in anyone, with the result that brother mistrusted brother and parents mistrusted their very own children ... And that is why everyone remained silent.

Now, after January, this became the first thing to change, and noticeably so. People not only began speaking again, but even carried it to excess. Strangers openly and passionately related the wrongdoings that had taken place. They detained foreigners and talked about everything under the sun. Perhaps they were carried away by the fact that they were no longer afraid. This way they learned not to be afraid any longer. They became stupefied by their own enthusiasm. Slowly and trepidatiously they were becoming internally free people. But the process was complicated. There were too many of those who had compromised themselves in the preceding era, who had been overzealous in the execution of their duties, who had caused harm to other human beings. And these people again became afraid—afraid of losing high positions, afraid of vengeance, afraid of responsibility. And so it happened that at times the most vocal exponents of truly progressive ideals were people who were dirty and compromised, who attempted in this way to eradicate their own past.

There were times when it was difficult to believe in the sincerity of all those who now were on the side of Dubček. Prague was at its loveliest. But it was the atmosphere more than anything else that captivated. Not only did progressive slogans appear to be triumphing, but human decency as well. It was worse, however, in the provinces. Various self-conscious manifestations of "progressiveness" appeared which at first showed no signs of being in any way dangerous. It seemed that for the time being anyway it was "proper" to be human and undogmatic. Thus it was that people attempted to demonstrate their personal political courage (which they could do at the time with impunity). Nothing was as yet settled; everything was still in the process of becoming, and not without difficulty and friction. We thought perhaps that democratization would in fact ultimately triumph over demoralization. If a person, we reasoned, was forced by circumstances, atmosphere, the mood of society, the press, and so on, to be decent, then perhaps eventually he would become still more decent. But then came the occupation.

There was something quite beautiful in this tragic period. People became a nation in the best sense of the word. A nation fighting—without weapons in hand—for freedom. Fighting not only for freedom, but also for its personal dignity as a nation. By the ideals which we were defending, we were creating ourselves. What showed signs of developing gradually, over a number of months, was realized now in the course of a short period of time. The wall of silence which arose between ourselves and the Russians closed behind us not only a long period of deceptions, of daydreams about Slavic brotherhood and unity. Not only did it divide us from people without a sense of personal responsibility, who only listened but did not think. It was as though the wall at the same time locked us up by ourselves on a single ship surrounded by turbulent elements. The sense of danger created solidarity, a fact which even surprised us.

For the time being we are living in an atmosphere of emotional tension and we pray for a miracle to happen. We do not reason logically, for if we did, we would have to confess at least to ourselves that what awaits us is sad. We live only in the present. What is now is good; we are together, we have found ourselves at last. But how long can this last? The human organism requires the creation of conditions in which it can exist. In excessive heat or excessive cold a person changes, degenerates, dies. He does not endure physically, but there exist at the same time certain minimal moral demands which have to be met in order for a person to live as a human being. When these do not exist, when there is nothing to breathe, human decency falls to pieces and disappears ... A blameless collective heroism is possible where a threat exists for a single day or at the most a few weeks. It is easier to be a hero when you stand face to face with an adversary. But in endless days and years, without an enemy one can see and touch, with fear ever present, together with uncertainty, mistrust, and fatigue, in conditions which force one not to think, which stabilize a system of unfair treatment and denunciation—how long is it possible to remain a hero?

At the moment we are sailing in a vessel threatened by a stormy sea. But ships sometimes founder on foul shoals or are thrust onto dead ones. Planks fall apart and rot, while people sentenced to death become cannibals out of despair, exhaustion, and their own baseness. I am afraid . . . at the moment we are sailing together, all facing the same threat and united. But can we defend ourselves against external attacks which are becoming increasingly more violent? And will we later be able to save ourselves in the face of our own fear and debasement? The occupation armies and the embassies of the countries that attacked Czechoslovakia are looking for assistants. They are haranguing and distributing inflammatory material about the "Czechoslovakian counter-revolution" and about the "brotherly assistance of the armies of the Warsaw Pact." And the Polish Embassy in Prague is distributing material which one should like to take to the Czechoslovak police as outrageous provocation. But now people are again a little afraid, so what they do instead is simply destroy the objectionable literature and say nothing more about it. We are still together and therein lies our strength. But morally unbearable conditions must not be created for people. Over an extended period of time one can live humanly only in human conditions.

Everything, however, is still changing. We are still overwhelmed at the absurdity of everything that has taken place and we still believe in miracles: perhaps the Russians will come to see and admit the error of their ways and simply leave the country, perhaps we shall never have to be afraid again, perhaps no one again will have to persecute another human being out of his own fear. Moreover, everything that a person can write or think today quickly loses its timeliness because the situation changes from one day to the next. In fact, I should be very grateful if these observations of mine had already lost their immediate relevance.

Written on the day of St. Wenceslaus.

Translated by Harold B. Segel

LAST WRITINGS

Andrzej Stawar

TYRANNY

IN THE FINAL PERIOD, some pathological traits of Stalin's personality came to the surface, favored by circumstances. Let us start by quoting Lenin, who recalled—when he felt the approach of old age—the words of Turgenev to the effect that a man's worst crime and failing is to reach fifty-five. Lenin, as we know, escaped that fate.

There is actually no reason to believe that Stalin was a particularly psychopathic type. He was, after all, under constant scrutiny, as though under a magnifying glass. An analogy comes to mind: If Tiberius had terminated his reign soon after fifty, he might have left behind him the record of a harsh, perhaps cruel, ruler, but one whose conduct was in the main politically rational. The features of personality that characterize Tiberius in history books did not become evident until old age.

German writers gave currency at one time to the term *Caesarenwahsinn*—the madness of caesars, the occupational disease of absolute rulers, especially those who may have usurped their power.

There are certain standard situations, following a. familiar pattern. There are the staggering contrasts of personal situation. Let us try to assume the part of a man treated by his entourage with adulation mixed with fear, fed a constant diet of flattery. Yet he feels surrounded by people who are waiting for his first false step to bring him down. He wonders whether there might be a plot among the seemingly loyal courtiers, whether the cup of tea might not be poisoned, or the physician approaching him with a hypodermic might not be an executioner. The severe tension of such a

48

situation, its violent transitions, giving full play to a suspicious imagination, would be enough to shake the balance of even the strongest nervous system, such as Stalin's undoubtedly was.

In the course of years the symptoms became aggravated, including self-delusion and a sadistic delight in degrading others, as for example when he ordered the highest state officials (Voroshilov among others) to strip naked and perform a Cossack dance. There were other significant touches, as for example when he added in his own hand, on the proofs of a book submitted for his approval, the term "great" next to his name. These tendencies, developing through the years, intruded eventually also into the field of policy. This was particularly evident in Stalin's last move, in the matter of the "criminals in white."

The atmosphere of the Kremlin court, and that of the pinnacles of state power in general, was strongly reminiscent of Byzantium or some sultanates of the east. It was often said that Stalin used doctors when he wanted to remove personalities whom it was not convenient, for one reason or another, to put on trial. This was rumored in connection with the death of Frunze (1924) and Pilnyak wrote a famous short story based on this theme, which reportedly cost him later his life. The privileged state clinics were under the *de facto* management of the GPU and MVD, which supervised the selection of their personnel. The first sensational medical trial was held in 1938, when the GPU chief Yagoda was charged with such methods, but it seems doubtful whether he could have done so without higher approval.

When Stalin, with the progress of age, began to see more and more of the men in white, it must have occurred to him that he might become their victim himself. Persons in his entourage could have easily stimulated the dictator's morbidly suspicious imagination in that direction, supplying an excuse for a major purge, according to some sources stated to reach the proportions of those of 1936–38.

It started with the so-called Leningrad affair—the liquidation of Vice-Premier Vosnesensky and his supporters. There is no doubt that a silent resistance was brewing at that time among the higher Party echelons. Vosnesensky dared to cast doubt upon Stalin's infallibility, especially in economic matters. He criticized the costly and unrewarding giantism, which found expression in many construction projects of Stalin's later years.

The war brought some degree of relaxation, both ideological and organizational. There was a slackening of the terror; men were needed. During the war the government was compelled to cancel many sentences of the 1937–38 period. Thousands of officers were released from concentration camps and often entrusted with responsible commands. Such moves could not be reversed afterwards.

There is no doubt that in the higher reaches of Party and army hierarchy, where the behind-the-scene facts of the conduct of the war were well known, the generalissimo's prestige declined appreciably (as Khrushchev hinted in his famous speech). Stalin sensed it and he decided to rebuild the cadres in the well tried way, by liquidating a sizeable portion of the higher ranks of the Party, in the 1936–38 manner.

THE SOCIAL RESERVES OF TERROR

Historians and writers generally view terror in its most obvious aspects: executions, atrocities, deportations, and other measures calculated to induce fear of authority. The other side of the coin, though significant, is often overlooked.

Edgar Quinet made some interesting observations on the subject (examples were not lacking in France at that time). When the secret police hounds the members of the opposition, when they are sentenced by the thousands, the reaction of the community is generally compassionate. But a dozen years go by—an amnesty usually comes sooner or later—and the survivors return. They are greeted by the community with mixed feelings, with some uneasiness.

Why? Their places in society have been taken, their rights usurped. The business of the deportee is now in other hands, someone else has the law practice, or the university chair, a wife may have found a new protector. All those who *de facto* profited by the disappearance of the victims of terror are now anxiously awaiting revindications, disputes, perhaps even revenge from those coming back.

In constitutionally governed societies, the process of legitimate social rotation is a very slow one. A government official, an army officer, a scholar, or even a professional man has to wait for a long time before he can reach the position to which he aspires. Competition is usually sharp. Incidentally, it is one of the causes of social unrest, which finds diverse forms of expression.

A period of terror creates a fluidity of personal positions and possessions. The jobs of liquidated dignitaries are taken over by others, who often take not only the posts of those executed or deported, but also their goods.

The style of life at the top is the same under all regimes. People furnish comfortable apartments, they collect antiques and art, they assemble libraries. Now all this goes on auction. In the aftermath of terror there is a macabre animation, a kind of market in bargains: everything can be picked up cheap—jobs, houses, art, rare books, and so on.

While some careers are broken, others see a meteoric rise. Many quick promotions are available. An assistant professor, the trusted aide of a great scholar, counted sadly the years or decades that might pass before he could take over his chair. Now he has his chance: a skilfully compiled selection of the senior professor's more careless remarks, sent to the right quarters, is sure to open a vacancy. And who could be better qualified to fill it than the man who alerted the authorities to the danger?

In Imperial Rome a delator received a portion of the property of the condemned man. The same practice was adopted by other despotic regimes, including Russia before Peter the Great. The informers always concentrated, naturally, on people from whom they could expect some profit. A fever of denunciation seizes thousands, in the capital and all over the country, in cities and in villages. We can understand the true nature of terror and its social consequences only in the light of such phenomena.

Soviet Russia has certainly set some records in this field. It would be inaccurate to credit one man with the establishment of this system. It was built over decades by an organization which bore different names in the various phases of the revolution. At the time of the Civil War it was the CHEKA, then the GPU, and later the NKVD and MVD. But it was always the same institution. Stalin, in making his often quoted remark: "We are all Chekists," supplied a doctrinal justification of the theory according to which the class struggle intensifies as socialism progresses.

At any rate this diabolical system functioned perfectly. In constitutional regimes a dissatisfied citizen constitutes an embarrassment for the government. But under this system any malcontent could be rapidly picked out—the concentration camps still needed free labor—so that the dissatisfied citizen ended up by serving the interest of the state.

It was a return to very archaic concepts of government. The author of a memoir entitled *Fifty Years in the Ranks* (one of the more noteworthy books of the period) recalls an interesting conversation with one of his diplomatic colleagues, at a time when he served as military attaché in one of the Scandinavian countries, shortly before the First World War. An intelligent man, a Stolypin supporter, an embassy counsellor, he maintained—mostly on economic grounds—that Tsarist Russia should be separated from Europe by a Chinese Wall, as a protection against disruptive influences. The tsarist regime was, of course, incapable of erecting such a wall. But a frontier bordered by a stretch of no-man's-land, with lines of barbed wire, bears considerable resemblance to the Wall of China. It was, in some ways, a return to the Russia of the pre-Peter period.

Archaic features were a typical characteristic of the Stalin regime. He has been compared to recent tsars, notably Nicholas I. But the latter wanted to be a Prussian style despot, clothing his absolute rule in administrative decrees, which he tried to observe himself. Stalin, who paid little heed to any laws, especially in his later years, kept his own execution squad for disposing of members of his entourage who displeased him—a method more reminiscent of an Oriental sultan.

GENERAL CONCLUSIONS

The fact that revolution came, in a sense, as a by-product of a war, was a matter of surprise for Marxists of the Second International type. It would have been no surprise for Engels, who made some penetrating comments on the role of wars and armies in economic development.

I have already referred to the military view of socialism as a means of awakening the consciousness of the Russian masses, and the consequences of this view. Actually they are still effective. The basic inner conflicts of the revolution survived through years of upheaval and changes of economic structure.

Lenin, in one of his speeches after the conclusion of the Civil War, replied to opponents who charged him with merely advocating things long familiar from Sunday readers: be honest, trustworthy, industrious, studious. The poet Alexander Bezymensky, then an elated Komsomol youth, relates the shock with which he and his friends received Lenin's speech. They expected—being the hope of the revolution—some marvelous promises for the future. They heard instead what the young are often told: study, learn, you do not know enough.

We encounter here the inevitable second phase of the revolution: the transition from battles, violent upheavals, and violence to a slow process of formation of a new social consciousness, based on new principles, a new reality comparable to what might result from a geological cataclysm. Such phenomena cannot be easily grasped by the participants. We should now examine some basic problems, which will remain long unsolved, but which may determine the fate of the new regime.

In the previous revolutions, called "bourgeois" by the Marxists, there was a certain concordance. These revolutions did not create the type of economic man unknown, or at any rate unrecognized, by the feudal era, they merely released him from bondage. This contributed to the economic growth of capitalist societies, as the establishment of that type was by no means confined to the bourgeoisie alone. It was adopted at all levels of society, permeating deeply the social and intellectual life of these nations, becoming part of their culture. There is no evidence of a similar phenomenon occurring in the Soviet Union, and this is clearly evident in attitudes toward economic problems. Such a statement might appear a paradox without foundation in fact. After all, there is undeniable economic progress, proved by statistics and by such technological achievements as the Sputniks.

But it has been known for a long time that economic effectiveness and high technology do not necessarily go together. In the United States the urge for technological progress has always been strong, but economic effectiveness was often left behind. It was said in the nineteenth century that when an American wants fruit, he cuts down the tree. Extravagance was inspired, of course, by a sense of inexhaustibility of resources—present also in the Soviet Union. I will endeavor to probe these basic problems.

Let us start with a matter of the most profound importance in shaping the economic philosophy of any society. I am referring to the philosophy of property.

The rigorous protection of socialist property in the USSR and in the people's republic is well known. Recently capital punishment was reinstated as a means of protecting such property (also in Poland).

The principle appears to work in support of socialism. A healthy respect for communal property among the citizens would certainly eliminate many harmful phenomena of economic and social life.

There are, however, other aspects of the situation. It has been pointed out that a particularly stringent protection of communal property emphasizes the fact that the personal property of citizens does not enjoy such protection. This is reflected in countless wisecracks current in the streets. No amount of punitive measures can change this fact.

Property and the powerful passions it evokes are not simple matters. There are two extreme manifestations of that emotion: one is the grasping greed for profit, to be accumulated with a view to further enrichment and exploitation of others. This is the meaning of Proudhon's famous aphorism: "Property is theft."

But we also know that some of the strongest passions are inspired by forms of property devoid of practical value. This includes all forms of collecting as, for example, the common urge for book collecting. Some people spend years, often at some personal sacrifice, assembling a library of books which they will never read. Aside from art, antiques, coins, people collect items without any intrinsic value, sometimes bordering on the absurd, but it is such collecting that arouses the keenest passion. It may be an expression of some cult of value, of rarity, and of human achievement—social achievement in the last analysis.

Why should a pair of shoes in the window of a government store merit special legal protection, while the same shoes, purchased by a citizen and stolen off his feet in a bus, are no longer so strongly protected, by reason of having become private property? Such distinctions are at the root of the sarcastic attitude of the population toward the whole matter.

That is why there may be much truth in the opinion that even a socialist society should promote respect for all property, as it would increase at the same time respect for communal property. This view seems to be confirmed by the experience of nations which do not extend any special protection to government property and yet report few violations, because of the general respect for property of any kind.

We are dealing here with a factor of primary importance for the development of economic effectiveness, an instinct for rational management of communal property, which is lacking in socialist countries. Severe penalties, such as capital punishment, are hardly conducive to a positive change in outlook. All they accomplish is to spread panic among the current offenders of that type. In a field as complex as national economy management, the scope and efficiency of terror are limited. Some measures could throw the economic life of the country into chaos.

But it is impossible to inculcate new economic ethics without a basis of general ethics, binding for both the governed and their rulers. Bolsheviks generally treat such reasoning with suspicion, as nothing more than intellectual talk, and they adopt the interest of the Party as the final and highest criterium of moral values. They also believe that the aims of the Party are so elevated and socially moral that they justify any action taken by the Party. It is an application of a principle formerly ascribed to the Jesuits: the end justifies the means. The analogy is not accidental—the ethics of a closed order may well include such a rule as its guiding principle. It gives the Party exceptional strength and freedom of action. Yet the overall effect on public ethics is disastrous. The non-Party citizen reacts defensively and tries to turn the principle to his advantage, finding many opportunities for doing so.

Another frequently proclaimed principle gives politics priority over economics. It can also have deplorable results, providing bureaucracy, especially at the middle and lower levels, with an excuse for stifling initiative.

The problem of improvement of the standard of living, the endless promises invariably ending in disappointment, is closely tied to the economic philosophy of the regime and of the people. There seems to be little hope of any significant progress in this field without a change of basic attitudes, a profound revision of the whole outlook.

It is not a matter of placing economics over politics, as some technocrats would suggest, but rather of establishing some workable balance between the two. Disregard for economic effectiveness results in waste on a gigantic scale, making all appeals for greater production efforts sound ludicrous. One could quote countless examples, reported in the press both in the USSR and in the people's republics.

Let us take the following case: A correspondent of *Krokodil*, a satirical journal which takes a very serious view of its duties, observed in a distant province of Russia a most remarkable phenomenon: several railroad carriages standing in a field, without any railway in the vicinity. His inquiries unfolded the following story: there used to be on the site a rail spur for a warehouse with building materials for a factory in the course of construction. Several state concerns participated in the construction. When the factory was nearly completed, a delayed shipment of building materials arrived at the site. The concern handling the construction refused to accept the shipment, because their books were closed and they were getting ready to move to another job. The transport authorities also declined to handle the shipment. The state railway administration refused to take the carriages back until they were unloaded. The construction concern soon wound up its operation and moved away. While the jurisdictional squabble went on, the transport authority, which had urgent work elsewhere, simply took away the railroad spur line and left only a couple of hundred feet of rails under the carriages.

The case seems to be a classic one in its disinterestedness. No one had any axe to grind, no one stole anything, everyone acted according to the regulations. The resulting waste was an automatic outcome of a strict observance of the rules. The Soviet press is full of similar cases, though not always as striking in visual impact.

Thousands of such leaks erode the economic well-being of the population. Economic life cannot be handled effectively under rules of bureaucratic routine, governed by a universal fear of overstepping limits of jurisdiction, meddling in other's affairs.

Some years ago Pomerantsev's article "Sincerity," published in one of the monthlies, aroused widespread interest, though it was later condemned for revisionism. The author described the following incident:

A provincial official received orders, under the plan of the assistance of cities to rural districts, to move with his office to a nearby kolkhoz and help with the harvest. A harvester combine was already there and work was started. The weather was wet, and the machine, instead of harvesting the oats, bent the stalks and crushed them under its tracks. On the first day some 20 hectares of oats were trampled into the mud. In the evening the city official assembled the kolkhoz workers and asked them whether they could think of any solution to the problem. The men replied that they could, but that they expected to get every tenth sheaf of oats. On the next day the kolkhoz men brought out scythes and sickles left over from the days of individual farming and they harvested the wet oats.

A few weeks after the official's return to the city, he was indicted by the district attorney, on the basis of charges filed by an informer. The indictment included three counts:

1. Demoralization of kolkhoz workers.
2. Causing valuable state equipment to stand idle (the harvester was standing by while the men used their scythes and sickles).
3. Waste of state property.

Fortunately for the official, this happened when the period of summary sentences was over, so he escaped punishment. A few weeks later, he was involved in an identical incident concerning the digging of potatoes, and was indicted again.

Such cases exemplify the application of formalistic bureaucratic rules to current economic problems.

INCENTIVES

Profit is said to be the god of a capitalist economy. The premium is then the god of a socialized one. It certainly provides an incentive for the implementation of the plan. But, just as capitalists sometimes may destroy merchandise to increase profit, so the premium incentive may lead to similar abuses, on an even larger scale. The classical case is that of a factory department, or even an entire branch of industry, substituting an unsuitable material, contrary to technological requirements, sometimes making the product virtually worthless. The factory gets its premium for carrying out the plan, but the consumer grinds his teeth and inundates the commercial distribution system with complaints. An even more complex chain of reactions is started if the item of sub-standard quality is delivered to another branch of industry and incorporated in its products, causing widespread disruption of production.

Such cases cannot, of course, be blamed on premiums alone. There are other contributing causes, but the chief economic planners do not seem to be aware of them.

THE PSYCHOLOGY OF POWER

Soviet leaders often say that the Bolshevik is an uncommon man, not like others. They may be right, especially as far as a certain combativeness, fighting spirit, and determination are concerned. There is a singlemindedness, a devotion to one dominant idea, which provides clear cut decisions at the top and blind obedience at lower levels.

Their politically consistent action in a relentless drive for power makes the Bolsheviks unbeatable whenever they are faced by parties based on other principles—they are then, as someone observed, like iron pots among clay ones. That is why all coalitions, alliances, and so on, invariably end with the other party broken to pieces, whether it be Social Democrats, Anarchists, or weaker states in diplomatic confrontations.

One should also take account of a talent for organizing mass emotion, directing and utilizing passionate social feeling, as well as the ability to hypnotize individuals with visions of boundless power. These capabilities sometimes assume an extreme form.

The Vikings, famed for their voyages of conquest, had a special elite of warriors. They were called the Berserkers. They surpassed their comrades in valor and fighting ability, but the ease with which they went into battle fury made them dangerous even to their own fellow soldiers, so that they were assigned separate boats and were kept apart from the main body of the expedition.

Bolshevism undoubtedly has its own Berserkers. Combativeness, when lacking visible external enemies, may turn inward. Various groups and factions are ruthless in their mutual opposition. Even minor policy differences give rise to the most violent accusations of treason. Those who witnessed factional conflicts and purges report that they were conducted in a state of frenzy bordering on intoxication, a kind of ecstasy of hate, which afterward slowly subsided into a more lucid state.

The berserk element represents, of course, only a very small fraction of the eight million members of the Communist Party, composed mostly of quite ordinary people. But it may be more

significant among the leading elite. The leaders of the Party and the
government are formed and recruited within that elite.

Relations with the great mass of the people remain dialectical.
The elite still sails in separate boats—its philosophy, its way of
thinking, and its personal life (with a few exceptions) remain alien
to the mass of citizens, despite the elaborate propaganda machine.
Propaganda therefore has to concentrate on popularizing the leader,
and it finds a fertile ground in a centuries-old monarchic instinct.
The political interests of the people are focussed on the person of
the leader, especially as far as the Russians proper are concerned.
These are, of course, not the tepid emotions aroused by British
monarchs among their subjects.

We are dealing here with a new caesarist formation—the leader
becomes known for his great deeds and achievements, through
famed feats of propaganda. Such emotions are explosive but unpredictable. Vast communal actions are undertaken to offer a total
solution of various problems. They may succeed or not, but
propaganda remains silent on the failures.

Success requires a total isolation of the citizen. In Stalin's time
the "capitalist encirclement" was pictured as a ring of famished
vultures ready to pounce upon the population of the Soviet Union.
Generally speaking, wartime emotions are the easiest to arouse and
the strongest, as well as those that the propaganda machine
controls with the greatest ease and virtuosity. Naturally, the
isolation of the citizens creates a peculiar world of thought and
feeling, well suited to the exercise of such arts of persuasion.

These little understood contradictions came to the surface in the
course of the last war. Under a liberal regime any war, even without
serious defeats, is seen by citizens as a major aggravation—bringing
with it economic and spiritual restrictions, a limitation of personal
freedom, and increased coercion by the state. In the Soviet Union
many citizens, especially the intellectuals, saw the war in a different
light—as a harbinger of freedom, a means of emancipation from the
dull formalistic rule of Party and state bureaucracy, the opening of
a window onto real reality. Such feelings were clearly reflected in
Pasternak's famous novel.

Such a reaction may, of course, seem paradoxical and startling.
But it carries with it some concealed dangers. An absence of a fear
of war (which is so widespread in the West) among large numbers of
the population means that the government has complete freedom of
decision in vital matters of war or peace.

The basic concept forged under Stalin remained unchanged.
The Twentieth Congress brought violent personal criticism—
aimed mainly against the cult of personality—but it was a limited

criticism. It failed to cope with the caesarean principle, in fact firmly rejected any attempt to do so.

The only force capable of carrying out a reform of the state and the regime is the Party, but it has no program of reform. Besides, such a move would jeopardize its monopoly of power. Yet only then would it be possible to activate elements which so far remain passive. The absence of legitimacy became evident in the course of the changes after Stalin's death—even though every effort was made to ensure a smooth transition of power. In such conditions every change of administration becomes a minor or major coup.

This is hardly likely to inspire the masses with loyalty. Outside the Party and its government and police machine, there are two forces which enjoy by their very nature a certain amount of organizational autonomy. One of them is the army. On several occasions in recent years it played a decisive role in the struggle for power. Some of the ambitions that came to the surface had to be curbed, which was not accomplished without difficulty, as in the case of Zhukov.

Another force with its own propaganda machine is the Orthodox Church, which seems to have been gaining popular support in recent years. There are also numerous illegal or semi-legal religious sects, which appear to be quite active.

The rejection of any program of reform by the Party is quite logical. After all, the Party professes that the present line of evolution is leading the Soviet Union to the highest form of human organization: a communist society. Soviet scholars, such as Professor Strumilin, who granted an interview on this subject to the Warsaw *Nowa Kultura*, seem to have already established a timetable for the gradual introduction of communism by stages. It is apparently scheduled for the forthcoming decades, with a completion date within this century.

There are among the political activists of the Communist Party of the Soviet Union many who are sincerely convinced that they will live to see communism established. The dissolution of a huge state coercion apparatus within decades does not appear impossible to them. However, according to Khrushchev's concept, the omnipotent Party would still remain the arbiter of human relationships in the new society.

It is hard to imagine the psychological transmutations required to make the functioning of such a new system possible. After some fifty years of the new regime the economic mentality remains unchanged—money remains the yardstick of well-being and citizens, just as in the West, strive to secure as much of it as they can—the only difference being that Soviet citizens make it more often by illegal means. If experienced politicians like Molotov and Malenkov were sceptical about the socialist character of the present regime only a few years ago, some doubt about the sincerity of the current predictions may be permitted. They resemble some of the sleight-of-hand tricks of the deceased leader, calculated to work mainly on the imagination of youth, a method taken over by his successors. The Chinese experience shows that such planning of new eras of social and cultural change according to the calendar results merely in chaos.

Translated by A. T. Jordan

THE DEATH OF AN OLD BOLSHEVIK
Reminiscences about Steklov

Aleksander Wat

> "Their eyes were dark and sunken,
> And their faces pale as if detached from their
> bodies,
> So that their skin assumed the shape of their
> bones.
> ... Their eyeholes were rings without bones,
> And whoever reads O M O on their faces
> Will at once recognize the sign of 'M'."

ONE OF the tortures of Lubyanka is its idle existence. For months on end nothing happens beyond the usual daily routine, and one cannot resist the feeling that it is going to remain this way eternally. In my cell, No. 34, which I shared with three other convicts, one of whom steadily drifted into insanity, we were stuck as in a tin can, isolated from the rest of the world. Out of this arises a complete disruption of the sense of time; the past and the present are interwoven paradoxically and complexly, as in the New Novel, and above all subjective time detaches itself from calendar time. I couldn't even tell you when we were evacuated from Moscow: in July or September of 1941? We had known about the war for quite a while—from trifling signs, which here assumed an unusual shape and gravity, as in dreams. Thus, the windows were first painted in a blue color; the prisoners were shifted around in different cells, which in the past were spacious—and now, as in the days of Jeż,[1] were crowded; the long dead corridors were en-

---

1 A Polish writer of historical novels in the 19th century. [Translator's Note]

livened from time to time only by the echoing of footsteps and the buzzing signals of the guards, occasionally by the screams of a beaten man from an office. Now, when they were taking us at night for a "grilling," we passed gesticulating groups of NKVD officers. The abbreviated time of the interrogation, the nervous distraction of the inquisitors attested to existing anarchy in the edifice of Absolute Order, as well as to the poverty of our tightly locked microcosmos.

Even though I don't remember the date, I won't ever forget the days of our evacuation. I see unknown faces and silhouettes today as though through a magnifying glass, and it seems that after twenty years I could still recognize them in a crowd.

They chased us all "with our things" into those long intricate corridors, where previously two convicts did not have the right to meet each other, onto wide, steep steps, fenced in with a metal net from the floor to the ceiling from the time Savinkov committed suicide there. Men implicated in the same affair met each other on them, brother found brother whom he had thought dead. We could not yet call out to each other and therefore made signs to one another either by blinking in an astonished sort of way, or by a joyful wrinkling of the brow, or by a spark in the eye. Everything took place in complete silence, which one could literally hear, not despite, but thanks to the sound of a few hundred stamping feet. Looking at people in other cells, we realized how we must look ourselves: bedraggled old jailbirds.

We made our way through the thick crowd, one after another— all of this was taking place effortlessly, as if we were shadows— past officers of the NKVD with stripes and rhombs,[2] lieutenants and generals, and young, pretty girls, well-groomed, with a European chic, girls the likes of whom I haven't seen anywhere else in Russia, creatures from another unattainable high world—among the crowd of the condemned. Every one of them was carrying armfuls of briefcases, tall stacks of files, and index cards. Down-stairs they were throwing them into the trucks at random! Those files—the books of destiny of 200 million people on the rigorous order of which the entire empire of Stalin was maintained. The end of the Empire, the Apocalypse—so we thought, shaken by hope and terror, watching carefully as our dog-catchers demolished the foundation of their power.

We stopped for the night in Butyrky—in narrow box-cars without air. I immediately found my friend Broniewski there. We were arrested at the same time in January, 1940. One of those wonderful accidents and meetings which are so frequent in the

2 Rhomb: from the geometric rhombus, an insignia worn by officers in the Soviet Army during World War II. [Translator's Note]

USSR, but which so upset Western critics of *Doctor Zhivago*. We were suffocating in this "box," but we hardly felt it, so great was our exhaltation at the sight of signs of the downfall of the Empire.

The following day they packed us as tightly as possible into cattle-cars on a railway siding. Nevertheless, during the daily check two dogs managed to open a wide path for the NKVD officers.

In my car the majority were victims of the first post-war catch, from a variety of proscription lists. The difference between them and us was almost a difference of species. Their very satiated faces still bore the special martial inflatedness of Soviet dignitaries; their eyes were like baited traps. Who wasn't there: generals, deputies of the Supreme Soviet, famous flying aces! Academicians, a group of biochemists. A group of Jewish managers of the Moscow department stores, who were selectively arrested as speculators, while their associates, native Russians—and high-ranking Party members to boot—remained free. Germans—leftist emigrants, among whom I met the editor of *Sturm*, whom I knew in the twenties in Berlin. Polish and Lithuanian officers, Erlich and Jewish Bund members from Vilna. We were fed with clay-like bread and herring covered with a layer of salt while we had a limited ration of water, etc., etc.—such things are well known and have been frequently described.

On the fourth day we were unloaded in Saratov. They rushed us practically at a trot to an Internal Prison of the NKVD several kilometers distant. The snake-line of short-winded, miserable wretches was several hundred meters long; the women brought up the rear, while nervous shouting soldiers marched alongside. Countless passersby in the streets pretended not to see a thing. The Poles tried to maneuver so as to remain together. Both of us, Broniewski and I, were helping Erlich, who seemed as though he were having a heart-attack. My friend Tadeusz Peiper, who was exhibiting all the signs of a persecution complex, whispered to me: "I saw your wife. Be happy, you'll be together again." I didn't know anything about my family since I was arrested—and I was full of the greatest fears. I don't need anything more! My sensitive, beautiful wife in such wretched misery. And my son probably lost. I tried to stay behind and get closer to the women so I could ask them a question: Is the wife of the Polish writer Wat here? As I was maneuvering in such a manner I heard from the distance a voice shouting "Stalin" accompanied by epithets which most of us then could not even dare to think to himself. "The old man Steklov," my companion whispered to me, "that's the way he was carrying on even in the train." The voice was sharp, barking, but not hysterical.

A few minutes later I found myself next to the curser. He was walking briskly at the very edge of the column. The soldier next to him did not say a word; his face just expressed fear, anger, and sleepiness. The prisoners at Lubyanka, generally speaking, aroused in the soldiers and the guards not respect, but a general fear; they knew that no matter how wretched we were, we were an élite, toward whom they had no rights. In this case they definitely took the bold fellow for a fool, which aroused their traditional Russian fear and respect for the "spiritually crippled." The ill wishes, epithets, and curses of my temporary neighbor were monotonous and vulgar. However, his overall bearing was striking. I didn't know too much about Steklov; I knew, however, that he was one of the first comrades of Lenin, for many years an editor of *Izvestiya*, the author of books about Chernyshevsky, Bakunin, and Dobrolyubov. Involved in my own troubles, I glanced at the fool—because that's the way I thought of him, because I had seen so many of them already. I looked at him with more and more attention, because his appearance contrasted so greatly with that of the others. Slender, tall, somewhat bent, with a narrow, well-proportioned head, he immediately impressed me as an old Englishman—an Eton nursling. He was dressed cleanly and carefully, and even though his suit hung on him, it looked well preserved. But like the rest of us, his skin was not of an earthly color but seemed to be splattered with ashes. And if he differed so much from us, the old convicts, how much more he differed from the new arrivals from freedom!

Have a careful look at the faces of official Soviet tourists, politicians, Party workers, writers over thirty. Whether fat or slim, attractive or repulsive, pleasant or unpleasant, the faces of the intelligentsia of a certain generation or of "promoted workers," energetic or passive, good-natured or sadistic—they all have a common stamp which one can hardly express in words. It is not necessarily a mask, but rather a general facade, under which one can imagine several layers of under-faces. A kind of a dead expression in their gaze, despite their disturbingly lively eyes. A monstrous self-assurance which in a moment—to our despair—can turn into a cry of mercy or perhaps madness. A jovial gaiety which insufficiently masks a cowardly smiling. A constant tense alertness, the vigilance of the fugitive who has to know what is happening behind his back. Not so much languor as heaviness. An unnatural readiness to smile cordially and the parvenu haughtiness of a clerk. And last, but not least, particularly among Party dignitaries and generally among other Party members even of the lowest ranks, what the Russians refer to by the untranslatable *poshlost*, a unique mixture of vulgarity, dullness, and coarseness. Sometimes one or the other ingredient is missing, but there remains their generally sympathetic "appearance," *Gestalt*. Of course, *we are speaking now about the typical Soviet face*. And precisely this typical Soviet stamp predominated on the faces of the newly arrived prisoners. They represented all the varieties of the Soviet physiognomy. Nothing remained in them of the almost musical counterpoint and physiognomical tension of the pre-revolutionary Russian intelligentsia. Nor did they have the amusing simplicity of the faces of the simple Russian people.

The contrast between the occasionally handsome upper part of the face and the lower, with its soft flesh and hard bone, is more striking than usual. But what is particularly unique here is that their eyes, the expression of their eyes, harmonize precisely with the lower part of the face, which must denote the preponderance of animalism. I stress: this is the phisiognomy not only of the new intelligentsia, but also of the old, though it is often less easily detectable after so many decades of an existence which determines not only "consciousness."[3] This is understandable and demanding of understanding, when one recalls that it was enough not to have the prescribed garb, appearance, and gestures in order to perish. Nature, as we know, is superbly inventive in mimesis.

What I have just written is a summary of my many years of observation. However, I believe that one can also deduce the same thing from the human condition in the Soviets, as if one were piecing together a synthetic criminal portrait.

Not a trace of any of this was in Steklov. His eagle-like profile corresponded to his lonely existence among us. But what really struck me most of all was not only his strangeness, but the particular humanness of his face. Very thinned out, bony, it seemed reduced to the simplest formula of humanness, the same one that is at the bottom of every "existence," unchanging despite all the changes experienced. Now, as I write this, a Dantesque vision comes to mind: "Chi nel viso degli uomini legge OMO, Bene avia quivi conasciuto l'emme." The letter "M" in medieval thought and iconography represented the most essential scheme of the human face. The appearance of Steklov thus was not Russian either—it was simply human.

The moment of attentive examination was not long, thus it was one of those moments when one truly sees. And never forgets.

Later, the ritualistic squatting down and blessing of water from barrels took place in the prison yard. This was followed by a disorderly crushing into a huge cell, and a running to grab the

3 A well known axiom of communism: "existence determines consciousness."

best bunks. The best bunks and their immediate surroundings were taken by three *urks*⁴—a frantic ringleader and his two adjutants.

The ringleader, a wild character, gnashed his teeth, spoke in a harsh voice, spat, turned his eyes up and down, stripped himself naked, and the flow of his words was a masterpiece of thieves' argot. There were only three of them, but hundreds of Soviets gave them a wide berth with fear and a carefully masked disgust.

I found out more about Soviet life in this hall in the course of two weeks than I did in the ten months I was in Lubyanka. We managed to form an intellectual club in the corner: five Poles; a Soviet microbiologist, whose only guilt was that he had a hobby—logistics, about which only four or five of his reliable friends knew; an academician—the only specialist in Russia on avalanches, which have devastated cities of Central Asia, and who was deported because he had a German name, even though his grandparents were Russified. Anyway, this is the way they explained their presence among us.

After a few weeks I was taken to a small cell. I found the young *urks* there. One of them was as handsome as the boys at the Café Flore. The other, a little peasant, illiterate, who after landing in a penal colony for some reason or other developed a taste for the *urks*, for their charming carefree existence. Without their ringleader, who demanded to be called "prince" (he gave his family name as Obolensky), they both were nice, accomodating, and peaceful. The younger one would throw strings into the neighboring cells, sometimes with my notes: "Is there a female citizen by the name of Wat among you?" He managed to do it with the skill of a circus performer; he even organized extensive communication with the lower floors, and that was when we were caught. Here they did not tolerate the kind of special telephone network with which the walls of the Kiev Prison, where tens of thousands of unbridled children live, was covered.

There was also an old professor from Saratov University, a historian, who had the misfortune to possess a piano and a beautiful daughter. Young university students gathered at his place, recited Mayakovsky, and once, someone, perhaps a provocateur, spoke about a pure "second" revolution.

There was a Volga German, a Party activist, who thanks to the early arrest avoided the general deportation of the Volga Germans from the booming collective farms—the only ones that were independently booming in the USSR. He talked to me about his expectation of Hitler's coming—in the language of Luther, because the

4 *Urki*: A Russian word meaning bandit or thief, which came into existence during the Revolution. [Translator's Note]

native Germans, who occupied the Volga territory from the time of Catherine the Great, preserved their native tongue and their bible.[5] After the deportation of the Germans, Saratov became one of the hungriest cities in the USSR.

I also came across the academician who specialized in avalanches. He was extremely talkative on the subject of politics. He told us what he "consumed" once—us, who toward the end were ready, like the mythical Erysichton, to eat our own bodies. Through this he gained some kind of a base predominance over us, of which he took advantage, even though he aroused antagonism among us due to his pettiness, a trait intolerable in prisons.

There was also a thirty-odd-year-old Moscovite, who claimed to have been the manager of the Theatre of the Red Army, an individual not without a certain charm, but at the same time repulsive, cynical to the very marrow. He was, as the inmates would say, a typical product of the Moscow marginalia of the Komsomol. A mixture of shrewdness, of scraps of information snatched here and there, and of unbelievable ignorance. However, he knew Moscow in and out, its bars, intrigues, the customs of its upper classes, facts, and personalities. He loved to impress others with such aphorisms as: "With us, you can have any woman you want for half a litre of vodka."

When speaking about the inhabitants of my cell, I must not omit the bedbugs. Nourished by our meager blood, they were big, exceptionally immobile, mopish, and seemingly immortal. I say immortal because in the evening, after they had their fill of us, we burned out their nests with the acetylene lamp each cell contained; however, the next morning, the same number of them would crawl slowly up the wall, stopping always at the same height, never crossing the invisible line—the bedbug taboo in the domain of Soviet law.

But even here the Apocalypse found us. As I described it else-where, during the night we were wakened by a loud shrieking, a spasmatic laughter, vulgar, scoffing, strikingly like the laughter of Mephisopheles in a provincial opera. We did not immediately discern that it was a monitor circling along the Volga River, giving signals of alarm. An air-raid siren over the Volga! Only a few months after the beginning of war! I detected a diabolic sign in all that.

The theatre manager told us a lot about Steklov. He was a close friend of his son. A celebration on the fiftieth anniversary of his revolutionary activity had been organized for Steklov with all the

---

5 In 1941, Hitler was repatriating all the national minorities, with the exception of the Jews.

usual Soviet pomposity, under the patronage of Stalin himself, who for a long time had a weakness for him. Steklov knew how to amuse him with his jokes, which were sometimes so bold that the courtiers were frightened to death. Almost on the eve of the celebration, Steklov was arrested with his wife and his son. However, his wife and son fairly quickly returned to Moscow and even—an unheard of thing till then—were given a part of their previous apartment. Moreover, they even got back quite a bit of their stamp-collection, which once belonged to a Russian tsar and which was Steklov's favorite possession. Soon afterward, the family was officially informed about Steklov's death in prison due to a heart attack. Among relatives and friends nobody doubted the truthfullness of the statement. It happened just before the war.

We were swelling from hunger, that is, some were swelling, others were drying out. Not only were we prisoners hungry. The guards who took us for walks down the iron staircase tried unobtrusively to pick up from the dust breadcrumbs spilled by the delivery man. One day, to our great joy, pieces of green tomatoes appeared in the hot water. This continued several days, for about a week. Immediately thereafter, an outbreak of dysentery erupted in the entire prison. In our cell I was the first to get it. After a week of high fever, which more than once surpassed 104, and the other miseries connected with the illness, I was taken to the hospital which was situated in another enormous prison, on the other side of the Volga. In the Black Maria I found myself face to face with Steklov.

Two, perhaps three hours later we sat unattended in a corridor, and here began a conversation that did not stop for a moment. It was rather he who spoke; I only interpolated some question from time to time. I realized that this was the only occasion for me to find out the true answers to the questions that bothered me so much. Also, despite my fever, I tried to pay attention and not to lose or forget anything. We both had high fever, but it was not making us lose consciousness; true—it was predatory, but it sharpened the aggressiveness of intelligence and at the same time the capacity for attention. However, at certain intervals I was overpowered by such fatigue that whole fragments of the conversation slipped into oblivion, and finally from the sum total of information from this "confession of a burning heart" of the old Boshevik, not much was left in the final analysis.

And this "not much" I am closely examining, in order not to attribute things to the deceased which stem from so many of my own experiences. I remember a few sentences just the way he spoke them; others I repeat faithfully, I believe, if not verbatim, at least the way my memory dictates to me, together with the living intonation of his voice.

It was bright in the corridor, the morning was sunny, and the autumn light mild, thus this time I could observe him closely and for a long time.

This time he made a different impression on me: that of a Polish intellectual aristocrat from the time of positivism. Narrow, elongated head, with aristocratic bone structure; dried face harmoniously etched yet seemingly smooth, with an energetic line over his lips; big eyes, without brilliance, which occasionally lit up, but also without any brilliance; piercing pupils, which very often narrowed in an expression of contempt, at which time the eyelids nearly closed; eyelids as thin as cellulose, so that his glance fell heavily upon the person conversing with him, on things; his lips must have once been full, soft, and maybe even feminine, now they were barely a trace of lips; his beard was hard; due to extreme thinness his nose protruded energetically, boldly, yet did not dominate his face, as his heavy glance did. The entire face, together with his cheek bones and his forehead, indeed formed the Dantesque letter "M".

He would either become morose, or again, after a moment of silence, become beautifully mild. For the most part, however, he demonstrated a contemptuous and scoffing aggressiveness toward everything. He gesticulated excitably and sharply, especially in moments of angry rage, in which he seemed to indulge himself, but which he could also immediately control. Generally speaking, he was able to discipline himself, and then for a change he was icily calm and haughty. He was distinguished by a special kind of lordliness which I observed previously in old Social Democrats from good families, carefully brought up from childhood. At the same time, perhaps, this lordliness was the cause of their downfall in the USSR; their very appearance provoked the Communist commoners and parvenues.

His voice this time was completely different, though still dry, filled with the richness of abrupt modulations, unpredictable— the voice of a seducer. And also the voice of a great parliamentary speaker, who after his work, changes into clean clothes and shoes within the four walls of his apartment.

To my question whether the tales about him told by the theatre manager were true, he answered affirmatively. And so it was the truth that there were festivities planned to celebrate his anniversary, and Stalin himself took an interest in their preparation. It was also true that he was arrested shortly before the date set for the celebration. After an exceptionally long and severe and rather formal investigation in Lubyanka, he was deported to Omsk Central. This wasn't even a death house. It was a coffin, where the arrested sits alone, in such solitary confinement that the world outside doesn't even know whether the convict is still alive. In this *one exceptional* case the family was informed that the convict died a natural death, as Steklov learned when he met friends in the transport about whom it was common and official knowledge that they had been dead for a long time.

But the war uprooted even that graveyard order. Some of the convicts were sent to Moscow in the first days of the war, others to Lubyanka, from which no one ever returns. Steklov, as it turned out, came with us from Lubyanka to Saratov.

In Omsk, Steklov was especially in favor. Even though he was buried alive like everyone else, he was still permitted to work in his cell on a new book about Chernyshevsky.

Apparently this work was initiated by Stalin himself, who was very much interested in Chernyshevsky. Every morning the convict would get a certain amount of paper and had to return the same amount to the guard in the evening. He was also supplied with whatever books he wanted, along with documents from archives. "The mere name of Chernyshevsky turns my stomach," he now complained to me. But how much of this disgust was reflected in his writing? This will remain a mystery of the manuscript, which alongside so many others—perhaps the most valuable part of Soviet literature—is resting peacefully in the archives of the MGB.

Most of all he talked about Stalin, but it was precisely these revelations about him which interested me most of all, which threw me suddenly into a state of exhaustion bordering on collapse, and at these moments an unceasing noise in my ears overpowered the voice of the speaker. It seemed that I was swimming farther and farther away from this voice, in my inner sea, and my memory control over words and facts seemed to me so shimmering that their recollection is full of holes.

I made every effort, forced my attention, ever mindful of the exceptional nature of this occasion when I was being made privy to phenomena of which I was ignorant at the time.

I remember that he spoke a great deal about Jenukidze, whom he knew intimately. He was, as he insisted, the only man whose contempt the vindicative Stalin tolerated for an exceptionally long time. But the daughter of Jenukidze was a Communist bigot of the Cult of the Leader (*nota bene*: As I have been assured on several occasions, these "Passionarias" were not put off by the repulsiveness of their idol, his short stature, big head, pockmarked face, red brush of hair, low forehead, and cold "white" eyes. On the contrary, it had a great effect due to the contrast with his power.) Jenukidze's daughter ran to Stalin to report on her father, presumably about his confidential sally against tyranny, which wounded him more painfully than ever before.

This genius from some miserable little province established for himself a home circus and surrounded himself with the most vulgar creatures. It was not a court, nor a clique, but a gang with a ringleader. The entertainments, the conversations at the table with vodka flowing freely were extremely vulgar, little more than hangman's jests. After some quarrel—(with his wife Aleluevna, or his daughter? I don't remember)—he called a henchman and told him to "give her a spanking," a bullet in her forehead. When the henchman returned with his report of the execution, Stalin fell into deep despair and ordered the executioner to be executed himself. "The Sultan from Sheherezade, a 'mythological knight,'" added Steklov. He imagined that the hangman would have hidden her in a hermitage.

(This story in other variations I later heard many times in the USSR and Poland. From the flow of Steklov's outpourings about Stalin, I came to the conclusion that not only was he suffering from his own experiences, but also that he was frequently citing rumors circulating in the highest and lowest spheres.)

He mentioned many famous names of heroes of the Revolution. Not one, as far as I can remember, was spared his biting, abusive invective and even such epithets as "scoundrel," "scum," "rag." It was either that "scum Trotsky" or that "rag Voroshilov" or that "scoundrel Ordzonikidze." As a matter of fact, from my own previous observations and later ones, I knew about the incredibly fast process of degradation of the "old Bolsheviks" and, generally speaking, of Communists who were once famed as heroic rebels. For example, "the tapper" in my first cell in Lubyanka was an old Bolshevik, the vice-minister of electric works in the Russian S.S.R. Why? For what? For the tea and cigarettes with which the interrogator treated him? Out of doggish love? Out of the need of a heart deprived under Stalin? Due to the dialectics of change by which a strong revolutionary is transformed into a servile executioner?

I asked Steklov, as I usually did everyone: how does one explain the manysided, complete, and mean degeneration of the Revolution? "Allmacht des Staates!" I heard this analogical answer many times; almost every Soviet intellectual became converted to one type of anarchy or another after prison. I told him, as I did the others, that this explains nothing, that many times and in many countries the omnipotence of the government repeated itself: during the reign of Philip I I, Louis X I V, Napoleon, Nicholas I, to say nothing of ancient empires. After all, they had nothing in common with the Empire of Stalin.

I was always stunned by the inability of Soviet citizens to comprehend how it happened that "proceeding from the foundations of absolute freedom, they reached absolute enslavement" (the words of Shygalev in Dostoevsky's *Possessed*). Even the prophetic Dostoevsky barely formulates the point of departure and the point of arrival and is absolutely silent about the path followed. But here it is indeed real; it is from the world of mystery. Among all the people under the Soviet yoke, my comrades-in-arms from the dungeon in Alma-Ata in the year 1943, the élite of great banditism, seem to me to be the most perceptive, the least derouted and mystified by a quarter of a century of ideology.

So I asked Steklov about the Moscow trials. As with the rest, I was distressed by the puzzle of self-accusations. True, I did not yet know Koestler's novel, and if we had known it in Lubyanka, it would have been the subject of gay mockery. However, we knew very well how confessions were obtained. Anyway, I once closely observed four men who were tortured. There were two young Ukrainian nationalists in the Zamarstynov prison in Lvov. But they could not deny that they killed a sizeable number of NKVD people and soldiers, especially at the time of their arrest, in Lubyanka. The enterprising Tietz, who in the immediate pre-Hitler years was the Berlin director of the Institute of Trade with Central Europe (and at the same time director of a subtly branching out subversion) was recalled in 1933 forthwith to the Institute of Marx and Engels. He returned (or more accurately was returned) to Beria himself, prepared like a meat-ball, with finely chopped buttocks, thighs and legs. He already had signed two confessions that he was a spy for the GESTAPO, thus an active saboteur, but twice he retracted his confessions and intended to stand trial and deny the accusation before the Military Tribunal Court. He wanted to confess only to sabotage. And because in those highest places of prosecution Socialist justice demanded that testimony have a logical structure and sequence of order, he asked me, as a writer, to help him prepare the scenario of his acts of sabotage.

I also had in my cell an old engineer, a Bavarian, whom unemployment drove to Russia in 1930; mercilessly tortured, he stubbornly refused to confess his guilt—most probably because his rigorous Lutheranism did not permit him to lie.

I was finally convinced that one can withstand torture, even threats toward one's family; Tietz, for example, had a wife whom he loved.

I asked Steklov whether the confessions in Moscow trials were forced by tortures? "Why tortures?" he shouted. "All our hands were dipped in blood, in sh . . ! All of us, all of us, without exception! From the very beginning! Up to the elbows!" These words I remembered, I believe, verbatum, because I felt such a shiver pass through me at the time. When he told me what he did, his hatred toward his own past reached a "crisis," his face was torn by convulsions, the movements of his hands were abrupt; indeed, he reminded me of one of Dostoevsky's characters—"A Jacobinian who was questioned once about wild massacres in prisons answered: Was the blood we have spilled, without any mercy, without any hesitation? No one had to be tortured, everyone had in his mind's eye a long list of his own crimes and misdeeds. So why not confess to this and that? It really didn't matter that much. Besides, those were already human rags." So spoke Steklov, and I agreed with him in spirit, thinking of a believing Catholic who would have finally lost all faith in salvation.

"When you return to Poland, please describe how old Steklov was dying."

I answered: I'll never return. He grew angry for a moment: "You will return, sir, I am *sure of* that." I had the impression at the time that I had before me a spoiled old egoist; I'll have to return because he, old Steklov, had given me an assignment to fulfill.

And a moment later: "When you return to Poland, write how old Steklov was dying."

Those were his last words, for they had already come for us.

We were separated, but we were divided only by a wall and a guard at the door. Before daybreak I heard his sharp "For God's sake"; no doubt he was begging for something, and then I heard, for a change: "Stalin . . . Stalin . . .," but he spoke those words probably in delirium. His voice grew weak, fell, the voice of an old man. The words no longer intelligible. Upon hearing the name "Stalin" the old woman who tidied up our place clandestinely crossed herself.

Twice I had the chance to stand at the door. I took advantage of the guard who only warned me that it was not permitted to talk there. The first time was on the afternoon of the fourth or fifth day after our arrival. I could only make a gesture of friendship and devotion. Steklov responded with a pleasant gesture, putting his hand on his heart. And again: "When you return to Poland, do write about how Nahamkes-Steklov was dying." But it sounded as though it were coming from a broken instrument.

The next time was on the same day, in the late evening: his lower jaw dropped and he seemed as though he were deprived of his body. He reminded me of the mummy of Rameses; his sunken eyes were closed, he was breathing heavily. His skull was that of a corpse, but still human. Despite all that, he was strangely beautiful: OMO.

This is how I shall remember him for the rest of my life.

The circumstances of my biography became so arranged that only after twenty years am I fulfilling the last wish of Steklov. Before that, however, I told everyone who was interested or wanted to listen how the old Bolshevik Steklov died. Now I can pay tribute to this victim of communism, one of the tens of millions, who appeared to me in his last days as a beautiful man. He sinned, sinned a great deal, but he had the good fortune and courage to redeem this through protest and courageous suffering.

A few days later, in a farther cell, Walden died, a victim, as he used to say, of his German Communist émigré friends.

Not long after, however, I returned to my cell, not badly cared for. Our head physician used to perform miracles in order to acquire for us such unusual items of food as rice, fish, and carrots in a hungry city, in a city of the hungry. He took particularly good care of a long-time leader of Latvian Jews, Senator Dubin, who in order not to become ritually impure, from the very beginning of his arrest ate nothing besides his "rations" of clay-like bread and was now lying next to me, transparent like a parchment, with a broken arm, which was the result of the artificial nutrition at Lubyanka. I told him that on certain occasions when there is a threat to life the Talmud permits one to break the law. "It permits, but does not order," he answered simply.

I now have the opportunity to say a few words about the health services in the USSR. How did it happen that, despite the complete brutalization of life there, most of the doctors, at least those with whom I had dealings, young or old, even Party members and even prisoners, preserved the Samaritan traditions of Russian medicine? Is it possible that even Stalin could not uproot all the noble traditions there? On more than a single occasion they fed me out of their own meager rations. Many times they saved my life.

At the end of November I was freed. My salvation was as much due to coincidence as to the theatre manager who shared my cell. As it turned out later, I weighed less than 45 kilograms, though my normal weight is around 80. I knew nothing about the amnesty toward Poles, which was already in force over three months. One night I was called in for an interrogation; the issue seemed very grave—supposedly I said something to the effect that Hitler is worth Stalin and vice versa. This means that the guard who knew Yiddish must have overheard me when I spoke to the Volga

German, a Communist Hitlerite. Besides, it was known in the cell that he was a "tapper"; the old German engineer, whom he treated with a son-like tenderness, was indebted to him for the special severity of his torture.

During the interrogation, when I was giving personal information about myself, the NKVD captain learned to his surprise that I was a Polish citizen. "Prove it!" he said. "How can I prove it, when you have all my documents?" "We'll check." As it turned out later, my file was misplaced somewhere; I was simply forgotten.

Soon afterward, with two other Polish officers I found myself at the barber's, where with devilish wickedness we were given a close shave for a haircut, and when evening came, we were released with rubles and bread for the road. Through the completely dark and empty Saratov we dragged ourselves to the railroad station—I, a skeleton covered with hanging skin, my two companions, one swollen, the other, like me, all skin and bones, all of us emaciated but free. Our steps were supported and hurried by the joy of the Apocalypse and the hope of salvation. If these words ever reach my comrades of that nightly wandering let them respond.

The prophecy of Steklov afterward began to come true. But my worse experiences came several months later. And for almost the next five years my greatest fear was that I might die in the USSR! That I might be buried in earth that had become contaminated. Let me die anywhere, but not there!

Perhaps it was precisely this fear and dissent that gave me the strength to survive all this calamity, misery, illness, and further imprisonment.

Translated by Vera Von Wiren-Garczynski

THE ROAD TO MOSCOW

Bogusław Miedziński

On the morning of April 30, 1933, I stepped out of the Warsaw train in Moscow. As I write these words I see the same date on the calendar—only it is thirty years later. Yet, the very matter that then carried me to Moscow is equally topical today: "peaceful coexistence" with Soviet Russia.

My Moscow visit was not the first step on that road. It had been preceded by confidential talks between I. Matuszewski and me with the Soviet envoy in Warsaw, Antonov-Ovseyenko, lasting several months.

It was in April, 1932—shortly after Hitler's talk in Bytom signaling "revindication" in the East when he assumed power, and several months after the initialing of the Polish–Soviet non-aggression pact—that Joseph Beck, then still Vice-Minister of Foreign Affairs, invited Matuszewski and me to his office. He told us that the Komendant [Joseph Piłsudski] had placed a stronger hand on the helm of foreign affairs, that he had ordered greater activity and initiative from the Polish side both in the West and in the East. In conjunction with this development there loomed for us, according to Beck, a clear task.

Namely, we were to make friendly contact with Antonov-Ovseyenko who, regardless of diplomacy, was a strong voice in the Party; obviously, during the Trotsky-Stalin conflict he had not offended Stalin. Said Beck: "Try to convince him that we would like to see in the non-aggression pact not only a diplomatic instrument but that we would also want to endow it with a living spirit; that as far as we are concerned—in addition to good will in maintaining the pact—we are ready to pass from a *sui generis* position of a 'cold war' to truly cordial and good neighbor relations.

"The Komendant considers a détente with Moscow as advisable

and possible in the present situation, both for us and for them. They are having great economic problems; apparently they have begun to build a big military base in the Far East, which would indicate fear of the Japanese; finally, what is going on in Germany cannot be conducive to peaceful sleep for the men in the Kremlin.

"Eventual improvement of relations with Russia," Beck went on, "will have a significant reverberation in the West. It will be received there with approval; further, it can assist in our effort—which we plan to undertake—to come to terms with Paris and London so that we might get an estimate of the situation and thereby explore the possibility of forming a mutual—but unlike Locarno—preventive policy vis-à-vis Berlin. As to the last point I cannot at this time tell you more."

Obviously, we accepted the assignment.

Establishing relations with Antonov-Ovseyenko was not difficult. At the next official reception we started conversation with him which went rather interestingly and ended with his invitation to lunch at the Soviet Legation, which naturally we accepted. During the following several months we met every few weeks at Matuszewski's, at my place, or as guests of Antonov, conducting on each occasion a lively discussion. Naturally, for the Soviet envoy the breaking away from a policy of isolation, as well as the opportunity for open talks with politicians who had considerable weight in government circles was a positive achievement. Like the majority of Russians, he also liked to debate. For us, however, at this early stage the talks were not progressing toward our real goal; except, of course, that they did create a certain free atmosphere, a definite openness, and an almost personal intimacy. Antonov was an uncommon individual, interesting and rather personable; he definitely was a man of deep ideological convictions who honestly expounded the canons of his Marxist faith.

Neither was the past of this revolutionary commonplace. Until 1906 he had been a career officer in the Tsarist army. As a young lieutenant he had been stationed in 1898 at the Warsaw garrison. After the unveiling of the Mickiewicz statue he deliberately made a point of ostentatiously and with formality saluting the statue whenever he passed by, for which he was transferred to the provincial garrison at Puławy. He was already secretly in contact with the Russian revolutionary movement, and in 1905 he organized a revolt of the garrison; imprisoned, disgraced, and sentenced to hard labor, he remained in Siberia until the outbreak of the revolution in 1917. In the fall of that year he found himself in Petersburg at Lenin's side.

Lenin entrusted to him the task of organizing a "mailed fist" composed of soldiers and sailors. Meanwhile, he was engaged by Trotsky to divert the attention of Kerensky and the Democratic Socialist leaders in a war of words during interminable public meetings. When Antonov was ready with his *force de frappe* Lenin had him storm the Winter Palace, disperse the provisional government, and assume power. From that time Antonov was one of the leading figures in the Party.

He had, however, a typical bolshevik vice: an infantile conception of conditions in the twentieth-century capitalistic world. He believed very simply that the important and deciding power in this world was the work of some international sanhedrin of capitalistic potentates, in whose hands individual governments were only marionettes in varying degrees of subservience. And so when after several meetings we proposed that though we highly valued the talks up to that point, we would prefer to pass from discussion of "principles" and away from past matters to the future so that we might bring up the non-aggression pact, we received the following answer:

"But you gentlemen are talking about an accomplished fact, and the pact is not yet ratified."

"There is no doubt as to ratification from our side."

"And I'll lay a wager with you that you won't ratify," answered Antonov with stubborn certainty.

"Such a bet would not be honest on my part because I'm too well informed; honestly, I don't understand what makes you so certain," I answered hiding my irritation with difficulty.

"Because France won't let you!" he answered undiplomatically. (André Tardieu was then head of the French government.)

The dispute got a bit hot and Matuszewski intervened humorously, proposing a temporary private non-aggression pact until the facts indicated who was right. But he added that he would accept the wager to the tune of a barrel of caviar.

Even though we parted graciously and calmly, we more than appreciated the stubbornness of our opposite number to continue the talks; they were resumed right after ratification, which took place in December, 1932.

During the first three months of 1933—after Hitler had been named Chancellor—we met several times, discussing ways of drawing closer and achieving better understanding between our countries as a concern grounded in principle. The talks then went smoothly. The whole discussion turned on what today is called "peaceful coexistence."

At this time there appeared my article in *The Polish Gazette* which gave in fact a *résumé* of our talks with Antonov. I expressed the conviction that there was no reason why neighborly relations between the two countries could not further develop amicably. Constitutional and ideological differences should not stand in the way, because there was no plan to "export" them by force; with regard to the Treaty of Riga and the recently signed pact all that was needed was a background of mutual cordiality and good will.

Several days after the publication of this article I visited Antonov and asked him if the contents of the article reflected what in my opinion was agreed upon between us. He had no reservations. Later he asked me if I did not think that our conversations ought to go further, on another level. This was an allusion which could be understood as a graceful withdrawal on his part, or as an affirmation of the need of accepting decisive policies. I did not ask him to clarify his meaning, wanting first to discuss this new development with Beck. He was of the opinion that we ought to take Antonov's hint positively, and that was also my opinion. Several days later Beck informed me—he was then Minister of Foreign Affairs—of the Komendant's decision: carry on further talks with Moscow. My instructions this time far surpassed the previous ones.

As to method—what with Stalin's obvious mistrust of diplomacy —it was suggested that I present myself as one of Marshal Piłsudski's old colleagues, delegated in this instance to reflect his opinion. As to content it was my job to convince the Bolsheviks that Poland under no circumstances would link herself with the Germans in any aggressive act against Soviet Russia.

Formalities for my trip to Moscow were arranged on the basis of my being editor of *The Polish Gazette*, and the purpose was to make personal contact with directors of the Soviet political press. This arrangement was accepted and the formalities were quickly and courteously settled.

One of Stalin's closest colleagues was Karl Radek, formally editor of *Izvestiya*, *de facto* director of the whole central press and propaganda apparatus in Moscow, and besides this advisor to Stalin in the field of international politics, a role independent of Litvinov, Minister of Foreign Affairs.

And so I found myself in Moscow on April 30 desiring, apart from my true goal, to see the May 1 celebration which—as we had been informed—that year was to be particularly noteworthy, especially the military phase.

At the train station I was greeted by Karl Radek, the Polish envoy, J. Łukasiewicz, and our correspondent from *The Polish Gazette*, Jan Berson.

At the train station I immediately told Radek that as a professional colleague I well understood how busy they all must be on the eve of May 1, and even for the next few days; therefore, I would prefer not to trouble them with introductory visits and would simply leave my calling card at the offices of *Pravda*, *Izvestiya*, and Tass. Radek accepted this proposal, affirming that indeed the next two days were filled up. He proposed, therefore, that we begin talks on May 2. We agreed that Jan Berson would act as intermediary and that we would not attach importance to formalities as to when and where the talks would be held. As it turned out we saw each other that evening.

At our Legation it had been decided to start my stay with a visit to the theater. However Łukasiewicz's secretary was informed that because every theater was presenting holiday performances in honor of May 1, tickets were not to be found. Several hours later, however, the Legation was informed that two tickets were available at the Vakhtangov Theater for the play *Intervention*. We were advised to arrive at the theater roughly three-quarters of an hour late, as the performance would be preceded by May 1 ceremonies. We set out punctually, nevertheless. Later we realized the misunderstanding: we had not been "advised," but rather asked to arrive late.

The moment we entered the theater and handed over our tickets, we received surprised looks, but just then the lights were dimmed; the curtain went up, so we hastened to our seats on the aisle, second row. On stage there began a ceremony clearly having a Party character. We listened to a report on the activities of the local Moscow group for which the Vakhtangov Theater had that evening been reserved. Next, there occurred the presentation of a standard to the leading Komsomol group in the area and, finally, the representative of the Moscow Soviet delivered a speech on the international situation and the foreign policy of Soviet Russia. The last we listened to with understandable interest. When that part of the program was concluded and intermission came, Karl Radek appeared and said smilingly: "Well, well, Editor, Colonel, or Minister, and let's face it, one time Chief of G-2 . . ." and he congratulated me that in the space of twelve hours I had managed to attend a Party meeting meant only for members. "But, no harm's done when all ends well. At least you were able to discern that in the report on the international situation, obviously not meant for outsiders, you did not hear a bad word about Poland." That was indeed true. As usual the speech endowed all the enemies of the proletariat and of Soviet Russia with unceremonial epithets; Poland had been omitted.

The play *Intervention* had its setting in Odessa at the end of 1918, during the Allied occupation, when the Bolsheviks were underground and the Red Army had retreated. The play was decidedly anti-French, well-acted, and actually the performance of the actors gave it yet another drift—it had an inadvertant anti-Semitic flavor. The bourgeoisie in Odessa was comprised primarily of Jews; the black characters in the play had to be the bourgeoisie, and true to the Stanislavsky tradition, these types were endowed with full local [Jewish] color in characterization as well as in speech and gesticulation.

After the first act the management invited Łukasiewicz and me backstage for tea. Of course, Radek came along and after introductions to the actors who played the lead roles we sat down to tea and cakes. A young woman sat beside me whose name I had not caught during the introductions. Twice I spoke to her in Russian. I noticed some hesitation in her answers. "A diehard Communist," I thought to myself. But after the third try, she said, "Please speak to me in Polish; I am Karl Radek's daughter."

Early next morning Łukasiewicz and I set out for the May 1 parade. From the diplomatic grandstand where high Soviet officials were seated (next to me sat Madame Yegorov, wife of the Chief of the General Staff), I watched with interest both parts of the parade; the military, in which for the first time the results of the modernization of the Red Army was shown. At one moment the mammoth square was filled with rows of heavy tanks, while at the same time up above squadrons of heavy bombers flew past. The sight was downright threatening, well-prepared, and well-executed. Stalin in the company of ministers and generals watched this from the Lenin Mausoleum. I was easily able to observe him; I also observed that during the last phase of the military parade, armored units, he carefully watched the diplomatic grandstand, obviously curious about spectator reaction.

As the army left the square a break in the proceedings occurred before the civilian part of the parade began. During this time we smoked cigarettes, rising with delight from the hard benches, while here and there lively conversations began, especially among foreign military attachés. I tried to engage in conversation Mme. Yegorov, who looked charming and agreeable and was distinctly well-dressed. I convinced myself, however, how very right was the advice not to ask anyone about anything. My question was an innocent one, something to do with the change in Moscow's views for the better, but Mme. Yegorov fearfully looked about and changed the subject as if to put a stop to any indication that she was revealing secrets to foreigners.

The civilian part of the parade was also well-organized. I distinctly recall one very characteristic thing: among the banners carried in the parade the most numerous bore the slogan: "Thank you,

Comrade Stalin. Life has become easier and happier." The old
faith still prevailed among the Russian Bolsheviks, that what was
projected in their plans, could be considered accomplished fact.
Those banners reflected Stalin's decree that the second Five Year
Plan would concern itself to a significant degree with consumer
products, articles of everyday use for which the populace was
desirous. This policy would unquestionably have brought about
significant relief and a great deal of happiness. But the fact is that
the anticipation proved hollow. The clouds were already gathering;
Hitler had risen to power in Germany and the second Five Year
Plan was again to concern itself completely with heavy industry and
armaments.

At the conclusion of the festivities in Red Square Łukasiewicz
and I spent the afternoon walking through the city. Delegations
from various parts of the Soviet empire made their way to designated
points where they received a holiday ration of food. It looked pretty
poor, nor could one see the touted "happiness."

As we toured the city by car as well as on foot, Łukasiewicz drew
my attention to the phenomenal détente that had pleasantly existed
for several weeks. Legation personnel could freely move about the
city without constant surveillance at infantry or armored check
points.

The next afternoon I had a talk with Radek. He was a bolshevik
type, completely different from Antonov-Ovseyenko, although even
less commonplace. Born in Tarnów [Poland], he finished Cracow
University, where he studied Polish Romanticism, and in particular
Mickiewicz, whom he revered. A capable and intelligent man, he
possessed a rare characteristic among Bolsheviks, a sense of humor.
Sarcastically witty, he was able to take a joke and even make fun
of himself. When once I expressed surprise that his relations with
Stalin, which started badly after the death of Lenin, had changed
so drastically, Radek answered: "Yes, in fact I thought at the
beginning that the best solution after the death of Lenin would be
the Trotsky–Stalin duumvirate, but while sitting it out in Siberia
I came to the conviction that Stalin would be enough." A note of
sour jibe resounded clearly in his answer. Radek also possessed
certain special rights in contemporary Moscow society and did not
accommodate himself to rules commonly required; to the question,
who was the greatest sage of the world, he allowed himself to name
Adam Mickiewicz and not Karl Marx. He was not afraid to repeat
malicious jokes about the Party if they were really good. He knew
the outside world, Western Europe, and that made conversation
with him easier. It is necessary to remember that in those days one
very often met people in high position, especially the young Party

members, who had never crossed the Russian border, people so unbelievably dense and so arrogant in their ignorance that it was impossible to come to any understanding with them on any matter.

Nevertheless, Radek was a confirmed Communist and Bolshevik. He was an ideological man just like Antonov-Ovseyenko, but a better student of Lenin with regard to reality and elasticity in political tactics. He had a typical bolshevik disregard for the individual and was totally lacking in sentiment. When once during our talks there was mention of the Soviet government's recent ruthless encounter with the Ukranian peasant and of the many millions who had died there from hunger, Radek was able to say: "Gentlemen, I don't understand why you attach so much importance to this affair. All right, let's say that you are right, that two million died in the Ukraine, and that the Soviet population will be, instead of 180 million, only 178 million. So what?"

Our first talk on May 2 at Jan Berson's had an introductory character. We both attempted to size each other up. With Berson Radek was already on intimate terms. We talked at length on the years 1919–1920, but more about that later. Radek arranged for me to have lunch at the journalists' club and confirmed the date May 4 by telephone with "Narkomindel." He excused himself on the grounds that he still had a great deal of work to do on the May 1 festivities and would not be free until two days later to take up such demanding and such constructive talks.

Before that came about it would be interesting to mention a few vivid moments connected with the May 3 reception at the Polish Legation.

For the first time there arrived at the reception a rather large Soviet delegation both civilian and military. Besides Litvinov there were several other ministers. Instead of the usual official reserve the behavior was relaxed and marked by friendly smiles—a clear indication of a détente.

Minister Litvinov, to whom Łukasiewicz introduced me as an editor and a member of the Diet, nevertheless insisted on addressing me as Colonel and opened the conversation with a question as to my opinion regarding the Geneva talks on disarmament then in session (with the same results today as thirty years ago). In reply I gave him some platitudes. I also talked with another member of the Soviet government, Rozenholts, Minister of Industry and Trade, decidedly a more ingratiating person than Litvinov, who clearly made much of his own friendly disposition toward us. Moving along the table I came to the military group. One of the legation officials to whom Łukasiewicz had entrusted me remarked that "here cognac rather than wine would be the thing."

I turned my attention to a mustached officer in the uniform of a komandarm (equivalent to a general) whose face appeared familiar to me. We were introduced, and General Budyonny cordially shook my hand and remarked that it gave him great pleasure to meet a Polish colonel in peacetime; I retorted with complimentary remarks on his great military reputation. We downed a cognac. I quoted Pushkin: "Soldiers recalled past days and battles in which they chopped at each other." Budyonny complimented me on my Russian and we had a second cognac. But when I refilled the glasses and the General and I reached out for them, his aide became concerned and "gingerly reminded" the General of a conference for which it was time to leave. Budyonny jovially retorted that he would make it and if he didn't make it on time, they'd wait, and besides the car hadn't been brought around. The aide went away, returned after a few minutes exactly when Budyonny, standing rigid like an old-time sergeant said to me: "Colonel, when you return to Warsaw please inform Marshal Piłsudski that until the day I die I shall always be proud of the fact that I had the honor to fight against such a great military leader."

"Komandarm," the aide intervened, "time to go, the car is ready." And so even the Red Army that day did not lack courtesy.

A lunch was given for me the next day, May 4, by the Moscow press with the participation of a couple of gentlemen from "Narkomindel," one being the director of Polish affairs, M. Stomonyakov. In addition to Radek there was—as I recall— Raevsky, director of Tass, the Editor-in-Chief of *Pravda*, and several leading journalists; on the Polish side there was Jan Berson, Moscow correspondent for *The Polish Gazette*. Radek and I agreed that we would not begin with any formal opening remarks. When wine was served Radek, as host, lifted his glass and addressed me in Polish: "We are happy to have you among us. To your health!" to which I replied in Russian: "All the best!" With Stomonyakov we spoke about Bulgaria, going all the way back to Byzantine times; I kept strictly to my instructions not to encroach on Łukasiewicz's domain nor conduct official conversations. Shortly there began a lively general discussion beginning, as is the custom among journalists, with the telling of jokes and stories. Berson bantered with Radek, who asserted that he could write better copy for *The Polish Gazette* than Berson, to which one of the Soviet reporters said that that was very possible, as Radek's articles were so full of Polonizations that they had to be translated into Russian. At one point when I could not find the right Russian phrase, Radek called out, "Sir, don't strain yourself to be perfect in Russian, there really are no Muscovites here—Stomonyakov is also a Bulgarian."

A more serious turn in the conversation came only when we retired to another room for coffee. Radek, Stomonyakov and I sat at one table; Stomonyakov shortly excused himself—duty called—and Radek and I remained alone. I warned him that I had to return shortly to Warsaw. I pointed out that diplomatic protocol seemed to be getting in the way of my mission, which was in fact to cut through that protocol, while at the same time making effective use of it. Perhaps we could talk like two old politicians, each of whom knew what the other represented. "Fine," answered Radek, "I am ready. Perhaps you could tell me, do many people in Poland think as you do about our mutual relations and do they want an improvement?"

"Surely you have guessed that I did not come here to acquaint you with the personal views of B. Miedziński. I am not going to give you a statistical report as to how many people share these views; won't the view of one man suffice—Joseph Piłsudski?"

"More than enough, but please remember that you just now said it. You are empowered by the deciding authority from your side but, up to now, I am only a go-between. In order to match your statement with an analogous authority on our side, it is not enough for me to say that I also 'guess'—to use your word." I interrupted, agreeing with him wholeheartedly. "Now that you have dotted the 'i', " concluded Radek, "I am ready to do my part." He asked me for a few hours delay—again editorial work called—and then we could get down to serious talk. We agreed to meet at ten that evening.

Radek greeted me with the request that I should not concern myself with the late hour, that he was at my disposal until morning if necessary. I assured him that I did not forsee the need, although I would indeed be happy if our meeting led to further discussions in the future. As a long-time student of Piłsudski I wanted to apply his method in intimate meetings when it came to finding an understanding. Piłsudski would state immediately at the beginning what he was ready to do and what he expected of others; the form was brief and then he awaited an answer: yes or no. He never allowed himself to "horse trade." And so I, too, put the matter briefly. But first I insisted on a short answer to the question: Do you Russians still hold to the idea that the role of Poland is that of a sallying-port or even the advance guard for all invasions of Russia?

Radek conceded, practically without any hesitation, that that indeed had been until then a widely held view; however, he stressed the "until then."

"So, I came here exactly to tell you that it is not so. In order not to speak in generalities, I'll come to the point. I tell you: Poland will not ally herself in any way nor under any circumstances with the Germans against Soviet Russia. I am fully authorized to make this statement by authority of the personal seal of Piłsudski, which I told you about today.

At this point I took advantage of a wall map of Europe, led Radek to it and concluded: "And now I'll tell you in my own words the basis of the position taken by Poland—not because we suddenly and passionately have fallen in love with you, but because our own interest dictates it. If we joined a German attack on Russia, what are the prospects? In case of failure the catastrophe is obvious. In the event of success? Now take a look at the map—imagine what kind of a situation Poland would find herself in, surrounded by the conquests of a fantastic empire, subject to its favors and piques. Do you suppose that we don't see this? As I see it, you ought to understand that this is a straightforward account of Poland's international situation, and you ought to give up an outdated suspicion of us. If on this score we understand each other, then the road to better relations between us is open; if not, then there's no point talking."

We sat on the couch looking in silence at the map. Finally, Radek said: "I have to concede to you, Colonel, that you have taken the bull by the horns. It seems to me that this is indeed a good beginning."

I clearly surmised that he wanted to digest what he had heard and I was sure that he understood me. I departed. The whole of the next day I spent with Łukasiewicz. In the evening Berson called me with the information that Radek asked him if it was true that I was planning to leave the next day. After Berson confirmed my pending departure, Radek alerted Berson that he would probably be in touch with him during the night so that information could be relayed to me. Berson assumed that Radek was on his way to the Kremlin with a report.

In the early morning Berson came with the following information. Radek indeed got him out of bed at three in the morning and asked him to relate to me—word for word—the following two sentences: "The meaning of your visit and our talks are duly appreciated. If you remain in Moscow a bit longer, it may be possible for you to be received by Joseph Vassily." I long pondered this turn of events. I came to the conclusion that it would be better not to stay. Strictly speaking, Radek's words did not constitute a definite invitation, only a "tenuous promise." As to talks with Stalin—I was afraid, obviously not of Stalin, but of Piłsudski and of my own unpreparedness. More important, I had no instructions for such an exigency. What had been assigned to me I had accomplished;

what I was to say had reached Stalin. I naturally turned to Łukasiewicz to confirm my reasoning. He didn't want to force my hand nor did I want to burden him with responsibility for my decision. As to the wisdom of requesting further instructions from Warsaw either by telephone or code, neither of us—for many reasons —was convinced that that was a good idea.

At the last moment I sent Radek my answer from the train station in the person of Berson, that I could not postpone my return to Warsaw. I would, however, welcome a return visit to Warsaw, where further talks along the same lines would gladly be undertaken. Łukasiewicz was a bit concerned about the possibility of ill-feeling on the Soviet side. It turned out, however, that there was none. Shortly after my return to Warsaw we received news from Moscow that Radek was planning a return visit in the very near future. He arrived just before Whitsunday.

During our first talk at the offices of *The Polish Gazette* Radek had already told me that Stalin received his report with the greatest of interest, that he was authorized to continue the talks begun in Moscow and that he would want from me only some further clarification, and then would be prepared to move on to concrete discussion as to what should be done by both sides in order to give relations between Poland and Soviet Russia a good neighborly turn.

Having received this declaration it was now feasible to seek instructions regarding further talks, but for this I had to gain time. Since the Whitsunday holidays were approaching I asked Radek if he did not want to start his visit to Poland after so many years absence with a tour of the country, or at least with a visit to his family home and to old Cracow. He replied that that would give him the greatest pleasure but, if it were possible, he would like above all to visit the Baltic coast. I assured him that he could travel wherever he liked and by whatever route he chose, that he had the *Gazette* car at his disposal and as a traveling companion I suggested the director of the news agency "Iskra," Colonel M. Ścieżyński, who not only would be an intelligent and well-informed guide but also a fine companion. We then sketched a journey through Kujawy and Pomerania to Gdynia, then through Posen and Silesia to Cracow, and finally to his family house in Tarnów, where I learned his brother lived. I did not forget to tell Radek—having in mind my experiences in Moscow—that the projected journey could be changed at will and that he should feel free to ask any questions about anything that interested him. Radek took this occasion to tell me of his last trip through Poland in 1919 when, as a Polish citizen, he was escorted from prison to the Polish frontier by the Germans, where he had been detained with Karl Liebknecht and Rosa

Luxemburg. Captain I. Boerner had transported him across Poland and delivered him to the advance guard of the Red Army. Of course I fully remembered this incident thanks to which Radek, instead of sharing the fate of his comrades, who were shot, landed in Moscow and, to boot, in the Central Executive Committee of the Bolshevik party.

Radek departed early the next morning to "take a look at Poland." I in turn informed Beck that Radek had a mandate from Stalin to continue talks, and requested further instructions.

Three days later Ścieżyński telephoned me from Cracow to inform me that Radek was leaving for Tarnów for a twenty-four hour private visit and then would be ready to return to Warsaw. I got an urge to talk to Radek in Cracow and that very evening we sat down together to supper at the Grand Hotel. Then we ambled through the mazes of the *Planty* [Public Gardens], along the Wawel walls, through the University where we had each studied at different times, finally ending up at the beautiful moonlit Square of Our Lady. In the Gardens we had sat a long time talking over the international situation. I had a definite feeling that the trip through Poland and especially the atmosphere of medieval Cracow had taken hold of Radek; he seemed to be a different man from the one in Moscow. It seemed to me that regardless of his bolshevism and marxism the Polish in him had come to the fore, and I felt he honestly thought that a détente and an accommodation of our relations were altogether possible.

Radek's stay in Poland lasted two weeks. We maintained a strictly unofficial routine, conducting talks tête-à-tête. The weather was fine, so I often took him to Wilanów or to Łazienki and our many talks often digressed to purely historical matters.

After our return to Warsaw Radek wanted certain additional clarifications. He began by repeating to me: "I assume that I understood the thesis that it is not in the interest of Poland to lend a hand to any kind of German action in the East, and that in the event of success Poland would find herself *de facto* at the mercy of the Germans; we can also assume that you Poles would not like a similar military thrust from East to West, that you don't want the map of Europe around Poland to be painted brown any more than you want it painted red." With all candor I acknowledged this additional interpretation.

We proceeded further. Radek stated that the Kremlin was convinced of the very simple reasons which motivated the Polish refusal to act with the Germans against Soviet Russia. "We believe in all sincerity that you won't do it. But we must take into consideration that you might be forced into such a situation. We see two eventualities. First, the Germans will hand you an ultimatum: Either go with them eastward, taking part militarily, assuring them a safe rear, helping them pacify conquered territories through your knowledge of the language and conditions in Russia, for which they will offer you this or that kind of share in the spoils; or, they will force their way through Poland, in which case you will constitute the first sacrifice to their *Drang nach Osten* policy, with all the consequences."

"The second eventuality: the Germans, not demanding from you open and actual participation, nonetheless will propose an arrangement based on your ceding to them the whole or at least the northern part of the Corridor, promising, of course, some kind of access to ports and a renunciation of further irredentist claims. In the event of your agreement, having procured free and uncontrolled access to East Prussia, they will be able to develop there a strong base of attack against us. Passage through Lithuania and Latvia, with or without permission, will be a simple thing for them. If, then, we believe completely that you do not succumb and there will not be any initiative or semi-initiative on your part with the Germans, you have to admit that in the event of a threatening ultimatum of which I speak, the situation will not be so simple."

At this point Radek attempted to persuade me that there would be nothing surprising if Poland, placed in such a dramatic position, fell under the first threatening alternative or decided to compromise with the second alternative. "We thought about this in Moscow, and frankly we weren't at all sure how we would act in your place."

"Neither do I know," I answered, "how you would react. But I do know without a trace of doubt how we would. Neither the first nor the second of the stated alternatives would meet with any other answer but a categorical "no" on our part. I am not surprised that there could be doubt among those in the Kremlin with whom you spoke about this. Neither Stalin nor Litvinov know Poland or the Polish character. But I am surprised at you who were raised in Poland, and know our history and our national character, both good and bad. You must know, regardless of your materialism, that such imponderables have played and continue to play a decisive role in Poland. And it wouldn't be irrelevant to remind you how seriously these scruples are rated by Piłsudski, the man who currently decides Polish politics. But let's be practical. Do you think that a nation, which for centuries has suffered at the hands of the Germans as we have, would believe that the German might would not be turned against us, or that we would lend ourselves to the strengthening of that might on the basis of some promise or proposal?"

I was angry and saw no reason to hide it. Radek observed my reaction closely. He added that as far as he was concerned, when he saw what we had done in Gdynia, the thought came to him that indeed that gigantic effort made no sense if we contemplated eventual surrender of our coast to the Germans.

Of course, I well understood that my emotional reply would not satisfy Radek. Without doubt those two questions he put to me had been dictated by Stalin. They would require a more formal answer at a later date. However, I did immediately relate to Radek with the greatest accuracy that part of my conversation with Beck on that very subject. After two days I was directed to assert briefly the point that Poland would not yield before danger or threat; also, I was given the authority to call on the Komendant himself—which I did.

In the meantime Radek and I talked over the matter of moving on to good-neighbor relations. He stressed how unfortunate it was when one relies too heavily on data culled from interviews, as that could lead to a completely false picture of the internal conditions of a neighboring country. Rather skillfully he voiced these views in the form of an attack on us implying, thereby, that we relied too heavily on "secret" reports about conditions in Soviet Russia, and about various situations which could threaten the stability of the Soviet government. He laughed about that, but at the same time used himself as a prime example of misinformation. He conceded that the picture of Poland which he saw during his journey differed markedly from that which he gleaned in Moscow from written or oral reports. "If not for the fact that in traveling with Ścieżyński from Warsaw to Gdynia I myself chose the route, then I admit openly that I would have suspected that you prearranged certain events which I saw in Łowicz or in Grudziadz. I was told, for example, of the extreme dislike of the populace for the army, which is virtually boycotted. And here at every turn I saw something absolutely different: I actually saw your soldiers dancing with the village girls. I heard and read about the tremendous poverty in the countryside—you yourself for that matter warned me that I would observe a country in a deep economic crisis—but then I saw the men and women riding to church in all their finery. I regret to say that in comparison with the Soviet countryside I got the impression of sheer wealth. I was forewarned in Moscow that I would be treated like a plague and that I must be careful not to allow myself to be insulted. I did have a bad moment or two at the Warsaw train station, as you probably noticed, when an old colleague from Tarnów threw himself at me and I did not immediately recognize him. But instead of an insult he greeted me in age-old Polish fashion. I'm an old hand, and I felt at the various meetings in Warsaw and Cracow—and Ścieżyński introduced me to Conservatives as well as Socialists—that I was being treated graciously. The same was true at your club in Warsaw, where after lunch I talked freely and frankly with your generals and colonels. I came away with the feeling that the initiative to improve relations between us—and you rooted that feeling in the views of one man only—must have a wide base in Poland."

We then talked about loosening travel restrictions between Russia and Poland, and of organizing a broader cultural exchange, which indeed several months later was undertaken. We then passed on to more concrete things. We talked about abandoning mutual tripping-up in the area of foreign policy, of also abandoning in the face of the situation in the West intervention in our countries' internal affairs. Finally, Radek touched on an obvious sore spot with the Bolsheviks, that our military attachés and members of our diplomatic corps in Soviet Russia need not give "lessons" to their opposite numbers from other countries who do not usually know the language and are not as informed about Russia as the Poles. I had enough instructions by this time, but we were reaching an understanding. In these "Wilanów Pacts" of ours there were several interesting moments. For instance, when Radek spoke of abandoning unfriendly acts he was quick to add that obviously neither the Russians nor the Poles would cease counterintelligence activities, because after all *sicher ist sicher*, and it would constitute no offense. But fanning the flames of national minorities, well, that was something else and that we could mutually put a stop to. Further, when I pointed to the actions of the Soviet envoy in Kowno as an example of malicious incitement of the Lithuanians against us, Radek told me that as far as Lithuania was concerned they were ready to give us *carte blanche*. Once he said in Polish: "Do with them as you like," and then at another time, in Russian, that if the Lithuanians insisted on playing games, "They will have only themselves to blame." When again he offered us that "free hand" in relation to Lithuania, I smilingly told him that that was the second time he wanted to sell me the same horse.

It was quite certain that Radek, who was staying at the Soviet Legation, was in contact with the Kremlin, that he sent on reports and was receiving instructions. Taking this all into consideration one could assume as significant our penultimate talk. Radek went rather far. This is what I heard:

"Our talks thus far reveal, we both admit, that it can come to armed conflict between Poland and Germany. Would it not be suitable then to think about something more than just a détente and an accommodation as well as good-neighbor relations? In such an eventuality we would be ready to come to Poland's aid. I well understand—he interjected immediately—that it doesn't suit you at all to have the Red Army defend your western frontier. But there are other benefits which you could receive from us (because help from your western allies would not necessarily be forthcoming)— we could supply, for instance, war materiel, ammunition, gasoline, for that matter. There could also be a useful concentration of our forces in the northwest, keeping watch on East Prussia. I'm a civilian, therefore, only outlining this or that possibility. Would not this indicate that our general staffs should come to an understanding and plan something purely defensive and, of course, mutually coordinated?"

I was taken aback by such far-reaching proposals. The proposal itself indicated clearly how positively our talks had been received by the Kremlin.

Naturally, I could not give an answer on my own initiative. I took advantage of the setting sun and proposed another walk the next day. I went immediately to Beck, informing him of this new turn of events: a proposal—something on the order of a defensive alliance between Poland and Soviet Russia. For Beck also this was a surprise, and that night he reported to the Belvedere. Rather late that night he informed me that he had received instructions from the Komendant, and these he passed on to me the next morning. Piłsudski advised me that nothing should be said verbally; to say only that Radek's suggestion would be taken under consideration by us, but at this time the suggestion was somewhat premature, that after so many years of more-or-less unfriendly relations between our countries, we must allow time for public opinion to adjust itself to a turn-about, but not to exclude a gradual tightening of the bonds of good-neighbor relations in the future.

That is the way I presented the case to Radek that afternoon at our last talk. I carried away the impression that he received the answer with due understanding. We agreed—foreseeing that in the future official and diplomatic personnel would concern themselves with implementing what we had discussed—that we would main-tain personal contact, and that if the official road became snagged we would try to clear it through private correspondence.

Because Radek was departing for Moscow the next day I invited him and Antonov-Ovseyenko for a farewell drink at Fukier's, in the company of a few others, and naturally there was no more talk of politics. The conversation was dominated by talk of Sienkiewicz's *Trilogy*, which it turned out both Radek and Antonov-Ovseyenko knew well. I asked if Stalin was familiar with Polish literature and

Radek answered that he knew for sure of one Polish book with which Stalin was familiar—Bolesław Prus' *Pharaoh*.

In summation, the Wilanów Pacts, undertaken no doubt with the approval of the leaders of both sides, had resolved the following issues: we would mutually stop meddling in internal affairs and in diplomacy; we would endeavor to animate relations between our countries starting with the arts and culture. We saw a road open to further rapprochement. On that road Poland immediately set forth. Polish military attachés received instructions not to share information and intelligence data with representatives of other armies. The Soviet legation in Warsaw from that time on enjoyed equal status with the other diplomatic outposts. Russia's former diplomatic isolation came to an end. Soviet receptions were freely attended by representatives of the political, parliamentary, and economic worlds; government as well as opposition leaders attended. In the area of cultural contacts, there appeared at first the special issue of the Warsaw *Wiadomości Literackie* (Literary News) dedicated to the poetry and literature of Soviet Russia, and in return there appeared a comparable issue of the *Literaturnoaya Gazeta* in Moscow dedicated to contemporary Polish literature. (Not however without distortions, humbugs, and excesses on the Russian side, but no matter.)

And so when Radek left Warsaw in June, 1933, it could be assumed that a favorable turn in our relations with Soviet Russia was well grounded. Evidence for this hope could be found in Realpolitik and, it so seemed, in the proper understanding of it by both sides. Naturally, I have in mind here not the mere indications of a détente, of which I spoke above, but those basic political developments that emerged from our Moscow and Warsaw talks when viewed in relation to the ominous turn of events in European conditions brought about by Hitler's rise to power in Germany.

Nevertheless, this understanding lasted not even a half year; it faltered by November. It was restored in February, 1934, thanks to steps taken by the Polish side, but during 1935 it appeared that Moscow returned to unfriendly and malicious behind-the-scenes guerrila warfare against us.

About that I'll speak again later. In the meantime, for a full understanding of these developments a look at simultaneous Polish activity in the West is indispensable, for there lay the chief goal of our politics. Negotiations with Moscow had a complimentary, auxiliary meaning, although they were very important and, as far as we were concerned, completely honest.

It concerns what is called in European political literature Piłsudski's policy of preventive war against Germany. Understandably, the matter was held in the strictest of secrecy; nevertheless,

I had at the beginning fragmentary knowledge and later fuller information from Beck, both from my talks with Antonov and Radek, as well as from my capacity as editor of *The Polish Gazette*. I will relate at first my information from these sources, beginning from June 14, 1932, when I received from Beck clarification of a famous incident of that day. The warship Wicher, despite protests from Danzig authorities, sailed into the port in order to greet an incoming English squadron and do the honors as host. Beck told me that the Komendant had ordered this step to guarantee our right to foreign representation of the Free City; moreover, another factor came into play involving not Danzig and London but Paris and London. We had already begun to "sound out" France and England in order to assess their reaction to Hitler's march to power, undertaken with the full intention of rebuilding Germany's military might. We came upon an astonishing phenomenon: French and English political circles were not considering undertaking any preventive measures against Germany but were, on the contrary, treating German aims as if they were accomplished facts, as if that "tiger" had already grown his teeth and paws. And they feared that somebody might pull him by his whiskers and provoke him to jump. Meanwhile they reasoned that even if the consent of the West continued, it would take several years for the "jump" to come about. Presently and in the next several years the disposition of forces would be such that the "tiger" could still be tamed without risk: French and Polish land forces and English and French sea and air power were quite enough. Beck continued: We wanted to show up this state of affairs by using the Wicher. We had the right to do it. And if the Wicher committed some procedural error or violated some League of Nations' regulation, well, so what. Comm. Morgensztern had orders that in the event of an insult to the Polish flag on the part of the Danzig authorities he was to fire into the harbor-master's office. But there was no need. It came about also that Berlin as well did not react.

After several days Beck told me: "As you know, the 'tiger' didn't jump; he only ran to Geneva with a complaint. *Quod erat demonstrandum*." He added with the greatest satisfaction that French military circles understood the Danzig incident and through unofficial channels he had received words of appreciation, outright satisfaction, and hope that their politicians would learn from the example.

In February, 1933, after Hitler had been named Chancellor of the Reich, the Danzig Senate on its own authority introduced a change in the special port police on the order of the *Schutzpolizei*; Piłsudski countered on March 6 with the doubling of the Polish military garrison in Westerplatte. Beck added a commentary that the two affairs were similar with one exception, and that was that Hitler was already in power and it was necessary to point up sharply that we were prepared to defend the rights of the Republic in Danzig.

Again nothing more happened than an appeal to the League of Nations. Beck came away with the impression that in this instance even in French political circles "our object lesson"—to use his words—had provoked reflection. Confirmation of this view can be seen in the pronouncements of the most prominent French diplomat, Ambassador A. François-Poncet, in his *Souvenir d'une Ambassade à Berlin*. He said there that Piłsudski, who understood that the danger of Hitlerism had to be crushed in the bud, through carefully created incidents wanted to test the Western mood: "Will they be able to take advantage of a situation which he offered them?"

The third definite step undertaken by us occurred May 2, 1933, this time a diplomatic rather than a military act: the *démarche* of envoy A. Wysocki in Berlin. In order to underscore the importance of this step he was first called to Warsaw, received by Piłsudski—this meeting was made known to the press—and then given instructions. After his return to Berlin he demanded an immediate meeting with Hitler. Citing innumerable pronouncements of Hitler, he put the matter in categorical terms: either a renunciation by Germany of border revision with Poland, or war. Hitler replied that the decided aim of the German government was action only within the framework of existing treaties. He had retreated.

Contemporary German weakness was a striking thing. Their confusion was compounded by the possibility of preventive action against Hitler's drive and, on the other hand, by the unbelievable stubborn blindness of Western powers, who at just this time were ready to offer Hitler participation in the European oligarchy. (The Four Power Pact—Italy, France, England, and Germany, proposed by Mussolini and not without the participation of the French ambassador in Rome, H. de Jouvenel, with the idea of "satisfying" Hitler at the cost of Poland and the recognition of Germany's "equality" in armaments.) This pact Poland energetically protested. Beck declared in the Diet that the basis of our politics was "Nothing about us without us. No decree concerning our interests promulgated without our participation can be obligatory." At the same time, and with Piłsudski's approval, he threatened withdrawal from the League of Nations and the organization of a revolt of the smaller powers.

In the middle of November, 1933, Beck gave me a sort of balance sheet report on the attempts to bring about preventive action. He spoke of his intimate talks with French and English statesmen, and of attempts to reach influential politicians of both countries through private personal connections. He summed up their efforts in a short sentence which was literally the answer we received from both the English and the French: "Public opinion will not accept a preventive action against Germany."

I was not surprised. As editor of *The Polish Gazette* I had a web of correspondents in the leading European capitals, intelligent and well-informed observers. The reports which they filed confirmed that line of thought. I related this view to Beck and asked him if he expected any change. He answered me openly that he did not entertain any hope but that the Komendant, given his intellectual make-up and military way of thinking, told him to seek persistently a victory of pure logic. And that logic said: If we know that a "potential enemy" is dominated by the idea of retaliation for defeat suffered in the last war, if we have indisputable data that he has already begun to build up the forces necessary, then the conclusion to be reached is simple—deter him while there is time. The Germans are repudiating the provisions of the Treaty which, wisely or not, was conceived in the form of an organizational charter dictating the life of European nations. Maybe finally someone will look at this state of affairs with open eyes and draw the necessary conclusions.

After the German Reich withdrew from the League of Nations in November, 1933, Beck reported to Piłsudski on the fruitless results of our efforts to bring about a preventive action. Piłsudski decided again to undertake a decisive *démarche* in Berlin and he advised Beck to give the French and English governments the following briefing on the action: Hitler's break with the League of Nations creates for Poland a new legal political situation. The League of Nations was after all the one instrument regulating Germany's relations with Poland. With the Western powers Germany bound herself by the Locarno pacts. As far as we are concerned Germany has no treaty obligations. Given the innumerable revisionist statements uttered by Hitler we can at any moment expect an attack when they feel ready for it. While that is not the situation today, nevertheless, if the Western powers will decide on a radical solution of the matter—preventive action—we are ready. If, however, the Western powers intend to permit German rearmament, putting their trust in the Locarno agreements, we will have to demand from the German government treaty obligations in the sense that all matters between us will be settled peacefully through conciliation and arbitration, and if they refuse, we will immediately apply precautionary military measures.

Beck told me further that he awaited news from Paris and London of the reaction to this confidential warning of our intentions. He added that he did not expect a change in their present position, that they probably will only advise restraint and not to push too far in embittering Hitler. Then Lipski—and he was prepared—will go to Hitler instructed to put the matter in the form of an ultimatum: "You know that the Komendant doesn't accept 'words without authority'; when he gave me these instructions the order to move several divisions to the western frontier was already on his desk ready to be signed. He also gave me to read a memorandum on internal measures to be taken, agreed to by the President in the event of war with Germany."

Two or three days later, exactly when Polish and German news agencies announced the so-called "Hitler–Lipski Declaration" containing the renouncement of the use of force and the settlement of conflicts in a friendly manner, Beck gave me pointers on how to throw light on this matter in *The Polish Gazette*. He suggested that I introduce the phrase "Eastern Locarno"; the value of the Locarno pacts lies in the fact—according to its adherents—that they were freely entered into and not "dictated," as the Germans call the Treaty of Versailles. We filled a significant gap in the treaty with respect to the eastern boundary of Germany, with this difference, that a renunciation of aggression in relation to us Hitler himself declares, while Locarno does not bear his signature. This is no small matter, as you are dealing with a man who regards his rise to power as the beginning of a new era, cancelling out the past from the year 1918. Not only has this agreement to do with Hitler, but also with Western public opinion. In the future, if Hitler perpetrates an armed attack on us, it will be his personal decision, an act in the name of the German Reich. This act could have an important influence in enforcing treaty obligations on the part of France, which fell in doubt after Locarno; it could even influence the English position.

After hearing out Beck I asked him if in these circumstances we could consider as done our attempts to bring about a preventive action. "I touched on this matter when reporting to the Komendant on the course as well as the result of Lipski's *démarche* in Berlin and asked him if we were to go ahead and turn the Hitler–Lipski Declaration into a formal non-aggression pact. But the Komendant told me not to worry about it. I have to tell you that the Komendant, regardless of his irritation and anger because of 'blindness in the face of reality' on the part of Western powers, demonstrates incredible patience in this affair; when I indicated to him that the last few days have brought more evidence of France's and England's intention to remain passive, the Komendant said that there was still time. To be sure, he doesn't hear the voice of reason, but that this state of dullness can pass, that Hitler himself can come to our aid, as moderation and tact are not his strong points, and he might utter some idiocy which would shake public opinion in the West."

After a two month delay the Polish–German Non-Aggression Pact was signed on January 26, 1934. Immediately after—even before the exchange of ratification documents, which took place in the middle of February, 1934—Beck paid a visit to Moscow. Its purpose was to manifest the fact that the Polish–German Non-Aggression Pact did not conflict with treaties entered into by Poland with other countries—not only our alliance with France, but likewise the non-aggression pact with Russia—and that we continue to aspire to good-neighbor relations with her. The visit passed favorably and in a friendly manner. The non-aggression pact was extended for ten years and it was decided to raise the legations in Warsaw and Moscow to the level of embassies.

Neither could the French or English governments object; after all, they knew best that Piłsudski sought other solutions up to the last minute and received only their stubborn refusal. I would remind the reader that three months later the French Minister of Foreign Affairs for the first time paid a visit to Warsaw. That was L. Barthou, one of the signers of the Polish–French Alliance of 1921. From that time representatives of France visited Poland every year. But more important, two years later—but unfortunately too late—we finally received from France a loan to build indispensable military equipment, which for twenty-five years we had been soliciting, but to no avail. English reaction was also positive. There developed an increased interest in Poland and her politics. I am noting here only the positions of the Western countries; attacks from other groups or persons I relegate to the background because the basis of such attacks was not the non-aggression pact itself, but rumored and exaggerated reports of alleged secret agreements and even a supposed "covenant reached with Hitler." The indisputable facts of 1939 gave the answer to that charge, so why waste words.

It would be a basic mistake to count the non-aggression pact with Germany as one of the successes of our policy. It was only an expedient measure, the result of losing a campaign, begun by Poland through the initiative of Piłsudski, and of the gloomy phenomenon of "blindness in the face of reality" in Paris and London. It was lost not through our fault and not only we felt the results. The whole world paid a frightful price. Perhaps Douglas Reed stated it the simplest: "In 1933 Piłsudski told the Western powers: You must stop Germany now or never. You can do it now with a minimal loss in people and money. Later it will be too late. When the powers remained deaf to his proposal he concluded a non-aggression pact with Germany. What else could Poland do?" (*Disgrace Abounding*, London, 1952.)

So much for the Berlin pact, except for this additional comment, that Hitler's agreement to conclude it was one more link in the chain of evidence that pointed up his weakness at that time, a weakness which Piłsudski's policy proved throughout the years 1932–1934.

The threat of armed action on the part of Poland was enough for Hitler to retreat, even though he knew of Paris and London's rejection of Piłsudski's plan, and even though they offered him "equal right to armaments"; the *right* he did not need because he simply took it, but he did need *time*, only time. And that time was given to him year after year, despite Polish warnings and the dissuasions of prominent French generals. Hitler eagerly took advantage, arming the country at an unbelievable pace. There were, it would seem, flashes of sobriety in Paris in the fall of 1935, to judge from the words of General George spoken at that time to General K. Sosnkowski: "I can happily inform you that we have come to a decision: if but one armed German steps foot in the Rhineland, we mobilize. And what will you do?" he added with meaning.

Several months later, on March 7, 1936, when regiments of the Reichswehr crossed into the Rhineland, Poland reacted immediately: with the first news Beck, after consulting with the President and Rydz-Śmigły, not waiting for the decision of the French government, informed the French ambassador that in the event of French military counteraction Poland would meet her obligations as an ally. Instead, Paris decided not to throw its forces in defense of her rights. England withheld her support.

In the French government there were voices which wanted to answer Hitler with the use of armed force and only then seek English cooperation. It is significant that Flandin informed neither the government, nor the General Staff, nor parliamentary circles of Beck's declaration of Poland's readiness to fulfill the *casus foederis*. He was clearly afraid that this could turn the scales on behalf of a military counteraction. Indeed in March, 1936, there was still time for this eventuality. The joint forces of France and Poland, even with English passivity, had a decided advantage over German forces. Hitler could then break his neck in this affair, and his General Staff so warned him.

It was in fact the last chance. From then on the balance of forces began to change. German military potential, taking into consideration its newness, began to leap ahead. The unpunished occupation of the Rhineland from another point of view—that of European relations—critically turned the scales: it markedly enhanced Hitler's authority in Germany, it earned him popularity in military circles, it gave him an unbelievable certainty of himself which before this time he had not possessed. At the same time it undermined the authority of France and England in Europe, and especially in Rome and Moscow. If not earlier, then certainly by then Stalin began to consider a policy of an eventual accommodation with Hitler regardless of the fact that the year before an agreement between France and Russia had been concluded.

*   *   *

The non-aggression pacts concluded then by Poland, the first with Soviet Russia, was signed before Piłsudski initiated his policy of preventive action, the second with the German Reich, after rejection of that policy by the West. The second was, as I have said, an expedient measure, the result of failure of the cardinal plan. The first represented a constituent part of Piłsudski's plans. They each depended on the liquidation of the German threat by West European forces without the participation of Soviet Russia which was, from a general point of view, totally unnecessary given the composition of forces in 1933 while, from the Polish point of view, downright dangerous. On the other hand, the guarantee of Moscow's neutrality was necessary and to the point. One could count on this guarantee of neutrality being observed chiefly on the basis of their own difficult situation: painful economic poverty, grave internal frictions (made public only years later), the Japanese threat in the Far East and undoubtedly, in connection with that, the fear that Hitler might begin his world-shaking deed with a march to the East.

Hence our "road to Moscow"; hence our Wilanów talks.

The Kremlin then knew the full scope of Polish policy at that time. Stalin had full confirmation of our good faith in the guarantees tendered in May and June of 1933.

In spite of these assurances at the end of 1934 or at the beginning of 1935 we could ascertain a definite return of Soviet policy to the practices of before 1933. It turned out unquestionably that Moscow inspired accusations of Polish secret ties with Hitler in the French press and in the German émigré and socialist press. It was necessary to admit that our attempts to arrive at an understanding were fruitless. The events of 1939 gave witness that every word uttered in that attempt six years before was reliable. We never entered into a treaty with Germany against Soviet Russia, either during Piłsudski's lifetime or after his death. And to ultimatums we answered with battle. The very thing Poland was accused of having done in the blatant propaganda of the time, it was precisely Stalin who did: entering into secret dealings and then forging an alliance with Hitler against us.

The question arises, Perhaps there was, despite our honesty, a lack of skill on our part, perhaps only we Poles do not know how to come to terms with Russia? The answer is patent: immediately after us France embarked on the road to Moscow. Moscow negotiated with her, indeed, willingly and amicably in 1934, indeed, signed a mutual defense treaty in 1935. And England too in the company of France embarked on the same road in August, 1939. Moscow indeed talked with them while at the same time preparing to sign the Ribbentrop–Molotov Pact.

This then seems to me to be the essence of experience: Whoever seeks a straight road to Moscow will never get there. Whoever, negotiating with her, brings honesty and good will on his part, let him not expect that he will be repaid in like currency.

Translated by Irene Sokol

MARXIST REVISIONISM IN POLAND: ITS BACKGROUND, SOURCES, AND MAIN TENDENCIES

Zbigniew A. Jordan

Marxism-Leninism always had to fight an uphill struggle in Poland. When it was introduced to the country after the end of World War II, it not only met a strong opposition on the part of the native philosophical tradition, but also was influenced, in its content and ways of thinking, by its opponents whom it set out to convert. Its dominant position in the years 1948–1954, gained by political means and supported by force, was not as firm and secure at it might have appeared at the time. When shortly after Stalin's death the censorship was relaxed (in order that the faction which was in control over the mass media of communication could use the Press against the other faction in its struggle for power within the Communist Party), the alleged genuine shift of intellectual allegiance to Marxism-Leninism turned out to be an optical illusion. Deprived of support, the ascendancy of Marxism-Leninism collapsed and vanished into thin air. The first signs of critical thinking, which was an important cause of its collapse, appeared in print in autumn, 1954, and gathered strength in the following months, culminating shortly before Gomułka's return to power in October, 1956.

This broadly based trend of critical thought and discontent—it was led and supported by both non-Party and Party scholars and writers—can hardly be called revisionism. Originally, it reflected the widely felt repugnance at the crimes and oppression of the totalitarian system—the extermination of opponents, the terror of the security police, the economic misery, the drabness of life, the regimentation of thought, and the suppression of freedom of speech. Only when the attempt to explain the "period of errors and distortions"[1] as Stalin's exclusive responsibility was made and rejected as sociologically inadequate and doctrinally incompatible with the basic assumptions of Marxian social theories, the search for their deeper causes located them in the principles of Marxism-Leninism. Some spoke of the "imminent evil of socialism" (meaning either Russian or Leninist socialism) or the end of "social mythology," and others of the deviation from the "Marxist revolutionary theory." Thus revisionism—the demand for a critical examination, evaluation, and modification of Marxism-Leninism—was born. It soon comprised the teaching of Marx, and its place and function in the contemporary world.

While the revisionist approach to the original doctrines of Marx and Lenin originated in historical experience, it was deeply influenced by the attitudes of mind and modes of thought prevailing in the native intellectual tradition. Therefore, this tradition must be briefly described before the form and content of revisionism itself is analyzed.

THE SCHOOLS OF PHILOSOPHY AND SOCIOLOGY

In the periods between the two world wars Poland had large and thriving schools of philosophy and sociology. At the end of the hostilities of World War II these schools resumed their interrupted development, reestablished their influence in teaching and research, and, owing to the excellence of their achievements, regained an academic ascendancy which no other trends could effectively challenge. On the other hand, Marxist-Leninist philosophy and sociology were non-existent. In the first post-war years there were only a few people acquainted with the more theoretical aspects of the Marxist-Leninist doctrine and, with one or two exceptions (of Oskar Lange in particular), nobody with a sufficient knowledge and experience to compete on an equal footing with non-Marxist scholars. The four leading Marxist-Leninists at that time were Julian Hochfeld, Władysław Krajewski, Adam Schaff, and Stefan Zółkiewski, of whom only Schaff had philosophical training, having taken his Ph.D. degree in the Institute of Philosophy of the Soviet Academy of Sciences in 1944.

The School of philosophy which gained a world-wide reputation was known as the Warsaw school or simply as the Polish school.

[1] This euphemistic phrase was coined to soften the impact of Nikita Khrushchev's secret speech denouncing Stalin's crimes.

Its best known logicians were Leon Chwistek, Stanisław Leśniewski, Jan Łukasiewicz, and Alfred Tarski, and its leading philosophers were Kazimierz Ajdukiewicz, Tadeusz Czezowski, Tadeusz Kotarbiński, and Zygmunt Zawirski. In the critical post-war years and in the Stalinist period only three of them—Ajdukiewicz, Czezowski, and Kotarbiński—were active, but their personal influence was wide and reinforced by a large number of their pupils who taught at the old and newly created universities.

Polish thinkers excelled in the philosophy of language, formal logic, and the philosophy of science. Together with the Austrian and German philosophers originally known under the name of the Vienna Circle and the Berlin Group respectively, they were the founders of an anti-metaphysical sort of philosophy and, in contradistinction to the supporters of traditional speculative philosophies, were mainly concerned with the logical analysis of scientific knowledge. They emphasized the importance of the study of language and set up high standards of precision in speech and thought, recognized the close connection between philosophy and science and applied scientific procedures to philosophical investigations, and distinguished sharply between the examination of the philosophical foundations of science and the philosophy given to the study of problems about which, as a matter of principle, science does not formulate any opinion.

Thus Marxism-Leninism was confronted in Poland with a well-established tradition of logically and empirically oriented philosophy, a strong attachment to the importance of matters of the mind, and a deep-rooted determination to abide by the verdict of truth, aided and supported by skills in the use of scientific method. Marxism-Leninism attracted a few new recruits and converts, in particular among literary and artistically-minded intellectuals. It managed to contain the influence of its philosophical opponents by depriving some of them of their right to teach (among them were Ingarden, a phenomenologist philosopher, Ossowska, a social philosopher, Ossowski, a sociologist, and Tatarkiewicz, a historian of philosophy) and by restricting others to the teaching of formal logic alone. It was in a position to silence public criticism, since it exercised full control over all publications and abolished the freedom of thought and speech. But Marxism-Leninism failed entirely to prevail against the tradition which it fought by all means, fair and foul. Geographically, Polish philosophy remained an island of logico-empirical tendencies within the Russian world of dialectical materialism.[2] Instead of supplanting these orientations and skills,

2 For the division of the recent philosophical trends into the three philosophical schools, see J. F. Mora, *Philosophy Today*. New York: 1960, pp. 82 ff.

Marxism-Leninism began being influenced by them. It was Marxism-Leninism which slowly changed its initial position, reducing its claims, revising its basic assumptions, modernizing its outlook, and discovering the value of objectivity, logical consistency, and free inquiry.

Sociology also was well advanced in Poland in the interwar period and compared favorably with its development in other European countries.[3] The founder of sociology as an academic discipline was Florian Znaniecki, who also exerted a considerable influence in the United States. Znaniecki had some distinguished predecessors and contemporaries, such scholars of international repute as Ludwik Gumplowicz, Leon Petrażycki, Stefan Czarnowski, and Bronislaw Malinowski, but none of them can be identified with the rise of modern sociology in Poland. It was Znaniecki who liberated Polish sociology from its connection with the speculative philosophy of history and established its modern empirical conception, provided a definition of its subject matter, gave it its method and research techniques, organized its teaching and research, and set up the Polish Sociological Institute (1927) and the first Polish sociological periodical *Przegląd Sociologiczny* (1931). Owing to his own sustained efforts and those of his students (of whom Józef Chałasiński and Jan Szezepański formed, together with Stanisław Ossowski, the big three of Polish sociology in the post-war period), there began a steady expansion of social studies, an increasing output of sociological publications, and a growing public interest in sociology. While the range of subjects for research and study was wide, the main interest was concentrated on Poland's basic social problems at that time. The sociologists wished to contribute to social reform, to the reduction of poverty and injustice in the country.[4] They shared the belief that sociology is both a branch of pure knowledge to be studied for its own sake, and an applied science, an instrument of rational control of social change and social processes in general. This belief they passed on to the younger generations of sociologists now active in Poland.

As soon as World War II was over the sociologists not only resumed but also greatly expanded their work. Old chairs of sociology were reactivated and new ones were set up, research projects were organized, contacts abroad were re-established, and sociological publications revived. The war, the post-war migrations,

---

3 For an independent assessment, see H. Barnes and H. Becker, *Social Thought from Lore to Science*, 2nd ed. Washington, D.C.: 1952, pp. 1077–78; E. M. Znaniecki, "Polish Sociology," in G. Gurvitch and W. E. Moore (eds.), *Twentieth Century Sociology*. New York: 1945, pp. 703 ff.

4 See, e.g., L. Krzywicki's introduction to *Pasiętniki chlopów*, Warsaw, 1936.

the vast hopes laid upon economic planning, and social engineering as an effective means of rehabilitating the country were all responsible for a wide-spread interest in sociology. The departments of sociology were flooded by numerous applicants, and some of the best brains among undergraduates chose sociology as their main subject of study.[5]

This revival was short-lived, for the end of 1948 marked the beginning of the Stalinist period. For numerous reasons Marxist-Leninists found Polish sociology as unacceptable as any other school of bourgeois sociology. Znaniecki, wrote a Marxist critic in 1950, represented a conception of sociology typical of contemporary bourgeois sociology. His followers, it was added with indignation, wanted to use his ideas for the studying and planning of the Socialist construction in People's Poland and ignored the fact that Znaniecki's sociology was irreconcilable with the great cause of building socialism.[6] These and other denunciations achieved their purpose. Sociology as an undergraduate subject was suppressed and replaced by historical materialism, to be taught by men who were neither sociologists nor competent Marxian scholars. But the tradition of empirical sociology was kept alive; fully trained sociologists were available, libraries continued to be used, the familiarity with the techniques of social research was cultivated, and the awareness of the social functions of sociology never disappeared. These were factors of considerable importance in the rebirth of empirical sociology in 1956.[7]

They also contributed momentum to revisionist thought and supplied it with invaluable knowledge in its clash with orthodoxy. For instance, it was a sociologist, Józef Chałasiński, who initiated the critical evaluation of Marxism-Leninism and, from a sociological point of view, exposed the "tragic consequences" of ignorance, stagnation, and sterility brought about by its claim to the monopoly of truth.[8] A. Malewski, another sociologist, a pupil of Ajdukiewicz

5 See T. Abel, "Sociology in Postwar Poland," *American Sociological Review*, Vol. 15 (1950), pp. 104–106.

6 J. Hochfeld, "O niektórych aspektach przeciwstawności materializmu historycznego i socjologii burżuazyjnej" (Some Aspects of the Antagonism between Historical Materialism and Bourgeois Sociology), *Myśl Filozoficzna*, 1–2 (1951), pp. 119–20. A. Schaff, who today is Chairman of the Institute of Philosophy and Sociology of the Polish Academy of Science, played a leading role in the suppression of sociology as an undergraduate subject in the Stalinist period.

7 See J. Szczepański, "Sociologie Marxiste Empirique," *L'Homme et la Société*, No. 1 (1966), pp. 46–47. The sociologists who were summoned by the Court during the trial of persons accused of crimes for their part in the Poznań riots in June, 1956, greatly influenced the verdict and sentence by pointing out that the riots were not the work of criminals but a demonstration of workers against a police regime.

8 I am referring to Chałasiński's articles published in *Nauka Polska* and *Przeglad Kulturalny* in 1954 and 1955. The larger and more fundamental issue of the freedom

and Ossowski, produced an impressive and incisive sociological and methodological analysis of historical materialism which set the pattern for the critical discussion about the place of Marxian theories in the contemporary world.[9]

Sociologically trained Party members—J. Wiatr and Z. Bauman —were in the front line of the attack against the long-established Marxist-Leninist dogma that social knowledge was an exclusive preserve of the Communist leaders and that the resolutions of the Central Committee were outstanding contributions to the advancement of sociological theory. They argued that this dogma destroyed science for the benefit of ideology and left enormous arrears in the domain of empirical studies and research techniques.[10] Sociologists exploded various myths in which Marxist-Leninist social theories abounded. They criticized the division of sociology into Marxist and non-Marxist, for there is only one science, one scientific method, one criterion of truth and validity, with which every scientific proposition must comply. Only reliable social knowledge can be useful in the construction of socialism, and only empirical sociology provides reliable social knowledge. Thus, ultimately, the conclusion was reached and implicitly accepted also by the Party leadership, that the "development of sociology and the training of sociological cadres are entirely in the interest of socialism."[11]

THE MARXIAN TRADITION

Marxian tradition in Poland originated in the eighteen eighties. At that time a group of young men, which included Ludwik Krzywicki, Kazimier Kelles-Krauz, and Edward Abramowski,[12] became acquainted with the works of Marx and Engels and popularized their views in Poland. Among them Kelles-Krauz was perhaps the best known abroad, owing to his publications in the French and German journals (*Revue Internationale de Sociologie, Sozialistische Monatshefte, Neue Zeit*) but Krzywicki was the more important.

---

of thought was re-examined by K. Ajdukiewicz in an admirable essay published in Polish (*Nauka Polska*, Vol. 5 (1957), No. 3) and in English (*Review of the Polish Academy of Science*, Vol. 2 (1957), No. 1–2).

9 A. Malewski, "Empiryczny sens teorii materializmu historycznego," *Studia Filozoficzne*, No. 2 (1957). This article was also published in German in *Kölner Zeitschrift für Soziologie und Sozialpsychologie*, 11 Jg., 1959.

10 J. Wiatr–Z. Bauman, "Marksizm a socjologia współczesna" (Marxism and Contemporary Sociology), *Myśl Filozoficzna*, 1/27 (1957), p. 8.

11 Z. Bauman, "O zawodzie socjologa," *Kultura i Społeczeństwo*, R. 4 (1960), No. pp. 166–67.

12 Abramowski is better known as a psychologist, but his essay *Le matérialisme historique et le principe du phénomene social*, Paris, 1898, is still very much worth reading.

Krzywicki, who edited the first Polish translation of *Capital*, published by private contributions in Leipzig in 1884, and translated Engels' *The Origin of the Family, Private Property and the State* and Lewis H. Morgan's *Ancient Society*, was himself a philosophical materialist, but he considered historical materialism as a set of self-sufficient hypotheses in no need of metaphysical foundations in dialectical materialism. In his exposition of the materialistic conception of history Krzywicki showed a considerable independence of thought and expounded what might be called its scientific version. That is, he conceived of historical materialism as a method of research and explanation, and not as a key to action. Moreover, he recognized from the very beginning, before Engels wrote his famous letters on the subject (1890–1894) and Plekhanov published *The Development of the Monist View of History* (1895), that historical materialism must involve mutual dependence between economic conditions on the one hand and social and political ideas on the other. Although the latter might be functionally a secondary phenomenon, they later became a factor of primary importance. Finally, Krzywicki accepted the fact of the diffusion of ideas in time and space and the existence of a "historical substratum," varying from one society to another and constituting a modifying medium of social change. Consequently, as the conditions of change are different in every society, there is no universal pattern of social evolution.

The Marxian tradition was carried on in the period between the two wars by such scholars as Stefan Czarnowski, Leon Chwistek, Oskar Lange, and Stefan Rudniański. However, all of them sharply differentiated between Marx's original works and their contemporary Leninist and Stalinist interpretations, of which they thought little. Chwistek and Lange, in particular, were outspoken in their comments on various aspects of Marxism-Leninism.[13]

Czarnowski, a pupil of Durkheim, a man of great erudition and versatility, was particularly influential, both because of his unswerving commitment to the cause of the working classes and his original application of historical materialism to sociology. Czarnowski, former lecturer at the *École Pratique des Hautes Études* in Paris, gained an international reputation by his studies on the sociology of religion published in French.[14] Apart from the sociology of religion his interests were wide and included the sociology of

13 See L. Chwistek, *Granice nauki: Zarys logiki i metodologia nauk ścistych*, Lwów, 1935, roz. 1; O. Lange, "Ludwik Krzywicki jako teoretyk materializmu historycznego," in *Ludwik Krzywicki: Praca zbiorowa poświęcona jego życiu i twórczości*, Warsaw, 1938. Chwistek's book, also available in English translation (*The Limits of Science*, London, 1948), did not appear in Poland in a new edition until 1963.

14 S. Czarnowski, *Le culte des héros et ses conditions sociales: Saint Patrick, héros national d'Irlande*, Paris, 1919.

literature, the sociology and history of culture, and problems of sociological method. Czarnowski combined Durkheim's approach with that of Marx and showed historical materialism at its best. Within the materialist conception of history Czarnowski practiced functional and multi-factorial sociological analysis, by means of which he revealed the variety and the relative role of different factors responsible for producing seemingly similar events. Thus, the ultimate determination of cultural phenomena by social and economic conditions was firmly set in a wide and concrete context of interdependent social facts; it worked its way from within the skeleton, as it were, of materialist assumptions, covered always with the living flesh of social, political, and cultural facts, with human strivings, ideas, and feelings. Some of the more important of Czarnowski's works were reprinted directly after the war, but his collected works did not appear until 1956, for they too were considered deficient from the point of view of Marxism-Leninism.

The scientific version of historical materialism, originated by Krzywicki and continued by other scholars, was reaffirmed in the early post-war years by the publication of a selection of Krzywicki's writings,[15] a new edition of Lange's important essay on Krzywicki,[16] and by Stanisław Ossowski's articles of 1947–1948.[17]

Ossowski, a philosopher by training, a sociologist by vocation, and a scholar of an admirable honesty and clarity of mind, undertook a searching examination of the Marxian theories which, in his view, could play an important role in the modern world and which he contrasted with the Marxist-Leninist orthodoxy out of touch with the knowledge and aspirations of the twentieth century. Ossowski's criticism faithfully reflected the views prevailing in the academic community, where Marxism-Leninism was gaining political adherents but intellectually made little impression. Most scholars were convinced that it did not deserve serious attention, because it was an antiquated, nineteenth-century doctrine, wanting in objectivity, detachment, and scholarly attitudes of mind.

Thus, despite the fact that Poland had a Marxian tradition, for Marxism-Leninism there was nothing in the past and the present to sustain its efforts to strike roots in Polish intellectual life. The works of Krzywicki were banned as containing a revisionist and erroneous interpretation of "Marxism."[18] Abramowski, Brzozowski,

15 L. Krzywicki, *Studia sociologiczne*, Warsaw, 1951.
16 O. Lange, *Ludwik Krzywicki jako teoretyk materializmu historycznego*, Warsaw, 1947.
17 S. Ossowski, "Doktryna marksistowska na tle dzisiejszej epoki," *Myśl Współczesna* 1947, No. 1/19; "Teoretyczne zadania marksizmu," *Myśl Współczesna* 1948, No. 1/20.
18 Not until 1957, that is, after the October upheaval, was the ban lifted and the Polish Academy of Science started publishing the collected works of Krzywicki.

Kelles-Krauz, and Czarnowski were treated first with suspicion and later repudiated altogether for the sake of the purity of the doctrine. Also, serious faults were found with Julian Marchlewski[19] and Rosa Luxemburg, who, in the public mind, were prominent representatives of the trends that culminated in producing Marxism-Leninism. When in 1949 Schaff read a paper on the development of Marxian philosophy in Poland at a meeting of the Polish Academy of Science and Learning in Cracow (PAU), he had to confess that apart from a history of errors there was nothing to build on. Although he announced that a new era in the development of Marxian philosophy had started, the start had to be from scratch.[20]

THE CONCEPTS OF ORTHODOXY AND REVISIONISM

Despite this hopeful announcement, Marxism-Leninism did not gain its dominant position in the intellectual life of the country through high achievements, but by government decree. At the end of 1948 Marxism-Leninism became the official doctrine of the State and the Communist Party, enforced by the administrative means at the disposal of the authorities. All free discussion ceased, all opponents were silenced, and Marxism-Leninism ruled supreme by being placed beyond any questioning and human doubt. The ascendancy of Marxism-Leninism lasted for about six years and collapsed as soon as it stopped being supported by the repressive powers of a totalitarian state.

As mentioned previously, toward the end of 1954 there began a searching scrutiny of the various Marxist-Leninist dogmas, and their supporters found themselves under constant pressure from all sides. This was the period known in Poland as the "thaw," the name given to the process of disintegration of a totalitarian state. The disintegration was due to the combined effect and interplay of various factors, such as an ideological split and factional strife at all levels of the Party organization; the discontent among the masses of the population, which was articulated and expressed by the intellectuals; the spontaneous rising of the Poznań workers; and, finally, the mass demonstrations in the streets of Warsaw, in which workers, students, and intellectuals joined hands to force the Communist Party to change its leadership and policies. Gomułka's

19 Julian Marchlewski (1866–1925), brother of a prominent biologist, was a well-known figure in the international Socialist movement and a founder, member, and leader of the Communist Party of Poland. He wrote little and his main interest was economic history.
20 A. Schaff, "Zarys rozwoju filozofii marksistowskiej w Polsce," *Sprawozdania Polskiej Akademii Umiejętności*, R. 50, 1949, pp. 597–98.

return to power in October 1956, marked the end of the "thaw" and the beginning of revisionism.

Gomułka's return to power can be regarded as symbolizing the emergence of the revisionist thought, because the factional struggle within the Communist Party and the defiance of the will of the Soviet Union in October, 1956 concerned the recognition of the principle of separate roads to socialism. Apart from the common revulsion against the crimes, inhumanities, and perversion of Socialist ideals in the Stalinist era, this principle constituted the strongest bond between Gomułka and one of the groups of former Stalinists (namely those who toed the Stalinist line out of fear and/or opportunism rather than out of conviction) on the one hand, and the prospective revisionists on the other. The successful outcome of the struggle for its acceptance gave to Gomułka the appearance of a revisionist leader and aroused great hopes for the future.

These hopes remained unfulfilled, and Gomułka turned out to be a revisionist *malgré lui-même*. Once the principle of separate roads to socialism was accepted the next most essential change, on which much else depended, was the demand for the freedom to discuss and revise Party doctrines and policies. At this juncture the ways of Gomułka and genuine revisionists began increasingly to diverge. One year after his return to power no doubt whatsoever was left any longer that Gomułka stood for ideological conformity, rigorous Party discipline, and a new orthodoxy of his own. Despite a revolutionary upheaval which was expected to bring about radical and irreversible changes, the events followed a spiral path similar to that described by Giambattista Vico as a universal pattern of historical advance. A heretical Communist himself, Gomułka abolished one orthodoxy to set up another. Having made orthodox what previously was heterodoxical, he also created new occasions or heresies, and revisionism was one of them.

In November, 1957 the Moscow declaration of the twelve Communist Parties, and among them of the Polish Communist Party, reasserted the "universal truths of Marxism-Leninism" (of which the right to separate roads to socialism was one) and named revisionism as its main danger. As defined by Gomułka for the purpose of clarifying his own policies, revisionism was a negation of or a deviation from the principles common to the entire international Communist movement.[21] However, since these common principles are not unambiguous, an additional provision is implicit in Gomułka's definition. Revisionism involves a rejection of or a deviation from the universal truths of Marxism-Leninism as laid

21 *Nowe Drogi* 1959, 4/118, p. 80.

down and interpreted by the Party leadership. In matters of ideology and policy, the Party leaders have a discretionary power of decision, and they alone have the right to distinguish between orthodoxy and heresy, the true Party doctrine and revisionism. Gomułka's definition of revisionism has certain merits. It somewhat reduces the ambiguity of the term "revisionism" and makes use of characteristics common to many cases to which the term had been applied in the past.

We cannot speak of heresy (and revisionism is a kind of heresy) without referring it, explicitly or implicitly, to a system of propositions which passes for or is accepted as orthodox doctrine. The concepts of heresy and orthodoxy are complementary and the former involves the latter. Furthermore, the concepts of orthodoxy and heresy are essentially sociological concepts, for orthodoxy is inconceivable without an organization and a ruling group or power elite within it. As Kołakowski put it, "the concept of orthodoxy is significant only in relation to an organized group, that is, a group with a stratum of organizers, in particular, with a caste of priests. Orthodoxy is the ideology of this stratum; it provides it with its *raison d'être*, which is to watch over orthodoxy. Whenever a heresy achieves an organized form, it becomes in its turn an orthodoxy and gains in strength by combatting its own heresies."[22] If orthodoxy is defined in sociological terms, then also heterodoxy or heresy should thus be defined. A revisionist, in the specifically sociological sense of this term, is a member of an organization who defies the organizational creed, alters some basic articles of its ideology, and is declared to be a revisionist by the guardians of the orthodoxy within that organization.[23]

If orthodoxy is a sociological concept and signifies the ways of acting, thinking, and believing shared by members of an organized group, an orthodoxy is an integrating force, sustaining the bond of group solidarity. Every organized society requires an orthodoxy of this sort, that is, a large body of beliefs held in common for the orderly conduct of its daily affairs. This use of the term "orthodoxy" is too broad, however, for the purpose at hand, because the word is not used to denote the way of life of any organized society but of a subclass of such societies. "Orthodoxy" in a narrower sense denotes the accepted creed of a society, an organization, a school of thought, or a denomination which is regarded as right and obligatory or

22 L. Kołakowski, *Świadomość religijna i więź kościelna*, Warsaw, 1965, pp. 52, 100.
23 See Lobkowicz, "Philosophical Revisionism in Post-War Czechoslovakia," *Studies in Soviet Thought*, Vol. 4 (1964), pp. 97–98; J. M. Bocheński, "Marxism in Communist Countries," in M. M. Drachkovitch (ed.), *Marxist Ideology in the Contemporary World*. New York: 1966, p. 72, where both writers seem to search for a sociological definition of revisionism.

which claims authority as truth. This claim of orthodoxy may rest upon a numerical preponderance, a position of strength and power of its believers, or upon a continuity, real or supposed, with an incontrovertible or saving truth. What is not orthodox is heterodox or heretic or revisionist. Heterodoxy or heresy or revisionism all refer to a divergence from the main stream of socially or organizationally held beliefs. While orthodoxy is said to sustain group relationships, heterodoxy is regarded as dangerous, because it is disruptive of the unity of a given society or organization, and may inspire action aimed at the destruction of the established order of things.

The term "revisionism," in its contemporary ideological or philosophical sense, came into use at the end of the last century to denote the position taken by Eduard Bernstein, who wished to modify certain basic assumptions of what then passed for an orthodox Marxian doctrine. The present-day revisionism does not try to reformulate the original doctrine of Marx but certain specific interpretations of it, namely, Stalinism or Marxism-Leninism, which before they became orthodoxies had been themselves heterodoxies. The revisionism of Bernstein and the contemporary revisionism of Ernst Bloch or Kołakowski are at variance with different doctrines and consequently are incomparable as to their content. We can refer to them by the same word provided that we understand by "revisionism" an intellectual attitude of rational criticism toward an orthodoxy. While it is true that a Party member becomes a revisionist in the sociological sense when he is declared to be one by the Party authorities, usually he is not called so without some reason, that is, unless he adopts the attitude described.

Now, revisionism defined as an intellectual attitude seems to be a very common and desirable feature of intellectual life, for intellectual progress mainly results from differences of opinion and cumulative changes of accepted views. Therefore, the question arises as to why revisions of political and social doctrines are frequently condemned or ruthlessly suppressed. Why is it that the supporters of an orthodoxy, to ask the question put first by Karl Kautsky, do not demand discussion but forbid it, do not press "for the refutation of contrary views but for the forcible suppression of their utterances"?[24]

This question admits of two answers. As a rule, social and political doctrines are systems of propositions about facts and values. They also include programs and policies said to be derived from those propositions. In other words, they consist of both factual statements and value judgments, and state not only what is the case but also

24 K. Kautsky, *The Dictatorship of the Proletariat*, Chap. 1.

what ought to be. For this reason, they are usually called "ideologies." For instance, they hold it to be self-evident that all men are created equal, are endowed with certain inalienable rights, such as life, liberty, and the pursuit of happiness. They may announce that the basic economic law of socialism secures the maximum satisfaction of the needs of society, or state that the political system of representative government secures the greatest amount of law, order, and freedom to the citizen. These are not declarative but normative statements and, as such, are neither true nor false. They express a certain choice of moral or social values on the part of those who accept and support them. Once a choice of values is made, we tend to disregard and dismiss not only other values and value judgments but also such factual statements as seem to affect psychologically our normative beliefs, that is, our will to believe in them or our determination to work for their realization.

There is, however, another and more compelling reason why revisions of ideologies are resented, condemned, or suppressed by the supporters of orthodoxy. As a rule, the term "ideology" is applied to a system of propositions which are accepted by large and numerous social groups or organizations. With respect to such groups or organizations ideology fulfils an important integrative function. It provides a common cognitive orientation, that is, a common way of looking at and conceiving of the world. It also organizes group values, provides some common commitments for action and the basis for an effective cooperation, which in turn strengthens social solidarity.

The integrative function of ideologies explains the fact that ideological assumptions are evaluated in a twofold way. They are evaluated from the point of view of their truth and falsehood and they are also assessed as either conducive to social solidarity or disruptive of it. In Marxism-Leninism the line of division between what is called a "creative development of the doctrine" and "erroneous revisionism" is very largely determined by the second criterion, that is, by the fact of whether it is held to unite or divide, to strengthen or to weaken social solidarity.[25] This is made apparent by the fact that the attack upon a dissenter frequently attributes to him a hostile design toward the organization, its ultimate values, and its very existence. The revisionist is not a man who errs in intellectual matters, but one guilty of either a contemptible or criminal and dangerous course of action. In his defence of the Marxist-Leninist orthodoxy Schaff accused his revisionist

---

25 For the distinction between "creative" and "erroneous" revisionism see W. Gomułka, *Przemówienia*, Warsaw, 1959, T. 2, p. 19; A. Schaff, *Spór o zagadnienia moralności*, Warsaw, 1958, pp. 30–34.

opponents of the intention to destroy the orthodoxy by depriving it of its distinctive characteristics. This, he said, was a "liquidationist revisionism," meaning one that ultimately does away with the orthodoxy altogether. One cannot question or modify or reject certain basic "Marxist" assumptions without cutting off one's connections with "Marxism" and inflicting an irreparable harm upon it.[26]

The evaluations of ideological propositions based on the two above-mentioned criteria need not coincide. A proposition may be considered unacceptable and rejected as revisionist in spite of being true because it is said to disrupt social or organizational unity. For instance, the supporters of the Marxist-Leninist orthodoxy often agree with John Stuart Mill's assertion that the freedom of thought and expression is the best way of discovering truth and of avoiding error. "Freedom of discussion, the free clash of opposing views," wrote Schaff, "undoubtedly provides the best conditions for the development of science and of culture generally." But they refuse to act in accordance with their belief, because in their view the present conditions make the limitations on freedom a "political necessity." There exists a conflict between the "cultural" and "social" advisability of releasing science and art from all controls. The demand for "unfettered freedom (of science and art) neither can nor should be realized in practice," for the realization of this demand would be harmful from a social (or rather political) point of view.[27]

On the other hand, a certain proposition may be ideologically acceptable and upheld by the Party because of its alleged favorable social implications, irrespective of whether it is true or not. The famous *Verelandungtheorie*, the law of increasing pauperization of the working class, is an instance in point. The law that in capitalist countries real wages tend constantly to decline is clearly negated by the findings of economic history. Yet the law continues to be upheld, with or without the addition of an *ad hoc* hypothesis of one kind or another, because of its obvious ideological usefulness. The theory of economic imperialism and exploitation worked out by Rudolf Hilferding, Rosa Luxemburg, and Lenin, which in the light of the post-Colonial developments is untenable, also continues to haunt Marxist-Leninist economics for the same reason as the *Verelandung-theorie*.

26 A. Schaff, *Nowe Drogi* 1961, No. 3/142, p. 81.
27 A. Schaff, *A Philosophy of Man*, New York, 1963, pp. 123 ff.; *Marksizm a jednostka ludzka*. Warsaw; 1965, p. 222. It is perhaps worth while to recall that Trotsky, faced by a similar dilemma some forty years earlier, gave practically the same answer. See *Literature and Revolution*, Ann Arbor Paperbacks, 1960, p. 221.

In view of the fact that ideological propositions can be evaluated by two entirely different kinds of criteria, it is sometimes held that orthodoxy is loyalty to an organization and revisionism is respect for truth, that orthodoxies are maintained by organizations in their own interest and revisionism is a product of a disinterested individual, or that the struggle between orthodoxy and revisionism is a trial of strength between an inquiring mind and conformity, reason and will, knowledge and political power. There is a certain simplification in these contrasting distinctions which also contain, however, a grain of truth. As a rule, we fare better, and our careers are more secure if we support the accredited beliefs of our society, do not defy them, or at least do not make our doubts about or dissent from them publicly known. Because we all learn in life, sooner or later, that it is not easy to assert our own beliefs against those socially approved, we tend to respect the heretics, to rejoice in their victories and applaud even their defeats. They always seem to be, and very frequently are, admirable men.

ORTHODOX AND PHILOSOPHIC REVISIONISM

The twofold way in which ideological beliefs can be classified allows us to distinguish between orthodox and philosophic revisionism. Orthodox revisionism is prompted by the awareness that a doctrine kept changeless is bound to depart more and more from truth, lose contact with reality, and consequently endanger the organization itself. The revisions of its tenets are made from above, in the light of experience and changed conditions, and the doctrine is modified in order to adapt it to altered circumstances, to modernize its outlook, or to make its policies more effective. Orthodox revisionism thinks first of the integrative function of the doctrine and consequently gives priority to social criteria of acceptability. As far as possible, it respects the rule that a proposition known to be false is bound to be suspected and ultimately disbelieved, although in the Stalinist period blatantly false propositions were publicly praised as important discoveries by men of undoubted intellectual prominence. But the concern with truth and falsehood is subordinated to organizational considerations. The revisions are evaluated as acceptable or unacceptable to the organization according to whether they are or are not likely to promote the social solidarity, institutional loyalty, and effective collective action of its members.

On the other hand, philosophic revisionism is primarily concerned with the truth and falsehood of ideological beliefs, and with the choice of values, and not with their acceptability from an organizational viewpoint. A philosophic revisionist, with his concern for truth and values, irrespective of their organizational effects, is a heretic in the original sense of this term. According to the *British Encyclopedia*, "heresy" meant originally "an act of choice" and later a "personal choice of an opinion or belief, or personal adhesion to a group or party advocating certain principles of belief." A heretic finds the prevailing doctrine to be false or morally wrong, and consequently proposes to change it in some significant way. The personal effort in the search for truth sharply differentiates a philosophic revisionist from a supporter of an orthodox doctrine who accepts truths and values in view of their being based on authority or being socially expedient. This difference is a source of hostility, conflict, and strife between them, with which the history of dogmas and ideologies is filled. While the organization demands loyalty and solidarity from its members, a philosophic revisionist asserts the rights of his intellect and conscience against the organizational claims upon him.

THEORETICAL AND PRACTICAL REVISIONISM

It is perhaps useful to make yet another distinction and to differentiate theoretical revisionism from practical (that is, political) revisionism. Theoretical revisionism tries to modify the principles underlying political programs or policies, and practical revisionism is concerned with these programs and policies themselves. The distinction between them seems, therefore, to reflect two different attitudes toward reality: one characteristic of men of action, and the other of men of ideas. Practical and theoretical revisionists have little respect for each other, even when they temporarily work together as allies. Napoleon made use of the *idéologues*, but later turned against them, and Gomułka dealt much more sharply with his intellectual revisionist supporters from the Left than with his authoritarian opponents from the Right, men of action and power like himself.[28] While Gomułka and the revisionists shared the belief that changes within the Party organization and corrections of errors in Party policies were necessary, Gomułka wished above all to preserve unity, and this meant keeping the ideology as much unchanged as possible. Therefore, he turned against those who, in his opinion, would disrupt organizational unity because they were anxious to modify the ideology, and stood for truth against falsity and expediency. The revisionists themselves now recognize that Gomułka had little choice if he wished himself and the Party to

28 For a closer analysis of the relations between Napoleon and the *idéologues*, see L. A. Coser, *Men of Ideas*. New York: 1965, Chap. 15.

remain in power, but they also emphasize that he had to bear the cost of his successful maneuver by having to assimilate at least some practices of his Stalinist opponents.[29]

If we ignore some extreme cases of political hostility between the intellectuals and men of power, the distinction between theoretical and practical revisionism is one of degree rather than of kind. While this distinction may sometimes be useful and instructive to contrast, for instance, the revisionism of Bernstein and the revisionism of Kołakowski, one has to concede that neither Bernstein entirely ignored theoretical and philosophical issues relevant to his attempt to revise the political program of German Social Democracy, nor was Kołakowski unaware of the political consequences inherent in his philosophical criticism of institutional Marxism.

THE THEORETICAL ORIENTATION OF POLISH REVISIONISM

While the distinction between theoretical and practical revisionism is not sharp and exhaustive, it is right to say that Polish revisionism was theoretical rather than practical. The fact that in Polish revisionism the theoretical problems predominated over practical ones was due to two main circumstances. First, although the leading Polish revisionists were politically committed men, few of them were politicians, and even fewer desired to share in political power. The most influential among them came from the ranks of philosophers, sociologists, economists, historians, writers, and even poets. Moreover, they were actively supported, in their intellectual revisionist activities, by skilled logicians, methodologists, social scientists, and also prominent natural scientists—I refer to such scholars and scientists as K. Ajdukiewicz, T. Kotarbiński, S. Ossowski, H. Ossowska, E. Lipiński, J. Konorski, and L. Infeld— who, of course, had no political ambitions and no knowledge of practical politics. They received this support because the revisionists were deeply concerned with the problems of the freedom of thought and expression that were of vital importance for the entire scientific community.

The theoretical orientation of Polish revisionism was also due to the circumstances of time and place. From the very beginning revisionism in Poland was handicapped by the self-imposed restrictions of not letting itself overstep the limits which would provoke prompt and decisive Soviet reprisals. The wisdom and even the necessity of this decision was tragically demonstrated by the Hungarian events. At the time when the struggle between the Right and the Left, the Conservative and the Liberal wings of the Communist Party, was

29 See L. Kołakowski, *Świadomość religijna i więź kościelna*, pp. 209-11.

still undecided, Kołakowski saw clearly where the main weakness of the revisionists lay. They were not in a position, he wrote, to rise above a purely moral protest and to translate their negative evaluation of the past into a practical program of reforms. Because in the prevailing "international situation" they could voice but not press their demands, they were bound to lose in the short run. The role they tried to play should not, however, be assessed solely by practical results, but also by the aims for which they stood. Illusions are necessary in order to actuate the non-illusory potentialities; disillusionment is unavoidable because it is the contrast between the goal and the achievement. Between the illusion and the disillusionment there is a lapse of time in the course of which the painful, hard, and slow realization of social progress is accomplished. It is also certain that the excess of hopes and of demands over possibilities is necessary in order to force reality to yield the maximum of its potentialities. The setting against the existing social conditions of a program essentially based on moral demands is not in itself as socially useless and unrealistic as it may appear.[30]

The self-imposed restrictions precluded, however, not only drastic political changes but also the possibility of the revisionist movement ever becoming an organized independent political force with wide support in the community. If the country were to avoid bloodshed and foreign occupation, and revisionism were to survive at all, it had to keep within the limits of general principles. Because the possibilities of direct action were limited, efforts were concentrated on influencing the minds of the power élite. The revisionists adopted the method of ideologically penetrating the ranks of the Communist Party with their ideas and of exercising influence from within and from below upward. They counted on the attractive force and appeal of these ideas and on their acceptance by the Party leadership as the orthodox doctrine despite their heterodox origin.

Their expectations did not remain entirely unfulfilled and their efforts were not entirely unsuccessful, for they did change the political atmosphere in Poland beyond recognition and greatly influenced the minds of all, including members of the ruling élite. While Poland continues to be an authoritarian, one-party state oppressive by its narrowness of outlook, mediocrity of aspiration, and thoughtlessness of action, the liberalizing tendencies within and without the Party have remained alive. In that way, at least some gains were not lost and the momentum of change—the revisionist utopia, as Kołakowski called it—was preserved. "I understand by 'utopia' this state of social consciousness," Kołakowski

---

30 L. Kołakowski, "Sens ideowy pojęcia lewicy," *Po Prostu* 1957, 8/423, pp. 2 and 4; "Odpowiedzialność i historia," *Nowa Kultura*, R. 8, 1957, 38/391, p. 5.

wrote, "which is born as an intellectual correlate of the social movement toward a radical transformation of the human world." The preservation of the revisionist utopia in the minds of individuals, Kołakowski commented in a style reminiscent of the young Marx and the Young Hegelians, was a prerequisite of its ever becoming the consciousness of a mass social movement and a social driving force which determines the practice of men and thus begins losing the characteristics of a utopia.[31]

But the Polish scene was not dominated as much by political strife between theoretically and practically oriented revisionists as by the conflict between orthodox and philosophic revisionisms, represented by Adam Schaff and Leszek Kołakowski as their chief protagonists respectively. In a certain sense, Gomułka has been the most outstanding orthodox revisionist in Poland, but Gomułka's revisionist policies are concerned with Marxism-Leninism as the ideology of the Soviet bloc and with the relations between the member countries and the Soviet Union. Consequently, they have the complexity which makes it impossible to consider them independently of the wider international issues. On this basis, Schaff may deservedly be regarded as the chief orthodox revisionist, at least until his last book *Marxism and the Human Individual* appeared early in 1965.

ORTHODOX REVISIONISM

Orthodox revisionism has preceded philosophic revisionism. Its first appearance should be explained as an attempt to break out of the isolation in which Marxist-Leninist scholars and intellectuals found themselves. This isolation was self-created, as it resulted from the absurdity of certain propositions basic to Marxism-Leninism. Among them none was more harmful than the assumption that internal contradictions are inherent in all things and in all phenomena of nature. From this assumption the consequence was inferred that the principle of non-contradiction had only a restricted validity and that in general logic, being responsible for a static and distorted view of reality, should be subordinated to dialectics, which alone is capable of supplying us with truly universal rules for the study of change and motion.

The rejection of the principle of non-contradiction meant that the distinction between valid and invalid arguments and between true and false propositions were no longer of any use. For, if two contradictory propositions are true at the same time, we can deduce from them, by means of the law of Duns Scotus, any proposition

31 L. Kołakowski, "Sens ideowy pojecia lewicy," p. 1.

whatsoever. Thus, Marxist-Leninist philosophy itself faces destruction. A Marxist-Leninist may reject a view with which he disagrees, but—because a conjunction of contradictory propositions is always true—he also must logically accept it. Similarly, and for the same reason, he is bound logically not only to affirm, but also to deny any part of his own philosophy. Furthermore, if the principle of non-contradiction is rejected, no reasoning, no argument, no discussion is ever possible, because without it and other logical laws we cannot establish our own assertion nor disprove that of our opponent. Finally, a man who makes contradictory statements says something and unsays it. He makes, therefore, some audible sounds, but these sounds carry no meaning and communicate nothing.[32]

For logically trained philosophers an inconsistent theory cannot be true, valid, or even significant. "It is very difficult to accept the rejection of the law of non-contradiction," wrote T. Kotarbiński, "and we should not accept it, because it entails absurdities and dooms the doctrine to failure."[33] Kotarbiński voiced an opinion which was shared by all competent philosophers and logicians, including those who were not unsympathetic to Marxism-Leninism on other grounds. Marxist-Leninists could spread their views among the uneducated and ignorant, but made no progress among the philosophically trained. The price to be paid for endorsing the "logic of contradictions" of Soviet Marxism was too steep for them and they had to abandon the doctrine if they wished to count in the intellectual life of the country.

Early in 1955 Schaff confessed that Marx, Engels, and Lenin were misled by Hegel into believing that there is no difference between a logical and dialectical contradiction. We speak of dialectical contradictions when we wish to state merely the fact that opposite forces or polar tendencies are inherent in all natural objects. This dialectical principle does not at all necessitate the rejection of logic and of the principle of non-contradiction in particular. On the contrary, a valid application of dialectics presupposes formal logic and cannot do without it. There is only one logic whose laws apply universally, both to objects at rest and to those changing and in motion. A Marxist-Leninist has to respect the law of non-contradiction as much as everyone else, because its rejection would make of Marxist-Leninist philosophy an inconsistent and, consequently, a false doctrine. Although this revision at first met a strong opposition, it ultimately prevailed and was accepted by all Marxist-Leninists.[34]

32 For a detailed description and analysis of the long debate concerning the principle of non-contradiction, see Z. A. Jordan, *Philosophy and Ideology*. Derdrecht: 1963, Part IV.

33 T. Kotarbiński, *Wybór pism*, Warsaw, 1957–8, T. 2, p. 516.

34 A. Schaff, "Dialektyka marksistowska a zasada sprzeczności," *Myśl Filozoficzna*

It can be shown, easily and convincingly, that Engels and Lenin did adopt their views about logic from Hegel, who in his *Science of Logic* recognized in contradiction the truly essential and profound determination of being. The fact that Engels and Lenin had adopted their views about logic from Hegel was not without significance, for it facilitated the abandonment of the "logic of contradictions." Many Polish Marxist-Leninists, including Schaff, thought little of Hegel and were anxious to minimize and reduce as much as possible any connections between Hegelian and their own philosophy. This anti-Hegelian orientation was not, however, universal. The younger generation of philosophers, educated in post-war Poland and deeply influenced by Marxian philosophy, split into two groups. Those among them who are oriented scientifically rather than humanistically and interested mainly in dialectical materialism tend to emphasize the naturalistic and positivistic elements in Marxian philosophy and to ignore its Hegelian influence. They conceive of dialectical materialism as a set of methodological rules for the investigation of the philosophical problems of science and do not feel at all that they are restricted to the orthodox doctrine of dialectics. They made use of the whole range of concepts and procedures that are available in modern logic and philosophy, and have become simply philosophers of science. They have remained, however, metaphysically committed, since they are without exception materialists in a broad sense of this term. The "dialecticians," whose leading thinker is H. Eilstein,[35] draw more and more closely to another group of philosophers of science, namely to the present-day descendants of the Warsaw school. The latter, in contradistinction to the "dialecticians," are logically and empirically oriented.[36]

There are, however, as has been mentioned earlier, some younger thinkers, former supporters of the Marxist-Leninist orthodoxy, who recognize, fully and emphatically, the Hegelian heritage in Marx's philosophy and have themselves adopted Hegel as their philosophical guide. They are attracted by Hegel's sense of order and transitoriness in history or—to put it in Engels's words—by Hegel's "fundamental thought," which "once and for all dealt

1956, 4/18; H. Eilstein, "Problem logiki w świetle marksistowskiej teorii poznania," *Myśl Filozoficzna* 1956, 5/25 and 6/26. Schaff's main opponent was Ładosz; see his "O sprzecznościach logicznych i dialektycznych," *Myśl Filozoficzna* 1956, 4/24.

35 The book edited by H. Eilstein *Jedność materialna świata*, Warsaw, 1961, gives a good idea of their approach, methods and considerable competence in the contemporary problems of the philosophy of science. The group includes Z. Kochański, S. Amsterdamski, Z. Augustynek, I. Szumilewicz, and an increasing number of younger people, less known as writers.

36 This group includes—to mention only those better known—Z. Czerwiński, J. Giedymin, L. Gumowski, M. Kmita, T. Kubiński, T. Pawłowski, J. Pelc, M. Przełęcki, K. Szaniawski, and R. Wójcicki.

the death blow to the finality of all products of human thought and action." The "Neo-Hegelians" are mainly historians of social and philosophical thought, for whom philosophy is a *Weltanschauung* or a historical study of *Weltanschauungen*. The best known among them are B. Baczko, L. Kołakowski, and A. Walicki, but they are much more numerous.[37] The "Neo-Hegelians" are responsible for a considerable revival of interest in Hegel, in the nineteenth-century writers—above all, Polish and Russian—who were influenced by Hegel, and in the problems of the traditional philosophy of history.[38]

The appearance of these new orientations was an unintended effect of the first orthodox revision of Marxism-Leninism, that is, of the abandonment of the "logic of contradictions." For the recognition of the universal validity of logic was only a first step in a long and still incomplete evolution of the orthodoxy that, described in general terms, is marked by an increasing respect for facts, objectivity, and the achievements of science and scholarship, irrespective of their origin. The old distinction between "bourgeois" and "progressive" science, the former a collection of falsehoods and the latter a repository of important truths, is gone, it appears, for good.

The second orthodox revision, hardly less important than the first, was a new interpretation of the principle of partisanship. This principle demanded from a Party member and everyone endowed with a sound respect for truth an unconditional submission to the pronouncements of the Party leadership in all matters concerning science, scholarship, art, and literature.

It also required a complete rejection of any propositions incompatible with the views of the Party, as such propositions expressed interests hostile to the working class and were false by definition. "Partisanship" was usually defined as "to be in agreement with the objective truth," the "objective truth" being what the Party leadership declared to be true in each particular case. The familiar justification of the principle of partisanship was the assertion that there is no "pure science," because all knowledge is class-bound and class-determined in its content. If all scientific knowledge contains an ideology and far-reaching social consequences, furthermore, if an ideology is held not on grounds of its conformity to scientific

37 The late T. Kroński, who was older than all of them and recognized as the leader of the "Neo-Hegelians," did much to revive the interest in Hegel but himself was an exceptionally woolly-minded thinker and an obscure and pretentious writer.

38 Apart from a new edition of the *Vorlesungen über die Philosophie der Geschichte*, published in 1958, there appeared the first Polish translation of *Phänomenologie des Geistes* (1963) and *Asthetik* (1964). A student's edition of Hegel (selected texts) was also made available (T. Kroński, *Hegel*, Warsaw, 1962).

procedure, but as a rationalization of class interests and aspirations, then the Party, as the guardian of social progress, has the right and duty to enforce submission to the principle of partisanship.[39]

The contention that the truth and validity of a proposition or a theory depends on its alleged social origin was strongly challenged by historical and logical arguments. Chałasiński argued that the history of science and civilization shows much evidence to the effect that irrespective of its origin science served not only the interests of the ruling class but was also a powerful factor in leveling class distinctions.[40] Czezowski, Lange, and Ossowski argued that the principle of partisanship was an instance of the genetic fallacy, that is, it confused the social and psychological origin of a belief with its logical validity.[41]

This criticism was to no avail at first, but in the period of the "thaw" has increasingly been accepted, at least in theory, because in practice the old habits of mind have occasionally reasserted themselves. The Party continues to regard itself as the supreme judge of truth in philosophy, the humanities, and the social sciences. There is a censorship of scientific publications and not everything can be published by any means. From time to time some writers are taken to task and their views are condemned, because they happen to be at variance with those of the Party leadership.[42] However, the important fact remains that the principle of partisanship has been revised and that the Party is under constant pressure to relinquish entirely any interference with science, scholarship, art, and literature.

The principle of partisanship has now been reduced to the distinction between two ideological attitudes, the conservative and the progressive outlook. The fact that scientific views originate in particular social and historical conditions does not in itself decide their truth and falsity. The truth of scientific statements depends exclusively on their agreement with reality and this agreement can be tested by actually altering reality. The truth and falsity of the statements of physics is established in the laboratory and industrial

39 For the details concerning the principle of partisanship, see A. Schaff, *Narodziny i rozwój filozofii marksistowskiej*, Warsaw, 1950, roz. II.

40 J. Chałasiński, "Socjologia polska w latach międzywojennych a prądy społeczne i umysłowe," *Myśl Wspołczesna* 1949, 1–2/32–33.

41 T. Czeżowski, *Odczyty filozoficzne*, Toruń, 1958, pp. 305–309 (the articles and addresses in this collection were published or delivered earlier); O. Lange, "The Scope and Method of Economics," originally published in the *Review of Economic Studies*, Vol. 13, 1945/46, reprinted in H. Feigl and M. Brodbeck (eds.), *Readings in the Philosophy of Science*. New York: 1953, see in particular pp. 750–51; Ossowski, "Teoretyczne zadania marksizmu," *Myśl Wspólczesna* 1948, 1/20, p. 8.

42 This happened recently even to Schaff, namely after the publication of his *Marksizm a jednostka ludzka*. See "Dyskusja nad książką Adama Schaffa," *Nowe Drogi* 1965, 12/199, pp. 170 ff. in particular, and Z. A. Jordan, "Socialism, Alienation, and Political Power," *Survey*, No. 60 (1966), pp. 132–33.

practice; the truth and falsity of medical theories in hospitals and operating theatres; the truth and falsity of political economy by the effectiveness of the economic policy based on it. But scientific discoveries are often stimulated by ideological motivation, by the passion for justice, the interests of the entrepreneurial stratum, or the desire to improve the life of the working classes. Moreover, there seems to exist some connection between the kind of ideological motivation and the rate or scope of scientific advance, for evidently ideological motivation may either favor or hamper the discovery of truth. We have to recognize, therefore, that there are two types of ideological attitudes, the progressive and conservative, with other intermediate types between them. While conservative ideologies, being interested in the preservation of the existing state of affairs, offer only limited possibilities of scientific advance or block them altogether, progressive ideologies, opposed to any permanency, reveal reality, favor attainment of truth, and promote scientific knowledge in every way. But it should be conceded that in certain conditions—Lange mentioned revisionist Marxism or the times of the "cult of personality"—the progressive attitude also may produce distorted knowledge and biased conceptions, and thus does not automatically guarantee the attainment of truth.[43]

The complete change in the style of thinking and writing about the views with which Marxist-Leninists disagree may provide the third example of orthodox revisionism. The old type of Marxist-Leninist criticism was based on the assumption that the opponent was not and could not ever be right in the slightest degree. The Marxist-Leninist critic did not take the trouble of discovering by study what in the opponent's views was false, and what was true. Such a discrimination was regarded as tantamount to academic objectivism and constituted an offence against the principle of partisanship. The writer who disagreed in any way with Marxism-Leninism was at once classified as an idealist of some kind or other, and, by the same token, as a supporter of bourgeois and imperialistic ideology. Therefore, the old type of criticism, now described as nihilistic, was confined to the abuse of the opponent and to a complete unconditional rejection of his views. This kind of criticism, Kołakowski wrote, was a struggle against an imaginary opponent and gained imaginary victories. Instead of trying to produce understanding and persuasion, it "became a part of a ritualistic ceremonial which could successfully combine ignorance of the subject with a contempt for the criticized writer."[44]

43 O. Lange, *Ekonomia polityczna*, Warsaw, 1959, pp. 276–94. This book is available
   in English translation (*Political Economy*, Oxford–Warsaw, 1963, pp. 322 ff.).
44 L. Kołakowski, *Światopogląd i życie codzienne*, Warsaw, 1957, p. 68.

Now this practice of the past has been repudiated, for such criticism, as Schaff emphasized, convinced nobody except those who shared the critic's opinion. The old assumption that certain trends have a monopoly on truth and others a monopoly on falsehood was simply inaccurate, if not entirely false. Truths, even important ones, can be found in systems that are otherwise full of errors; and falsehoods, even serious ones, may occur in systems otherwise entirely correct. The criticism of the nihilistic kind failed to carry conviction and, thus, was ineffective. Moreover, it atrophied the intellectual function of Marxist-Leninist philosophy and thus harmed Marxism-Leninism more than its opponents.[45]

The cumulative effect of these orthodox revisions was considerable; they encouraged objectivity, impartiality, professional competence, and other qualifications in which Marxist-Leninist scholars did not excel in the past. They reestablished the conditions necessary for teaching, research, and scientific discussion and raised the status of Marxism-Leninism in the universities and academic community. They also tended to enlarge the traditional scope of problems considered in Marxist-Leninist philosophy. Questions before neglected because of their origin in Western philosophical thought were taken up one after the other. Schaff himself pressed relentlessly for the inclusion of problems and whole disciplines in the Marxist-Leninist program of studies and for the modernization of the Marxist-Leninist conceptual framework. He urged and supported the revival among his fellow Marxist-Leninists of interest in sociology, social psychology, ethics, the philosophy of language, the philosophy of science, cybernetics and, finally, even the "philosophy of man," that is, an existentialized historical materialism.

In all these matters Schaff showed much mental energy, agility, and adaptability. He extolled lavishly the same thinkers, schools of thought, and fields of inquiry that he used to condemn, and made it a rule to dabble in them himself. While in the past he fulminated against semantics, "semantical philosophy," or existentialism, in the new period he published *Introduction to Semantics* and *The Philosophy of Man*. In general, it could be said that he faithfully reflected the light and pressures of his intellectual environment. To put it differently, he criticized the opponents of Marxism-Leninism—whether they were logical empiricists, analytical and

45 A. Schaff, *Wstęp do semantyki*, Warsaw, 1960, pp. 90–93, 350–51. This book is also available in English translation (*Introduction to Semantics*, Oxford–Warsaw, 1963). See A. Schaff, *A Philosophy of Man*, p. 19. For a more competent criticism of the idealism-materialism dichotomy on which "Nihilistic criticism" was based, see L. Kołakowski, *Jednostka i nieskończoność*, Warsaw, 1958, pp. 619 ff. By endorsing Kołakowski's views, Schaff made them orthodoxically respectable.

linguistic philosophers, revisionists, or existentialists—only to be influenced by them and adopt their views as his own in due course. He was prompted by the awareness of the fact that Marxism-Leninism could not compete with its opponents successfully unless it assimilated their ideas in one form or another.

Finally, he might have exemplified a more general regularity. According to Kołakowski, orthodoxy and heterodoxy are, as a rule, mutually dependent, the one determining and being in turn determined by the other. In the past the Catholic Church managed somehow to counteract the impact of the Reformation and the Reformed Churches to contain the Counter-Reformation by assimilating some of the tendencies that the revolt against them had produced. Similarly, while Marxism-Leninism firmly opposes and is genuinely hostile to many new ideas, it has ultimately to absorb them in order to neutralize their erosive influence and turn them to its own advantage.

The ultimate goal of orthodox revisionism was political. Schaff believed that the Party should modernize its outlook and methods of action in order to gain genuine social support and to compete successfully with the new trends of thought. He wanted the Communist Party to revise its ways of thinking and acting because terrible mistakes had been made in the past which were harmful to the dissemination of Socialist ideas and held up and impoverished the development of Marxism-Leninism. Because Schaff's revisionism is kept within the Marxist-Leninist framework and is subordinate to the supreme objective of making the power of the Party more secure and effective, it can justly be called "orthodox revisionism." [46] One can say about Schaff that he had enough of the revisionist in him to tinker with Marxism-Leninism, but not enough to press for its basic modifications.

PHILOSOPHIC REVISIONISM

Philosophic revisionism as represented by Kołakowski is not a doctrine, but an intellectual attitude or a critical method by means of which orthodox beliefs, accepted on the authority of the founders and other accredited interpreters of Marxism, are analyzed and evaluated. Although being a method rather than a doctrine, philosophic revisionism establishes certain general principles as the foundation stones of any alternative ideology. Kołakowski did not try to list these general principles and to establish them systematically, but the following three ideas seem to be central to his

46 See A. Schaff, *Marksizm a egzystencjalizm*, Warsaw, 1961, p. 47; see *A Philosophy of Man*, pp. 102–103.

thinking: (1) the moral autonomy and responsibility of the individual; (2) the distinction between the institutional and intellectual Marxism; and (3) the concept of rational or permanent criticism.

The principle of the moral autonomy and responsibility of the individual—which Kołakowski owes to Spinoza rather than to Kant [47]—is psychologically closely related to the experiences of the Stalinist period.

Stalinism provided the model of a doctrine which accepts the monism of facts and norms and deduces moral obligation from historical necessity. Kołakowski used the Hegelian—or pseudo-Hegelian, as he preferred to call it—and Stalinist view of history to show the horrors and corruption resulting from a doctrine which claims a complete and infallible knowledge of the future.[48] For it follows from such a doctrine that the moral problem of the individual does not lie in measuring historical events by the standards of one's own sense of justice, but in adapting one's own sense of justice to historical necessity. This leads to the identification of moral obligation with obedience to the will and commands of the rulers and thus to opportunism and ultimately to the destruction of morality. On the other hand, once we free ourselves from the fantastic belief that the standards of moral evaluation are logical conclusions derived from the knowledge of historical laws, we are faced by the simple and important truth that the facts of social life are not unalterable; that we cannot shift the responsibility for changing these facts to anyone else; and that thus the responsibility is entirely ours. "No one is exempted from the moral duty," Kołakowski wrote, "to fight against a system of government, a doctrine, or a social condition which he considers to be vile and inhuman, by resorting to the argument that he finds them to be historically necessary."[49] This argument ignores the nature of moral obligation and is materially false.

The argument is false, because value judgments are never logically derivable from the statements of facts.[50] We discover the facts, but

47 L. Kołakowski, *Jednostka i nieskończoność*, pp. 565 ff.
48 While most philosophers in Poland (and probably elsewhere) could endorse L. T. Hobhouse's view that Hegel's philosophy of history is a "false and wicked doctrine" (*The Metaphysical Theory of the State*, London, 1918, p. 6), this evaluation is a controversial matter. In Poland T. Kroński took up the cudgel for Hegel and defended him against the objection of moral blindness and indifferentism. See T. Kroński, *Rozważania wokół Hegla*, Warsaw, 1960, pp. 59 ff, 91 ff. Kroński's arguments are hard to follow, for he not only admired Hegel, but also emulated his style.
49 L. Kołakowski, "Odpowiedzialność i historia," *Nowa Kultura*, R. 8, 1957, 36/389, p. 4.
50 See L. Kołakowski, "Odpowiedzialność i historia," *Nowa Kultura*, R. 8, 1957, 38/391, pp. 4–5; "K. Marks i klasyezna definicja prawdy," *Studia Filozoficzne* 1959, 2/11, pp. 64–66.

we make the norms and rules of conduct ourselves. The perception of the moral world of value and obligation is irreducible to the knowledge of facts, events, and natural laws. While historical necessity is not entirely a figment of the imagination, we can never know its limits with sufficient precision to discover in any particular case what is and what is not predetermined by the historical process. The future differs from the past, for the future is never irrevocable; it always leaves room for choice and a realistically conceived decision. Therefore, no doctrine and no faith can release us from the moral choice and moral responsibility that each individual has ultimately to face.

If the moral act is a choice of values and values have no existence outside human consciousness, this does not mean that our moral decisions are entirely arbitrary or "subjective" in the Hegelian sense of this term. The moral beliefs and value commitments of the individual are subject to determinations of various kinds, some being inherent in the universal conditions of social life, others resulting from specific limitations of historical epochs and their class structure, or from membership in a definite class, in a professional, political, or ethnic group.

The social determination of our view of the world and moral beliefs does not deprive us of the freedom of choice, for social determination does not imply compulsion, and only compulsion precludes free choice. The rejection of the Hegelian monastic or barracks-like concept of freedom leaves open alternatives other than the autonomous, entirely self-determined individual of existentialism. The allegedly self-evident proposition "man is completely and always free or he is not free at all" is clearly a falsehood.[51]

The distinction between institutional and intellectual Marxism was related to the endless controversies over authentic Marxism, but its origin and significance lay elsewhere. The distinction became imperative as soon as the teaching of Marx was accepted as mass ideology, the ideology of ruling élites and states, the function of which was to enhance social stability and solidarity, to provide a firm purpose and effective method of collective action. Although there is an authentic Marxism, if Marxism refers to the doctrines of Marx to be found in his works, there is no authentic Marxism, if Marxism refers to an interpretation of Marx's teaching which in conditions entirely different from those during Marx's lifetime is

---

51 L. Kołakowski, *Światopogląd i życie codzienne*, pp. 102 ff., in particular pp. 116–17; "Determinizm i odpowiedzialność," in *Fragmenty filozoficzne: Seria druga*, Warsaw, 1959. The antinomies of freedom and determinism, including M. Schlick's solution of it, is discussed in detail in M. Ossowska, *Podstawy nauki o moralności*, Warsaw, 1947. Schlick's *Fragen der Ethik* is a book widely known in Poland. Its Polish translation appeared in 1960.

to provide an ideology and a political program of a mass movement.

Institutional Marxism is a set of doctrines which are selected by political authorities or one single person because of their ideological acceptability and their usefulness in providing the explanation of and justification for political decisions, policies, and programs. These doctrines, ascribed to Marx, are presented as eternal verities, but in fact are modifiable in the light of experience, changing conditions, and other requirements of time and place. The supposed incontrovertible truths turn out to be the beliefs of the hour imposed as the necessities of thought. For instance, until February, 1956, only an anti-Marxist, a reformist, a metaphysician, in brief— an idealist, could believe that socialism might be achieved without revolution. Since February, 1956, the former idealist has become a genuine Marxist and the former genuine Marxist has become an anti-Party idealist. Institutional Marxism cannot be defined by its content, but solely by its social and political function. We cannot describe its content by giving a list of propositions, but only by indicating an Office or an Authority with which the doctrine obligatory at a given moment is deposited. A supporter of institutional Marxism is not a man with definite views but one ready always to recognize institutionally approved beliefs.

There is one authentic Marxism only, that is, the doctrine of Marx contained in his own works, but this authentic Marxism is now mainly a historically significant fact. We should remember that some theories of Marx have been refuted and others have been modified, that whole new areas of facts have been opened to research, new theories, concepts, and methods have been devised and applied; and that a number of views which originated with Marx have been universally accepted. This is what normally happens in the advancement of knowledge, and there is no reason to mourn over the fact that Marxism as a distinct school of thought in philosophy and the social sciences has lost its importance and is gradually to disappear altogether.

This does not mean that the doctrine of Marxism has no permanent value. The teaching of Marx is and will remain an intellectual force, a powerful influence, and a revealing way of viewing men, society, and history. This intellectual Marxism is not a doctrine, not a system of propositions, but—to use Kołakowski's own words —"a vibrant philosophical inspiration, affecting our whole way of looking at the world." Intellectual Marxism as a vision of the world retains its original greatness and importance, and no passage of time can deprive it of these qualities.[52]

52 L. Kołakowski, "Aktualne i nieaktualne pojęcie marksizmu," *Nowa Kultura*, R. 8, 1957, 4/357, pp. 2 and 7.

Intellectual Marxism involves the third main principle of philosophical revisionism, the principle of permanent or rational criticism. Writing in a lighter and more literary vein, Kołakowski called it the "philosophy of the jester," a philosophy which in every epoch denounces as doubtful what appears as unshakable, and contrasted it with the philosophy of the priest, the priest being the guardian of the absolute who upholds and protects its cult.[53]

The scientific attitude means criticizing everything. The test of the rationality of our beliefs consists of their being permanently subject to discussion, to further investigations and logical control. Every view is tentative and provisional, for no view can claim conclusive evidence in its favor. There are always approaches which are unexplored and solutions yet unknown, and there is always the possibility of error. Because all men are fallible, it is absurd to assume that any single man or any group of men has a monopoly on knowledge and truth, whether in matters of theory or of practical significance. Neither observation nor reasoning justify the claim that there are any incontrovertible truths. Therefore, unfettered freedom of thought is the only guarantee in our possession that errors may be discovered and knowledge may advance.[54]

Restrictions on the principle of rational criticism lead to dogmatism, and dogmatism paves the way for an overt or concealed oppression of thought. Truths do not come from nowhere. If there is a list of incontrovertible truths, there must be a group of individuals who decide which truths are to be included in the list. These individuals must be powerful enough to protect them from the destructive impact of rational criticism. No dogmatism is able to survive on its own; it needs the support of an organized power which by means of various restrictions and controls makes dogmatism secure. But under the protection of authority and administrative prohibitions the difference between truth and falsehood, myth and reality disappears. Freedom of thought and political freedom are linked together; people cannot have one without the other. A minority which maintains its authority by the suppression of the freedom of thought is an obstacle to the development toward Socialism.

The principle of rational criticism assigns to communist intellectuals an important role. "The Communist Party," Kołakowski wrote, "does not need intellectuals in order that they admire the wisdom of its decisions, but only in order that its decisions be wise. Thus, they are needed by communism as men free in their thinking; as opportunists they are expendable . . . Communist intellectuals

53 L. Kołakowski, "Kapłan i błazeń," *Twórczość*, 1959, No. 10.
54 L. Kołakowski, "Racjonalizm jako ideologia," *Argumenty*, R. 3, 1959, 20/49, p. 8.

defending independent thinking from the pressure of politics are acting not only in the name of an abstractly conceived freedom of science, but also for the sake of the interests of communism." Only as men free to search for truth can the intellectuals be useful to a revolutionary movement.[55]

It is perhaps the principle of rational criticism which differentiates most sharply the philosophical revisionists from the orthodox revisionists. While the orthodox revisionists reduce the number of incontrovertible truths and "correct views," they have never abandoned them entirely and unconditionally. They were in full agreement with the leadership of the Communist Party that "there can be no creative Marxism against the ideological principle of the Party policy." Schaff said explicitly that "There are definite limits which no one can transgress if he does not wish to sever his connections with Marxism." When recently, driven by the logic of his assumptions, he almost crossed the line dividing orthodox and philosophic revisionism, he turned back at the last moment to declare, "I recognize (the Party's right) to intervene in certain problems of science and art." Because to grant the scientist, the scholar, the writer, and the artist an unfettered freedom of thought and expression would weaken the political power of the ruling élite, one has to accept these restrictions as a "necessary evil" and only stipulate that the Party's intervention should not go beyond what is absolutely unavoidable.[56]

Strange as it may appear, the thought that he may confer an excessive certainty upon his beliefs never occurs to an orthodox Communist. Thus his own hope becomes the sole law of life, the only source of moral values, and the only measure of integrity.

THE EARLY WORKS OF MARX AND THE PROBLEM OF
SOCIALIST HUMANISM

The question of the relation between the works of the young Marx (in particular, of *Economic and Philosophic Manuscripts of* 1844) and those which he wrote later in life was not discussed in Poland until 1959. It started with the publication of Kołakowski's article "Karl Marx and the Classical Definition of Truth" from which his philosophical ally, H. Eilstein, dissociated herself and which was sharply criticized by Schaff and others.[57] Little of any importance

---

55 L. Kołakowski, "Intelektualiści i ruch komunistyczny," *Nowe Drogi* 1956, 9/87, p. 31.

56 Dyskusja nad ksiąską Adama Schaffa," *Nowe Drogi* 1965, 12/199, p. 166.

57 H. Eilstein, "O stylu filozofowania Leszka Kołakowskiego tudzież o 'marksistowskiej' i 'engelsowsko-leninowskiej' teorii poznania," *Studia Filozoficzne* 1959, 6/15; A. Schaff, "O studiach nad młodym Marksem i istotnych wypaczeniach," *Nowe*

was heard of the "young Marx" in the following years. The problem was taken up again only in 1965 in Schaff's *Marxism and the Human Individual,* and given a sharp ideological and political turn.

Kołakowski's main objective was limited. He wished to emphasize the important difference between the "anthropological realism," as I propose to call it, of the young Marx on the one hand, and of the theory of knowledge of Engels and Lenin on the other. The latter is the copy theory of knowledge, which owing to Lenin's efforts in *Materialism and Empirio-Criticism* is considered an essential part of "Marxist" materialism. Kołakowski did not raise the question as to whether Marx is a dialectical materialist in Engels and Lenin's sense, although a negative answer is implicit in his examination of the Marxian anthropological realism.

Marx did not present his anthropological realism in a systematic form but in the course of his critical and polemical analysis of Hegel's philosophy to be found in the *Economic and Philosophic Manuscripts of* 1844. Its fundamental assumption is the belief that the relation between man and his environment should be investigated as the relation between individuals living in society and the objects satisfying their biological needs. The world is not the totality of things-in-themselves but of things for us. The material world, causally independent of man, does exist, but is entirely beyond his reach. Man shapes his environment according to his needs, and the needs determine the articulation of the outside world into separate things and their connections. If our needs were different, the world would look different to us, as it does to other animal species. The world is knowable, because it is determined by ourselves.

The world of Marx differs entirely from the world of Engels and Lenin. They believe that they can describe the world *an und für sich,* as it exists prior to any attempt to know it. On the other hand, Marx's world, being articulated by man's wants, impulses, aspirations, joys, and sufferings, is always a subjective world. Because man is a social individual, trying to satisfy his needs together with other men, the subjective world is socially subjective. Being socially subjective, it has some permanency due to the relatively durable, though not unchangeable, characteristics of the human species.

Anthropological realism emphasizes the primacy of human activity over reflection and makes metaphysics impossible. If the humanized world is the only one that man can ever know, it is futile to speak of the world as it exists independently of man. On the other hand, because anthropological realism conceives the outside

---

Drogi 1959, 13/127; M. Fritzhand, "Spór o spuściznę filozoficzną młodege Marksa," *Nowe Drogi* 1960, 1/128; E. Kuszko, "W sprawie artykułu L. Kołakowskiego 'Karol Marks i klasyczna definicja prawdy'," *Studia Filozoficzne* 1959, 5/14.

world as socially constructed and consciousness as a social product, it recognizes the possibility of scientific knowledge and the adequacy of the correspondence conception of truth. As the world accessible to knowledge is socially created, man's creativeness informs all scientific thinking. Scientific knowledge is true and valid, but this does not mean that it reproduces imitatively the world as it exists independently of man.

Anthropological realism has certain important consequences for the theory of value and the evaluation of historical knowledge. It justifies "ethical nominalism," that is, the view that values are determined by acts of choice and thus, being of purely human origin, are man-made. In turn, "ethical nominalism" supports the principle of moral autonomy and responsibility of the individual. Anthropological realism makes it clear that value judgments cannot be deduced from statements of fact.

Anthropological realism also implies that in historical knowledge total objectivity can never be achieved. In relation to its material the historian is in a situation similar to that of the human species in relation to its environment. History is a creation of historiography; there exists no historical process independent of us and yet completely knowable. While the historian does not create his material *ex nihilo*, he imposes on it a definite order. This order is determined by his conceptual framework, which is not, however, arbitrarily chosen, for it is conditioned by one or the other of the various world views existing at the time. But the choice of conceptual apparatus is practical, and not speculative. We do not choose a theoretical premise, but express a preference and adopt an evaluative attitude toward the world.

Thus the fundamental idea of Marx can be summarized in the proposition that "man the cognitive creature is only a part of the whole man." The claim of the old materialism that man is a creature of nature, determined by and depending on his environment, is only a half-truth; it leaves out the fact that the physical and social environment is the outcome of man's social activity. Man is the product of his own work. There is a constant action and reaction of the natural and social environment on man and of man on his natural and social environment, both being determined by and determining each other. The environment acts upon him through his sense organs and is acted upon and changed by his exertions. But if the environment that determines man's behavior is in turn constantly made and remade by man's labor, the world always remains an "unfulfilled world" and man a "permanently unfulfilled man."[58]

58 L. Kołakowski, "K. Marks i klasyczna definicja prawdy," p. 67; "Racjonalizm jako ideologia," p. 8.

In his spiteful article of 1959, Schaff rejected Kołakowski's "crazy constructions," describing them as a combination of "pathetic nonsense" and "unbelievable ignorance." But today he is no longer so sure that Kołakowski is wrong in everything he says. In his book *Marxism and the Human Individual*, published in 1965, Schaff has adopted Kołakowski's basic position, namely that the young Marx deserves being taken seriously, and that his youthful ideas are indispensable for the right understanding of the mature Marx.

Schaff believes that there is only one Marxian doctrine which contains both continuity and change, that is, which was expanded, modified, and improved upon at the various stages of Marx's intellectual development. In the course of his life Marx was changing his language, conceptual framework, and method of thinking, but certain basic ideas remained unaltered throughout. Among these basic ideas is his philosophical conception of man, developed in his early writings, which is the basis of Marxian humanism and which helps us to understand Marx's interest in political economy, his criticism of capitalism, his theory of social classes and socialism, and his other views expounded in his mature age.

Humanism is the belief that men have an intrinsic value and hence should be treated as ends in themselves. As Marx put it in his *Contribution to the Critique of Hegel's Philosophy of Right*, "man is the highest being for man." It follows from this axiom of humanism that men have to accept the "categorical imperative to overthrow all those conditions in which man is an abused, enslaved, abandoned, and contemptible being." Socialism is an attempt to realize this categorical imperative of humanism and to secure for every individual a free, full, happy, and dignified life.

Because a social revolution begins as a protest against an inhuman world, its aim is to secure for every man a really human life. Humanism is the foundation of all socialism and Marxian socialism too is based on the humanistic premises to be found in Marx's youthful writings. They underlie all other works of Marx, including *Capital*, and all his activities.

This interpretation of the thought of Marx has important practical consequences. It puts all his contemporary followers under an obligation to support actively Marx's humanistic premises and aims. They require that the well-being and happiness of men— concrete individuals, living here and now—should be the highest goal of Socialist construction. But this part of the Marxian heritage has been forgotten, not only in the Stalinist period, but also in the more recent years. The new evaluation of the content of Marx's early writings and of their place within Marx's life work leads

Schaff to a critical examination of "life under socialism" and to the conclusion that the Socialist countries have failed to secure for man the conditions of a free and happy life.

The failure of the Socialist countries is due to false doctrines and wrong practices. Together they explain the fact that under socialism man continues to suffer all kinds of alienation as much as he did under capitalism. Alienation does not disappear in Socialist society, because the coercive force of the State does not wither away and, consequently, men are subject to all kinds of compulsion, constraint, and oppression. It does not disappear because class distinctions, social injustice, and inequality are not abolished, but persist under a different guise. It does not disappear because the dehumanization of the worker arising from the application of advanced technology survives the Socialist revolution. Finally, discrimination on the basis of race, religion, and nationality so continues to be practised and encouraged. In *Marxism and the Human Individual* Schaff gives a detailed justification of these general propositions. His outspoken and courageous criticism caused a storm in the Party and much public humiliation for himself.

The discussion on the young Marx has brought orthodox and philosophic revisionism more closely together than ever before. This rapprochement can be accounted for in terms of the distinction between the two kinds of criteria by means of which ideological propositions may be evaluated. When the question of truth and falsity of ideological beliefs, that is, the disparity between words and deeds, ideals and reality, grows so wide that it cannot be ignored any longer, the orthodox and philosophic revisionists are bound to join hands, be it only a temporary alliance. This is bound to happen because the question of orthodoxy and heresy, of what unites and divides the organization, becomes indistinguishable in its effects from the question of truth and falsity.

They both lead to the demand and evoke the effort to introduce the necessary changes and modifications. The rapprochement may last only as long as the original pressure of circumstances remains in existence, or it may be more permanent. Our knowledge provides no basis for prognosis, and therefore, the only reasonable course is to wait and watch the development of events. This also means that the history of Polish revisionism must remain unfinished for the present.

Translated by the author

FROM THE DIARY OF AN EYE-WITNESS
Notes on the Hungarian Revolution of 1956

George Gömöri

October 22. In the morning I went to the University Library. Afterward I did not feel like going back to the Faculty of Philology; the weather was too good. As I was standing in front of the Library wondering what to do, I saw a friend hurrying toward me. "T. and some other fellows are looking for you," he said, "over there," and he beckoned in the direction of Kecskeméti Street. "They want to tell you something about the Poles."

We knew that something extraordinary was going on in Poland, but nobody was quite sure exactly what it was. The day before, Gomułka's speech was printed in the Party daily *Szabad Nép*, but many people did not read it and even those who did were a bit perplexed. What was happening in Poland? I hurried up and soon caught sight of T. and his friends, all students like myself. They were greatly agitated. I greeted them, but before I could open my mouth to inquire about Poland someone said: "Haven't you heard? Soviet troops surrounded Warsaw." They heard this news on the radio; it was relayed by the Hungarian service of the BBC. We did not know that by that time, that is by October 22, the Soviet tanks had already been stopped, if not withdrawn, on Khrushchev's orders. What we knew was the reason of the Poles' unrest: they wanted more freedom and national independence—this is why they elected Gomułka. The Russians tried to prevent these changes. Something had to be done. "We could organize a demonstration," suggested V., the only girl in the group. "I heard this morning that the Writers' Union is going to organize a solidarity march with the Poles."

As I learned years later, this rumor was started at the Academy of Fine Arts, where V. was studying. It was quite unfounded, but it served us well at that moment. After a short discussion we agreed to spread the news (which we accepted without question) and mobilize all our friends and colleagues for a peaceful demonstration—in support of the beleaguered Poles. We agreed that the demonstration was to take place the following day, on October 23.

The possibility of such a demonstration seemed self-evident to all of us; it was, as they say, in the air. Since the memorable mock-funeral of Rajk, the rehabilitated Hungarian "Titoist," which took place on October 6, Hungary had not been the same place. The air was charged with tension, the whole country was buzzing with rumors. The students of Szegbed University formed MEFESZ, the first non-Communist student organization since 1948. The students of the Polytechnic held crowded meetings where demands were voiced for the reform of higher education and for the further "democratization" of the country. They actually threatened the authorities that they were ready to take to the streets if their demands were not met.

This was only a threat, but my friends and I sprang into action. The demonstration was fixed for early next afternoon, to start from that intersection of Gorky Avenue where the Polish Embassy faced the Writer's Club on the other side of the street. We set out to spread the news—this was greatly helped by the fact that most faculties were about to form their discussion clubs modeled on the (by then) famous Petőfi Circle, and the first meetings of these clubs were scheduled for the afternoon of October 22. So the politically more active students of our faculty learned about the plan of the demonstration that very afternoon, at the first meeting of the "March 15 Circle."[1]

This was, incidentally, a crucial meeting for the advocates of the demonstration. There were only a few of us who felt the need to do something for the Poles, but there were many students who thought that the political improvements (rightly or wrongly) expected after the fall of Rákosi, a few months earlier, had failed to materialize. The leadership of the Party was still 90 per cent Stalinist, that is to say, compromised; Geró, the new Party Secretary, was not re-garded as a more "liberal" man than Rákosi.

The meeting of the debating society was held in a large hall

---

[1] March 15 is the day when the Hungarian democratic revolution of 1848 erupted. It was on this day that the so-called "March youth," led by the poet Petőfi, proclaimed and printed the "demands of the Hungarian nation."

generally used for theatrical preformances. It was opened with an announcement by Pozsár, the DISZ Secretary of the Faculty:[2]

"Comrades," said Pozsár, a thin young man with a sharp voice, "there were rumors about a demonstration of sympathy with the Poles, allegedly organized by the Writers' Association. Now I called up the Writers' Association and its Party Secretary made an official denial. They are not organizing a demonstration of any kind . . ."

On the spur of the moment I jumped up (I was sitting in the first row) and, turning toward the audience, shouted:

"Whatever the Writers' Association is doing, the students will be out on the streets tomorrow!"

My words were greeted with a thunder of applause. I was too excited to be surprised—but Pozsár was visibly taken aback and quickly changed his position. He waited for the applause to subside and then said in a firm voice:

"Well, if you decide that we should demonstrate, we shall demonstrate; and in that the case the DISZ will march in the first lines!"

The main question being settled by Pozsár's *volte-face*, we began to go into details. What sort of slogans should we use in the demonstration? I was asked to the stage to announce the proposed slogans. I had just scribbled down a few of them before the meeting: they were mainly about Polish–Hungarian friendship. I proposed a slogan hailing Gomułka which was, however, rejected by the majority of the students—the only thing people knew about Gomułka was that he was jailed by the Stalinists, and that did not seem to be enough recommendation. A red-haired linguist suggested that we should throw in some "national" slogans as well, but when pressed for concrete proposals, he did not have any. We adjourned this problem—and, indeed, the next day some good slogans were coined and accepted before and during the solidarity march.

The march had to be peaceful—in this we all agreed. We feared a provocation which, it was rumored, was being prepared by the followers of Rákosi within the Party. This is why we rejected the suggestion that we should get in touch with young workers and organize a joint march. No, ours should remain a student demonstration, a show of strength but not a reason for provocation and police repression. "And if the police shoot?" asked someone. This was a risk we had to take. But it was made clear that what we wanted was an orderly demonstration, with "constructive slogans." Nobody could foresee the drama of the next day.

2 DISZ (Dolgozó Ifjúság Szövetsége) was the Hungarian counterpart of the Polish *ZMP* [Polish Youth Alliance] and the Russian *Komsomol*.

October 23, Tuesday. About nine o'clock I went to the Faculty. General excitement and activity, people dashing around. Yesterday evening a committee was formed from students of various faculties and of the Polytechnic, and a final decision was taken about the route of the march. According to this we were to meet at Petőfi's statue on the Pest side of the Danube and march from there to the statue of General Bem, on the Buda side of the river.

The room of the DISZ committee was full of people. Enthusiasm for the demonstration apparently spread with the speed of an avalanche. Pozsár was on the phone talking to various faculties. I was trying to get some Polish flags from somewhere: the glass door of the Polish Reading Room on Váci Street was locked, the employees peeping at us from behind the door with frightened faces, motioning: "Go away!" Their fright could not spoil my mood— this was my day. I was a fourth-year student of Polish and I had been following events in Poland ever since my visit there in 1953. I liked the Poles, the whole crazy and charming lot. Upon returning to the Faculty I got a white and red cockade from the girls. It all looked like March 15 once again.

In the meantime a delegation had arrived from the Polytechnic. They wanted a silent march, but we were sticking to our decision (no demonstration without slogans!), so it all ended in an argument. The engineering students thought that a silent march would be more impressive. Finally we agreed to differ: let them have their "quiet" parade on the Buda bank of the Danube (the Polytechnic was at Buda, anyway) while we are going ahead with our demonstration. It was to start from the Petőfi statue. The delegates from the Polytechnic claimed they could bring out fifteen thousand students. For the first time I became worried—just how big a demonstration was it going to be?

At that point a new guest burst into the committee room— someone from the Petőfi Circle. "Be calm, my friends, the Circle is taking over the coordination of the march!" This was inevitable, I suppose. For the first time since the spring the Circle was caught unawares by the accelerating trend of events—they tried to catch up with us. (With *us*? But I was a member of Petőfi Circle as well.) Apparently, even the local Party organizations, those of the various faculties, were alarmed to the point of deciding to join us, in the belief that they could "take over" the demonstration. The Party stalwarts soon found themselves outnumbered and many Party members joined the demonstration enthusiastically.

At noon another meeting took place at the Faculty of Philology. The Party committee of the Faculty announced its decisions—in the main identical with the "points" accepted by the students of the

Polytechnic, which had been stenciled and pasted all over Budapest in the morning. Tibor Kardos, the Dean, told the meeting that the teaching staff would also take part in the demonstration. His statement was warmly applauded when, all of a sudden, someone let out a shout:

"The Russians should go home!"

After a moment of terrified silence people in the front rows began to turn around, asking their neighbors excitedly: "Who was that? What did he say?" Kardos saved the situation. With a half-smile, he translated the demand:

"That Comrade wanted to say that it would be desirable if only units of the Hungarian People's Army were stationed on Hungarian territory."

Everyone laughed and clapped. The meeting was about to be closed when the news that the Minister of Interior Affairs had put a ban on the demonstration poured new fuel on the fire. A delegation was elected without delay, in order to ask Party Headquarters to rescind the ban. The delegation consisted of about fourteen people, among them the Dean, members of the staff, and some students, including myself. As we squeezed ourselves into taxis, we told our friends to start the demonstration at three o'clock no matter what happened to us.

The building of the Communist Party's Central Committee in Akademia Street was crowded with delegations from various institutions, all asking for the same thing: the ban must be lifted. Only a few members of our delegation could get a hearing "upstairs"—we waited in the hall, talking in muted voices, not without some anxiety. After about twenty minutes someone burst into the hall: "The ban has been lifted!" We swarmed into the street, then hurried back to the University.

It was not yet a quarter to three, but it seemed that all of Budapest was out in the streets. People stood in groups along the curbs, locked in discussion. The withdrawal of the ban was apparently announced on the Radio—thus even those who would have failed to notice the demonstration otherwise went to the streets to see what was going to happen. The square behind the Faculty building was full of people—they were listening to Sinkovits, a popular actor, who was reciting "Rise, Hungarians!" a well-known poem of the 1848 revolution, at the base of Petőfi's statue. It was a theatrical yet curiously moving performance; people responded to the poem with an excitement rarely experienced. It was a perfect, rather mild October day; flags were slightly waving in the breeze, nodding their approval to Petőfi.

As newer and newer groups arrived with flags, songs, and

posters, I ran along the queue that was stretching now into Váci Street. I put on my "organizer's" armband and took off my tie. The sky was blue, people were chatting with each other with relaxed expectation, and someone far, far away was playing the old song "God who has saved Poland . . ." (Boże, cos Polske . . .) on the trumpet. It was five to three. Most students we expected had arrived and many others in addition. We could get going. I ran to the front and the march began.

It was a breathtaking moment—there's no other word to describe it. As soon as we set off, people in the windows of the neighboring houses began to applaud and cheer. After the first slogans, which we shouted in chorus, the applause became even stronger: "Independence, freedom/Polish–Hungarian friendship!" "We want a new leadership/our trust is in Imre Nagy!" "We won't stop half-way/Stalinism must perish!" We sang the *Marseilles* and patriotic songs of 1848–1849, and even some left-wing songs of the post-war years when there was still a genuine left-wing movement in Hungary. The street was lined by shouting, waving, cheering onlookers. Some elderly people began to cry.

As we turned from Kossuth Lajos Street into one of the main arteries of Budapest, some of the onlookers tried to join the march. At first we, "the organizers," objected to it, but soon it became impossible to stop people from joining us. There were some journalists whom I knew—they simply stepped into line. Only a joke would help: "Only students can march with us . . . but we opened a correspondence course." The number of our "external" students was growing steadily.

The march reached the Danube and passed on to Buda through the Margaret Bridge. We were to meet the "silent" students of Buda at Bem's memorial. It was easier said than done: the Bem Square was crowded like a can of sardines. Only the first few hundred people of our march could reach the square; the rest got stuck in a side street. There was a continuous roar like that of a soccer arena—one could hardly hear the voice of the writer Peter Veres, who was reading out the decisions or demands of the Writers' Association from the top of a Radio car. We sang the National Anthem, there was a recital, and I suddenly caught sight of the characteristic face of Déry at the base of the memorial. He was trying to speak, but his voice was drowned in the roar of the crowd—there were no loud-speakers. Next to Déry I spotted a short man with glasses. I suddenly remembered that that must be Ważyk, whose arrival in Budapest was announced in the morning. "Let us hear Ważyk," I yelled and someone turned back his head from the crowd; it was E., also a writer. He looked upset. "They're not letting him speak," he groaned. It was not a question of good or ill will; in such conditions even Lajos Kossuth himself would have had a hard time making himself heard. The noise was deafening; nobody knew what to do next.

The building behind Bem's statue was an Army barracks; dozens of soldiers were watching the crowd from the open windows. Suddenly one of them stuck out a Hungarian flag with a hole in the middle—the Russian-style coat-of-arms, which the people have never accepted, had been neatly cut out. The crowd roared its approval and soon all the flags were restyled in this fashion. In the meantime, a man from the Petőfi Circle who climbed the base of Bem's statue, managed to out-yell the crowd, telling those standing nearest that everyone should go to the Parliament, where there would be loudspeakers.

The crowd started surging toward the Danube; I had the luck to catch an open lorry which raced back to Pest over one of the northern bridges, originally called Árpád Bridge[3] and renamed "Stalin Bridge" in the bad old days of the Great Leader and Linguist. The lads on our lorry, judging by their looks mostly young workers, took up the chant, while crossing the bridge, of: "Árpád Bridge! Árpád Bridge!" The Hungarian past was rehabilitated in such a simple manner.

By the time we reached the Parliament the sun had already set, and it was getting dark. People ignited bunches of newspapers and lit the square with these torches. There was an enormous crowd—tens of thousands of people, waiting for something. For what? For somebody to give direction to the mass movement begun that afternoon. They were waiting for Imre Nagy, who had failed to arrive, and when he did arrive later he could not satisfy the crowd. But at that time he was still eagerly awaited, and from time to time a ripple went through the crowd and the defiant shout so familiar in Hungarian history went up: "NOW OR NEVER!"—but occasionally one could hear people shouting "Russians, go home" as well.

It was getting cool and I suddenly felt very tired. After half an hour or an hour stay at Parliament Square I walked home. As soon as I entered our flat, I fell on my bed and slept. How much time passed? Perhaps an hour. As soon as I awoke I called up Warsaw. It was important, I thought, that the Polish press should be properly informed about our demonstration—I telephoned the *Sztandar Młodych*.[4]

3 *Árpád* was the prince who led the ten Hungarian tribes into the territory of present-day Hungary in 896 A.D.

4 The daily of the ZMP, replaced in 1957 by the ZMS [Socialist Youth Alliance].

My choice was based on a personal acquaintance. I visited Poland in 1953, but most of my acquaintances were writers; I knew practically no journalists. On the other hand, I happened to know Hanka Adamiecka from the *Sztandar*. She was a nice, soft-hearted, plump girl whom I met in Budapest in the summer of 1956 and immediately befriended. We discussed every possible subject from literature to politics. Hanka, once no doubt a starry-eyed ZMP-member, now had her own share of doubts. She talked with indignation about certain Polish Communists whose close contacts with the Russian leadership were an open secret in Warsaw: "Imagine, they proposed an openly anti-Semitic program at our last Plenum . . . And these people have the cheek to call themselves Communists!" I knew that if I could count on someone in Warsaw it would be Hanka.

Unfortunately, she was not in the editorial office that night. I talked to a man whose name I have since forgotten, but who was willing to note down the information I gave about the aims and size of our demonstration. He promised to call back later for further details. He phoned around ten o'clock when the rifles were already coughing in the streets, only to hear my laments about the worsening situation. I told him I thought we were in for a Hungarian Poznań. The Polish journalist kept silent for a moment and then he said slowly: "I hope that everything will work out well for you. All the best!" I wondered whether he could hear the shooting over the telephone.

What happened in the meantime was this: Gerő made his idiotic broadcast at around eight o'clock. Not much later the Secret Police opened fire at the demonstrators who had surrounded the Radio building. It was actually the usual story of a students' delegation which entered the building with some demands and was never seen again—they were let out through the back door. The crowd, however, did not see them coming out and trouble began. Teargas bombs, a stray bullet, a volley—and the "siege" of the Radio followed. I talked to people afterward who got arms from soldiers, even from members of the secret police in the crowd: they did not want to fight, but handed over their weapons to volunteers. During the night the Russian tanks arrived, acting, by the way, on the request of the Hungarian government which had resigned the same night.

October 25. Yesterday was a day of uncertainties and hesitation —not for the lads fighting at various points of the town, but for me personally. Imre Nagy became Prime Minister (but Gerő did not resign yet as Party Secretary) and his appeal and offer of amnesty to the insurgents was broadcast throughout the day. All in vain, the fighting continued. One could see it from our window, from the sixth floor; a blazing tank was running in mad zig-zags through the deserted Somogyi Béla Avenue. Later on an armored car came and machined-gunned some of the houses in the neighborhood. It was not exactly a happy sight.

My dilemma was this: if we trusted anyone, it was Imre Nagy. Yet now Imre Nagy was Prime Minister and made an appeal for surrender. Why are people fighting on? Is it a national uprising? Or is there any truth in the allegations of the Radio about "counter-revolutionary elements" among the insurgents? But it was *we* who started the demonstration; it was *they*, the Secret Police, who began shooting—it was not unlike Poznań. And I knew one thing: the uprising in Poznań was *not* a counter-revolution.

On the 25th I went to the Faculty to find out what was going on. This was in a sense a decisive day, if not *the* decisive day for the course of the revolution. The massacre in front of the Parliament took place on this day. It all started with the announcement of an armistice and with fraternization between Russian soldiers (tank-crews) and Hungarians, who thronged with them to the Parliament Square. Suddenly unidentified "provocators" opened fire from the rooftops around the square. It was a senseless and mad provocation by the Secret Police and it became the source of much arbitrary bloodshed later on. To add to the confusion, a Soviet tank approaching from the other end of the square saw the shooting and joined in, killing many people who were running for cover. There were several hundred dead and wounded—and after this incident Gerő had to go and people began to demand the suppression of the Secret Police (ÁVH) and the abolition of the one-party system.

This is all said in retrospect: at the time the news of the massacre was just another shock that made people more defiant and filled them with fury. Soon after the shooting before the Parliament I took part in another demonstration which had the good luck not to be caught in the crossfire of the ÁVH and the Russians—on the other hand, we did not go near the Parliament. We marched through town shouting angry slogans: "The Radio tells lies! We are not Fascists!" There were students, workers, clerks among us, all sorts of people; I remember a girl dressed in the Hungarian national flag. In front of the Yugoslav Embassy (goodness knows, why exactly there) my friends and I began chanting demands for free elections and a multi-party system. On the way back, part of the crowd stopped before the US Embassy (situated very appropriately on Liberty Square) and chanted demands for a United Nations Special Committee. People had an almost childish faith in the United Nations in those days.

October 28. I have spent most of the last few days at the Faculty of Philology, going home only for short snacks and some sleep. On the 25th the Students' Revolutionary Committee was formed, with Pozsár as Secretary. The Committee was not elected by ballot; it was simply formed by a group of students and staff who felt that something had to be done. Most of its members had belonged to the DISZ—there was among them at least one formerly notorious Stalinist, or hard-liner, P., who went through an amazing transformation after October 23rd. He came to the Committee and offered his services, which were accepted. P. was not a scoundrel; he was just dogmatic-minded—and thereafter he became one of the most devoted workers of the Committee. A Press Section was formed under the Committee's auspices and some of us were appointed to edit a newspaper. In fact, the Faculty had a regular paper before the revolution, a weekly called *Egyetemi Ifjuság* (University Youth) which was now reissued as a daily—or rather this was what the Committee wanted. So far the situation had been extremely fluid, almost chaotic; for days Imre Nagy had been a virtual prisoner of his Stalinist colleagues on the Central Committee—it took time until he extricated himself from their embrace. We were in touch with Nagy through his friends and it was with relief that we heard the news about a new government being formed on the 28th. It was not a really good government (some people from the *ancien régime* managed to keep their positions in it) but now, we felt, Nagy was in control. The sporadic fighting at various points of the town had also subsided. Our people, with some individual exceptions, did not fight there, but we had plenty of weapons and were ready to use them in case the Russians tried to force their way into the University building.

In the evening of the 28th the first issue of our paper was almost ready. The most exciting article in this first number of the revolutionary *Egyetemi Ifjuság* was one by A. S., who refuted the slander spread by both the genuine reactionaries and the ill-informed man-in-the-street, namely that it was Imre Nagy who called for the intervention of the Soviet troops. We knew that this was nothing but a slander, but there had been no official statement to discount it—this is why a clarification seemed necessary.

As a curfew was imposed days before, we did not know how to get our articles to the printer. We were promised an armored car, but it failed to materialize. At last, around eleven o'clock we decided to walk to the printing house where *Szabad Nép* used to be printed—a distance of a mile and a half from the Faculty building. Ladislas Márton was coming with me. A short man with glasses and a large nose, Márton used to talk himself hoarse about injustice in the world in general and in Hungary in particular. He had every reason to do so: he came from a Jewish family, both of his parents were killed by the Nazis. Márton emigrated to Israel, but he did not like it there either and returned to Hungary in the fifties, just in time for the anti-Zionist campaign. For some time he had been a student of journalism at the University (he was, in my opinion, a born journalist) and could be often seen in the corridors quarrelling with someone or other. He was frank to the point of exhibitionism, which suited him well, but did not make him very popular.

It was pitch-dark outside. Manuscripts tucked away in our pockets, we set out on the street. At a corner I was stopped by a man with a tommy-gun: "*Kuda?*" It was a Russian sentry, one could see the silhouette of a tank behind him. What an opportunity to use my Russian, an utterly useless language for five years in school! "We are students on our way to the printing-house. To print our paper." No arms? No arms. The Russian motioned with the tommy-gun that we could go. For a second I was caught by the fear that he might shoot us from behind, but he was probably as happy as we that he did not have to use his weapon. We reached Rákóczi Avenue, normally a busy street, now completely deserted with torn tram cables rustling and broken glass grinding under our feet. Everything was quiet, but it was the silence of a paralyzed, dead city.

In the *Szikra* printing-house the windows were lit up, the printing machines humming. The Party daily *Szabad Nép* ceased to exist; in its last number it hailed the revolution as a just, democratic, and national movement. Three other papers continued to be printed here, edited by journalists like Péter Kende, or the Lenin-bearded Gimes, whom I had met before. They accepted our claim for a paper without any discussion. The typesetters read our manuscripts and waxed enthusiatic: "This is good stuff, boys. We'll print it even if we won't sleep a wink tonight." Then someone took me by the arm and lead me through winding corridors, muttering: "A friend of yours is here." A door opened: in the empty room, on a stack of old newspapers, Hanka Adamiecka was lying asleep. When we entered she blinked into the light with tired, red eyes but refused to go back to sleep. Back we went together to the printing hall. Hanka came with the first group of Polish journalists to cover the events which made her both sad and excited: "What a tragedy, George ... But those boys, you know, the ones who fought on the streets, aren't they marvelous? I talked to them. Some of them showed me their Party cards ... they told me that they are for socialism but first the Russians should go home." She mentioned the other journalists who flew in from Warsaw; one I knew personally was W. They were all to stay at the Polish Embassy.

At half-past six in the morning the first number of the *Egyetemi Ifjuság* was out. I was terribly exhausted, but happy. A lorry-driver volunteered to take Hanka back to the Embassy; she, too, was badly in need of sleep.

November 3. On the 30th the Russians withdrew from Budapest and Imre Nagy regained much of the popularity he had lost through his indecision or inactivity in the first days. The former editor of *Egyetemi Ifjusag*, E., turned up at the University and we formed an editorial committee. On the 31st there was a chance to go and see what was happening in the country: a University bus was sent to the western border for Red Cross supplies, food, and medicine. The Committee was looking for people who could bring the supplies to Budapest. I volunteered. E. and some others would take care of the newspaper. We stacked the bus with the current numbers of the *Egyetemi Ifjusag* and some leaflets, which called for confidence in Imre Nagy and his policy and protested against the presence of *any* foreign (Russian or Western) troops in Hungary. There was much talk about UN troops, but at that point we believed that their presence would be unnecessary.

As our bus progressed westward we stopped in some smaller towns, only to be surrounded, almost mobbed by people who were hungry for news from Budapest and snatched our newspapers out of our hands in their eagerness to learn something new. They asked our opinion about everything. "We have no confidence in anyone, only in you. You are students, tell us what to do." Never has the student's reputation been higher in Hungary than in those days. We told them to keep quiet, form their National Guards and trust Imre Nagy.

We spent two days traveling, the second night at *Hegyeshalom*, near the Austrian border. We met quite a few foreign journalists, particularly a Swede on the staff of the *Aftonbladet*. He asked me (the others spoke no English) what I thought about the Anglo-French attack on Suez. I shrugged my shoulders. He looked worried and said to me "I think the Russians will come back to Budapest." I could not see how these two things were interconnected, but on our way back we picked up reports that some more Russian troops were entering Hungary. Admittedly, this looked suspicious.

Arriving back in Budapest our suspicions were calmed. The city looked quiet enough, the arbitrary lynchings of real or suspected security police that had plagued the streets for two or three days had stopped, and students and armed workers were walking everywhere wearing the armbands of the National Guard, asking for papers of identification. Order was restored and most factories decided to resume work on Monday, November 5. In the printing house where we were setting the new number of *Egyetemi Ifjuság*, people seemed almost completely relaxed, they were exchanging jokes. Yes, Imre Nagy abrogated the Warsaw Pact, formed a genuine coalition government, and Russian troops occupied Budapest airfield—but we had information from the Parliament that the negotiations which were proceeding between the Russian and Hungarian high commands at Tököl were going well. The Hungarian delegation was led by Maléter, the new Minister of Defence.

Perhaps the Russians will agree to leave Hungary on "Austrian" terms? Everybody was optimistic that night, and Cardinal Mindszenty's short radio speech was dismissed by a wave of hand. "He is just a stubborn old man." About two o'clock in the morning we were on our way home with E., my fellow-editor. We were making ambitious plans: when all returns to normal, we shall transform *Egyetemi Ifjuság* into a weekly once again—it will be something like [the Polish] *Po Prostu*, a paper that is never afraid to be outspoken or controversial.

November 4. Bang! Bang-bang! They were shooting outside. How annoying. My mother jumped out of bed and remarked: "There's shooting outside." I turned on the other side: "Shooting? What's so unusual? Let them shoot!" "But those are guns!" and she turned on the radio. Just in time. The cannonade was shaking our windows and the Radio played the National Anthem. Then we heard Imre Nagy's voice; he reported the treacherous Russian attack. "The government is in its place."

The Faculty building was about a ten minute walk from us but I managed to make it in three. Most people were still asleep in the makeshift bedrooms of the dark building—they got used to shooting and just failed to pay attention to the cannonade. On hearing the news they started jumping up and dressing themselves in a hurry, some of them running toward the basement where all our arms and ammunition were stored. In the meantime, the radio stopped repeating its last solemn message.

What could have been done? We had wild thoughts: to print leaflets, calling for a general insurrection. Should we arm all civilians? The confusion was general. We jumped on a lorry and rushed to the printing-house to salvage some copies of our paper. What a silly headline to our last issue: "The Russian flood has stopped!" Alas, it didn't. Near the printing-house a barricade was being built.

Had there been a military commander to give orders, Budapest would have been prepared to fight like Warsaw did in 1944. But there was no one to command: the Russians arrested Maléter at midnight. Kopácsi, the head of Budapest police forces, disappeared. Nobody knew what happened to Imre Nagy. By noon it became clear that Soviet tanks were in control of most strategic points of the city.

Some fighting was still going on, but now we knew that we did not have a chance. Imre Nagy's appeal to the United Nations was in vain. The UN was discussing Suez and could not care less who was "restoring order" in Hungary.

Was it all in vain? Did we fight for a cause which was discarded by history?

No; we *made* history. Nothing will be the same again.

Translated by the author

THE SEVEN DEATHS OF MAKSIM GORKY

Gustaw Herling-Grudziński

L'histoire, décidément, ressemble de plus en plus à un roman policier, I recently read in one of the French papers. About the same time a number of the *Literaturnaya Gazeta* came into my hands with the following remarks: "We don't seem to have novels of crime and adventure in the Soviet Union. A bit of Jules Verne, Alexandre Dumas, Jack London, or Conan Doyle would do us no harm. It cannot be said that Russia has no detectives. Moreover, it seems likely that detectives might provide very useful examples for raising Soviet youth and for developing in Soviet citizens quick-wittedness, mettle, and initiative."

These two observations suggested the idea of a semi-mystery story about the seven deaths of Maksim Gorky.

I

Death Number One. Gorky died in 1936. His death was attributed to natural causes, and its propaganda value was wrung out to the last drop during the period of the funeral ceremonies. Foreign guests of honor (including André Gide, who then began his famous *Retour de l'URSS* to the measure of the funeral march) joined members of the Politburo in Red Square to review the Russian Army, and the powerful echo of the farewell artillery salvo resounded throughout Moscow.

Pravda published the following communiqué: "The Central Committee of the All Union Communist Party (Bolshevik) and the Council of Ministers of the USSR regretfully announce the death of the great Russian writer, genius, artist with words, devoted friend of the working masses, and champion of the victory of Communism, Comrade Alexey Maximovich Gorky, which occurred at Gorky near Moscow on June 18, 1936."

The medical report on the death of A. M. Gorky published on June 20 stated that Gorky had been taken ill on June 1, "with grippe, later complicated by catarrh of the upper respiratory tract and catarrhal pneumonia." The course of the illness was aggravated by "chronic paresis of the heart and blood vessels, particularly in the lungs, because of his past history of tuberculosis," and death ensued "as a result of paralysis of the heart and respiratory tract." The communiqué was signed by the Minister of Health of the Russian Federal Republic, Dr. Kaminsky, the head of the Kremlin medical office. Dr. Khodorov, Professors Pletnev, Lang, Konchalovsky, and Speransky, Doctor Levin, and Professor Davidovsky, who performed the autopsy.

Death Number Two. Two years later, in March, 1938, the trial of Bukharin and his "Rightist-Trotskyite bloc" began in Moscow. During the trial former NKVD chief Yagoda made the sensational declaration that he had murdered Gorky. He claimed to have done so in a rather unusual and original fashion. He had ordered Gorky's secretary, Khruchkhov, to arrange for the great writer to catch cold. When that happened, Yagoda sent two Kremlin doctors—Levin and Pletnev—instructions to apply the wrong treatment. As a result Gorky contracted pneumonia and died, in accord with the calculations of that medical achievement of Socialist planning.

Yagoda's secretary, Bulanov, gave the court several interesting details on the subject. "Professor Pletnev, Doctor Levin, and Gorky's secretary, Khruchkhov, were directly involved in the murder of A. M. Gorky. I can, for example, testify personally that Yagoda often summoned Khruchkhov and ordered him to see to it that Gorky caught a chill so that in this or some other way he would fall ill. Yagoda stressed the poor state of Gorky's lungs, emphasizing the fact that an illness brought about by a chill would have more chance of being fatal. Pletnev and Levin were to do the rest, and they had already received their instructions."

Death Number Three. In 1940 a collection of essays and reminiscences about Stalin was published in Veronezh. Stalin's private secretary, Poskrebyshev, in collaboration with Boris Dvinsky, contributed a highly instructive sketch entitled "The Master and the Friend of Mankind" to this anthology. In it he went back, at least semi-officially, to the story that Gorky had died from natural causes. At least semi-officially, for one must remember what Poskrebyshev was in Stalin's life—certainly something more than an ordinary private secretary to a head of state. It is not surprising that after Stalin's death the first triumvirate ritually cremated the faithful squire at his master's feet, or in any case they despatched him to the valley of the shadow of political death.[1]

Death Number Four. We owe the fourth version of Gorky's death to Herbert Morrison. In 1951 Moscow *Pravda* invited Morrison (then Minister of Foreign Affairs in the Labor government) to contribute an article, in order to show that there was complete freedom of the press in Soviet Russia. The article was written, submitted, and published, but its author committed an unforgivable offense against journalistic practice: invited to show the world the complete freedom of the press in the USSR, he used the columns of *Pravda* to expose its total absence. The editors of *Pravda* supplemented Morrison's article with a commentary full of indignation, in which one can read, among other things, the following sentence: "Freedom of speech does not exist in Russia for incorrigible malefactors, subversive agents, terrorists, murderers sent by foreign intelligence services, and the criminals who shot Lenin, killed Volodarsky, Uritsky, and Kirov, and poisoned Maksim Gorky and Kuibyshev."

It is worth noting that notwithstanding the basic similarity of Death Number Two and Death Number Four, they differ from each other in one rather significant detail: in 1938 Gorky was murdered "medically"—if one can use that term without slandering the noble practice of medicine; in 1951 he was simply poisoned. As for those who performed the deed, the differences between the two versions do not seem particularly material. Ultimately the entire "Bukharin bloc" together with Yagoda was merely, in Vyshinsky's by-now classic description, "a tool in the hands of foreign intelligence."

Death Number Five. The year in which, thanks to Morrison's article, we learned of the poisoning of Gorky, was also the year of the solemn commemoration of the fifteenth anniversary of the writer's death. Not one of the countless memorial articles that appeared in the Soviet and Communist papers alluded to the puzzling circumstances of Gorky's death. Which implicitly means a return to Deaths Number One and Number Three.

Death Number Six. In the long article on Gorky in the latest edition, the second, of the *Great Soviet Encyclopedia*, published in 1952, there is a brief mention of his death: "Gorky died on June 18, 1936. He was murdered by enemies of the people belonging to a Rightist Trotskyite organization, agents of the imperialists, against whom he had so valiantly fought. A short time earlier, in 1934, they

[1] 1963. Patricia Blake (*Encounter*, April, 1963) claims that Poskrebyshev is living in Moscow and writing his memoirs.

had killed Gorky's son, Maxim Peshkov." The same article reports that during his "last illness" Gorky still managed to read the project of Stalin's new constitution, which was published in *Pravda*.

In essence Death Number Six resumes the versions of Deaths Number Two and Four, differing from them in only one particular. It does not specify whether the assassin's fatal blow was delivered to the writer with the assistance of catarrh and pulmonary complications or with the assistance of arsenic without complications. Nevertheless, the reference to Gorky's "last illness" may be either a delicate allusion to "medical" Death Number Two or an unguarded slip of the tongue made under the influence of the competing lines of Deaths Number One, Three, and Five.

Something on the order of a compromise formulation appears in L. I. Timofeyev's *Russkaya Sovetskaya Literatura*, a handbook for the study of literature in the tenth grade of Soviet high schools, a publication approved by the Ministry of Education of the Federal Russian Republic (1952); "The hired assassins, who worked their way into his confidence, gradually caused the writer's mortal illness, which ended his life on June 18, 1936."

II

With such scanty official information at our disposal, we must obviously avoid such questions as "Who murdered Gorky?" or "Was Gorky really murdered?" A legitimate and carefully framed question ought to sound something like this: "Why in the course of the eighteen years that have elapsed since Gorky's death have two completely contradictory versions of his death been offered to the public on six different occasions?" But it is hard to answer that question without a certain, gradually unraveled working hypothesis.

In all of the Moscow "witch trials" the central point, aside from those charges that served a specific political end, was the defendants' relations with Stalin. Gorky, to be sure, never sat on the bench of the accused, but there is no reason why we should not also consider *his* relations with Stalin. And there is a particular circumstance that makes such an inquiry seem worthwhile. A photograph was published in all the Soviet papers to give a particular tone to the commemorations that marked the fifteenth anniversary of the writer's death. The organizers intended this photograph to testify to the long, unbroken, and intimate friendship of Gorky and Stalin. The place was Red Square; the year, 1931.

The photograph shows Stalin in a military cap and Gorky in an Oriental skull cap in what was expressly meant to be an affectionate pose, but it is not very convincing. Gorky gives the impression of being a beaten down, tired, and embittered man. He wears a slightly alarmed expression that makes him look more like a Russian muzhik face to face with that diabolical machine, the camera, for the first time in his life than like the most frequently photographed, painted, and sculptured writer in Soviet Russia. Stalin, on the contrary—Stalin lives up to his assumed name.[2]

Of course, it may mean nothing at all. After all, Gorky was considerably older than Stalin, and we know that, unlike his great chief, he did not enjoy particularly good health. But still the 1931 photograph suggests an animal tamer who has finally managed to subdue a wild animal and drag him half alive before the eye of the camera. The emphasis put on this picture in the reminiscences and memorial articles is highly suspicious. The similar photograph of Stalin and Lenin, reproduced in millions of copies over a period of years, obliterated the traces of the death-bed codicil to Lenin's testament.

It seems proper to go back and rummage through Gorky's revolutionary and post-revolutionary years to uncover the roots of this "unbroken friendship" of the writer and the dictator.

Even the 1952 edition of the *Great Soviet Encyclopedia* admits that Gorky committed several "serious mistakes" in the first days of the October Revolution. He did not sufficiently appreciate the organizational strength of the Party and the revolutionary proletariat and the possibilities of its alliance with the peasant class, fearing the whole time that anarchic-individualistic elements would in the end come to the fore. On the other hand, he exaggerated the importance of the old intelligentsia and its progressiveness in the later development of the revolutionary struggle. Gorky uttered these "erroneous views" in a series of articles published in 1917 and 1918 in the pages of the "semi-Menshevik" periodical *Novaya Zhizn*. The position he maintained was sharply criticized by Lenin and Stalin. Stalin "warned him personally" (in the periodical *Robochy Put*, October 20, 1917) that "one day he might easily find himself in the camp of those who have been repudiated by the Revolution."

It might be worthwhile to set the official biographer to one side for a moment and give a sample of Gorky's "erroneous views" *in extenso*. This is what he wrote in *Novaya Zhizn* on November 21, 1917: "Blind fanatics and unscrupulous adventurers are rushing breakneck toward 'social revolution,' but that is basically the road to anarchy, to the ruin of the proletariat and the revolution. The working class must realize that Lenin is experimenting with its blood. He has strained the proletariat's revolutionary spirit to its

2 Stalin's name derives from the Russian word for "steel."

extreme limits and is waiting to see what will happen. The working class must not allow adventurers and madmen to foist onto the proletariat the responsibility for infamous, senseless, and bloody crimes, because some day the proletariat and not Lenin will have to pay for it."

In the summer of 1921—the *Great Soviet Encyclopedia* continues—Gorky's tuberculosis flared up again and, at Lenin's urging, the writer went abroad for his health. The period from the autumn of 1921 until the spring of 1924 he spent in German and Czech health resorts, and in April 1924 he settled permanently in Sorrento.

Gorky's previously mentioned errors—the encyclopedist continues—did not pass without leaving their mark on his artistic production; in fact, he stopped writing for some time. But living abroad he maintained active contact with his native land. The abundant correspondence of these years bears witness to the "intense attention" with which Gorky followed all the developments of the life of Mother Russia. He visited the USSR twice (in 1928 and 1929), he wrote a travel sketch, *Across the Soviet Union*, and he returned to Russia for good in 1931.[3]

And now the final brushstroke of the *Encyclopedia* portrait: "Gorky was a friend and adviser of Stalin. The artistic and journalistic work and the political activity of the greatest Soviet writer were inspired by the teachings and ideas of Stalin. In 1932, on the occasion of the fortieth anniversary of Gorky's writing career, Stalin wrote him the following letter:

> Dear Aleksey Maximovich, I greet you from the bottom of my heart and I grip your hand in mine. I wish you many years of life and work, to the joy of all the workers and the dismay of the enemies of the working class.

"During his illness Gorky read the project of Stalin's new constitution in *Pravda*. He was so deeply moved that he exclaimed: 'Even the stones sing in our country!' His untimely death prevented him from carrying out his plan to write a series of works about contemporary life in Soviet Russia. In the last years of his life he was collecting material for an artistic profile of Stalin. Death interrupted this work. But in his journalistic articles Gorky sketched the

3 The date of Gorky's return to Russia as given in the *Great Soviet Encyclopedia* does not agree either with the inscription on the commemorative tablet at Villa Sorito in Sorrento ("From 1924 until 1933 the great USSR writer Maxim Gorky lived and worked here") or with Vsevolod Ivanov's account of his visit to Gorky in Sorrento at New Year's, 1933. It may be that, after his final decision to return to live in Russia, Gorky spent another two years, or at least the greater part of two years ("lived and worked here") in Sorrento. But for the *Great Soviet Encyclopedia* this would be a direct and unwelcome admission that his two previous trips to Russia had been exclusively reconnaissances safeguarded by the reservation that "it was still not too late."

splendid image of the leader of the first Socialist nation in the world."

After taking stock of this official portrait, how can one resist the insistent suggestion that, apart from illness, there must have been some deeper connection between Gorky's first instinctive reaction to the Revolution in its bloody swaddling clothes and his sudden and rather unexpected departure abroad?

III

It would be a mistake, of course, to minimize altogether the importance of considerations of health in Gorky's decision to leave Russia. Actually what the *Great Soviet Encyclopedia* has to say about "Lenin urging Gorky to go abroad for treatment" is in all probability at least partially true. There are, for example, two letters from Lenin to Gorky that have been preserved, testifying to the concern that the leader of the Revolution had taken for several years in the health of the Revolution's bard.

The first comes from Poronin and is dated September 30, 1913: "What you write about your health disturbs me immensely. Are you really getting better, living on Capri without treatment? The Germans have splendid sanitariums (e.g., at St. Blasien, near Switzerland), where they treat and completely heal lung diseases, obtain complete scarification, and then systematically accustom one to cold and build up one's resistance to chills, and release people fit and healthy for work. And you after Capri—winter in Russia??? I am terribly afraid that will harm your health and undermine your ability to work. Are there first-class doctors in Italy? Really, go to a first-class doctor in Switzerland or Germany, spend a couple of months on a serious cure in a good sanitarium. Because to squander the national patrimony, i.e., to get sick and undermine one's ability to work, that is inadmissible from every point of view."

The second, dated August 9, 1921, directly proposed Gorky's departure from Russia. "I have passed your letter on to Kamenev. I am so tired that I feel absolutely incapable of doing anything. And you, you are spitting blood and you do not leave! Believe me— that's neither right nor wise. In Europe, in a good sanitarium you will get well and be able to do three times as much work—I swear it to you. Here there are no possibilities of a cure or useful work— nothing but agitation, vain agitation. Leave, get well. Don't balk, I beg of you. Yours, Lenin."

But in this second letter an attentive eye will also catch, besides Lenin's undoubtedly sincere concern for Gorky's health, a rather surprising tone. "Here there are no possibilities of a cure or of useful work—nothing but agitation, vain agitation." Who is speaking, when, and to whom? The leader of the Revolution, four years after its victory, and to its most illustrious writer. What was the point of this unexpected outburst of fatigue and bitterness?

Lenin, one may imagine, was anxious to send Gorky abroad not only because he was concerned for the writer's health but also because he wanted to spare him all the shock and disillusionment of the post-revolutionary period, certainly for fear that they might strain even more his already so shaken faith in the Revolution. There are many instances of the rather forbearing and good-natured tone that Lenin assumed toward Gorky. Here, for example, is a passage from Gorky's book *Lénine et le paysan russe* (Paris, 1924): "I often had occasion to talk to Lenin about the subject of the cruelty of revolutionary tactics and behavior. 'What do you want?' he would ask, surprised and irritated. 'Can one be humanitarian in such a bitter struggle?' I bothered him continually with requests of all kinds, and I felt that my intercession in the case of certain persons aroused in him a feeling of pity, almost of disdain for me. 'Don't you realize that you are concerning yourself with nonsense?' I continued, however, to do what I believed necessary. I was not discouraged by the irritated and disapproving glances of the man who kept the accounts of the enemies of the proletariat. He shook his head painfully and said: 'You are compromising yourself in the eyes of the comrades, in the eyes of the workers.' I pointed out that the comrades and the workers were in a highly irritable and excited state that very often led them to treat with excessive lightness and 'simplicity' the liberty and life of valuable people, and that in my view needless and often absurd cruelty not only compromised the honest and difficult tasks of the Revolution, but in practice actually harmed the Revolution, driving away a large number of not-inconsiderable forces."

Finally, let us hear Trotsky. Immediately after Gorky's death, he wrote a piece about him for his Paris monthly, *The Bulletin of Bolshevik-Leninist Opposition* (July–August 1936). "He greeted the Revolution almost like a museum director." "Lenin, who appreciated and liked Gorky, was very much afraid that he would become a victim of his connections [with the intelligentsia] and of his weakness, and in the end he attained his object—he persuaded Gorky to leave Russia of his own free will." "He was a satellite of the Revolution, and like all satellites he passed through various phases; the sun of the Revolution sometimes illuminated his face and sometimes his back."

The general impression, then, is that the genius of pure political action that was Lenin considered Gorky the writer an asset to the

Revolution chiefly because of his literary activity and not because of his amateurish sallies into the sphere of active politics. Was Lenin afraid that direct political activity would infect Gorky with an incurable loathing for communism? Did he prefer to keep his falcon in readiness in the West rather than watch him exhaust himself and break his wings beating them desperately against the wires of a Moscow cage? Even the *Great Soviet Encyclopedia* makes a very subtle distinction between Lenin's attitude, on the one hand, and Stalin's, on the other, toward Gorky's rabid anti-revolutionary outbursts of 1917–1918. While Stalin openly warned him that "one day he might easily find himself in the camp of those who have been repudiated by the Revolution," Lenin "pointed out Gorky's errors to him and helped him find the way to surmount them in revolutionary activity itself, urging him to learn from the Revolution and advising him to have a careful look at the immense work achieved by the laboring class." The *Encyclopedia* closes the matter with the following seal: "Gorky later admitted his errors more than once, he acknowledged the total correctness of both Lenin and his advisers, and he acknowledged the correctness of the Party's wise policies." In this discreet manner the great Stalin of the post-revolutionary period was—at least as far as Gorky was concerned—reduced to the rank of an anonymous and modest adviser to Lenin.

IV

In the light of available material, this is what Gorky's trip abroad looked like from Lenin's point of view. And from that of Gorky himself? Of course, it was assumed that the reasons that led Gorky to his strangely precipitate departure from post-revolutionary Russia could not have been as simple as the writer's official Soviet biographers would have one believe. For example, Ilya Gruzdev, assures us that Gorky was never "a voluntary exile," a man who had "broken away from the Soviet Union," or "alienated himself from his native soil." But we still need more concrete evidence of what Gorky thought and felt during the first years of his "involuntary exile." Fortunately, the recently published first volume of *Harvard Slavic Studies* includes some hitherto unknown letters written by Gorky in the years 1922–1925 to the poet and critic Vladyslav Khodasevich, with whom Gorky edited the Berlin-published literary and scholarly periodical *Beseda*.[4]

4 *Beseda* "was designed as a medium both for Soviet writers and for Russian writers and scholars living abroad—a program which would be patently impossible today and proved impracticable even in the 1920's. Letters sent to Gorky from Russia by Soviet

Khodasevich, who was still in Russia the year Gorky went abroad (1921), says in his memoirs (*Nekropol' Vospominaniya*, Brussels, 1939) that Gorky finally decided to pack his bags not only for reasons of health but on account of his strained relations with Zinovev, at that time head of the Petersburg Soviet. "Things had reached the point," Khodasevich writes, "where Zinovev was having Gorky's apartment searched and was threatening to arrest various close associates of his. At the same time meetings of Communists hostile to Zinovev were actually held in Gorky's room, camouflaged as moderate drinking parties in which outsiders participated."

And here are a few passages from letters that "the involuntary exile" wrote to Khodasevich.

A letter from Günterstahl, undated, received by Khodasevich on June 28, 1923:

In London, Pilnyak and Nikitin managed to get into the "P.E.N. Club," an international but apolitical union of writers. The chairman is J. Galsworthy and there are members of all sorts: R. Rolland and Merezhkovsky, S. Lagerlöf and Hauptmann, etc. Our dashing young lads seem to have said a bit too much and I, being likewise a member of that club, have received an inquiry from the Administration, asking me whether I regard as feasible an apolitical organization which would include both Russian writers living in Russia and those who are scattered around abroad. I replied in the negative, citing the example of *Lef* [a magazine published in 1923–1924 by Mayakovsky, to whom Gorky was hostile, by the way] and its attitude to the writers, on the one hand, and the authorities, on the other. I also pointed out that some of us acknowledge the Soviet regime, while others impatiently await its downfall, sustaining themselves on this belief, but still are not in agreement and will not congregate with the third category of writers, who are counting on the assistance of Curzon, Poincaré, the plague, and leprosy. But—besides that, there exists a Soviet regime which cannot allow any *apolitical* organization *in Moscow*, for it does not recognize the existence of any persons not infected with politics from their cradles. It would be worth while to find out just what sort of Pilnyaking they did in London. Couldn't you discuss the subject with Nikitin?

A letter from Günterstahl, dated July 4, 1923:

The letters I get from Russia are far from good. There is some sort of morass there of weariness and depression. You don't even get a feeling of simple skin irritation in the letters.

---

writers were held up and examined by the Soviet censorship. Manuscripts destined for *Beseda* were likewise delayed by the censors, and some of them never arrived at all." (From Sergius Yakobson's introduction to "Letters of Gor'kij to Xodasevič, 1922–1925," *Harvard Slavic Studies*, I, 1953.)

A letter from Günterstahl, dated November 8, 1923:

Of news which stuns the mind I can inform you that *Na kanune* has printed this: "Gioconda, a painting of Michelangelo," and in Russia Nadezhda Krupskaya and a certain M. Speransky have forbidden for reading: Plato, Kant, Schopenhauer, Vl. Solovev, Taine, Ruskin, Nietzsche, L. Tolstoy, Leskov, Yasinsky (!) and many other similar heretics. And it is decreed: "The section on religion must contain only anti-religious books." All this, supposedly [Gorky inserted the word "supposedly" above the line], is by no means fiction, but is printed in a book entitled: *A Guide on the Removal of Anti-Artistic and Counter-Revolutionary Literature from Libraries Serving the Mass Reader.* I affirm that I have written in "supposedly" above the line, for I still cannot make myself believe in this intellectual vampirism, and I will not believe it until I see the *Guide.* The first impression I experienced was so strong that I started writing to Moscow to announce my repudiation of Russian citizenship. What else can I do if this atrocity turns out to be true?[5]

A letter from Sorrento, July 13, 1924:

Almost every day there are fireworks, processions, music, and "popular celebrations." "And at home?" I think. And—forgive me!—I am overcome to the point of tears and fury by envy and anguish and disgust and everything else.

A letter from Sorrento, September 5, 1924:

Truly,
> Times have been worse,
> But never more vile!

In order fully to appreciate the immensely important passage in the letter below, sent from Sorrento on May 15, 1925—which delivers a blow to the Soviet myth of Gorky's involuntary exile— one must bear in mind that only seven issues of *Beseda* appeared under the joint editorship of Gorky and Khodasevich. Not one of them was admitted to Russia, despite Gorky's endless efforts, protests, and pleas. Nor was it any use for Gorky to refuse to write for Soviet papers and magazines as long as *Beseda* was censored.

---

5 That "if" somewhat weakens Gorky's indignation. He was actually leaving himself a loophole in case he might want to back down from his attack sometime. In a note to this letter Khodasevich writes that some two months before the letter he had seen the *Guide* handed to Gorky's secretary, Baroness Budberg, in the Russian bookstore in Berlin. That same day Khodasevich went to Günterstahl with Baroness Budberg. Gorky was given the *Guide* as soon as they arrived, and during Khodasevich's three-day visit there was a great deal of talk about it. When Gorky wrote this letter two months later he evidently wished to forget the fact.

On the question—a question of the utmost urgency!—of whether or not to let *Beseda* into Russia, an extraordinary conference, attended by numerous wise and mighty men, was called. There were three who voted for admission: Ionov, Kamenev and Belitsky; all the rest said, "Don't let it in—then Gorky will come back home." But he won't come back. He is stubborn too.

The correspondence and friendship between Gorky and Khodasevich came to an abrupt end in July–August 1925. The cause was so petty that one can dismiss it as a mere pretext on the part of the Sorrentine co-editor of *Beseda*. In July Gorky expressed indignation in a letter to Khodasevich over his enthusiastic article about the efficiency of the great Belfast shipbuilding dockyard and his use of it to reproach the incompetence of Soviet shipyards. But behind the mask of this factitious indignation over nothing lurked something far more serious and to the point. In the same letter, Gorky wrote that P. P. Khruchkhov "has been living here with me for the past three weeks. He is a down-to-earth individual with no tendency to exaggerate things, and what he tells me is very significant and important."

Who was this Kruchkhov? In the years with which we are here concerned, he was Gorky's confidential literary and financial manager, and director of the Soviet book outlet in Berlin, the *Mezhdunarodnaya Kniga*. At the same time, he was probably an agent of the GPU assigned to Gorky to oversee and rectify his course of action. Khodasevich writes that Khruchkhov "wormed his way into the management of Gorky's literary and financial affairs. Consequently a rivalry grew up between him and Maxsim [Gorky's son, Maxsim Peshkov, also looked after his father's affairs], which was already clearly evident even then."

To say that Kruchkhov was "probably" an agent of the GPU by the 1920's is extremely cautious. He was *certainly* that after Gorky's return to Russia, when he became the writer's personal secretary. This is the same Kruchkhov who during the last Moscow trial of 1938 was accused of having murdered Gorky and Maxsim Peshkov on Yagoda's orders (see Death Number Two) and was executed.

What then was so "significant and important" that Kruchkhov had to say to Gorky during his three-week stay in Sorrento? We shall never know with total certainty, but in any case the direct result of his visit appears sufficiently obvious.

The hard-headed guest clearly managed to straighten out the waywardness of his impractical host, for in the same letter in which the mouse of Belfast brought forth with such difficulty the glacier freezing Gorky's relations with Khodasevich, we also learn that

Gorky was beginning negotiations for printing *Beseda* in Russia while editing it abroad. The reasons for this decision were in perfect harmony with the arguments that this "down-to-earth individual" probably advanced. Printing costs, Gorky pointed out to Khodasevich, were considerably lower in Russia than in Germany.

Thus, the match between Gorky and Moscow was over in the first round, ending apparently with compromise but actually with Moscow's victory. Of course, the man who was "stubborn too" did not himself return to his homeland, but he sent on his *Beseda* before him.

V

There are still people in Sorrento who were friends of Gorky and his family, or in any case remember well the former residents of Villa Sorito. And there is no difficulty in getting them to talk. The numerous, motley, and constantly changing Gorky entourage won for itself, in Sorrento in the years 1925–1933, the reputation of being exceptionally worldly and pleasure-loving (*mondano e gaudente*). Gorky himself impressed those who knew him as a "humanitarian Socialist" who hated the atrocities and abuses of the Revolution and was suspicious of any form of violence. This trait, by the way, is confirmed by Gorky's significant avowal in *Lénine et le paysan russe*: "I have an organic disgust for politics and I am a very dubious Marxist, because I do not believe in the competence of the masses and particularly of the peasant masses."

Gorky's son, Maksim Peshkov, betrayed a particular weakness for the bottle, parties, and extravagance. But all the residents of Il Sorito, permanent and transient alike, perhaps with the sole exception of Gorky himself, spent most of their time in diversions. They often built huge bonfires on the beaches in honor of sightseers, they spent a great deal of money, and they even indulged themselves in that slightly perverse pleasure of the *nouveau riche* which is conspicuous philanthropy. Gorky's daughter-in-law, Nadezhda, was usually referred to as *la bella* or *la bellissima*. In a couple of accounts Khruchkhov was mentioned as a disagreeable, suspicious, two-faced, and gloomy habitué of Il Sorito. Maksim Peshkov, as well as being *un gagliardo bevitore*, was also an automobile enthusiast and spent a fortune on new cars. Gorky's financial means were so great that the entire family with their hangers-on were able to live on a scale with the most rampant bourgeois. In keeping with the Russian tradition of hospitality, *de rigueur* at Il Sorito, the villa's doors never closed. Particularly in the evening crowds of guests descended and alcohol flowed freely. When there were not enough glasses to go around the guests drank from ashtrays, flower pots, and egg cups. In Sorrento it was generally believed that Gorky received a monthly check from Russia for a million liras (in the 1920's!). This was certainly an exaggeration but it is sufficiently indicative.

Where did this golden stream of money originate? What was its source? It is almost certain that Gorky's royalties could not have been large enough to provide him in exile with a life the extravagance of which amazed even the *grands seigneurs* of Naples. Then where did it come from? Probably not just from Soviet publishing houses. This conjecture, together with the fact that despite his contacts with Neapolitan Communists Gorky was never seriously inconvenienced or annoyed by the Fascist police, lets one suppose that after the compromise with Moscow in 1925 Gorky lived, to all intents and purposes, under Soviet protection—financial as far as his material welfare was concerned and semi-diplomatic in everything that concerned his immunity from the Italian Fascist authorities. (Gorky's exceptional status is partially confirmed by the interview he gave to the well-known Fascist writer Sibilla Aleramo, published in the *Corriere della Sera* on May 21, 1928: "He is grateful to our government for allowing him to live in ideal peace.")

Against this background, how can we describe the figure of the *shaman* of the Gorky tribe, the writer himself? He took money from Russia to maintain his gay and greedy court. He was in constant contact with Soviet periodicals and publishing houses in order not to lose touch with the Russian reader. At the same time, in the hothouse atmosphere of his Sorrentine *buon retiro* he still felt cut off from life; he was often depressed and even afflicted; he was corroded by the rust of nostalgia. It gave him the greatest pleasure to sit before a blazing fireplace and listen to his daughter-in-law sing Russian songs. One day a delegation of Russian workers came to Sorrento on "a holiday awarded as a prize for exemplary work." Gorky talked with them a long time and at a certain point broke down in tears. He explained that it was not easy to listen calmly to the choral relation of the sufferings of one's own countrymen. Could he then, after all he had seen himself and heard from others, have been an enthusiastic supporter of the Soviet regime? Maksim Peshkov once told a Neapolitan friend: "We are not Communists." But never mind whether or not Gorky was a Communist. After the decision of 1925 he could not back down. All he could do was accept the consequences of what he had done and return to Russia. For financial reasons, because Khruchkhov's clever tactics had put him deep in the Soviet pocket; for reasons of prestige and personal pride, because he did not want to admit, even to himself, that he had made a mistake; partly for political reasons, because he sincerely hated the rigid and inflexible anti-Soviet attitude of the Russian émigrés; and for reasons of natural human vanity, because he wanted to savor in Russia the privilege, fame, and authority due to the greatest contemporary Russian writer; and, last but not least, for sentimental reasons, because he was homesick.

From Sorrentine accounts, it seems clear enough that his two trips to Russia, in 1928 and 1929, were something in the nature of reconnaissances. In the year of his first trip the interview with Sibilla Aleramo was published with such phrases as "He is returning soon to Russia, but only for a few months. It seems that he can only work here." It is hard not to believe one of the most frequent visitors to Il Sorito that each time Gorky's family returned from Russia they fell into a long period of torpidity, anxiety, and discouragement, and that their chief topic of conversation were the changes wrought by the first years of Stalin's regime. Especially Maksim Peshkov, who always talked a lot (particularly when he drank), complained openly of the intolerable police surveillance and bitterly confided that during both visits he had not been allowed the slightest freedom of movement. But the die was cast. Stalin was not concerned with Gorky's health or with preserving at any cost (even that of staying abroad) his benevolent forbearance. Stalin wanted him in Russia right then, when he was preparing for his final show-down with the opposition.

Thus began the last act of the drama. In the wake of *Beseda* the man who was "stubborn too" finally returned to Russia—so that both would cease to exist. But in the case of *Beseda* everything went smoothly and all but automatically; in the case of Gorky it took three hard years.

VI

Among the many assessments of the Moscow trials the prevalent one, which is both extreme and frivolous, regards them as an entirely repugnant spectacle of lies and absurdities fabricated during the preliminary interrogations. That this view is frivolous is demonstrated by the incident of Krestinsky during the trial of Bukharin. At the public hearings Krestinsky withdrew the confession he had made during his interrogation, and the very next day, after a night spent in the Lubyanka dungeons, he reconfirmed his confession in a broken voice. Had he been a coward concerned only with saving his own skin, he would have smoothly recited the prayer "agreed upon" during his interrogation by Vyshinsky and not waited to be rather emphatically prompted. But Krestinsky was not a coward. Neither was Bukharin. If their deaths had been marked in red on the calendar the very day they were arrested, that mark of doom must have been underscored several times after what they dared to say at the trial. Why, then, didn't they deny the fictitious charges totally and consistently to the very end, for they knew that nothing could save them, that they must surely face the firing squad? There are three usual replies: that they could not endure further torture; that they agreed to perform their assigned roles faithfully in exchange for the lives of their families; or that despite everything they remained loyal to the Revolution and yielded to the iron dialectic of their adversaries. One can immediately dismiss "the iron force of the dialectic of their adversaries." It is very efficiently evoked in *Darkness at Noon*, but in the light of real analysis it is unconvincing. As for torture, could they possibly have thought it could be avoided by half-confessions and vacillation? And as to their families? Very few people believe that Bukharin and Krestinsky did not know what had happened to the families of their predecessors, who recited their lessons with alacrity. Is it really possible then that they imagined one could redeem potential hostages at half price, that they haggled with Stalin at a public hearing over the inflated price of the tribute? It is hard to take such a possibility seriously.

There is a way out of this labyrinth: the accusations at the Moscow trials had one leg to stand on, and the other danced in the air to the accompaniment of Stalin's rendition of Vyshinsky's melody. There is nothing strange or unnatural, after all, about Krestinsky, an adversary of Stalinist policies, meeting with envoys of Trotsky abroad. But Stalin wanted more. Stalin also wanted Krestinsky to turn out to be a German spy, disguised in the dress coat of the Soviet Ambassador in Berlin. This was too much for Krestinsky. He refused to swallow that absurdity. He tried to spit it out in disgust like castor oil, but they finally forced it down his throat. That the operation worked, that the patient made his appearance before the court thoroughly purged we know from the next day of the trial. What about Bukharin? One can be almost certain that a man of his stamp and temperament must have criticized collectivization very severely in the closed circle of his political intimates. And he probably would have readily admitted this without torture, because when there is no escape from death it is better to die as an opposition ideologue than as an opposition nonentity. But again Stalin wanted something more. To round out the charges, Bukharin had to have ordered his subordinates to put broken glass into the butter produced in the kolkhozes. In the annals of the Moscow trials one has to sift the chaff of Stalin's sick and sadistic imagination for the grain of truth. This is likewise true of matters that were only indirectly concerned or peripherally connected with the trials: among others, the matter of Gorky.

The portrait of Gorky sketched thus far has some rather distinct outlines. He was certainly not all of a piece; he did not distinguish himself by either strength or incorruptibility of character. Those who knew him intimately were aware that under a cloak of false modesty was hidden a mania for greatness, as well as a tendency to pose as an infallible oracle and moral super-arbiter in political controversies. Nothing could be more revealing, albeit in a minor key, than a comparison of the French and English translations of his book on Lenin. In *Lénine et le paysan russe*, published in 1924, he cites Lenin's opinion of Trotsky: "Show me another man who in the course of one year could succeed in organizing a model army and winning the esteem of military experts. We have such a man. We have everything. And we are working miracles." In *Days with Lenin*, published in 1931, he suppressed this passage. But what Gorky never lost was his natural and spontaneous passion, the soul of the eternal rebel, simple and instinctive human goodness mixed with some of the idealistic traits of the Russian Populists. With the extremism typical of most self-made men he twisted himself into solemn and haughty conformity when he was flattered and stiffened into dogged and intransigent opposition when he was criticized or merely insufficiently venerated.

If he sold out to Stalin in the end, he certainly did not do so for the same motives as, say, Aleksey Tolstoy, who as soon as he returned to Russia put Stalin on the same granite pedestal next to Peter the Great and happily (he acknowledged it himself to Bunin in Paris) collected his reward in the form of luxurious villas, cellars full of wine, and the most expensive automobiles. But Gorky intended to collaborate with Stalin on an altogether different plane—as the titan of Soviet literature with the head of the Soviet nation—and it never crossed his mind to humble himself, truckle, or lay on Stalin's altar his human, political, and artistic dignity. Even more, he reckoned on becoming Stalin's real adviser, and believed that he could succeed in introducing a more conciliatory and moderate tone into Stalin's absolutist policy of extermination, personal vengeance, and slavery. But that is not what Stalin expected of him. Stalin preferred Tolstoys.

If Maksim Peshkov had been content to bathe in champagne, play cards, seduce women and, in his rare moments of lucidity, indulge his passion for driving, certainly nothing would have stood in his way. Alas, he felt that everything, absolutely everything could be said out loud. Even more unfortunate was his attempt to deprive Khruchkhov of the chamberlain's staff he bore in the administration of his father's court. As for Nadezhda, suffice it to say that she soon had occasion to discover how much more dangerous were flirtations in the Kremlin than romances in Sorrento and Naples.

Under these circumstances there is no reason not to believe the official charges of the 1938 trial that when Yagoda decided, partly for political and partly for personal reasons (it was an open secret that he was in love with Nadezhda), to despatch Maksim Peshkov to the next world by getting him drunk and leaving him out in the snow all night, he found in Khruchkhov only too willing an executor of his plan. One can assume that Gorky did not know the real cause of his son's death, which occurred barely a year after the family returned to Russia. But he must *at least* have felt that there was something unusual about it, something that could only have been a conspiracy or a warning. The murder of Maksim Peshkov by "Trotsky's agents" was not mentioned at once. On May 12, 1934, immediately after Maksim's death, Stalin wrote the following letter to Gorky:

I share your sorrow in the misfortune which has so unexpectedly and brutally struck all of us. I believe that your steadfast Gorky soul and great will can overcome this heavy affliction.

Perhaps as Gorky read this letter, he realized that an elusive and ominous shadow had crept into his relations with Stalin.

VII

Two years after the death of Maksim Peshkov, according to the 1938 trial, Yagoda turned again to the infallible Khruchkhov and ordered him to get ready to assist the Kremlin doctors in the "medical" disposal of Gorky. But who issued this order to Yagoda? The charges maintain that it was the "Bukharin-Trotsky bloc," because Gorky was too loyal to Stalin and admired and esteemed Stalin's policies too highly. The emphasis on just this point is extremely suspicious. There is not one single deposition or testimony of the accused in the 1938 trial that does not stress the perfect symbiosis of Gorky and Stalin. Here are a few extracts from the official *Report of Court Proceedings in the Case of the Anti-Soviet Bloc of Rightists and Trotskyites*, published by the People's Commissariat of Justice of the USSR.

Yagoda: "For a long time the Center of the Rightist-Trotskyite organization tried to influence Gorky and draw him away from his close collaboration with Stalin. To this end, Kamenev, Tomsky, and others associated with Gorky. But they achieved no real results. Gorky remained loyal to Stalin. He was an ardent supporter and defender of Stalin's political line. Since the Rightist-Trotskyite bloc were seriously planning to overthrow Stalin's government and seize power themselves, the Center could not ignore Gorky's extraordinary influence in Russia and his authority abroad. As long as Gorky was alive he would raise his voice in protest against us. We could not allow that. When the United Center realized that it was impossible to alienate Gorky from Stalin, it decided to eliminate Gorky."

Rykov: "I know Trotsky, of course, realized that Gorky considered him a villain and adventurer. Furthermore, the intimate friendship between Gorky and Stalin was common knowledge, and the fact that Gorky was an adamant political supporter of Stalin aroused our organization's hatred of him." Bukharin declared that Tomsky had told him in 1935: "The Trotskyite group in the United Center bloc has decided to make an attempt on the life of A. M. Gorky, because of his support of Stalin's policies." Beshonov testified that during one of their meetings Trotsky said: "Gorky is on extremely intimate terms with Stalin. He plays a colossal role in winning for the USSR the sympathy of democratic world opinion, particularly in western Europe. Gorky is very popular as Stalin's best friend and as a spokesman for the general party line. Our former supporters among the intelligentsia abandoned us primarily because of Gorky's influence. Therefore Gorky must be eliminated. Give Pyatakov the following instructions in the most categorical form: Gorky must be physically eliminated at any cost."

As one can see, the organizers of the 1938 trial went considerably out of their way to emphasize Gorky's friendship with Stalin.

But to get back to Yagoda. Who really ordered him to have Peshkov and Gorky murdered? Of all the defendants at the last Moscow trial, Yagoda was probably the only one against whom the charge of endorsing the ideology of the opposition sounds absurd and altogether unlikely. As the chief of the Soviet police, he was simply a blind executor of Stalin's orders, nothing more. Why then put him among the accused too—and in a political trial at that? Why not just get rid of him, if that is what the circumstances required, in a discreet administrative proceeding? The answer to this question explains not only the mechanism of the trial itself but throws considerable light on the way in which assassins in Soviet Russia carry out political murders.

Immediately after the trial ended, Trotsky published an extremely interesting article, "The Role of Yagoda," in his *Bulletin of Bolshevik-Leninist Opposition* (April 1938). "According to Yagoda's own words (during the hearing on March 5), he instructed his subordinates in Leningrad not to obstruct any terrorist act being prepared against Kirov. As an instruction issued by the chief of the GPU it was tantamount to an order to organize the murder of Kirov." Where did this order originate? Let us briefly recapitulate the incident to which Trotsky is referring. Kirov was murdered on December 1, 1934, by a Leningrad student named Nikolaev whom no one had ever heard of before. The trial of the murderer and his accomplices was held behind closed doors. All fourteen were sentenced to death and shot. But on January 23, 1935, a rather puzzling thing occurred. A military tribunal sentenced, to terms of two to ten years, twelve senior officers of the Leningrad GPU, including the department chief, Medved. The text of the sentence, published in the Soviet papers, maintained, among other things, that the "accused knew of the terrorist act being prepared against Kirov, but the criminals demonstrated their irresponsibility in not taking the necessary steps to protect him." Can one seriously imagine that Medved and his colleagues in the Leningrad GPU could have known about the plans to kill Kirov and not reported the fact to their superior, Yagoda? There are only two possibilities. Either they did not make a report (at that time in a country where neglecting one's responsibility to inform in matters of particular national importance automatically meant a death sentence) and hence deserved more than the light sentence of two to ten years; or they did make a report and then Yagoda, who likewise failed to take the proper steps to protect Kirov's life, probably ought to have been charged along with them in January 1935, and not just in March 1938. Hence it seems more than likely that Yagoda, too, reported the terrorist act being prepared against Kirov to his highest superior, if he did not simply organize the whole thing on Stalin's orders. Someone in the Kirov affair was desperately looking for an alibi and found it in the persons of the twelve scapegoats of the Leningrad GPU.

Trotsky has the following to say. "The circumstances of Kirov's murder must have started whispers in the upper reaches of the bureaucracy that in his struggles with the opposition the Leader had started playing with the heads of his closest collaborators. No one in his right mind had any doubts that Medved, the chief of the Leningrad GPU, submitted daily reports to Yagoda on important operations and that Yagoda in turn reported to Stalin and received all his instructions from him. The only way the rumors could be stopped was by sacrificing the Leningrad executors of the Moscow plan."

Following Trotsky's very precise and logical line of reasoning, one easily arrives at the following conclusion. Although the casual alibi of the twelve scapegoats of the Leningrad GPU was sufficient for Stalin and Yagoda in 1935, it was too narrow a blanket to cover *two* bodies for very long. Someone had to pull it over on his side and expose his partner. A simple matter, and Stalin did it. At the 1938 trial Yagoda made his appearance as the man responsible for killing Kirov. The alibi now became Stalin's exclusive property. Something similar happened in the case of Gorky: Yagoda faced the court charged with what he had done on Stalin's orders.

A question arises. Why wasn't the mere *fact* of the killing of Gorky announced immediately in 1936, as the comparable fact had been in the case of Kirov? After all, the guilty parties could still be apprehended later. In 1936 the memory of the Kirov slaying was probably still too fresh for Gorky's death to be exploited as a new terrorist act by the opposition. Hence the first version of the writer's natural death. Two years had to pass before the time was ripe to tell the world that Gorky had been the victim of the opposition and to cut down Yagoda with a well-aimed double-barrel shot. But the scapegoat maneuver—first applied in the Kirov affair alone to the twelve Leningrad GPU officers and subsequently to Yagoda himself in both the Kirov and Gorky deaths—not only failed to silence the whispers at the highest levels of the Party but, on the contrary, its very repetitiveness kindled more suspicions concerning the real perpetrator. That is why the irreplaceable Poskrebyshev received instructions in 1940 to go back to the version of natural death. And that is why the mystery of Gorky's death still oscillates between two extremes. Stalin fell into his own trap, at least in part. For the most cautious conclusion must be the following. Unless Gorky's death was the natural result of catarrhal pneumonia, all the psychological and political circumstances of his last years in Russia suggest that his *seventh* death was brought about at Stalin's express wish.

Finally, there is a curious document that deserves attention despite the fact that Trotsky considered it semi-apocryphal. It is the anonymous *Letter of an Old Bolshevik*, written directly after the Zinovev and Kamenev trial of August 1936 (i.e., a few months after Gorky's death) and smuggled to London from Russia. According to the author of this letter, Gorky hoped to play the arbiter after his return to Russia and to effect a reconciliation between Stalin and the opposition. For a short time his endeavors had some results, but about 1935 Stalin finally decided on the course of liquidation. He stopped seeing his "friend and adviser," and he did not answer his telephone calls. Matters went so far that an article by David Zaslavsky appeared in *Pravda* attacking Gorky. The enraged writer demanded a passport to leave the country, but the post-revolutionary story with Lenin was not repeated.

POST-SCRIPTUM

A few months after writing this semi-mystery story about the seven deaths of Maxsim Gorky, an article appeared in the *Socialist Courier* (the Russian-language Menshevik periodical published in the United States), entitled "Who Poisoned Gorky?" It was written by the German Social Democrat Brigitte Gerland, who was given an early release in 1953 from the Vorkuta camp and sent back to the German Federal Republic. I give her text here with only minor abridgements.

One of the most colorful and unforgettable figures I had occasion to meet in Vorkuta was our hospital doctor, an old man almost eighty. I worked as a nurse for some time under his supervision and we became very friendly, if one can speak of friendship between people so different in age and background. This doctor was Dimitry Dimitrevich Pletnev. His name had created considerable stir at the time of one of the famous trials against the Old Bolsheviks [see Death Number Two; and Death Number One, where Pletnev figures as one of the signers of the official medical bulletin]. One day the professor told me the following story:

"We were treating Gorky for heart trouble, but his sufferings were not so much physical as moral. He never ceased tormenting himself with reproaches. He could no longer breathe freely in the Soviet Union and passionately longed to return to Italy. Actually he was trying to run away from himself. He hadn't the strength left to protest. But the mistrustful despot in the Kremlin feared that the famous writer might make an open statement against the regime. And as always, when the right moment came, he found the most efficient means to this end. This time he decided on a box of chocolates—yes, a light pink bonbonnière tied with a silk ribbon. Gorky had it on the night table by his bed; he liked to offer a treat to his visitors. Soon after he received it he offered the chocolates to two attendants and ate several himself. An hour later all three suffered acute stomach pains and an hour after that they were all dead. An autopsy was ordered immediately. The result confirmed our worst fears. All three had died of poisoning. The other doctors and I said nothing. Even when the Kremlin issued a completely false account of Gorky's death we said nothing. But our silence did not save us. Rumors began to circulate in Moscow, 'whispers' that Gorky had been murdered: Soso[6] poisoned him. Stalin did not like that at all. People's suspicions had to be diverted and pointed in another direction by finding other culprits. Naturally, the simplest course was to accuse the doctors of the crime. Why did the doctors do it? A naive question. At the order of Fascists and their agents, of course. The end of the affair? Well, you know the end . . ."

6 The Georgian diminutive of Joseph, by which Stalin was known to his intimates.

In concluding her account, Brigitte Gerland adds that "Pletnev's tale was engraved in my memory forever," and that is why she had repeated it with the greatest fidelity, "not adding and not changing a single word." Finally, she says that she would never have believed in "all the cheap mystery trappings of the pink bonbonnière and poisoned chocolates" if she had not herself experienced "Stalinist methods combining arrests, hearings, and trials," and that she "would not have told about this meeting in Vorkuta if Pletnev were still alive." But "he died in 1953, over eighty years old, and there was nothing more that the NKVD could do to him."

Translated by Roland Strom

UNDER CONRAD'S EYES

Gustaw Herling-Grudziński

O F ALL CONRAD'S novels probably none has had such varying fortunes as *Under Western Eyes*. When it first appeared in 1911,
it attracted no notice; it would be no exaggeration to say that it was
greeted with an indifferent shrug of the shoulders. After the First
World War it briefly became the fashion to quote the novel at almost
every step in articles dealing with Russian affairs, especially in
those which attempted to explain and evaluate the Bolshevik
Revolution. In the introduction to a new edition published in 1920,
Conrad himself commented on the fact with evident satisfaction
as "testifying to the clearness of my vision and the correctness of
my judgement." A long oblivion of forgetfulness followed, but after
the Second World War came another renascence. Professor G. D. H.
Cole's assertion that *Under Western Eyes* is one of Conrad's best
novels, because in it Conrad interpreted one half of Europe for
the benefit of the other half, is very significant from this point of
view, for it indicates that the story of the right-thinking student
Razumov, who betrayed his terrorist colleague, had come to be
considered something on the order of a Russian-Western dictionary
of psychology. And it was that much more valuable because it had
been prepared by a man who was a Pole by origin and an Englishman by choice, that is to say, a man possessing the virtues of his
blood without its vices (the feeling of Russia inherited from his
forefathers, but without partisan national involvement) and the
virtues of his mentality without its vices (the objectivity of one who
is not nationally involved, but without a hereditary blindness to
things Russian). And as we have just seen, the West reaches out
for that dictionary with revived interest whenever "the enigma of
Russia" arouses uneasiness as well as the usual curiosity.

It must be admitted that Conrad did everything he could to
assume the guise of an interpreter explaining one half of Europe
to the other, and if the fortunes of his novel have so closely depended on the ebb and flow of the tide of Russian history, he has

in large measure only himself to blame. From Conrad's remark in a letter to Galsworthy during the period he was writing the book, a remark that sounds like a bulletin from a research institute ("I am trying to capture the very soul of things Russian"); to the rather unnovelistic title of the book, defining in advance, and with the tone of an object lesson, the goal he set himself; to his assurance in the introduction of "scrupulous impartiality" imposed on him "historically and hereditarily, by the peculiar experience of race and family"; and to his choice of a narrator in the person of a teacher naturally didactic in temperament—Conrad did not miss a single detail in preparing his public for his role as a guide to the psychology of Russia.

My object in this essay is to demonstrate that this is actually the chief cause of the circumstantial fluctuations of the success of *Under Western Eyes* and for the deep artistic flaw that runs through the entire story of Razumov. Five Conrads make their appearance in this novel. There is Conrad the Pole, who despite his anxiety for "scrupulous impartiality," was filled with hatred of Russia and contested its history and, more particularly, its literature. There is Conrad the Englishman, raising his lance against the "senseless tyranny" of Russia and wearing the visor of English liberal institutions. There is Conrad the skeptical conservative, terrified by the reflection "That all these people [the rogues' gallery of terrorists depicted in *Under Western Eyes*] are not the product of the exceptional but of the general—of the normality of their place, and time, and race. The ferocity and imbecility of an autocratic rule rejecting all legality and in fact basing itself upon complete moral anarchism provokes the no less imbecile and atrocious answer of a purely Utopian revolutionism encompassing destruction by the first means at hand, in the strange conviction that a fundamental change of heart must follow the downfall of any given human institutions. These people are unable to see that all they can effect is merely a change of names. The oppressors and the oppressed are all Russians together; and the world is brought once more face to face with the truth of the saying that the tiger cannot change his stripes nor the leopard his spots." There is Conrad the tragic pessimist, for whom life is "a sinister jungle" and who scorns "senseless desperation" as an answer to "senseless tyranny." And finally there is Conrad the stern moralist, who condemns Razumov's betrayal in the name of a chivalrous code of principles of conduct and honor because they are the only ones capable of saving human dignity in the name of that "conventional conscience" which is scoffed at equally by Razumov, by the representatives of autocracy, and by the terrorists. It is evident that in the first two Conrads the role of Russian-

Western "interpreter" predominates; in the third Conrad the conviction of the vain Utopianism of all revolutions assumes the
character of the discovery of a specifically Russian character
("place . . . and race"); while only in the last two does the humane
philosophy of life we have come to know so well in the author of
Heart of Darkness and *Lord Jim* again make its appearance. Here,
then, is the vein of the flaw; what Conrad had to say, or rather to
reiterate, in Razumov's story were two or three of his imperturbable
universal truths, but instead of using Russia as a background for
the story, he treated it as the main subject. The "interpreter" took
precedence over the writer, and thus the book was doomed to be a
work of historical topicality. Had it not been intended chiefly as a
handbook of the psychology of Russia for a Western audience, the
book might have been a work of art. In other words, what is profound and immutable in this novel takes place under Conrad's eyes
and is generally unnoticed by the eyes of the West. What is superficial and transitory occasionally catches the eyes of the West, but
too much is a result of Polish atavism passed through an English
filter, and too little comes from the direct experience of the author
for it really to engage Conrad's own vision.

*   *   *

Before turning to Conrad's novel, I would like to quote a passage
from that beautiful miniature of Conrad in Bertrand Russell's
Portraits from Memory.

Of all that he had written I admired most the terrible story called *The
Heart of Darkness*, in which a rather weak idealist is driven mad by horror
of the tropical forest and loneliness among savages. This story expresses,
I think, most completely his philosophy of life. I felt, though I do not
know whether he would have accepted such an image, that he thought
of civilized and morally tolerable human life as a dangerous walk on a
thin crust of barely cooled lava which at any moment might break and
let the unwary sink into fiery depths. He was very conscious of the various
forms of passionate madness to which men are prone, and it was this that
gave him such a profound belief in the importance of discipline. His
point of view, one might perhaps say, was the antithesis of Rousseau's:
"Man is born in chains, but he can become free." He becomes free, so I
believe Conrad would have said, not by letting loose his impulses, not
by being casual and uncontrolled, but by subduing wayward impulse to
a dominant purpose.
He was not much interested in political systems, though he had some
strong political *feelings*. The strongest of these were love of England and
hatred of Russia, of which both are expressed in *The Secret Agent*; and
the hatred of Russia, both Czarist and revolutionary, is set forth with
great power in *Under Western Eyes*. His dislike of Russia was that which

was traditional in Poland. It went so far that he would not allow merit to either Tolstoy or Dostoevsky. Turgenev, he told me once, was the only Russian novelist he admired.

Except for love of England and hatred of Russia, politics did not much concern him. What interested him was the individual human soul faced with the indifference of nature, and often with the hostility of man, and subject to inner struggles with passions both good and bad that led towards destruction. Tragedies of loneliness occupied a great part of his thought and feeling.

*   *   *

What strikes one immediately in the first Conrad is that his picture of Russia is so banal in its conventionality: "... the hard ground of Russia, inanimate, cold, inert, like a sullen and tragic mother hiding her face"; "an almost physical impression of endless space and of countless millions"; sacred inertia, "unhappy immensity," "doomed," gloomy expanse. The Russian people are "as great and as incorruptible as the ocean," and the nation is "under a curse"; Razumov's existence "was a great cold blank, something like the enormous plain of the whole of Russia, leveled with snow and fading gradually on all sides into shadows and mists"; "an immense, wintry Russia which, somehow, his view could embrace in all its enormous expanse as if it were a map." "Under the sumptuous immensity of the sky, the snow covered the endless forests, the frozen rivers, the plains of an immense country, obliterating the landmarks, the accidents of the ground, leveling everything under its uniform whiteness, like a monstrous blank page awaiting the record of an inconceivable history."

And what does that "page" call to mind? Is it not the *Ustęp* ("Digression") of the third part of Mickiewicz's *Forefathers' Eve*?

> An empty, white, and open land
> Like a page laid out for the writer's hand ...

Conrad's arch-priest of revolutionists, Peter Ivanovitch, "had one of those bearded Russian faces without shape, a mere appearance of flesh and hair with not a single feature having any sort of character." And Mickiewicz:

> The face of every man is like that land
> Empty, open, and bland.

No doubt about it, this is the picture of Russia which the child Conrad kept before his eyes after the journey he made to Vologda with his mother in the wake of his exiled father and which his

youthful reading later fixed in his memory. All these "immov-
abilities," "immensities," and "expanses" express three characteristics of his Polish historical, hereditary, racial, and familial
attitude to Russia—hatred, instinctive scorn, and instinctive dread.

But the mature Conrad tried to rationalize these feelings and did
so by disputing with Russian literature and primarily with its
two giants, to whom he did not "allow merit." In the rationalized
and atavistically stamped layer of his novel, the ceaseless echo of
his polemic with Dostoevsky resounds like the crash of rocks hope-
lessly and helplessly bombarding the abyss. Thus, for example,
there is the "illogicality of [the Russian] attitude, the arbitrariness
of their conclusions, the frequency of the exceptional . . . some
special human trait . . . [the Russians'] extraordinary love of
words . . . they are always ready to pour them out by the hour or by
the night with an enthusiasm, a sweeping abundance, with such an
aptness of application sometimes that, as in the case of very
accomplished parrots, one can't defend oneself from the suspicion
that they really understand what they say"; "the moral corruption
of an oppressed society where the noblest aspirations of humanity,
the desire of freedom, an ardent patriotism, the love of justice, the
sense of pity, and even the fidelity of simple minds are prostituted
to the lusts of hate and fear, the inseparable companions of an
uneasy despotism." Then, of course, there will be "the Russian
soul" unscathed by "philosophical scepticism" and "what's
divine in the Russian soul . . . resignation"; "the land of spectral
ideas and disembodied aspirations"; the Russian need "to pour
out a full confession in passionate words that would stir the whole
being of that man to its innermost depths; that would end in
embraces and tears; in an incredible fellowship of souls—such as
the world had never seen." There will be visionaries: they "work
everlasting evil on earth. Their Utopias inspire in the mass of
mediocre minds a disgust of reality and a contempt for the secular
logic of human development." There will be—and here we come so
close to The Possessed as to feel its infernal breath—"Russian
simplicity, a terrible corroding simplicity in which mystic phrases
clothe a naive and hopeless cynicism"; "Russian simplicity often
marches innocently on the edge of cynicism for some lofty purpose";
the omnipresence of "certain tones of cynicism and cruelty, of
moral negation, and even of moral distress"; the inability to tell
"truth from lies"; an atmosphere in which "it is more difficult
to lead a life of toil and self-denial than to go out in the street and
kill from conviction"; "the peculiarity of Russian natures, that,
however strongly engaged in the drama of action, they are still turning their ear to the murmur of abstract ideas"; and finally—as if

these indirect allusions were not enough and the thing required a pointing finger—the belief "that there are plenty of men worse than devils to make a hell of this earth." And one would probably have to be totally blind to miss the source of the ukase of the tsarist dignitary murdered by Haldin: "the thought of liberty has never existed in the Act of the Creator. From the multitude of men's counsel nothing could come but revolt and disorder; and revolt and disorder in a world created for obedience and stability is sin. It was not Reason but Authority which expressed the Divine Intention. God was the Autocrat of the Universe. . . ." How could one fail to recognize the masterly pen of the Grand Inquisitor of the *Brothers Karamazov*.

It's hard to believe that such a rich "poor man's anthology of Dostoevsky" could be fitted into the pages of a single novel. But our eyes do not deceive us. Here Conrad looks like the tragic Polish figure of the orphaned boy who protests against the crime that a strong aggressor perpetrated against his parents by beating his fists in impotent rage against the rock from which the aggressor has already made off. But in carrying out his baleful work, the orphan is too pained and angered even to see that rock clearly. A shocking reaction—and how vividly I feel it myself! How intimately I experience that terrible instinct! But Conrad's blind and unjust impulse appears in its entirety only when we see that what separated him from Dostoevsky was not so much his outlook on life as his view of how one must walk "on a thin crust of barely cooled lava."

Looking more deeply into the first Conrad we discover in that "proper Russian driver" Ziemianitch (everything in the novel is "truly" and "properly" Russian) our old friend Platon Karataev, small in appearance but the great comforter of Pierre Bezukhov of *War and Peace*. Ziemianitch, "a true Russian man" is for Conrad the novel's worthless example of the "bright Russian soul." Razumov hates him with his whole heart and continually calls him a "beast," and on the fatal night of the betrayal Razumov breaks a stablefork over the back of the sleeping drunk. Unjustly! Because Ziemianitch is the best representative of what Razumov himself feels at a certain point: "What is this Haldin? And what am I? Only two grains of sand. But a great mountain is made up of just such insignificant grains. And the death of a man or of many men is an insignificant thing." And at once one hears the echo of Tolstoy's words in Book Four of *War and Peace*:

Sometimes Pierre, struck by the force of his remarks, would ask him to repeat them, but Platon could never recall what he had said a moment before, just as he could never tell Pierre the words of his favorite song.

Mother, little birch-tree and *my heart is sick* came in but they made no coherent sense. He did not understand and could not grasp the meaning of words apart from their context. Every utterance and action of his was the manifestation of a force uncomprehended by him, which was his life. But his life, as he looked at it, held no meaning as a separate entity. It had meaning only as part of a whole of which he was at all times conscious. His words and actions flowed from him as smoothly, as inevitably and spontaneously as fragrance exhales from a flower. He could not understand the value or significance of any word or deed taken separately.

Conrad must have shaken with indignation and disgust when he read that this wretched mote, for whom "his life . . . held no meaning as a separate entity," was the source of Bezukhov's inner rebirth. But replying to Tolstoy's Platon with his own Ziemianitch, he fell into a contradiction between the writer's imagination and the "interpreter's" ferocity. For exactly that "bright open soul," that "vile beast," that really Russian grain of sand floating in the limitless ocean of vodka, ultimately emerges as one of the few figures in the novel endowed with that "conventional conscience" which was so dear to Conrad's heart. The circumstances of Ziemianitch's death are lost forever in the impenetrable gloom of Russia, but everything seems to suggest that he hanged himself in despair when he thought that his drunkenness had been the cause of Haldin's arrest. When Razumov learns of Ziemianitch's end, he feels "pity for Ziemianitch, a large neutral pity, such as one may feel for an unconscious multitude, a great people seen from above—like a community of crawling ants working out its destiny."

All that remains in the field is the one "Russian novelist he admired." Of course, it is the Turgenev who frequented the salon of the Goncourt brothers, the author of *Fathers and Sons*, the creator of the very concept of nihilism, the portraitist of that Bazarov whom Pisarev canonized as the saint of nihilists, the Bazarov who said, "We have nothing to boast about beyond the sterile capacity of understanding to some extent the sterility of existence." But we must not anticipate our encounter with the third Conrad.

* * *

It is a relatively easy matter to dispose of the second Conrad, the Conrad who pelted Russian autocracy from the island fortress of liberalism, the Conrad who provided the West with a concept too constricted and decidedly strained the English grounds of his Polish rages. This is the least convincing Conrad, exaggeratedly proud and too conscious of the luxury of his chosen national allegiance—so that one might almost call him (without the sarcastic connotation of the phrase) a *nouveau riche* looking down on the wretches.

One can very well imagine the criticism of Russian autocracy from such Western standpoints which underline its strangeness, which scorn, mistrust, and even hate it, albeit without rising to the towering regions of superiority that others cannot reach. There is hatred without aristocratic hauteur, contempt without pride, a sense of strangeness without any elemental disgust, mistrust without a belief in the irreversible curse of history and innate qualities, in a word, the conviction that nations do occasionally manage, unlike tigers and leopards, to change their stripes and spots. For Conrad, Russia was nothing. When Edward Garnett reproached him in a review of *Under Western Eyes* for suffering from the emigrant Pole's Russian trauma, Conrad, who was always so tactful with his friends, lost control of himself. In a private letter to his accuser he chucked in his face the charge of Russification, called him the "Russian ambassador to the republic of letters," and demanded credit for the wealth of tenderness he had heaped on the characters of Tekla and Sophia Antonovna in the novel (we'll return to this point later), and what then? Did he boldly pick up the gauntlet thrown down before him, like a born Pole and fugitive from Russian tyranny? He couldn't do that, for the English reliance on the belief in the immutability and otherness of that "corrupted dark immensity" forced him to the extreme of having the English teacher of languages advise Natalia Haldin to return to Russia. Thus Conrad limited himself to remarking sternly to Garnett that any discussion of Russia was an undertaking of the most chimerical kind because everyone could see how matters stood. He reminded Garnett that Bismarck in 1864 had said that Russia was nothing and had demonstrated the fact by the contempt manifest in the policies he had followed for twenty years in dealing with "that great power." Conrad concluded by repeating that Russia was nothing. Anyone with eyes can see that!

I remember a meeting of the Fabian Society in 1948 chaired by Harold Laski, at which three Labour MPs gave an account of their trip to Poland. "Certainly," one of them said, "an Englishman couldn't live under such a regime, but the Poles have never known real democracy." The second Conrad of *Under Western Eyes* expresses a similar attitude to Russia.

Nations, muses the narrator, the English teacher of languages, it may be have fashioned their Governments, but Governments have paid them back in the same coin. It is unthinkable that any young Englishman should find himself in Razumov's situation. This being so it would be a vain enterprise to imagine what he would think. The only safe surmise to make is that he would not think as Mr. Razumov thought at this crisis of his fate. He would not have an hereditary and personal knowledge of the means by which a historical autocracy represses ideas, guards its power, and defends its existence. By an act of mental extravagance he might imagine himself arbitrarily thrown into prison, but it would never occur to him unless he were delirious (and perhaps not even then) that he could be beaten with whips as a practical measure of investigation or of punishment.

In the interest of exactitude, but with no intention of suggesting absurd comparisons, it is worth mentioning that in 1920, some ten years after Conrad's words were written, the English Parliament made provision to keep in force, in special cases, the law concerning flogging with the cat-o'-nine-tails. So a young Englishman need not have had particular imaginative gifts to conceive of at least one detail of Russian autocracy at a time when the British lion (or cat, in this particular case) was slowly changing its claws.

So Natalia Haldin is right when she says to the narrator of the novel, "You belong to a people which has made a bargain with fate and wouldn't like to be rude to it. But we have made no bargain. It was never offered to us—so much liberty for so much hard cash." In other words, the curse of Russian history and innate qualities is irreversible only for those who, thanks to "a bargain with fate," have the good fortune to belong to a nation which pays the price for the blessing of its own history and its own innate qualities.

Conrad, probably unconsciously, realized the extremism of this theory of national blue blood, because at a certain point he tosses off, as if in an aside on the lips of his narrator, a reflection in which there suddenly rings out a note of shame and human revelation:

It is strange to think that, I won't say liberty, but the mere liberalism of outlook which for us is a matter of words, of ambitions, of votes (and if of feeling at all, then of the sort of feeling which leaves our deepest affections untouched) may be for other beings very much like ourselves and living under the same sky, a heavy trial of fortitude, a matter of tears and anguish and blood.

*   *   *

We are now ready for our meeting with the third Conrad. In the letter to Garnett mentioned above, the author of *Under Western Eyes* dipped his pen in the ink of amazement and asked if it were possible that Garnett had not perceived that he had only ideas, exclusively ideas, in view and that nothing else concerned him— that he had not been influenced by any kind of hidden motives. This amazement of Conrad's was doubly illegitimate. In our analysis of the novel thus far we have already catalogued a few of those hidden motives, and later we shall also see that he had his eye on, above all and as always (albeit this time with less concentrated and more diffuse attention), his main philosophy of life. But in one respect Conrad had actually earned a certain right to the complaint that reverberates in the question he asked Garnett. In no other novel of his do ideas play such a large role—and, in fact, one idea: revolution. But he has no one else to blame if—by interpreting it narrowly as an exclusively Russian creation and by dismissing with thunderbolts the "conviction that a fundamental change of hearts must follow the downfall of any given human institutions" as the mere delusion of "a change of names" that is only possible in a world in which "the oppressors and the oppressed are all Russians together"—he barely achieved half his object in transmitting the suggestiveness and perspicacity of his views on revolution.

Stendhal observed that the Germans, in contrast to other nations, were excited rather than soothed by meditation. "That is true," adds Camus in *L'Homme Révolté*, "but it is even more true of Russia." These words (with the exception of "Germans") might well have served as the motto for the entire revolutionary section of *Under Western Eyes*. However one ought to supplement them with Pisarev's remark about children and adolescents being the greatest fanatics as well as the explanation that the Russians are the children, or at most the eternal adolescents, of nations.

Totally neglecting the exciting influence of meditation on other nations and ignoring the "thirty years' apostolate of blood" (to use Camus' words) which, after the first terrorist revolver shot fired at General Trepov by Vera Zassulich, thundered in the echoes of assassination attempts in Germany, Italy, Spain, Austria, France, and the United States (in the year 1892 alone there were more than one thousand dynamite outrages in Europe and almost five hundred in America), Conrad sat down to describe people who were the product "of the normality of their place, and time, and race," and turned his back on the raging torrent of European revolutionism in order to fix his angry gaze on the shadows of Russian revolutionaries looking at their reflections in Lake Leman and the Neva. It is true that the history of the "thirty years' apostolate of blood" does not include the founding of a missionary station in England, but after all England is not the entire West.

It would be a glaring understatement to say that Conrad depicted his revolutionists in the colors of grudging irony becoming to the representatives of "Utopian revolutionism"; the primary colors he uses in his picture are chiefly bile and venom. It is worth stopping for a moment for a closer look at this world of "visionary and criminal babble" and "passions that can never be sated," this world that emerges from the cradle of Russia "lapped up in evils, watched over by beings that are worse than ogres, ghouls, and vampires." There is the "Russian Mazzini," Peter Ivanovitch, a combination of the Asiatic physical characteristics of Bakunin and the feminist exaltation of Herzen: "the great author of the revolutionary gospels grope[d] for words as if he were in the dark as to what he meant to say," a man who "suggested a monk or a prophet, a robust figure of some desert-dweller," who had "something Asiatic" in his appearance, a leech clinging to the unfortunate Tekla, "the arch-revolutionist" and "preacher of feminist gospel for all the world," and in fact a shameless gigolo, "burly, bull-necked, deferential" to his Egeria, Madame de S——. There is Madame de S——, "a galvanized corpse out of some tale of Hoffmann," an "ancient, painted mummy with unfathomable eyes," a ghost of an eighteenth-century "atmosphere of scandal, occultism, and charlatanism," the heiress of Madame de Staël, but with this difference, that "Napoleonic despotism, the booted heir of the Revolution, which counted the intellectual woman for an enemy to be watched, was something quite unlike the autocracy in mystic vestments, engendered by the slavery of a Tartar conquest." There is Nikita nicknamed Necator, the terror of Russian gendarmes and police agents, the legendary "Necator of bureaucrats, of provincial governors, of obscure informers," actually a "creature so grotesque as to set town dogs barking at its mere sight," "horrible ... burlesque of professional jealousy," with a voice like the "squeak ... of some angry small animal," and, as we discover later, like his model Azev, simultaneously a great master-terrorist and Okhrana agent. The diminutive and grotesque "genius of invective" Julius Laspara sits "with his little feet twined tightly round the legs of his stool like an imp in an alchemist's laboratory." Sophia Antonovna was "the true spirit of destructive revolution" with her "thick hair, nearly white" and her black "Mephistophelian eyebrows." Certainly there are also exceptions. But what exceptions! There is Tekla "the Samaritan ... of unselfish devotion," the victim of victims of tyranny and revolution. There is Victor Haldin, who for his "cheerless and muddy dreams" paid with his life: "But, at any rate, the life now ended had been sincere, and perhaps its thoughts might have been lofty, its moral sufferings profound, its last act a true sacrifice." Only with Haldin does Conrad manage to strike that same note of embarrassment which we found in his reflections on "mere liberalism" as a "heavy trial of fortitude, a matter of tears and anguish and blood," writing that "it is not for us, the staid lovers calmed by the possession of a conquered liberty, to condemn without appeal the fierceness of thwarted desire." And finally there is Natalia Haldin, the victim of her pure, trusting, and naive heart.

With these three exceptions (the motif of the offering in its two aspects of sacrifice and victim is used to provide these three characters with their only absolution) the world of Russian revolutionists is described in *Under Western Eyes*, with that matchless Conradian gift of evoking the uncanny and the terrible, as if it were a gloomy den of thieves observed through a key-hole by "old, settled Europe." But no, there is one more exception, and it is a very significant one. For the twinkling of an eye there appears in the person of Sophia Antonovna *l'homme révolté*, the propagator of the deepest revolutionary instinct common to mankind. "Life," says the incarnation in woman of the "spirit of destructive revolution" with her gray hair and black "Mephistophelian eyebrows," "life, Razumov, not to be vile must be a revolt—a pitiless protest—all the time." And then "Razumov looked at her white hair: and this mark of so many uneasy years seemed nothing but a testimony to the invincible vigour of revolt . . . as though in her revolutionary pilgrimage she had discovered the secret, not of everlasting youth, but of everlasting endurance." But immediately after that, "How un-Russian she looked, thought Razumov. Her mother might have been a Jewess or an Armenian or—devil knew what."

When one has read all this and then looks at the short history of the revolutionary movement in Russia in Camus' book, it is impossible not to feel a grievance against Conrad for his injustice. Camus says of the Russian revolutionists that they were "men of the highest principles: the last, in the history of rebellion, to refuse no part of their condition or their drama. . . . History offers few examples of fanatics who have suffered from scruples, even in action. But the men of 1905 were always prey to doubts. The greatest homage we can pay them is to say that we would not be able, in 1950, to ask them one question that they themselves had not already asked and that, in their life or by their death, they had not partially answered." Kalyaev, the murderer of the Grand Duke Sergei, was seen before an assassination attempt holding a bomb in one hand and making the sign of the cross with the other. "But he repudiated religion. In his cell, before his execution, he refused its consolations." "For Dora Brilliant, the anarchist program was of no importance; terrorist action was primarily embellished by the sacrifice it demanded from the terrorist. 'But,' says Savinkov, 'terror weighed on her like a cross.' " "The first attempt on the Grand Duke Sergei failed because Kaliayev, with the full approval of his comrades, refused to kill the children who were riding in the Grand Duke's carriage." "Savinkov was opposed to an attempt on Admiral

Dubassov in the Petersburg-Moscow express" because of his fear
for the life of other passengers. "Jeliabov, who organized the
attempt on Alexander II in 1881 and was arrested forty-eight
hours before the murder . . . asked to be executed at the same time
as the real perpetrator of the attempt." "Five [gallows] were erected,
one of which was for the woman he loved," Sofia Perovskaia. She
"kissed the man she loved and her two other friends, but turned
away from Ryssakov," who had broken under interrogation. At his
trial Kaliayev finished his testimony with the exclamation: "I
consider my death as a supreme protest against a world of blood
and tears." Against that real world of blood and tears—on which the
"ordinary English liberal" of Conrad's novel reflects only once—
Sazonov, the author of the murder of Minister Plehve, took his own
life in prison "to earn respect for his comrades."

Camus continues: "Necessary and inexcusable—that is how
murder appeared to them." After them would come others
"consumed with the same devouring faith as these, [and] will find
their methods sentimental and refuse to admit that any one life is
the equivalent of any other. They will then put an abstract idea
above human life, even if they call it history, to which they themselves have submitted in advance and to which they will also
decide, quite arbitrarily, to submit everyone else." But these will
already be the times of Chigalev of *The Possessed*, who starts out
"with the premise of unlimited freedom" and arrives at "unlimited
despotism"; the times of the half-prototype of Conrad's Peter
Ivanovitch, Bakunin, who started out with hopes of achieving total
freedom by means of total destruction, in order to come "to the
conclusion that to found an indestructible society it must be based
on the politics of Machiavelli and the methods of the Jesuits:
for the body, only violence; for the soul, deception." Conrad feels
(albeit completely incorrectly, as far as the chronology and mechanism of events are concerned) the deeper menace of these times,
when he had his narrator say in conversation with Natalia Haldin:
"in a real revolution the best characters do not come to the front.
A violent revolution falls into the hands of narrow-minded fanatics
and of tyrannical hypocrites at first. Afterwards comes the turn of
all the pretentious intellectual failures of the time. Such are the
chiefs and the leaders. You will notice that I have left out the mere
rogues. The scrupulous and the just, the noble, humane, and
devoted natures; the unselfish and the intelligent may begin a
movement—but it passes away from them. They are not the leaders
of a revolution. They are its victims: the victims of disgust, of
disenchantment—often of remorse. Hopes grotesquely betrayed,
ideals caricatured—that is the definition of revolutionary success."

Razumov, full of barely suppressed hatred for "the bearers of the spark [an allusion, perhaps, to Lenin's *Spark*] to start an explosion which is meant to change fundamentally the lives of so many millions in order that Peter Ivanovitch should be the head of a State," goes ever farther: "In this world of men nothing can be changed— neither happiness nor misery. They can only be displaced at the cost of corrupted consciences and broken lives—a futile game for arrogant philosophers and sanguinary triflers." This acute but excessively severe observation, however, has nothing to do with the Russianness or un-Russianness of the revolutionary instinct—it expresses only the fatalism and tragic nature of the general human "revolt . . . all the time"—and in no way does it diminish the greatness of "everlasting endurance." Here for the first and only time rings out the true voice of Conrad, the pessimistic and tragic glorifier of the valor or the weakness of the solitary man in this unchanging world of men. But unfortunately we do not hear it very distinctly because it is drowned out by the bitter philippic of the herald of English conservatism and the child of the fate prepared for Poland by Russia.

Poor Sazonov did not then "earn respect for his comrades" with the author of *Under Western Eyes*. How can that be? one may ask. Isn't Victor Haldin one of them, one of "the men of 1905?" No. Against the background of the Conradian terroristic-revolutionary den on the one hand and the high intellectual values of the Russian variety of the *homme révolté* on the other, Victor Haldin is a sympathetic raw youth, and one can without any scruples dismiss him with the remark Conrad made about Axel Heyst: "The young man learned to reflect, which is a destructive process, a reckoning of the cost." Unfortunately however, Haldin died before his reflections could pass beyond the teething stage. "What do you imagine I am?" he asks Razumov. "A being in revolt? No. It's you thinkers who are in everlasting revolt. I am one of the resigned."

What is the upshot of all this? Not only the Russophile Edward Garnett but even V. S. Pritchett, anything but a Russophile, considered Conrad a reactionary. The old despotism and the new Utopianism represented two complementary forms of moral anarchy for Conrad. Their fruit is cynicism, a higher degree of despotism, and a greater amount of destruction. Many people came to that view, however reluctantly. But, according to Pritchett, Conrad was a rigid reactionary. He never tried to understand the sense of the revolutionary current. He hated the Russian revolution as only a Pole could hate it, a Pole who was a generation removed from the passion of the day. Pritchett concludes that Conrad's hatred was rooted in the past and there it remained forever. But Pritchett's judgement is only a part of the truth, just as, in the reverse sense, was Cole's superficial faith in Conrad as an "interpreter." One must clean out the muddy bottom of this novel to see what is hidden under layers of Russophobia, arch-Polishness, and ultra-Englishness.

Setting up the problem as he did in *Under Western Eyes*, Conrad made two mistakes. By depriving "revolt . . . all the time" of its characteristics of "plastic shape and a definite intellectual aspect" (as the English possessor of Western eyes says), by denying universal characteristics to a matter of specifically Russian cynicism and stupidity, Conrad lost his chance for a deeper and more evocative statement of his sound conviction of the futility and disastrous results of Utopian revolutionism *despite* the fact that it may be born in great minds and hearts. By the insistent straining of his philosophy to fit the Russian monopoly of "place, and time, and race," he creates a non-homogeneous and artistically overstated impression throughout the novel. (Gide, who in his *Journal* called *Under Western Eyes* a "masterly book," scowled however—too lightly!—at the excess of Conrad's consciousness in the continuity of the design, at the traces of too great effort, at the lack of ease, the insufficiently convincing irony, the longueurs, and the diffuseness.)

*   *   *

We can consider the fourth and fifth Conrad together, for they represent in relatively the clearest form the author of *Heart of Darkness* and *Lord Jim*. "Senseless desperation" as a reaction to "senseless tyranny." Why senseless? What kind of desperation is sensible or senseless? Natalia Haldin says (and her words serve as the book's motto): "I would take liberty from any hand as a hungry man would snatch a piece of bread." Hence even from the hand of a "criminal idealist" or a "piteous imbecile," as Razumov mentally describes the red-nosed Petersburg student. Here through layers of mud the real bottom begins to emerge. Russia, revolution, these are mere synonyms for the "ominous jungle": man walks through it alone, despairing, hungry, he is ready to snatch a piece of bread from any hand, he casts his uneasy glance around him, he goes forward cautiously, again he runs unconsciously into the depths, not always remembering that under his feet is "a thin crust of barely cooled lava." Too bad for him if his weak idealism cracks under the strain of the horror of the tropics and his isolation among wild beasts. Doubly bad for him if he drops the reins of his impulses, surrenders to the hands of chance, ceases to be master of himself, and does not subordinate his capricious drive to a higher goal. Have we any right to be surprised that he sometimes gives way to despair? But that is not senseless desperation. It is inevitable despair, and hence tragic. He is surrounded, of course—later, beyond the jungle!—by the immortal Conradian sea: "a great cold blank ... levelled with snow and fading gradually on all sides into shadows and mists," "a monstrous blank page."

He can write something of his own on that page and rescue his threatened dignity, because man, although he is born in chains, sometimes becomes free. But he must have at least a "conventional conscience," *at least* that conscience which the men of 1905 had, believing that "any one life is the equivalent of any other." It is not a matter of chance that Razumov (a typical representative of what Russell calls the Conradian "tragedies of loneliness," who once dreams of "walking through drifts of snow in a Russia where he was as completely alone as any betrayed autocrat could be," a man in reference to whom Conrad is to say that "no human being could bear a steady view of moral solitude," a man "lonely in the world") writes his first report from Geneva to the Okhrana in the shadow of a statue of Jean Jacques Rousseau. And certainly that scene was vivid in Russell's memory when he defined Conrad's philosophy as the antithesis of Rousseau's. It is really a symbolic scene: "the exiled effigy of the author of the *Social Contract* sat enthroned above the bowed head of Razumov in the sombre immobility of bronze," the head of Razumov who was betraying other people and feeling "the bitterness of solitude." And more: " 'Perhaps life is just that,' reflected Razumov, pacing to and fro under the trees of the little island, all alone with the bronze statue of Rousseau. 'A dream and a fear.' "

But before Razumov comes to fulfill his Genevan duties as an informer, he is gripped by a spasm of hesitation muffled at once by the exclamation: "Is it possible that I have a conventional conscience?" This is what his classically Conradian drama really depends on: until the moment of his "repentance," evoked perhaps more by love of Natalia than by moral necessity, he did not have a conventional conscience. How could he have acquired one, if he fell into the hidden traps of his own logic. "Betray. A great word. What is betrayal? They talk of a man betraying his country, his friends, his sweetheart. There must be a moral bond first. All a man can betray is his conscience. And how is my conscience engaged here; by what bond of common faith, of common conviction, am I obliged to let that fanatical idiot drag me down with him? On the contrary—every obligation of true courage is the other way."

In these words and in their consequences is lodged the blemish, if not, to put it bluntly, the artistic flaw, of the hero of *Under Western Eyes*. Up to this point everything has been clear and Conradian: having substituted Russia for the sea, the element or pitilessly

indifferent nature, and revolution for the menacing jungle or thin
crust of barely cooled lava, we have a picture of the perils that lie
in wait for the weak man fighting against both the good and the bad
passions that lead toward destruction. But the point is that Razumov,
like his distant cousin Raskolnikov, is not at all a weak man. On
the contrary, he is a strong man. And if he betrays Haldin and
"conventional conscience" with him, it is not out of weakness and
cowardice but because he knows full well where his strength, his
unconventional conscience, and his "obligation of true courage,"
impel him. As Raskolnikov hated the disgusting old money-lender,
so Razumov hates revolution, and from their own points of view
(and, up to a point, the point of the inviolability of the commandments "Thou shalt not kill" and "Thou shalt not betray," also from
the points of view of Dostoevsky and Conrad) they are both right
in defending their futures—the one against guiltless misery and the
other against the "lawless forces" of revolution. But the catch is that
one must read Conrad's work with the same feelings of hatred and
loathing for revolution with which it was written in order to identify
revolution with the disgusting money-lender. And this is, at least
for me, impossible. To express this a bit more clearly: the moral
problem is similar in the two novels, but while in *Crime and Punishment* the evil that drives a man to unpardonable crime must seem
objective to the reader, in *Under Western Eyes* it is at least—very
delicately speaking—subjective to the degree of glaring and unjust
exaggeration. Hence Raskolnikov has the power of convincing while
Razumov does not.

Conrad maintains that "Razumov is treated sympathetically."
This assurance strikes me as a euphemism. To a certain extent
(as I have already indicated) Razumov is Conrad's spokesman as
far as his views on revolution are concerned. Why should it be
otherwise? His very name assigns him the role of the only *reasonable* man among people who probably deserve only strait-jackets.
But anyone who does not share Conrad's prejudices against revolution, anyone who is not blind and not inexorably stern and also
manages to see some greatness and nobility in it must immediately
regard this reasonable young man with deep antipathy. Gide
accurately sensed that *Under Western Eyes* was a novel about the
disastrous consequences of the hero's inconsequence. Conrad's
greatest philosophical and artistic error is that he does not make it
absolutely clear when this inconsequence begins: when Razumov
first wants to help Haldin in his flight, or when he goes out in the
streets of Petersburg to betray him, or later, when he goes to the
gathering of revolutionists in Geneva to "repent." In any case the
Conradian betrayer remains faithful to the end in his hatred of

revolutionists. And he is driven to confess not by the discovery of moral baseness or the unforgivability of betrayal but by a moral stuffiness evoked by his love for the sister of the man he betrayed. Perhaps that is why almost simultaneously he draws up two inconsistent declarations. In his confessional letter to Natalia Haldin he writes: "I am independent—and therefore perdition is my lot," and at the gathering at Laspara's he exclaims: "To-day, of all days since I came amongst you, I was made safe, and to-day I made myself free from falsehood, from remorse—independent of every single human being on this earth."

*   *   *

His safety is illusory; in Conrad one must pay without hope of redemption. My sketch is finished. Let us then say farewell to two young men. In "a little two-roomed wooden house, in the suburb of some very small town, hiding within the high plank-fence of a yard overgrown with nettles" Conrad's reasonable man is slowly dying for breaking the moral laws of "conventional conscience." He is "crippled, ill, getting weaker every day," deaf and cut off forever from the world. Meanwhile his distant cousin, Dostoevsky's reasonable man, is serving his punishment in distant Siberia for breaking the divine moral law of the ten commandments. He is reading the Gospel with tears in his eyes.

Translated by Roland Strom

YEGOR AND IVAN DENISOVICH

Gustaw Herling-Grudziński

T HE ELEVENTH and final volume of the Polish edition of Chekhov's *Works* (Warsaw, 1962) includes the first Polish translation (abridged) of *Sakhalin*. In an afterword Natalia Modzelewska describes the origin of the book.

Toward the end of the nineteenth century Chekhov decided to visit the "convict island" of Sakhalin. He was then enjoying the fullness of creativity and success, and consequently his decision came as a surprise to his friends. Today one can see that he himself had a clear view of the signs of his approaching "crisis." He wrote and wrote and again and again was unable to touch bottom. He felt like a swimmer who is too easily carried forward and forcibly buoyed to the surface by everyday banalities: "I still haven't developed a political, religious, and philosophical *Weltanschauung*. I change it every month, hence I must settle for descriptions in themselves—how my heroes love, marry, are born and die, how they talk." It is sufficiently probable that it was in Sakhalin that he expected to touch the bottom of contemporary Russian life and of human life in general. If Lev Shestov was partially right years later in calling Chekhov's tales "creations out of nothing," it was nevertheless necessary to uncover the roots of that nothingness. "The penal colony," Chekhov is alleged to have remarked before his departure for Sakhalin, embodies perhaps one of the most terrible absurdities that man has managed to devise with his conventional notion of life and truth."

He prepared for the trip with his genuine conscientiousness and scrupulosity, despite a certain coquettishness about his "modest" status as a writer, investigator, and public figure: "I go altogether convinced that my expedition will contribute nothing new to literature or science. I haven't the time, the knowledge, or the ambition for that. The only thing to be regretted is that it is I who go and not someone else more competent in the matter and more gifted in arousing society." But Chekhov understood perfectly well why he was going. In the same letter he added, "Sakhalin is the place of the greatest anguish that man, be he free or imprisoned, can bear" and the responsibility for the "convict island" weighs "on all of us." The following statement also dates from the period in which he was making his preparations. "Thanks to books which one ought to have studied more deeply [Russian penal codes, extracts from the history of prison administration, historical documents concerning the colonization of Siberia], I have learned what everyone should be compelled to know, under threat of forty lashes, and what I in my ignorance did not know before."

He set out on April 21, 1890. On July 10 he reached the shores of the island.

He spent three months there. It is almost unbelievable how much he managed to accomplish in such a short time. He visited all the prisons and settlements, he made a census of the island, he recorded dozens of conversations, and single-handed he initiated investigations like those undertaken nowadays by university teams of skilled investigators and survey specialists. He was only forbidden access to political prisoners. "I saw everything except capital punishment. When I recall Sakhalin now, it seems like hell itself."

He worked on his book at intervals over a period of four years, treating it like a kind of dissertation in settlement of his "debt to the science of medicine." "Doctor Chekhov," however, expressed himself in this vein: "Before my departure Tolstoy's *Kreutzer Sonata* was an event for me, and now it makes me laugh and strikes me as pointless. Either I became a man because of the journey or I have lost my reason—the devil only knows." In fact, the mixture of expedition report, official inventory, statistical yearbook, and investigation encompassing the fields of psychology, sociology, medicine, and law contained in his book about Sakhalin could not fool the reader, though it might deceive the censor.

"In the Korsakovsk outpost lives the deportee-convict Altukhov, an old man in his sixties, but perhaps even older, who again and again escapes in the same way: he takes a chunk of bread, closes his cottage, and scarcely half a verst from Korsakovsk sits down on the hill to look at the tayga, the sea, and the sky. He stays there for three days and then goes home again, only to gather up his victuals and return once more to his hill. They used to flog him, but now they only laugh at his flights. Some people run away with the hope of having a month or a week of freedom, while others are satisfied with a single day. 'One, but it's mine!' The longing for freedom completely overwhelms some of the convicts at intervals, and in this respect resembles drunkenness or even epilepsy. It is said to come on in specific seasons or months of the year, so that loyal convicts warn the authorities of their escape every time they feel an attack coming on. Usually all escape attempts—without exception—are punished by flogging or even caning. But the very fact that these flights from beginning to end are so striking in their absurdity and senselessness, that often completely reasonable and modest people with families run away without clothing, without bread, without a destination, without a plan; with complete certainty that they will be caught, knowing that they are risking their health, the confidence of the authorities, their relative freedom, and sometimes even their salaries, and that they are running the risk of freezing to death somewhere or being shot—this very senselessness ought to have shown the Sakhalin doctors, with whom the decision rests whether or not to punish the fugitives, that in many cases what is involved is not an offense but an illness."

But the "illness of freedom" did not afflict all the prisoners of Sakhalin. Only one chapter of the book has a title, which indicates that the author somehow wanted to stress its importance. That chapter is entitled "Yegor's Story."

Chekhov met a convict named Yegor in the house of a certain clerk from whom he rented a room shortly after his arrival on the island. He was a forty-year-old peasant "with a simple-hearted, seemingly half-witted face." He would go to the clerk's house not out of duty but "out of respect" to help the elderly serving woman. Everlastingly busy with something, handy at fixing anything, and always on the lookout for work, he slept barely a couple of hours a day. Only on holidays could he be seen at the crossroads wearing a jacket over his red *rubashka*, his stomach protruding and his feet spread wide apart. He called this his "stroll."

He had been sent to Sakhalin for "manslaughter." From his naive and rather intricate account it emerges that he was convicted without evidence and sentenced unjustly because there were no witnesses. In court he was told simply, "Here everyone says the same thing and makes the sign of the cross, and it's all lies." He was almost happy with his lot in Sakhalin. When asked if he was homesick, he replied that he was not: "Only one thing bothers me—grief for the children." What did he think when they led him to the penal colony ship in Odessa? "I prayed to God that He would grant the children wisdom and understanding." Why hadn't he brought his wife and children to Sakhalin? "Because they're just as well at home."

Natalia Modzelewska justly observes in her afterword: "We encounter the most tragic figure of the penal colony in the apparently dispassionately recorded "Yegor's Story." Yegor is almost a paradigmatic picture of those poorest in spirit, who can no longer distinguish justice from injustice, who have lost all sensitivity to their own and others' sufferings, in whom not even a spark of protest burns. They bear their fate with inexhaustible humility and even manage to be happy. This horrible force of inertia and humility, as Chekhov displays it to us, constitutes one of the pillars that support the penal colony."

For the author of *The House of the Dead* the anguish of those condemned to the penal colony had an inexplicable quality, as if it were the epitome of eternal human destiny. The Polish convicts, as Pawel Hostowiec perceptively observed, irritated Dostoevsky with their attempts at rational or mystic explanation. For Chekhov the humble anguish of Yegor was a condemnation of society; the author of the book about Sakhalin would have been entitled to set Marx's exclamation on his title-page: "How wretched is the society that must turn to the hangman for protection!"

* * *

Sixty years later we behold Yegor's grandson or great-grandson in the penal colony, Ivan Denisovich Shukhov. Did God send him "wisdom and understanding?" Did the Revolution help him to discern his own fate? Did the new order ignite "even a spark of protest?" Did the new powers restore his "sensitivity to his own and others' sufferings," did they invest him with the ability "to distinguish justice from injustice?"

Reading Alexander Solzhenitsyn's novel one may doubt it. Nor is the most horrible fact that in comparison with the Soviet prison camps of 1941, described in my *A World Apart*, the conditions in Ivan Denisovich's camp in 1951 seem to have become considerably worse: that programmatic cruelty, brutal and inhuman maltreatment of prisoners had openly become part of the structure of the system. What is most atrocious are the brief remarks, likewise dispassionately recorded and scattered in passing throughout Solzhenitsyn's text, as in "Yegor's Story" in Chekhov's book. "How time flew when you were working! That was something [Shukhov had] often noticed. The days rolled by in the camp— they were over before you could say 'knife.' But the years, they never rolled by: they never moved by a second." "You wait, Captain. When you've been in for eight years you'll be picking [fag-ends] up yourself. We've seen prouder ones than you in the camp . . ." "Earlier there'd been a spell when people were lucky: everyone to a man got ten years. But from '49 onward the standard sentence was twenty-five, irrespective. A man can survive ten years—but twenty-five, who can get through alive?" And the sentence that concludes his story: "A day without a dark cloud. Almost a happy day!" A day without a dark cloud even after the description of nine hundred minutes, each one full of anguish and degradation! Almost a happy day! Can't one hear the echo of Yegor's voice? In one respect his grandson or great-grandson finally learned to distinguish "justice from injustice": "But who benefited, then, from all these work reports? Let's be clear about it. The camp. The camp got thousands of extra rubles from the building organization and so could give higher bonuses to its guard lieutenants . . . And you? You got an extra two hundred grams of bread for your supper. A couple of hundred grams ruled your life."

"Now [Ivan Denisovich] didn't know either whether he wanted freedom or not. At first he'd longed for it. Every night he'd counted the days of his stretch—how many had passed, how many were coming. And then he'd grown bored with counting. And then it became clear that men of his like wouldn't ever be allowed to return home, that they'd be exiled. And whether his life would be any better there than here—who could tell? Freedom meant one thing to him—home. But they wouldn't let him go home." "Tell me, Yegor, why didn't you bring your wife and children into deportation with you?" "Because they're just as well at home." "Alyosha," said Ivan Denisovich to the young "Baptist" in the neighboring bunk, "I'm not against God, understand that. I readily believe in God. But I don't believe in paradise or hell." This Alyosha irritated him a bit as the Polish convicts had irritated Dostoevsky: "You see, Alyosha, somehow it works out all right for you: Jesus Christ wanted you to sit in prison and so you are—sitting there for His sake. But for whose sake am I here?" For nothing. By ordaininment of the eternal anguish of the humiliated.

In Solzhenitsyn's novel the Revolution is referred to only once. One of the prisoners, the film-maker Tsezar, is discussing Eisenstein's *Potyomkin* with a companion in adversity, the navy captain Buynovsky. They are discussing the famous scene in which the sailors see the maggots in the meat and raise their clenched fists in mutiny: the scene, of course, that Eisenstein conceived as a great metaphor of the decay of tsardom. Buynovsky remarks: "Well, if they were to bring that meat here to our camp . . . and dumped it straight into the cauldron we'd be only too . . ." Listening to the conversation, the other prisoners howl their agreement. This is the comment that the "damned and oppressed" of 1951 have to make on the events that shook tsardom fifteen years after Chekhov's journey to Sakhalin.

How wretched is the government that must turn to the hangman for protection!

*   *   *

To read Chekhov's book on Sakhalin today arouses other thoughts. Strange times they were in which it took a famous and sickly writer three months to reach the convict island forgotten by God and man. "From Krasnoyarsk to Irkutsk," he wrote en route, "atrocious heat and dust. And add to that hunger, dust in the nose, eyes drooping from constant insomnia, and the continual dread that the coach might break down. But despite all this, I am happy and thank God that He gave me the strength to undertake this journey. I have seen a great deal and experienced a great deal, and it is all uncommonly interesting and new to me, not as a man of letters but simply as a man." He saw and experienced still more, "not only as a man of letters but simply as a man" in Sakhalin.

Nowadays the gathering of information does not require such exertions, but it is not for that reason any simpler or easier for the modern man of letters or simply man. Ten years ago Sartre wrote in his famous debate with Camus in the pages of *Les Temps Modernes*: "I too consider the Soviet camps intolerable, but I also find intolerable the use that the bourgeois press makes of them everyday." The Polish Communist poet Broniewski said exactly the same thing to me three years ago. Which in practical terms means that the existence of the camps and writing about them are equally "intolerable," for the "non-bourgeois" press either encompassed them as a rule with a conspiracy of silence or saw in them an invention of the advocates of "cold war." Hence Ivan Denisovich ought to have waited patiently until his fate was called up before a purer court.

Thanks to Solzhenitsyn's novel, we now have such a tribunal: it is presided over by Khrushchev himself. At last the "proper" press has made "proper" use of the camps. And although one observes with satisfaction the deliberations of a "pure court" (never mind that it is a quarter of a century late!), I cannot drive out of my mind an old photograph of 1935 that Borys Lewickyj reproduced in his splendid book *Vom roten Terror zur sozialistischen Gesetzlichkeit*. It shows an inspection of one of the White Sea Canal camps. (According to a rough estimate these camps consumed three hundred thousand convict lives in building the canal.) In the foreground, a pair of masters, Yagoda and Kaganovich. A bit to one side, with a cyclist's cap cocked on one side of his head and wearing a *rubashka* over his trousers, with a simple-hearted and seemingly half-witted face, his hands behind his back and his stomach protruding is the apprentice, Nikita Sergeyevich. Perhaps he too is a grandson or great-grandson of Yegor.

Translated by Roland Strom

THE LITERATURE OF BORDER LINE SITUATIONS

Jurij Ławrynenko

Austria, 1947. After fifteen years of wandering over the vast areas of Soviet Eurasia, with my thoughts still tormented by the memory of the Great Eastern Crisis, one day I came across a publication in a newspaper which revived my interest in the problem of "borderline situations." It was the first published account of a discussion which took place in Munich in 1932 among five German intellectuals led by Oswald Spengler. In the course of the discussion the immediate historical moment (it was the eve of Hitler's coming to power) was described as an imminent catastrophe looming over Germany and Western Europe. The question was raised: What stand should an aware and self-confident individual take in this situation? Since everyone seemed to expect an answer from Spengler, he gave his views on the matter. From the point of view of attaining results—he said—it may already be too late to make either a physical or spiritual sacrifice. And under the particular, exceptional circumstances, the uselessness of sacrifice justified the individual's temporary abnegation of duty.

Here one of the participants interrupted Spengler to argue that the moral instinct did not recognize such things as a "useless" sacrifice. Spengler let this remark pass and went on with his argument. There exist moments, he said, when an active opponent may help the enemy more than one of his followers. Every object inside a violent whirlpool speeds up its motion so that it is impossible even to distinguish the forces which restrain its motion from those which drive it on. This is the moment when (as in the case of a defeated army) the entire burden of responsibility is shifted from the group onto the individual. As a result, the responsibility of the individual transcends its own limits and man is confronted

198

with an *ultimate decision*. Almost miraculous things may occur at this point: the individual's "ultimate decision" may take on un-expected values and have a serious effect on the future fate of man-kind. Moral decisions made at this stage may be transformed into physical energy.

However, the final condition necessary for this type of decision is a sense of perfect orientation. There are times when partial orientation becomes completely impossible, and then everything depends on faith, a faith produced by the interplay of two forces in a man: moral strength and the ability to see and comprehend. It is no longer the individual's moral and cultural roots as distinct factors which are decisive, but rather the faith and intuition born of the interaction of these two integral parts of human nature. Then there appears in the individual those elemental forces that are found at the sources of the continuity and eternal regeneration of history. Then man seems to acquire the ability to penetrate the darkness of the historical moment with his glance, and to perceive the "new" which until then had escaped his notice.

I was especially struck by this inspired improvisation, because in it Spengler had overcome the expressly pessimistic fatalism of his earliest book *Untergang des Abendlandes*, and did so at precisely that moment when his own cultural-historical group found itself on the verge of decline. So then he himself became an example of his theory (although he did not physically experience the crisis). However, Spengler's theory, limited as it is to the experiences of western Europe, does not give an adequate explanation of the problem in the form which it took in the countries of the Soviet Union and lately in the "Peoples' Democracies" as well.

According to Spengler's theory, the "old" and the "new," "birth" and "death" cannot coexist. He is not aware of the death of that which is newly born. Evidently the crisis of the West (in comparison with that of the East) had not yet become a true border-line situation. The totalitarianism of the West—at that time the culminating point of the Western crisis—was essentially only a cancer-like growth, removed by the surgical knife of the Second World War. Neither the disease nor the operation were actually the "birth of the new," but represented rather the self-defense of the "old."

Moreover, Spengler was not familiar with the "borderline situa-tion" as a continually developing crisis, a permanent state. His "moment of ultimate decision" was a dramatic zenith, not the dynamic curve of a crisis. Finally, Spengler's "responsible man" was not yet confronted with the division of his own personality because the struggle as yet was being waged only in the outer world and not within the human soul. He did not yet have to face directly the compromise with the devil as the iron command of history, the will of God.

Before the downfall of Stalin, the situation in the "Peoples' Democracies" was not substantially different (except in degree of intensity) from the picture drawn by Spengler. Nothing "new" had been born; only the "old" was defended, and defended with some success. The individual could still hide his true face under a mask and remain on neutral territory, thereby preserving the precious heritage of the "old" in his soul. But still, when this situation is compared with Western European totalitarianism, it does recall the more authentic "borderline crisis" of the East. Despite the proximity of the West, here there were more elements of uncertainty in the air, and the feeling of impending disaster was more expressly voiced.

In 1945 and 1946, the *White Eagle* published the memoirs of Richard Wraga, in which he recalls his stay in the Ukraine in the late twenties. Writing about the play *The People's Prophet* by Mykola Kulish, Wraga adds with a sigh that Poland could consider herself lucky if her own literature, enslaved by bolshevism, could produce a play as powerful as that of Kulish, a work which would strike so violent a blow to the occupying power. At that time I did not share Wraga's pessimism, for I thought that he underestimated the spiritual capacities of his own people. Hence when Milosz's *The Captive Mind* appeared in 1953, I was particularly struck by the following passage:

We should not be surprised if a writer or painter doubts the value of resistance. If he were sure that a work created in opposition to the official line had a lasting value, he would probably make up his mind at once without worrying about its publication or exhibition. He believes, however, that such a work would be artistically weak—and in this he would not be far wrong.

Let us emphasize that the essential factor here is not external resistance, which would be utterly pointless, but the individual's inability to come to terms with his own ego. "A writer," as Milosz says, "does not believe in writing for the drawer." He believes, then, that his art acquires greater vigor when subjected to official sterilization. In the light of the experiences of writers in all the Soviet Republics, such a statement sounds rather paradoxical, because in the national literatures of the USSR true art and opposition have become practically synonymous. Exceptions to this rule are without significance. This unwritten law has held sway in the Soviet Union for nearly forty years.

But no sooner had many translations of *The Captive Mind* appeared than events in Poland and Hungary proved Milosz's pessimism to be unjustified: both countries had been nurturing the seeds of the "new." We are not speaking here of a "victory"; on the contrary, I see in all this the deepest defeat and the source of a borderline situation with all its eastern and dynamic implications. If you try to picture the emotional state, the spiritual impasse of the Hungarian writers who were abandoned by the West and are now in prison or returning from it in spiritual bondage, you will understand what I mean. And yet, even the suppressed uprising showed Hungarians that all was not lost, that although there was no use counting on help from the West, there still remained the possibility of an inner regeneration, a regeneration which can occur only within the human soul.

And at this point we find the origins of the "borderline situation" where birth and death exist in the closest conjunction.

"Silent is the fog where death and birth sleep in one shroud." These words were written by the Ukrainian poet Teodozy Osmachka, and they reflect quite accurately the present situation in the Ukraine.

In the course of a decade historical circumstances had produced a situation of extreme crisis in the West. Those who lived during this crisis experienced two catastrophes. In the first (1919–21), the newly independent republics of the Ukraine, Belorussia, the Caucasus, and Asia were once again annexed to the modernized Bolshevik empire. In the second (1931–36), planned destruction attacked not only national and cultural groups but the spiritual core of a man as well. Forty years of a borderline situation— Spengler had no idea such things could occur. Measured by this new scale, human life seems shorter. Man can neither defeat fate nor outlive it. Painful compromises with the devil (even at the price of partial spiritual capitulation) become the order of the day. The protective ramparts of the last stronghold of resistance—the human soul—are broken down; the battle is moved to the terrain of man's inner being. Henceforth, the individual will wage war not only against the external enemy but also against a part of his own ego. The borderline situation begins to resemble the "ladder of damnation" descending into the pit, to infinity. The ladder is the same for everyone, but each man must make the descent completely alone and on his own, like the Spaniards condemned to death in Hemingway's *For Whom the Bell Tolls*.

The editor Karka, a character from a novel by Mykola Chvylovy, could be speaking for all the writers of the Soviet Ukraine when he declares, "We are destroying our souls in the name of victory, but no one will ever know exactly *how* we committed our share of the destruction."

In my sketch I wish to show how four of the greatest writers of the post-revolutionary Ukraine "destroyed their souls," each in his own way, in the name of victory over evil. The writers are Pavlo Tychyna, Mykola Chvylovy, Mykola Kulish, and Teodozy Osmachka. I have limited myself to these four examples in order to give some idea, however approximate, of several variations of the "ultimate decision," using the word in its Spenglerian sense.

PAVLO TYCHYNA, OR "PLAYING WITH THE DEVIL"

Sixty-six year old Pavlo Tychyna, once the greatest Ukrainian poet after Shevchenko and today only the president of the Ukrainian Workers' Republic and Deputy Chairman of the Soviet of Nationalities of the USSR, belongs to the elite of the greatest empire in the world. Apart from his qualifications as a man of state, poet-laureate Tychyna has a perfect command of all the European languages and a dozen Asiatic ones, is a fine translator of poetry and a great lover of music. Unusually sensitive in his private life, he has the habit of walking almost on the tips of his toes, of speaking in a subdued voice and isolating himself from noise rather like Proust.

His first volume of verse, *Clarinets of the Sun*, won him literary fame. Its poetry was so universal in its love, light, and music that each line seemed to resound with all the strings of the universe. Tychyna's next three volumes, *Instead of Sonnets and Octaves*, *The Plough*, and *Wind from the Ukraine*, established his position as a master of tragic and lyric poetry. At the same time he began to publish fragments of his long poem *Skovoroda*, which was expressly intended as the Ukrainian counterpart of Faust. All this was written between 1918 and 1926. Fate turned out to be stingy with the poet and did not give him even ten full years for artistic realization; yet Tychyna worked so intensively that the next three decades of his absolutely conscious poetic suicide could not destroy the poetic edifice raised during the first decade.

Clarinets of the Sun sang of the spring of peoples. Shortly after, Tychyna was the first who warned that death had already stolen into the cradle of the newly born:

> Open wide the doors—a young lady is approaching
> Open wide the doors—to the clear blue sky
> Eyes, heart, chorales have become silent, waiting
> And the doors opened—to the dead night
> And the doors opened—all the roads were filled with blood
> Through the darkness—unshed tears, a heavy rain.

This was the first borderline situation of the East—the year 1919. The catastrophe closed in as quickly and unexpectedly as the darkness that falls at noon during an eclipse of the sun. In the midst of the general terror and destruction Tychyna appeared with his powerful and openly tragic lyrics centered around the deathless image of the Mater Dolorosa and her crucified son—the nation, and all humanity. Later he threw aside his golden-stringed parnassian lute and published the amazing book *Instead of Sonnets and Octaves*, a classic example of the poetry of a "borderline situation."

In his poem *The Twelve* the well known Russian poet Alexander Blok has no qualms about identifying the twelve blood-thirsty red guardists with the twelve apostles led by Christ himself. Tychyna seems to be responding directly to this image when he writes, "Oh cruel aestheticism! When will you stop admiring a cut throat? Beast will devour beast." And to those who justify terror for the sake of a lofty goal, Tychyna replies, "A great idea demands sacrifices. But is the devouring of one beast by another a true sacrifice? A great idea will justify everything except spiritual emptiness." And again, "To play Scriabin to jailors is not yet a true revolution. Instead of sonnets and octaves, I curse you, I curse all of you who have turned into beasts."

But no one heeded the poet's warnings either in his native land or in the West. Tychnya clearly foresaw the triumph of evil, although everyone still expected changes for the better. He knew that the moment of "ultimate decision" had arrived. The value of open resistance, even spiritual resistance, was questionable. God himself seemed to have made a pact with the Devil. The unforgettable strophe and anti-strophe of his *Instead of Sonnets and Octaves* is suddenly interrupted by a question filled with bitter irony, "Shouldn't I too go and kiss the slipper of the pope?" (Obviously he means the pope of the Third Rome, the pope of the Bolshevik Empire.)

Wind from the Ukraine is the last work in which Tychyna still displays signs of resistance and the first in which he seems reconciled to compromise. But if for Tychyna compromise was a carefully observed law, to the contemporary devil it was only a pause, a springboard for new pressures. Between 1931 and 1934 twenty-five per cent of the Ukrainian peasants and seventy-five per cent of the Ukrainian intellectuals perished under the unexpected blows of the Kremlin. The second "borderline situation" was revealed in all its brutality and for a second time writers were faced with an "ultimate decision." What form did this "ultimate decision" take? The majority of writers chose the path of annihilation, like the girl in the poem by Lesya Ukrainka who proudly announces:

> You can kill me if you want
> But you can't force me to be alive.

Only fifteen per cent of the writers agreed to become "Stalin's singers." Foremost among them was Pavlo Tychyna, the greatest, most profound poet of the Ukraine!

Tychyna's position has all the external features of total self-renunciation, but still such signs may be *only* external. Ukrainian literature had already known the example of a great romantic genius—Taras Shevchenko—who wrote "for the drawer," and kept the light of his unhappy people alive deep in his heart. In the sentence condemning Shevchenko to ten years of exile, Tsar Nicholas I added in his own hand, "And let him be forbidden to write and draw." Tychyna's case was different and more complicated. He was not *forbidden*, but rather *ordered* to write. Lest the soul of the poet should become the shelter for a secret spiritual light the occupier stuffed it with dross. Only then did Tychyna enter the phase of a true "borderline situation" which has lasted for twenty-five years.

Will his life appear longer as a result of that crisis? And if not, how can he hand down to posterity a sign or proof that his spiritual suicide was not in vain? If he does not even hope to write for the drawer for future generations, as Shevchenko did, then his state of mind must be one that no pen could describe.

MYKOLA CHVYLOVY, OR "DEATH DEFEATED BY DEATH"

This controversial figure posthumously won two epithets: Stalin called him a "literary bandit," while part of the émigré Ukrainian press accused him of being a "Communist matricide."

In reality, Chvylovy was quite modest, a devoted son and a friend faithful to the extreme. On the other hand, the manly sincerity of his works combined lyricism with biting satire and irony. At a time when Stalin had not yet been deified and no one foresaw the new crisis, Chvylovy proclaimed the slogan "Long live disorder" and threw the whole weight of his talent into the struggle against the all-embracing whirlpool. His was not only a critical negation but also a program and the act of a great "beginning." Chvylovy was certain of two things: the triumphant early rebirth of the captive nations of the East, and his own premature death. These two convictions gave rise to two contradictory feelings which run parallel through his works: joy in the rebirth and a painful premonition of doom. Fate gave him only six years (1921–26) for his writing and the formulation of his confession of faith.

The seven years that followed were a period of struggle conducted first in stubborn silence and terminated by a bullet through
the head. But, filled with inspiration, Chvylovy managed in the
course of those six years to publish nine books (the rest of his
literary production, including two long stories, was destroyed with
their author) and to create his own literary school and style. His
style, the so-called "romantic vitalism" or "active romanticism,"
represented the direct opposite of the "Socialist Realism" of the
Stalinists. In his satirical works he succeeded in exposing the
ethical vacuum of communism. He led thirty of the greatest
talents in the Ukraine in a break from the Party and formed the
strongest, most radical of the literary groups, VAPLITE. He cast a
living seed into the mind of youth, presenting his program in a
few words: Know how to think and feel. He resisted Moscow's
claims to cultural hegemony, proclaimed loudly his battle cry
"Away from Moscow" and advocated an alliance with "Faustian"
Europe, predicting the coming of the "Asiatic Renaissance" as the
Spring of Peoples in the East. The Party threw the whole weight of
its apparatus into the struggle against "Chvylovism," but it spread
to the other Soviet republics. Then Stalin decided to intervene
personally and Chvylovy was condemned. The verdict reached him
in Vienna where he had gone for a cure in January, 1927. The
writer was confronted with an "ultimate decision." He could have
remained abroad, but this would have meant deserting the ranks
which he himself had formed and led into battle. From Vienna he
wrote an "act of contrition" for the Soviet press, in which he threw
himself upon the "mercy of the Communist party." From that
moment on he was dead as a writer.

But this was not all. If he returned from the West, it was not to
bask in the sunlight of "Communist mercy." The Party ordered
him to write a new book in the spirit of Socialist Realism. Chvylovy
never carried out this order. In the meantime a new cataclysm
erupted and an avalanche burst upon the Ukraine. Just as mass
arrests were beginning among Ukrainian intellectuals Chvylovy,
who had recently returned from a tour of the Ukrainian villages
devastated by the deliberately induced famine, invited some of his
fellow writers to his home on the pretext of reading his new book.
That was on May 13th, 1933. Gay and sparkling as always, he
excused himself for a minute and went into the next room to
get the manuscript. There he shot himself. On the table lay letters
to his friends and to the Communist Party. The one for the Party,
written in "his own blood," was truly heart-rending and was taken
by thinking youth as a heroic declaration of independence. Since
then, for a quarter-century, the Kremlin has hunted down the

ghost of Chvylovy in the Ukraine, always raising a hue and cry against the "seeds of Chvylovism."

Tychyna, who did not belong to the Party, arrived at communism. Chvylovy, who was a Party member from 1919 on, left it. The whole threat of Chvylovism lies in the fact that its creator was a Communist and yet found in himself enough strength and courage to break away from his own ideological roots.

In the story *My Istota*[1] Chvylovy gave a classic portrayal of the division within an individual soul torn by the forces of self-destruction. "I am a Chekist but I am also a man" says Istota, chairman of a Chekist tribunal since 1919. All the other characters in the story symbolize the two halves of the hero's soul. The members of the tribunal stand for the Chekist line: Doctor Tahabat, whose appearance and pitiless rationalism remind the reader of Lenin, and a sentry named "Zvyrodnialtsa" ("Degenerate") who personifies the extreme point of the Chekist line. On the human side stands Andrey, a young student rebelling against his compulsory attachment to the Cheka tribunal (which he calls a meat-grinding machine). The human line culminates in the figure of the hero's mother, who in the eyes of her Chekist son grows to the dimensions of a "miraculous Mary" standing on the border of unknown centuries." The tragedy develops swiftly and inexorably: Istota struggles with himself pulled by two magnetic poles. On one side is the ethics of the distant goal, the Utopia of "unattainable communism behind the distant hills, a paradise created by man." On the other is his loving and beloved mother for whose sake eternal Mary lives on, the symbol of the divine origins of the world. The Nietzschean "love for the distant" is opposed to Christ's "love for one's neighbor"—two feelings which are irreconcilable and yet exist side by side within a single human soul. What is the solution? The Chekist tribunal led by Istota orders a group of nuns to be shot, and among them is Istota's mother. Under the force of Tahabata's logic, Istota kills his mother with his own hand, pressing her to his breast in an attack of hysteria. Then the hero is forced by enemy troops to retreat north into the moonlit night. The tragic moon over his native village changes before his watery eyes into the magic flame of "unattainable communism."

This is the destruction of life itself, of its truest and deepest roots. In this story Chvylovy breaks open the nut of communism and shows that it is empty, devoid of ethical content. At the same time he has drawn the figure of the mother in the foreground as that "Ewig Weibliches" with which Goethe ended Faust's search. The image of the mother introduced by Tychyna and Chvylovy started

1 Istota—essence, being.

a real epidemic in Ukrainian literature of the 1920's. Almost every writer of the period wrote at least one work in which the figure of the mother was central.

MYKOLA KULISH, OR "THE ROAD TO GOLGOTHA AS THE ULTIMATE DECISION"

Mykola Kulish, born in 1892 and last heard of from the camps at Solovki on June 15, 1937, was a close friend of Chvylovy. The writers had many things in common, including an innate personal modesty and a decorous, chivalrous manner. Kulish, like Chvylovy, had been a Party member since 1919. As artists, both liked the pathetic style, with the difference that Chvylovy's pathos was embittered with irony and sarcasm or else burned with the pure fire of tragedy, while Kulish interjected accents of humor and tragicomedy into his romantic pathos. The difference between their respective "ultimate decisions" derives from this subtle dissimilarity in their talents. The outwardly even-tempered Kulish even differed from his friend who was endowed with an unusual temperament. And, unlike Chvylovy, Kulish was unwilling to be drawn into political discussions, although his comedies and tragicomedies were highly charged politically. He made his debut with the play *Ninety-Seven* in which against the background of the mass famine and bestiality of 1921, Kulish shows how humanity succeeded in maintaining an unusually high spiritual and ethical level at the very moment when its last spark of life was being extinguished. In the tragicomedy *The People's Prophet*, which in plot and insight is twenty years in advance of Giraudoux's *The Madwoman of Chaillot*, Kulish depicts the schizophrenia created by the social reforms of the Revolution. Like Chvylovy, Kulish, a Communist, pointed out the bankruptcy of communism in general and Ukrainian communism in particular.

The Spanish philosopher Ortega y Gasset says that during a period of crisis it is not known what man really is and what his true ideology should be. What seems simple for everyone on close examination becomes a complicated problem and vice versa. In the midst of this chaos art becomes the first link joining man to his own ego and to reality. *My Istota* by Chvylovy and Kulish's *The People's Prophet* represented the first vigorous confrontation of Soviet man with reality and with himself, an eruption which came from within to burst open the petrified shell of Communist dogma and system. It is not surprising that these works brought about the spiritual ebb of communism in the Ukraine.

The Party was merciless in its attacks on Kulish. Scandals and violence accompanied every premiere of his plays. He was especially criticized for bringing up the sensitive problem of nation-ality in the USSR. This problem was treated in his play *The Pathetic Sonata*, which was a direct response to Bulgakov's *The Days of the Turbins*. Tairov directed *The Pathetic Sonata* in Moscow; the premiere enjoyed an overwhelming success, but the play was soon after removed from the repertoire. It was never put on at all in the Ukraine.

"Only the man who mounts the scaffold and makes a speech looking death in the face will conquer through his idea." These words are spoken by Marina, the heroine of *The Pathetic Sonata*. On June 19, 1931, they were delivered from the stage of a Moscow theatre and three years later, in the prison of the NKVD Kulish had to supply a concrete meaning to his heroine's proud "ultimate decision" by his own actions. How did he do this? In 1933, after Chvylovy's suicide and in an atmosphere of wide-spread terror and despair, Kulish's wife hid his revolver. The author of *The People's Prophet* reassured her, "Don't worry, I won't follow in Chvylovy's footsteps. I'll find enough strength within myself to hold out to the end." He was finally arrested and put into the camps at Solovki. News of him stops in 1937 and from then on nothing more of him is known. For twenty years it was not even permitted to mention his name. Recently, *Literaturnaya Gazeta* carried the following notice, "A special committee has been appointed to make an inventory of the literary heritage left by M. Kulish." In the jargon of the Kremlin, this means that the writer whom Moscow theatre critics once called "the greatest dramatist in the Soviet Union" had been physically wiped out by his torturers.

TEODOZY OSMACHKA OR "WEAKNESS AS THE ULTIMATE ESCAPE"

Teodozy Osmachka is the only one of our four poets who survived his ordeal both physically and as a poet.

This truly invincible poet was one of the first candidates to be "put against the wall"—and yet he did not agree to the slightest compromise. With the obstinacy of a peasant he remained true to his convictions as a singer of individualism and the search for truth. During a period of universal self-criticism on the part of writers, Osmachka, though threatened by pistols pressed to his temples, refused to utter a word. When arrested, he feigned mental illness. Tortured by examining judges and madmen in the psy-chiatric hospital of the NKVD, Osmachka in the course of many years touched the depths of hell, and only during the German occupation of Kiev in the fall of 1941 did he return to the outside world. He was free, but instead of the sun of freedom he found himself in the murky darkness of the most atrocious of wars. He escaped to the West, realizing his long cherished dream of presenting to the world the truth that the "borderline situation" of a man knows no limits.

One of the leading poets in his native land, in emigration he held a leading position in contemporary Ukrainian literature by his three volumes of verse and three novels. But there is something unfathomable in his poetry and prose, because the infernal situations of human existence which he describes are unfathomable and will remain forever the curse on his soul. You cannot pretend certain things and remain unscarred by them. A man of an amazing sincerity, an ardent heart, and gigantic metaphors, he bit deeply into the live body of the devil and in his despair often threatens the entire universe and God himself. Osmachka is a mixture of fierce hatred and lack of faith and a longing for lost love. There are flashes of genius in him, but in the impenetrable darknesses of night. In any case, we are dealing here with a truly indestructible force.

And in the borderline situation of the 1930's it was this same force which sought escape in "weakness." In Osmachka's autobiographical story *The Rotunda of Murderers* the hero, the writer Ivan Brus, has the following thoughts on the night before his arrest: "To struggle against danger is the same as to fall from an airplane onto the surface of the sea, there to struggle against the waves . . . There exists another power which can defy the forces which destroy life . . . It is weakness . . . No one ever fought against weakness . . . But instead, since the fifteenth century Christian civilization has sent crusaders to come to the aid of weakness. But what kind of weakness should one have? Obviously one which is repeated from generation to generation: mental illness. And Ivan Brus decided to simulate schizophrenia . . . Then he would even be able to come to terms with certain people and could feel himself a soldier in the trenches fighting against historical injustice, although at times pessimism born of contact with real life would try to persuade his heart to abandon resistance . . . And Ivan Brus nervously rubbed his forehead with both hands . . . This would be his path of salvation and struggle . . ."

Ivan Brus drank the bitter cup of his "ultimate decision" to the last drop. When all their attempts to detect his pretense had failed, the inquisitors transferred the writer from the prison hospital to behind the walls of an insane asylum.

Four writers, four types of "ultimate decisions." Tychyna chose to play the devil's game—the poet became the commissar. Chvylovy gave a concrete meaning to his uncompromising stand; by physical destruction he conquered spiritual death. Kulish pronounced his credo looking death in the face and with humility bore his cross to Golgotha. Osmachka hid his infinite strength under the mask of weakness. But behind these four stood hundreds of other writers and thousands of other intellectuals.

On June 20, 1954, The Association of Ukrainian Writers, "Slovo," sent the following telegram from New York:

Moscow, USSR. Second Congress of Soviet Writers.

Ukrainian writers abroad greet the Congress and express their deep solidarity with the writers of all the captive nations of the USSR. In 1930 the works of 259 Ukrainian writers were published. After 1939, of those 259 writers, 36 were left. You must carry out an investigation into the police organs to find out why and under what circumstances 223 writers vanished from Ukrainian literature.

Because no answer was given to this telegram, *Slovo* published in the press the following communique:

The losses to Ukrainian literature can be enumerated as follows: 17 writers were shot, 8 writers committed suicide, 175 writers were deported or removed by other police methods, 16 writers disappeared without a trace, and seven died natural deaths.

With this handful of statistics which are admittedly neither complete nor conclusive, as they only refer to the best known Ukranian writers, we can conclude our examination of the problem of man's spiritual position in a "borderline situation" when society is crumbling under the blows of the forces of destruction, when even the factor of public opinion ceases to matter and man can depend only on his individual resources, on his own "ultimate decision."

Can "spiritual man" triumphantly survive the trials of an inhuman situation? In the quiet of one's room sitting before one's desk, it is easy to reply optimistically "Yes" and even easier to utter sceptically "No." It is more difficult to get to the bottom of unexplored reality. As far as I am concerned, there is no doubt about one thing: "Spiritual man" of the East is not only continually confronted with "borderline situations" but is also always being reborn in the embrace of death. As we have had the opportunity to show, he knew how to express his faith in rebirth. In the name of that rebirth, he also knew how to destroy his own soul— completely alone, in the darkest night of Soviet Eurasia, there "where birth and death sleep in one shroud."

Translated by Colleen Taylor

SOME CONTRADICTIONS IN MODERN ART

Konstanty A. Jeleński

FROM AMONG the many ways of describing the evolution (or involution) of contemporary art, I should like to choose an absurd one that makes this movement seem logical and that led lyrical abstraction (in the sense of Action Painting, Tachism, *Art Autre*, etc.) to its triumph (and failure). It is the story of a contemporary painter who discarded one burden after another so that he might feel free.

First he discarded the subject (or object) in his paintings. For so many centuries the painting of the subject had produced the painting; the painting had contained the subject within itself. In turn, he discarded the picture, leaving the canvas that then served as a material base for an existential gesture. Next, he gave up the canvas for the bare, uniformly blue or white walls (Yves Klein) where the existential gesture still functioned in the color. But why bother with color? The gesture of choosing, of making the decision (now the only important consideration) could be demonstrated by stuffing the "box" with an accumulation of common, banal subjects. This return to the subject (fortunately, the subject was not being "represented") was considered yet another burden. What emerges, at least, from this return is Neo-Realism or the New Realism. The painter eventually came to the pure event. (American happenings are psychodramas played in art galleries.)

The painter in the story is so unburdened now that he looks around for his easel, paints, and canvas. Who knows, perhaps he will return to his picture, maybe even to the subject, before he again feels they are a burden.

This story requires a commentary. That commentary will be

some observations on the contradictions that modern art, in the fifty or so years of its existence, produced from within itself without giving those contradictions very much consideration.

PAINTING OR ANTI-PAINTING?

Since the beginning of the twentieth century, there have been two currents in contemporary art that are in opposition to one another, though not always consciously. One of them is the trend of "pure painting," art for art's sake, *Peinture-Peinture*, under the seal of Cézanne and Maurice Denis. The second, paradoxically, seems to be trying to destroy painting through painting, or to be using painting to realize a particular concept of man. In the first, the painter serves the painting; in the second, the painting the painter. The object of the first is the "perfect painting." In the second, intention and choice are important; however, most important is the act of painting. The painting is a by-product. At best, it is a kind of evidence.

At the bottom of the first current, obviously, is Maurice Denis' famous *Définition*: "Remember that the picture of a battle-horse, a naked woman, or some incident is in the first place a plane covered with colors put on in a particular order." All this began so very calmly. Cézanne's first apples conformed *consciously* to a general understanding and perception of apples (as did Manet's naked women). But soon those apples were swept from the table (and the naked women from the beds). Even apples and women as Denis described and conceived them were swept away. Nothing was to tear the viewer's attention from the composition of space and color. The vulgarizers of modern art frequently annotated Uccello's *Battle* in terms that made it appear to be a nearly perfect abstract painting. Why not complete it by removing the horses and travelers? Why these pretexts? These circuitous roads? Once these are eliminated, one can paint the painting. The present crisis in painting is paradoxically connected to the understanding among painters of what painting is all about. In the Western tradition painting was a process of creation similar to alchemy. Today, we know that the alchemist accomplished a series of material operations without knowing what the "philosopher's stone" was. The point of his efforts was to find that "stone." In contrast to the alchemist, the painter often found his "philosopher's stone" (the miracle of painting). But that "miracle" was not the final achievement in itself; it was, in a way, an unintentional reward. The painter painted a picture, putting into it all of his potential. The painting itself lay at the end of a long voyage whose actual destination was not known. Every so often, the values upon which the painting were supposed to depend were stored in the hold during this voyage, and the painting itself survived somehow. What then is painting? We shall ask past generations and they will reply: *Cose sublimi, maniera nobile, thèmes dignes d'être peints*, feeling, psychology, reality—never painting. But for Cézanne painting mattered, and Maurice Denis knows this. Elie Faure and Worringer finally codified that principle (long before their popularizer Malraux did): painting is the play of space, form, and color. Why make a long, exhausting voyage if one can call up a miracle consciously?

But contemporary art was not satisfied to launch an attack against "pictures" in order to liberate "painting." That is not the only contradiction in contemporary painting, for soon after it turned against painting itself. The Futurists naively, Dada treacherously, and Marcel Duchamp and Picabia consciously introduced the notion of anti-painting. Now, not only are the apples swept from the table, but also the perfect composition of space and color is swept away. Duchamp divides painting into "retinal" (*peinture rétinienne*) with or without apples, because for him what is especially important is space, color, and "cerebration" (*peinture de la matière grise*). He will eventually throw away his palette and brush for a game of chess, and will shout: *C'est fini, la Peinture!*

Of these two currents, the first, which at the dawn of contemporary art was exalted because it annihilated the subject of the painting, and the second, which annihilated painting itself for the sake of the painter's freedom—his choice, ideas, and caprices—obviously the second one tipped the scales in favor of abstract painting in that triumphant period after the last war that seems to have passed so imperceptibly under our noses a few years ago. Today, where do we find painting that has conscious aesthetic values, that can make its point directly without the mediating aid of a subject? The first current found its ultimate expression in geometric abstraction, which has a marginal existence in the optical illusions of Vassarely. On the other hand, one forgets easily how much so-called post-war lyrical abstraction (Tachism, Action Painting, *Art Brut, Art Autre*, and so on) is the fault of Dada and the surrealists.

These two quotations from Aragon's *Peinture au Défi* (1930) will suffice:

1. "Undoubtedly, when Picabia spoke about the ink spot he signed, he was pointing out the characteristic of *not being able to imitate* that splotch. He congratulated himself that no one could

copy his ink spots as well as they could a painting by Renoir. And so it is that basic criticism of painting, from its dawn to our time, has become influenced by Picabia's endeavor."

Wouldn't the young Tachists find something to ponder here?

2. "Some important stages of this process have been Duchamp's adding a moustache to the Gioconda and signing it; Cravan's signing his name to a urinal; and Picabia's signing an ink spot and calling it 'The Blessed Virgin.' For me these are the logical consequences of *collage*. What has now been established is the negation of technique, as in *collage*, and at the same time the negation of the personality executing that technique. The painter, if we are still to call him such, is no longer connected to his painting by some mysterious, physical relation analogous to birth. Instead, from these negations arises an affirmative idea that is the *personalization of the functioning of choice*."

Wouldn't the young Neo-Realists find something to ponder here?

The truth is that since turning from an idea of painting as "static beauty," the sources of aesthetic pleasures have been strengthened since the last war by a new argument: existentialism. When we see today's (or yesterday's) splashes by the Tachists (they really have ancient ancestors) filling miles of walls in museums and galleries from Valparaiso to Reykjavik, we can not forget that the "ancestors" in this case are two phenomena of exceptional importance: Jackson Pollock and Wols. About Wols, his friend and chosen witness to that era, George Mathieu, writes: "In this work, he engaged in a decisive struggle with existential honor, this work of tragic freedom, of living freedom, that was supposed to wipe away what was left of the western awareness of existence."

New American painting is indebted to Harold Rosenberg and his article ("The American Action Painters," *Art News*, 1952) for its name Action Painting. In that article Rosenberg did an analysis of painting using a method he borrowed from Heidegger and Sartre. "At a certain time," he writes, "for one American painter the canvas seemed to be a canvas, while for another it was, instead of a plane, an arena intended for action, an arena in which to create, to analyze, or to express the realistic or imaginary subject. What is put onto the canvas from that time forward is not a painting but an event."

Actually, not only the most actute critics of this "formless" (*peinture informelle*) school (a term that takes in Action Painting, lyrical abstractionism, and Tachism), but also the artists themselves have often repeated to us during the past fifteen years that what is significant for them is not the picture but the act of painting it. On the other hand, only a few exceptional and honest minds like Harold Rosenberg had the courage to draw the logical consequences from such an artistic stand and to admit that such a stand precludes the use of all aesthetic criteria for painting. If the point of "formless" painters is not art, but the revelation of what they are (probing their identity) through a series of more or less spontaneous "acts" (spontaneous because they are uncontrolled), and that this revelation is helped by putting paint onto canvas, then the painting, once painted, is a by-product of this existential form of seeking one's self. Rosenberg admits that "If the picture is an act, than it is not possible to give reasons for its *being an act of genius* in a certain genre because the apparatus for judging it has gone to hell. Its value must be found beyond art."

Mary McCarthy made a famous response to Rosenberg's analysis: "One cannot hang an event on the wall, only a picture." The point is that the owners of art galleries and the painters themselves sell paintings and not events. Collectors and museum directors also want to buy paintings. It is not strange, then, that the defenders of "formless" art continue to bow in the direction of Maurice Denis' *Définition*. A keen mind like Georges Mathieu became oriented in the situation early. In 1947, he had already designated as "dangerous" the positions of Arp and Bryen who "recognize *existence* as the only criterion." In 1948, "foreseeing the anarchy that will result from similar positions" (this time the reference is to the criticism of Michel Tapié and Picabia), Mathieu answered with *Freedom—a Desert*. Later he wrote: "For me, actually, overcoming the medium by producing a particular effect, or in other words, the achievement of the maximum expression through the minimum means, i.e., the perfect matching of content to form, will remain the one *criterion* I shall defend against both Bryen and Tapié, who will open wide the gates for "formless" anarchy (*Au-delà du Tachisme*).

At least Mathieu has the illusion that his criterion is new. Clement Greenberg's answer to Rosenberg is very revealing in this instance. Greenberg is the one American critic who matches Rosenberg in prestige. They are almost a pair like Rosencrantz and Guildernstern in *Hamlet*. From the beginning, Greenberg was a warm supporter of the new American painting, and the New York School owes him a great deal. But, like Mathieu in France, Greenberg came to realize that Rosenberg was cutting the branch on which the whole organization of modern art was sitting—the museums, galleries, prices, criticism, art lovers, and the investors—from under himself. He decided to "break off" both the picture and painting.

"I do not see anything fundamentally new [in abstract art]," he writes in *Encounter*, "which one could not discover or which was not revealed in either Cubism or Impressionism, just as I do not seen anything basic in Cubism or Impressionism which one could not trace back to Giotto, Masaccio, Giorgione, or Titian."

Modern art sometimes says: I destroyed everything that came before me. But if that remark disturbs you, I will add: seriously speaking, I am also Braque, Renoir, Titian, Giotto. . . .

A CONTINUATION OR A REVOLUTION?

We see that the dilemma of painting vs. anti-painting comes to grips with another dilemma: continuation vs. revolution. More than half a century ago modern art announced its revolution. During this half-century the tradition of revolution has been established. Klee is revolutionary: "I want to be like a new-born child, not knowing anything, absolutely nothing, about Europe . . . I want to be almost primitive." Mondrian says the same thing, but differently: "The creation of something like a paradise is not impossible if one really wants it." Frequently, and it is the crux of the way of thinking in this century, revolutionary art and revolutionary politics join forces, as in the U.S.S.R. in 1917–1922.

The revolution in modern art wanted to overthrow aesthetics, as the Marxist revolution wanted to overthrow history. History, however, clings so obstinately to life in the Soviet Union; perhaps, similarly, aesthetics will continue to cling, at least in the sense that aesthetics does not seem to be divorced from human experience. Modern art contains this self-contradiction: While causing an insurrection against traditional art and always calling for the "end of art," modern art was simultaneously imposing itself as the only real art, and it endured. The "end of art" meant closing the doors of the past, but the doors of the future remained open. It meant revolution—but constant revolution. Frequently, then, "continuation" and "representational art" find themselves in the same bag through a misunderstanding. That is how Mathieu speaks of art "whose originality converged with the emergence of pictorial thought, and art that was the basic expression of man for man by helping to exhibit forms born in visible reality—that was art from the Quaternary to 1910." Mathieu adds that today we are "fifty years after the properly certified death of that art" (*L'Autopsie de l'Art Figuratif*, 1960). Here at least is a kind of simplistic division of art: from the Quaternary to 1910 and from 1910. . . .

This revolutionary credo can be embarrassing, especially for the revolutionary critic. Sir Herbert Read says in *The Philosophy of Modern Art*: "The modern movement in the arts which began to reveal itself in the first decade of the century was fundamentally revolutionary ... When I characterize this movement as *fundamentally revolutionary*, I attach a literal meaning to these well-worn words." As an art critic, Read states further, "My aim has been to represent a consistent revolutionary attitude." But in that same book Sir Herbert reflects upon whether surrealism (which according to his definition is "absolutely revolutionary") "is still art." "Just as we would not call 'science' a direction if it denied the acknowledgement of inductive proof, so we have the same right to deny the name 'art' to a direction that discards the law of harmony. . . ."

What kind of revolution can this be if from the Greece of Praxiteles an old friend—harmony—winks at us! That contradiction seems not to have been contraverted from the Quaternary to the fifth century B.C. In all his essays about art Jean Paulhan opposes, although he has a predilection for the cubists, the abstract or "formless" painters such as Bonnat, Meissonier, and Carolus-Durand. He treats them as though they were not the contemporaries of Degas. Are Manet and Renoir, whom he admires, not to be treated, in turn, as though they were contemporaries of Buffet, Carzou, and Jean-Gabriel Doumergue? Paulhan likes to mock the salon painting of the nineteenth century (*Peinture de Genre*): "Cardinals with Kittens," "First Ball Gown," "After the Betrayal," and "The Return of the Father." He surely thinks in this case that modern art is a springboard of the absurd. In the past few years, however, salon painting has been returning to the museums of modern art in a new form as Pop Art. David Sylvester, one of the devotees of Pop Art, writes: "Pop Art serves the same needs as the 'problem' paintings of the old Royal Academy, or as some anecdotal Victorian painting—'Last Day in the Old House,' 'Seeing Father for the Last Time,' etc." (*Sunday Times Magazine*, June 2, 1963). David Sylvester is one of the best western authorities on Malevich and Suprematism; he is the author of the best monograph of Henry Moore; and although it certainly does not matter here whether or not Pop Art has some kind of value, it is not insignificant that Sylvester admires the same artists to whose pictures Paulhan refers and who were the source of the same joke for Paulhan. The cardinals, debutantes, and prodigal sons that banal avant-garde criticism has always been using as a bugbear are now returning to the bosom of good company, to the rustle of the royal purple, to the coronets, through the great doors. . . .

The dogma of revolution in modern art and the uncertainty that influences it seem to me one of the chief diseases of art today.

THE ART OF ALL ERAS IS CONTEMPORARY

The contradictions and paradoxes do not end there. At the same time that modern art announced its break with the past, the parallel evolution of aesthetic consciousness uncovered not only the "past" in the sense of the western tradition, but also all pasts and all presents in all cultures. What's more, cave paintings, the masks of African witch doctors, the sculpture of Egypt and primitive Greece, Chinese painting and Byzantine mosaics, and utilitarian objects from the Polar regions achieved, all at the same time, the rank of "works of art" and on the same basis as modern works. The Futurists passionately wanted to burn down the Louvre. In 1913, Apollinaire's pamphlet screamed into the void *Merde aux Musées*. The museum was to be transformed into the museum of the imagination and was to greet the Futurists with open arms.

After Elie Faure and Worringer, the art of all eras became contemporary. In this enormous scheme for the history of an art that overthrew time and space, the contemporary artist was frequently helpful. The updating of history and the universalization of space are but one aspect of a process whose second aspect is the end of local western traditions.

Certain *moments* in modern art seem to put a spotlight on *moments* in the art of all times and places, and these moments come to be regarded as visible and actual. Cubist painting allowed for the discovering of such different works as African masks and the paintings of Paolo Ucello. Looking for ancestors, surrealism ministered to the rebirth of Bosch, while it recalled from obscurity Fuseli, Blake, and the German romantics. Action Painting and lyrical abstraction turned the interest of art lovers in the direction of the caligraphy of the Far East and the drawings of the masters of Zen Buddhism. In this way the aura of modern art takes in more than the works of the present. Ancient sculpture can be contemporary, just as Byzantine mosaics can. While modern art includes objects that never were considered works of art but served some purpose in magic or in everyday life, it has also added other objects that are not "art" or "works"—stones found on the beach, roots, bark, and strange pieces of junk from the trash heaps of factories.

But the spotlights work in the opposite direction, too. Over the years the enlightened contemporary artist has succumbed to the influence of the endless shuffling of centuries and continents that does produce an "artistic output," increasing the number of exhibitions dedicated to eras, schools, countries, and works, and that does cause these exhibitions to be sent around the world. The attention of the contemporary painter is brought to bear, sometimes notwithstanding, on various elements that painting always contains, but which certain painters, certain schools, and certain eras especially accentuated: again and again the focus is on color, structure, movement, space, imagination, and choices. We need only recall the influence on matter, resonance, and color in some "formless" paintings at exhibitions like the one of Spanish Painting in Paris in 1955, or the great retrospective show of Rembrandt in Rotterdam. We must be thankful to contemporary painters for a series of ectoplasms of Rembrandt, Goya, and Valdés-Leal. This phenomenon was especially evident at the Exhibition "Homenaje Informal a Velásquez" in Madrid in 1961, when on this occasion of the four hundredth anniversary of Velásquez's death, all the Spanish Tachists splashed and rubbed and poured paint (often with great taste) on the Infante, Bacchus, and Breda. . . .

CONTEMPORARY ART AND INDUSTRIAL SOCIETY

I have tried to point out the contradictions in contemporary art with regard to the concept of art and in view of tradition, continuity, and the past. There is another contradiction: the relation between the social implications of the present and the prospects for the future that are imposed by industrial society. If I return to ideas expressed in my article, "Pure Painting or Poetry," I do so because certain intuitions, in a field that is so hypocritical as art criticism, perforce repeat themselves as well as develop. In that article I proposed an approach to contemporary art that was in the form of an answer to the challenge thrown to the artist by the sociological mutations in industrial society (where the services and distribution sectors predominate over the productive sector). Such an answer can be either positive, an attempt to integrate industrial society into the frame of a new utopian mythology; or negative, that is, as a form of compensation. In either case, art acts as a storehouse of the eternal and individual mythologies of industrial society.

Abstract art was born under the sign of the positive answer. Futurism, Suprematism, and Constructivism were projections of the dreams of the utopian future fostered by the new technology. Machines and technology, however, are not only airplanes, radio-telegrams, automobiles, and reinforced concrete; not only that "electrification" that Lenin said need only be connected for the Soviets to enter the era of communism. The war of 1914–1918, the first industrial war, signaled new dangers: not only mass death, but also the anonymous social compulsion to scale unknown heights. Dada and the forms of surrealism that grew out of it, therefore, were a kind of unconscious protest against the anonymous power of technocracy and against the new forms of organization that do not help so much to broaden human freedom as to clamp new, subtle and inexorable bonds on man. Lyrical abstraction, whose connection with surrealism becomes more and more obvious, emerged after the last war as the final violent test for preserving individual freedom in its ultimate and fundamental fortress of instinct, the autonomy of dreams, and the unconscious.

Never has so much been said about the freedom of the artist as in industrial societies today, as though people felt the need to transfer their freedom to the artist who does not feel very deprived of it in his everyday life.

Since the end of the last war a young man may sometimes decide to become a painter not because he wants to reproduce his relation to the world in plastic form, but because among the many fields of endeavor, contemporary painting is where an aggressive temperament can find the most immediate and certain expression. We saw earlier that the most authoritative critics of Action Painting agree that such paintings cannot be judged by any other criteria than by tension and the intensity of the struggle taking place in the arena of the canvas. And so Kmicic,[1] one of the contemporary French types, still had a choice not so long ago: he could remain a paratrooper in Algeria or become a painter for the Stadler Gallery.

Incidentally, one of the characteristics of contemporary art is that painting, for instance, draws upon people who once found their outlet in other fields. I turn to a fact that grapples with yet a different problem: today painting is a means of expression for *intellectuals*. Frequently, writers and philosophers are also painters and vice versa. That is not all. These often charming characteristics of the petty, eccentric inventors, who for a hundred years have taken their ideas for an underwater fork, or a bicycle that converts to a camp bed, or shoes that are built on springs to the patent office, can lead the Neo-Realist painter to triumph. There is nothing very revealing in the resemblance of the eccentrics who display and have displayed their inventions for a hundred years at the *Concours Lépine* in Paris, to certain others who display theirs in the *Salon de Mai*. What would Casanova do? Would he risk the dungeons of Venice, get mixed up in some petty spy intrigue, or swindle at cards if he were alive today? The keenness of his mind, his spontaneity, his adventurousness, and the resources of his imagination would open all the art galleries and all the museums of modern art to him. Such a statement is not groundless. Yves Klein was the paid guard (with a revolver in his pocket) of politicians of various parties,

1 A bold, adventurous character from one of Sienkiewicz's novels. [ed.]

a professor of jujitsu in Madrid, and a novice in a Buddhist monastery before he converted to painting and made a brilliant career for himself in the last seven years. I know a group of young painters who have similar biographies.

But let us return to the problem of the artist vs. industrial society. The success of Pop Art in New York and London in the last three years gives the problem a new dimension. Little is known about Pop Art on the Continent—so little that an esteemed critic like Genviève Bonnefoy says that Pop Art is quite frankly the Anglo-Saxon name for Neo-Realism (*Les Lettres Nouvelles*, February, 1963). Pop Art in America is Ray Lichtenstein's gigantic, blown-up episodes from the comics and Wesselman's colored, glossy advertisements from *Time* and *Life* (somewhere between *collage* and *trompe-l'oeil*) of marvelous turkeys, fabulous ladyfingers, the most wonderful beer, and a cigarette as the key to success. In England it is Hockney's scenes from the life of the "new class" of the working aristocracy, an amusing commentary on the twist, juke boxes, and television.

We agree that mass culture is often kitsch. But kitsch became nature and entered the landscape. We can extract from kitsch the elements of the "opera fantasy" that Rimbaud saw in it. He said: "For a long time I have boasted of possessing all the possible landscapes and have found amusing all the notoriety of contemporary painting and poetry. I liked idiotic little pictures, wallpaper, sign boards, and small print. . . ." (*Un Saison en Enfer*)

Pop Art, in opposition to the argument stemming from Dada through surrealism to lyrical abstraction, is not at all opposed to industrial society and its superstructure—mass culture. It is the art of young people who since childhood have been brought up on television, the juke box, and advertising propaganda, and who, at best, try to turn their attention to the new elements of the landscape that ultimately have the same value for them as mountains, forests, cathedrals, and tenements. This amusing and by no means hostile commentary on mass culture is the first effort by American sociologists like Shils and Bell to oppose the elite criticism that considers this a new standard of amusement, variety, and communication among people. I consider Pop Art an authentic and witty form of social realism, and conclusive evidence that art is experiencing a profound crisis. The articulation of the sociological implications of Pop Art is, however, meaningful.

CONTEMPORARY ART AND POLITICS

The paradox of the revolutionary quality of contemporary art and of its duality in relation to industrial society is strengthened by an external factor: the alliance against contemporary art by all the authorities and powers who practice social order and naively believe in it. There is no doubt among today's Fascists and Communists that contemporary art is an "element of corruption." Among the various camps of liberals, the humanists argue the lamentable dehumanization of art, its "contempt for the public," and so forth. The argument is so strong that the Vatican, the American conservatives, and the readers of *Le Figaro* need only have police put at their disposal. The most frequent reaction by the self-esteemed intellectuals to the hostility to modern art of the fascists, Khrushchev, the Pope, and the simple-minded representatives of the western bourgeoisie is a shrug of the shoulders and ridicule. Such a reaction is proof of the total lack of respect for contemporary art and of its being shoved into the field of pure aesthetics, as though art were only a picture on a wall or literature merely a book on a shelf and not a measure of reality. Let me introduce a reservation, however. I do not for one moment believe that Hitler would not have carried on the war and would not have built Auschwitz and Bergen-Belsen if he had not liquidated *Entartete Kunst*. I am convinced that the Soviet abstract artists are not responsible for the problems in farming or for the dispute with China. But in a certain sense Hitler and Stalin were correct and Khruschev is correct: their societies support a fictional view of man to which contemporary art is not only strange but hostile. The "good thinking" western bourgeoisie demonstrate such a hostility. Neither Dada, nor surrealism, nor the post-war flood of Tachism came forward with anything new for the social order, which changes under other influences anyway. But for *Osservatore Romano, Le Figaro*, the Pentagon, Saint-Cyr, and for all who use the term "Christian civilization," the basis, and it is their conviction that it is also the reason, for running the machine of society is *values*, or the fictional view of man to which contemporary art is not only strange but also hostile.

Without question the common characteristic of contemporary thought, literature, and art is the struggle over the integration of all aspects of man, making man "whole" again. Marxist alienation, Freudian analysis, and Heidegger's "inauthenticity" dissect contemporary man; they are causing his internal dissolution. Marxism, psychoanalysis, and existentialism are different forms of searching for freedom and eliminating dishonesty. But the problems touching upon the freeing of man are more often the subjects of studies and theories rather than practice. *Practical Freedom* is revealed in literature (Joyce and Gombrowicz) and only sometimes in art (the surrealists). Actually, the work that says that "one must be freed" is stating nothing more than an open, enlightened humanism. This humanism bred values after the death of God; it was a secular form of morality. Consciousness and unconsciousness and being and existence were divided into upper and lower, showing that truth inheres in the lower level and that calling that level "lower" is a traditional error of humanism. A liberating work allows us in practice to come down to the lower level and to understand that we are not impoverished by being there, but enriched. Such a work does away with the artificial divisions among the various areas of human experience. But let us be more careful. No literary work, no work of art liberates our behavior; it does not knock down psychic walls. Liberation is at most its creator. In spite of everything, such a work is an *example* to the reader or viewer; for a brilliant moment it gives an intuition of what freedom might be. If it does not liberate the man who reads it or looks at it, perhaps, ultimately, it will contribute to the liberation of man. In a contemporary society that needs morality and discipline to function properly (to lengthen that period when production overtakes natural growth) works that liberate are dangerous.

Liberal society permits (even surrounds with esteem) all humanist undertakings that strive for the complete liberation of man now, when what is always at stake is liberation for some future time. Contemporary liberal society knows that it is mortal (this differentiates primitive societies from stable ones), and allows itself to contemplate at leisure the prospect of its death. This society was raised, in large part, on the spirit of historical experience; it knows now, for instance, that revolution does not overthrow morality and discipline but strengthens them. If western society does not feel endowed with a metaphysical mandate to allow it to suppress liberating works, that is, works that liberate immediately and knock the bottom out of morality and discipline, it is because that society raised freedom to its greatest value. Soviet society believes (or pretends to believe) that it is endowed with an analogous mandate and does not tolerate any liberating work. Here is the paradox of that society that derives its mandate from its mission to integrate man into his wholeness—at least from the Marxist point of view— but which, instead, actually discriminates against and excludes man more than any other contemporary society.

What kind of paradox results for the artist? In a liberal society an artist may produce a liberating work, and the indignation of the humanists may even sustain him for a while; however, sooner or later, greedy liberal society will shower him with prizes, money, and honors. In communist society, where the artist's work could have a certain revolutionary potential, the artist is quite frankly cut off from the public. In the last few years the situation in Poland has been the worst. (How superbly Milosz analyzed this situation in literature in *Kultura* not so long ago.) There the forms of freedom are, in general, respected so long as they are vacuous. One may use the language of contemporary art, but one cannot finish what one wants to say in that language.

CONTEMPORARY ART AND LITERATURE

There is no insult greater to the contemporary artist than to say, while making a face, "That is very literary." On the other hand, art has never been closer to literature than it is today. I recalled earlier that for the first time in years painting has converted openly to the *intellectuals' camp*. The intellectual is often a contemporary painter; he is always a lover of contemporary painting. In 1908, late as usual, Matisse wrote: "What I dream of is an art of balance, of purity and serenity devoid of troubling and depressing subject-matter, an art which might be for every mental worker, be he business-man or writer, like an appeasing influence, like a mental soother, something like a good armchair in which to rest from physical fatigue."

Exactly fifty years later, Jean Dubuffet announced the characteristic position of contemporary art: "Is art like a garden with garlands, a good bed, a luncheon for gourmets? We shall leave that for others. For us there are more adventurous seas, farther voyages . . . The work of art does not speak to the eyes but to the mind . . . The justification for its existence is to function as a connector of the high intensity current to the light that throws an unheard-of illumination on life and things. . . ." I open Mathieu's book on contemporary painting and *on one page* I find the following names: Parmenides, Empedocles, Plotinus, St. Gregory Nazianzan, Meister Eckhardt, Henry of Ghent, Siger of Brabant, Cantor, Gödel, Bohr, Heidegger, Dionysius the Areopagite, Nicholas of Cusa, Lupasco, Henry Lefebvre. . . . Such an intellectual company is hard to take. One of Mathieu's flashy essays is entitled, not more and not less than, "From Aristotle to Lyrical Abstraction." It turns out to be a devastation of western thought via Aristotle that has in part been rehabilitated by the ideas of Jackson Pollock, Wols, and the author himself. We know from another source (actually from the circles of the lyrical abstractionists) that Lupasco's prestige and his logic of contradictions were so great that painters considered his pictures a contribution to philosophy. The advancement of structuralism from Paris into the foreground of ideas by Lévi-Strauss (and the interest in structuralism by young, informed Marxists) led, in turn, to a structural interpretation of painting.

The most advanced artists see in their paintings a relation to the work of ethnologists like Dumézil or economists like C. G. Granger on the pretext that structuralism relies upon functional analogues and not substantial ones. Art can be most literary when it has forgotten about painting scenes from [Henryk Sienkiewicz's] *Quo Vadis.*

CONTEMPORARY ART AND NATURE

Although art has never been at such a distance from the subject as in its "formless" phase, it has, at the same time, never been so close to nature. That statement seems paradoxical. Isn't nature made up of objects and subjects? Nature is not, however, only a cliff. A cliff is, above all, a slowly made formation of crystals. A tree is a life-giving thing that makes chlorophyll. The non-representational painter does not want to "paint nature"; his object is, through the medium of painting, *to create* like nature.

It has been noted more than once (this universal observation has been misused in a number of prefaces) that "formless" paintings are like photographs of bark and trees, and microphotographs of tissues and the internal structure of metals, and macrophotographs of the heavens. Certainly this mimesis in painting of the deep processes of nature has filled a void in our daily lives. As the anonymous mass of artists covers the revolving planet, depriving us of immediate contact with the organic world, eliminating those raw, plastic ideas that are rough trees, a porous stone, mildew lichens, or spots of moisture on the walls, it is not so strange that an art should have been created for Antaeus who was not able to touch the ground. In the same way Dubuffet's paintings are "stones in a salon," and Burra's rags in the skyscrapers of the Milanese bourgeoisie prevent contact with the waste being eliminated without trace from a series of mechanical gadgets. Characteristically, if the "formless" artist turns to the material and industrial works of man, then his only point is the exploration of their waste by rummaging through their garbage. The "formless" painter also filled a void left in the poetical and imaginative experience by the decline of craftsmanship. The profound function of craftsmanship was to act as a medium between consciousness and matter, nature, and substance. "Formless" art undertook the function of expressing once again matter in its fluid and unstable form.

But in order to open (or to tempt to open) the creative processes of nature, the painter has to do away with consciousness and produce within himself an emptiness that will allow him to plunge headlong into the power of instinct. It seems to me that the "formless" painter accepts the paradoxical humanist position against his will, for the fact remains that he himself, the whole man, is nature, nature with intelligence, awareness, and the ability to choose. The creative process of the "formless" painter deprives him of those resources by which nature can express itself exclusively through man without competition from anyone or anything in the world. If a volcano makes lava better than man, it is because the volcano has more strength and time. The internal structure of metal and of mineral strata is made up of thousands of years of fine precision sedimentation.

We see that the artists are not in competition with nature, which is really impossible, but are evolving a new mythology. This mythology is linked to the exhibition of post-war American painters. The act of creation for the "formless" artist is not so much the beginning of a work of art as an action, an action that is important in itself and has sacral elements. The act of the painter is like a prayer, in that it aspires to a different and universal existence, to the cosmos, and to the absolute. But such acts are actually states of being and their nature is close to what we know about mystical experience. It is not strange, then, that in the vocabulary of "formless" painters appear allusions to all the mystical traditions. Siger of Brabant and Meister Eckhardt are the patron saints of Georges Mathieu. Action Painters ponder the Vedas. Not so long ago every foolish preface by a third-rate Tachist referred to Zen or the Tantraic mystics. The transfer of the sacral elements to painting is generally well known, for it is the chief (vague) thesis of Malraux as art historian. In all civilizations, however, sacred arts and rituals played their part in dance, music, orgies, prayers, and liturgical ceremonies. *In time, the act of painting comes to play its part; later, the painting cools off, immobile in space.* At this point, if the sacred potential of painting is what matters, that potential seems very limited—one can repeat a prayer endlessly, or the music of a jam-session endlessly, but the problem in painting is more complicated, for one can only live through an act of creation that is at every moment becoming static under the hand of the artist.

"Formless" art wanted to take on the dynamic function of joining itself to nature, in its ceaseless work, and the function of the world of panic. The one indispensable function of art, however, is the evocation of static uniqueness.

IS ART DEAD?

Let us return to my little story. It has been going around in my head for a few years, from the time, after fifteen years of Tachist euphoria, when a certain anxiety began to reveal itself among some of the most engaged critics and among some of the painters, too. The last Venice Biennial was a sheer disaster—the Waterloo of Tachism after so many Austerlitzes. This anxiety was reflected by the art lovers, business, and prices. Napoleon's and de Gaulle's one principle for art—*L'Intendance suivra*—really applies here. When prices entered the game, the press became interested, so that in the course of the last year dozens of naive articles have appeared about the crisis in abstract painting, the return to the subject, and so on. One of the most overplayed banalities is that "formless art has become academic." In a certain sense academism is always one of the roads open to every artistic style in its decline. A second, frequently wonderful result is mannerism. Thus far I have tried to show that the accelerated decline of "formless" painting is not due to some general laws, but is connected to a certain internal logic of that painting itself (often in its most interesting manifestations). "Formless" art attempted to achieve a continuity of gesture, to mingle in the streams of painting, but the bounded rectangular frame of the painting destroyed its internal dynamism. If Vladimir Slepian, a young Russian abstractionist, devoted two or three years to painting a canvas a few kilometers long, pouring paint on it from a truck, it was not for the scandal that he might provoke but because his logical (contradictory) idea (in the Soviet Union he was a mathematical philosopher) led him to the apparent resolution of one of the contradictions. I also appreciate Mathieu's speed record for having painted a picture of the ceiling of the Paris Opera on a Tokyo street in half an hour. The futile, caricature-like quality of these efforts allows one to understand why, after Pollock and Wols and after fifteen years of exploring all the possibilities of gestures in the arena, the Tachist who still politely associates himself with the little arena of a bounded canvas is condemned to dullness, superficiality, and banality. The Tachist academy is condemned to a quick death. At the same time, Tachism has certainly produced some more interesting mannerists. Yves Klein threw gold dust about and sold his "gesture" (for the price of a painting) to naive (or perhaps rather eccentric) collectors. Alberto Greco and his Arte Vivo School gave their "signature" to lived-through or experienced situations and to scenes glimpsed or seen on the street—these are their "paintings." These paths reach the height of dandyism. I do not use the term in a negative sense, not only for the sake of Baudelaire's memory. These paths, however, are blind alleys. The other paths that emerge from "post-tachism" seem to me to be regressions. Neo-Realism is a return to Dada; Pop Art is a better, more authentic form of social realism; and non-representational art is the same old story of a return to post-impressionism and post-expressionism through pretentious pop artists via naive critics. I shall believe in neo-representational art when I see a "neo-nose," a "neo-apple," or a "neo-chair." The darling of current Paris criticism, the ex-Tachist Bernard Dufour, paints women looking at themselves in mirrors, scenes of open windows, and combinations of mirrors and windows. It is evident to everyone that the pictures whose subjects (that's correct, subjects!) are mirrors, windows, but especially the mirrors and windows together have a certain power of attraction. They are so attractive that in this kind of painting Dufour is much better than Czapski. Too bad that Czapski is not in his early thirties and that he never escaped from Tachism.

Is art dead? Or, are we at least at the end of an artistic era? We can not forget that in this time of crisis there are a few living painters whose prestige is growing and who make, in a sense, a new constellation, though they are very different from one another. While Picasso has made history, he is at once great and at as great a distance from us as Daumier and Courbet. Max Ernst, who is not much younger than Picasso, is also a painter of great talent. We add a few other names: Giocometti, Balthus, Francis Bacon, Brauner, and Dubuffet. What are the links between the completely representational Balthus and Dubuffet, who came so close to becoming a Tachist? First, neither one allowed himself to be drowned in the deluge of abstraction, and at the basis of their work is reality seen from a new point of view, one that implies objectivity and psychic distance. From the younger generation I would add John Lebenstein to this group. Clearly, I am not proposing a new school whose patrons would be these very different painters. On the contrary, I was quite frankly appalled at the last *Salon de Mai* by the imitators of Francis Bacon. I also know of the very banal imitators of Lebenstein in Poland and even in Venezuela and Korea. For someone to follow in the footsteps of Balthus, someone without his talent and his "being," is probably to produce kitsch. In spite of all, the position of these painters is in a certain sense an *example*, an example of the freedom of the imagination, of the freedom to act, and of not giving in to the fads of the times. I dream of a time when painters will again paint what they want, how they want, without outside pressures (governments, galleries, and museums), and without internal censorship (intellectualism and snobbism). The two worlds—one, the day with its new look on the horizon of reality, and the other, night with all the fetishes of our time—remain inexhaustible.

Translated by Hubert Babinski

HOW CAN ONE NOT CRY OUT?

Józef Czapski

The entire world press reported an event which took place the third of January of this year in Moscow: thirty-two sectarians (Evangelists) called on the embassy of the United States of America with a request for asylum. This was the first time that this type of wholesale petition for help at a foreign embassy ever happened in Moscow. The Evangelists were handed over by the American authorities to the proper Soviet agents and were taken away under police guard to an unknown destination. The State Department, in refusing asylum to the Evangelists, who were requesting it on grounds of religious persecution, announced that it had acted on the basis of fixed instructions and regulations binding their diplomatic posts.

On the fourth and fifth of January, the whole press spoke of the incident. Certain newspapers also added that this news would undoubtedly receive *un énorme retentissement* in the world—colossal publicity. Beginning with the sixth of January, the press ceased to write of it, and the removal "to an unknown destination" of 32 "sectarians" (as they are called in Russia) was submerged, not only in France but in America, in millions of new sensational events, political, criminal, or the like.

We shall examine in detail the *facts* gleaned from overlapping and mutually confirmatory accounts supplied by various journalists.

At 9.30 *A.M.* on the third of January, 32 persons—men with their wives and children—from Chernogorska (Central Siberia, the Krasnoyarska district) reached the American embassy, in order to gain refuge, as has been stated, from religious persecution. After a distance of 3000 kilometers, after a four-day journey, this handful of mourners were begging for help *from those who believe in Christ*. The Americans took them to the embassy dining room, converted on the spot into a waiting room, and treated them to eggs, coffee, and toast. Meanwhile the officials of that self-same embassy ran and telephoned to apprise the Commissariat of Foreign Affairs of the situation.

At 11.30 *A.M.* Richard T. Davies, the political officer, returned in the company of two Soviet officials and conducted them to the room where the sectarians had been placed. We do not know how the "negotiations" between the Siberian men and the Soviet officials progressed in the presence of American diplomats. They continued an entire hour. At the very same time the ambassador, Foy D. Kohler, received a representative of the Commissariat of Foreign Affairs in his own office, while diplomats of a more subordinate rank prevented the penetration of self-invited journalists into the dining room. They were forbidden not only to photograph anyone and anything—having been forewarned that, in the event of their noncooperation, their cameras would be confiscated—but in addition the doors to the dining room (they were probably glass-paneled) were also shielded by a plywood screen.

At 12:30 *P.M.* embassy officials demanded that the journalists leave the embassy building; one of them conducted all the reporters out to the street. Not one of the journalists had gained the right of meeting with or speaking to the refugees. Then, at last, before the locked doors in the courtyard of the building, Soviet officials, in company with embassy officials, set about loading the "sectarians" with their wives and children into a large Soviet vehicle. This process took another forty minutes. According to information included in the despatches, there were many heart-rending scenes then.

At 1:15 *P.M.* the vehicle began to move. Police dressed in plain clothes prevented anyone's approaching the vehicle during its departure from the embassy.

The journalists succeeded only in gathering the scraps of the sectarians' cries which were audible or which were repeated by embassy personnel. Many of them were sobbing, "We want to stay here; send us to any country whatever, where is all the same to us; there's no place for us here." Others were begging that they be sent to Israel; embassy officials were not sure whether they meant modern Israel or that biblical land "flowing with milk and honey" which nourished with hope the imaginations of those apart from the world, the diligent readers of and adherents to the Bible.

While they were being helped to leave the embassy they kept repeating, "We want to stay here; if you hand us over, we will all be shot. *You who believe in Christ*, help us." They all averred that the Soviet authorities wanted to take away their children.

Soviet officials promised the Americans that they would do no harm to these people, that they would only take them to a hotel—they even indicated which, the Northern Hotel. But the journalists who set out for that hotel were told that nothing at all had been heard of such guests. Official spokesmen, except for one representative of the Committee for Religious Affairs of the Council of Ministers, refused any explanations. He gave assurances that that committee would investigate and determine whether the local authorities were guilty of any abuses in the case of these people. But another representative *of that very same committee* categorically denied that the matter was in any way within the province of that agency and advised the journalists to return to the Commissariat of Foreign Affairs.

There officials refused to give any explanations.

But the next day—the fourth of January—that same Commissariat of Foreign Affairs informed the foreign correspondents that all the travelers from Chernogorska were already on the way back to their district. Of the whole incident the Soviet press gave not even an inkling; only the Soviet television and radio broached, during that same period, the subject of all the misdeeds and irregularities perpetrated in Soviet Russia by antisocial "sectarians."

And now let us imagine how these events of the third of January in Moscow really looked.

Writing about the contradictory explanations given to the correspondents, *Figaro* comments elegantly and diplomatically: "cette mise aux point laisse planer l'incertitude sur le sort reserve au réfugiés de Tchernogorsk"—or, in a free translation: "over the fate of the refugees from Chernogorska hangs a cloud of uncertainties." But here there is not a single uncertainty. The "sectarians" will pay for their frantic move, perhaps not by 10 to 25 years in a prison camp (the classic term of the Stalin period), but pay they will, severely and cruelly. In spite of great changes which have taken place (above all the cessation of mass deportations to prison camps—but was there a complete liquidation of these camps?), the liberalism of present-day Russia is still thousands of miles removed from what may be called liberalism in the western sense. The fate of Mme. Ivinska—Lara in *Doctor Zhivago*—her deportation for eight years to a prison camp immediately after the death of Pasternak—is an adequate and sufficiently well-known example.[1]

Today's difference from the Stalin period—aside from a certain liberalization—consists also of the more frequent substitution of hypocrisy for cynicism. Mme. Ivinska was convicted for violations of the currency exchange regulations—God forbid that it have

[1] The noble-minded, incisive article by Mme. Pelletier-Zamoyska in *Esprit*, accurately based, as it was, on the facts, gave the best possible account of the affair.

anything to do with Pasternak. The "sectarians," if advantageous
for the authorities, will be punished for other "crimes," and not for
seeking shelter in the American embassy. The Stalinist "vsyo
proglotyat," [2] as Stalin said about the reaction of the West to the
terror, thus becomes easier to swallow for us, looking after our own
good consciences, our clear consciences; for us who so wanted to
believe in the painless evolution of the Soviets and in all the little
"automatic machines of progress."

The official of the Commissariat of Foreign Affairs, negotiating
with the ambassador in the latter's private office, [3] those other
Soviet officials who, behind closed and screened doors, were
"persuading" the sectarians to leave the embassy are, after all,
certainly either NKVD operatives, under one cognomen or another,
to avoid recognition, or their outright agents. But the Americans,
having so hastily assembled the additional plywood doors so that
none of the reporters could either observe or overhear the *moans*
of these people, who at the risk of their entire futures, arrived
there seeking rescue; these diplomats [i.e. the Americans—trans.],
then, were most closely allied with the officials of the NKVD. The
liquidation of the unpleasant incident was in their mutual interest.
To the cry "You who believe in Christ, help us," the only answer
was the "Black Raven" [i.e. the Black Maria—trans.]—for so were
these vehicles, nowadays repainted in another color, called, twenty
years or more ago. So what if each president of the United States in
each speech talks about God and the fact that all religions have the
absolute right of existence in America.

The slander, at this same time, of the "sectarians" as an antisocial and criminal element is an altogether classic ploy. Long ago
the Roman Empire, on this very basis, used to sentence the first
Christians, who were suspected of all crimes; and this analogy is
not at all strained. These "sectarians" are the most defenseless of
defenseless people among the Soviets. They have no temples, they
have no church hierarchy on whom the persecution is concentrated
above all. The Orthodox Church (in the last three years alone three
seminaries, the Kiev and Pochayev Monasteries, and many churches
have been shut down) is still, in comparison with these, *considerably*
privileged.

In Solzhenitszyn's story *One Day in the Life of Ivan Denisovich*
we meet Alyosha, who is so close to Alyosha Karamazov; he was a
brother to these refugees from the embassy, deported with his

2 "They'll swallow everything."
3 Gian Carlo Menotti, in his *Consul*, over which for a year the New York public was
   moved to tears, presented a scene almost identical to this; but that was an opera—
   tears and emotions were in place.

coreligionists on account of his prayers; he continues to pray in the prison camp, concealing a copy of the Gospels in his plank bed, and comforts the others and augments their strength "with eyes like candles."

"Sectarians" were suppressed in Russia even in the time of the tsars. In those days there were a few million of them: from the Old Believers, the Khlysts, with their dark sexual undercurrent, from the self-mutilating Skopts-eunuchs, to sects approaching Protestantism such as Stundists, Adventists, Evangelists, Baptists, Dukhobors, and the like.

In 1895 the Dukhobors, who were settled in the Caucasus, threw into a fire the weapons which had been given to them for defense against bandits. They wished thus to manifest their absolute pacifism and refusal of military service. They were deported to Siberia, as today, and were imprisoned, as today. But over the course of many years writers, civic leaders, and politicians rose to their defense, examined their faith; even Rozanov, contributor to the reactionary *New Time* (Novoe Vremya), stood for their defense in a rational way. That repressive world provided them with friends, students, sympathizers, defenders. Tolstoy fought for them for years, most energetically and most effectively—he was then the world's unequalled moral author. He secured for the Dukhobors the right of emigration to Canada. Could that recollection have pushed today's Evangelists to the American Embassy?

Who is today interested in the religious sects of the U.S.S.R.? Even we have forgotten about them, despite the fact that, according to the Soviets' statistics, the number of Evangelists and Baptists is over 250,000.[4] For militant atheists their world is only medieval darkness which must, in one way or another, be annihilated in the name of progress.

Their slander by the Soviets is understandable. But why this silence about them in the rest of the world? Why this silence from the press of North America, with innumerable sects denominationally so close to the Soviet Evangelists? The pressure of official censorship is no excuse; the press there is really free. Lack of information? Fear that writing about them might harm them? Or is it simply indifference to events which are too far away? Is it not precisely by *silence* that we will harm them the most?

I have no intention at all here of burdening especially the conscience of the American ambassador in Moscow and of making him responsible for everything. What would I have done in his place? (Assuredly I would not have barred entry to the journalists,

4 According to our information, the sectarian movement within the territorial limits of the USSR is spreading in recent years with vital strength.

nor would I have ordered the erection of the plywood screens. But that is, in the final analysis, just a detail.) Would I have dared, moreover, in spite of the orders of my country, without a glance at the unpredictable political consequences of this act, to keep the sectarians in the embassy?

I am concerned here with an attempt to *evoke* a picture of what happened; with an awareness of what befell a group of people who believed that they would be saved by those who believe in Christ; with an awareness of our impotence—impotence verging on betrayal and present in every one of us. Where are those people who in truth "believe in Christ" and want to hasten to help, *exposing themselves*?

* * *

When "a certain man was going down from Jerusalem to Jericho and fell among thieves . . . a priest traveled that very same road and, having seen him, passed by. Likewise a Levite, having reached the same place, approached, and seeing him, passed by. But a certain Samaritan . . . seeing him, took pity on him. And coming up to him, he bound his wounds, pouring on oil and wine, and having laid him on his beast, carried him to an inn and ministered to him."

That priest, that Levite—they are all of us. Not just the Ambassador of the United States. That priest, that Levite likewise had a certain hierarchy of things; more important and pressing matters did not permit them, perhaps, to save the man on the road who "fell among thieves."

I know that more than one reader will blame me for the fruitlessness of my emotional reaction, but *how can one not cry out?*

When Mickiewicz, in 1848, in an audience with Pius IX, admonished him vehemently "to fulfill his obligations," he was reproached after the audience by Polish priests for shouting at the Pope. "And how can one not cry out," answered Mickiewicz, "when my fatherland is struck down?"

Today one need not be a Mickiewicz; it is enough to be the most ordinary of the men who traveled across Russia; to desire the same, and in the same helpless way to cry out after reading in the daily newspapers about the incident at the American Embassy.

In the name of higher—higher?—political and diplomatic ends, hope and mercy, the refuge of the innocent, were struck down. No one took pity on "the man who fell among thieves." Not a priest or a Levite, nor yet a Samaritan.

Translated by William J. Sullivan

MAKING A LIVING IN POLAND: HOW TO MAKE MONEY (WITHOUT TOO MUCH WORK, AND AS LEGALLY AS POSSIBLE)

*George J. Flemming**

As is commonly known, the minimum wage for Communist Poland, arrived at by the ceiling method (that is, dreamed up by staring at the ceiling) comes to seven hundred and fifty Polish złotys, and the statistical average earnings are about fifteen hundred złotys. It is easy to see that such sums do not even let you die decently, if we consider that a small plot of cemetery land costs anywhere from five to fifteen thousand. In the light of the above facts it becomes clear that no one in his right mind abandons himself completely to the mercy of an official income, but must work out his own methods, which do not always enjoy the approval of the Communist authorities, but which are extraordinarily valuable for physical survival.

The individualism of the Poles does not allow them to make use of stereotype methods, and the variety of ways to make money is unlimited. It could be said that there are as many methods as there are citizens supplementing their incomes, and the fact that during twenty years of building socialism the people have survived somehow is the best proof of the efficacy of the path chosen beside the main road.

We therefore reject with distaste all suggestions that we acquaint the reader with the distorted picture of the world as observed by the superficial spectator—which may be found in countless number

* A pseudonym of Jerzy Dzialek. [ed.]

235

of reports, articles, and books appearing in the West—and will occupy ourselves with more profound matters, the real essence of life. This will enable us to determine how thirty-two million people have managed to remain alive, to look healthy, and even to multiply in moments free from "shady moonlighting."

As mentioned previously—there are endless ways of making money. And they are not necessarily connected with the occupation forming the basis of one's income, which is used for the payment of rent, light, gas, heating, telephone, subscription to radio and television—because it does not stretch further than that. The rest, that is to say daily bread, decent clothing, and entertainment must be secured by other means.

If you have no definite profession, a technical one, for instance, enabling you to supplement your income in nearly limitless fashion—then it is necessary to look around in the closest proximity, where there is always a good opportunity for the willing.

In the deluge of exhibitions of all kinds—technical, trade, instructive, progress in development, and so on endlessly, opportunities invariably arise for an energetic person in the preparation of "scenarios" of the exhibitions. It is not necessary to be very knowledgeable for this; it is enough to know how many meters of stands or planks the exhibition is to run and what its subject is to be. Such an exhibition plan is of no use whatsoever to the artist who is to execute it technically, because who would even bother to read such nonsense, but the budget of the exhibition provides a certain sum for the scenario, and that is the whole point. A clever, sociable and industrious person can produce two or even four such scenarios monthly—and that already is not a bad income.

The State has the ambition—and even ideological compulsion— to take over everything and to invade every phase of life. This fact offers many possibilities for people with a head on their shoulders. If the State has money for everything and, what is more, wants to be the only mentor and instructor—it must be helped along. For this purpose a fellow who never in his life has seen how a well is dug begins to put out a mimeographed periodical, under the protection of the proper ministry, devoted to this most vital problem. The material is not hard to come by; it is enough to turn to the competent chair at the Cracow Mining-Metallurgical Academy, and to crib as much as one can, or rather *for* as much as one has to.

An acquaintance of mine, immortalized by Leopold Tyrmand in *Zły*[1] as Count Lolo, maintains a small turnery in his home, employing one laborer, and this deal enables him to produce medallions depicting Queen Nefertete or decorative belt buckles—and the

1 English title: *The Man with The White Eyes.*

income from this is sufficient to support his would-be wife with two children and her parents, his current wife and her parents, and his future wife—not counting his own costly way of life.

The Stalinist period was less favorable for people not endowed with talent, whereas those possessing talent could spread their wings far and wide. At one time during this period, the Central Council of Labor Unions had its own publication staffed with people who could not tell the difference between a linotype and a piano, and whose only occupation—according to the words of a certain gentleman—was to throw satchels of gold back and forth to each other; all that was required was that they enter at the proper moment to catch such a satchel in mid-air. This publication had an ambitious politico-publishing scheme, and at one time paid through the nose for a poem on Stalin numbering several hundred lines in print. The affair ended in scandal, when it was discovered that the poem had been dashed off by two hungry young poets in two days. This seemed suspicious not so much for artistic-professional reasons, but rather it was judged to be an insult to Stalin. (A poem about the Generalissimo in two days? Without the proper retreat to meditate?)

Of course, for lively minds there remain a great many ways to do little but to get some money out of it. For this purpose it is a good thing to become a wandering lecturer for *Wiedza Powszechna* (Popular Knowledge), for the Society of Polish-Soviet Friendship and the like, because then one can maunder on about any assigned subject in provincial club houses, reading rooms, and libraries at five hundred złotys an evening plus travel and hotel costs. There are masters of this art in Poland, who can give lectures on such seemingly divergent subjects as, for instance: the ballet, astronomy, the secrets of French cuisine, or the latest biological discoveries. I say "seemingly" because the secret is the ability to say nothing that could be attacked by anyone. It has been a disappearing profession, however, since specialization, backed by studies, began to be demanded from the meanest journalist.

One profession that does not require the slightest qualifications, is not badly paid, and entails very little work is the administration of organizations such as the Polish Committee of the Defenders of Peace, the Society of Polish-Soviet Friendship or Polish-other Friendship, the Society of the Science of Dog Breeding, the Hunting Association, the Fishing Association—although the last three must be a calling to some extent. Being a hunter one can live— and not badly at that—out of hunting for wolves and wild boar, for which there is no closed season, taking part in an expedition of the zoological museum to bring down the required specimen for a good price, and accompanying hard-currency hunters, when besides game it is possible to bring down a few dollars as well.

A person who knows foreign languages (that is, foreign to the lower classes) can spend his vacations as an *Orbis* (Polish Travel Bureau) guide, living and traveling at the expense of this institution, and can even earn the appreciation of the tourists from abroad, in the literal meaning of this word. Therefore—O tourist from abroad—regard such a guide as a poor starving creature, and not an ace of the secret service and a crypto-Communist, which is a meaningless term in Poland, absolutely unknown and exotic- sounding.

If someone already has everything at home that his heart desires, such as furniture to his taste, kitchen equipment, a television set—money made on the side can be invested in accordance with one's possibilities. Thus, one can buy a car and run it as a taxi with a hired chauffeur, preferably in a town located in another province—in order to confuse the Treasury authorities. One can buy several such cars, or even a dozen or more, as many as can be managed, since there are some seventeen provinces and it is only the State taxis that run at a deficit.

Or one can, as a certain enterprising genius did, buy out portraits of Marx from shops selling "material for cultural use" and after a slight retouching and coloring job sell them at church festivals as Saint Joseph.

One can also collect two-cent pieces taken out of circulation by the government and, leaving the eagle on the reverse side, print an Our Lady on the front with a primitive die and sell it, together with a chain, as a souvenir of baptism or participation in some indulgence. By paying a slight sum into the pocket of the manager of a scrap iron purchasing center, one can get permission to forage around in the collected scrap, and this digging can sometimes pay off extremely well. Not long ago a happy hunter found bracteate from the time of King Chrobry and Renaissance arms. Money invested in a trip to the most God-forsaken one-horse town can also pay a fair return, since one of my friends bought for twenty złotys, at a rummage sale near Cracow, an original table made of royal Kolbuszewo manufacture, worth at least a thousand times more. At open-air markets and fairs one can still find, if he knows where to look—although it is becoming more rare—old furniture, books, china from ravaged estates, palaces, and museums, either taken away from the Germans or traded for a bottle of vodka by the Russian liberators. More than one of these objects has found its way to the West, and the only set of Voltaire first editions offered for sale since the war, auctioned off in Paris a few years ago, was among objects taken out of Poland.

For industrious people there remains the possibility of taking several jobs at one time, most often with conflicting hours, which is managed by wandering from one place to the other. You accept commissions for tasks to be completed on office time; you undertake these projects, about which you have not the slightest idea, in this way letting someone else make money "incognito" (called *à la Nègre*), because this someone does not have access to the connections you have.

A couple I know hold seven jobs between them, he four as a physician, she three as an engineer—and at long last they are not only making ends meet, but already are driving their own car and traveling abroad.

After the overthrow of Nkrumah in Ghana, it is said that a great number of "Communist technical advisers" from China and Russia were chased out—but the Western press did not mention the rather sizeable group of Poles working on various constructions. Do they know even in Ghana that such jobs are received through *Polservice*, an export concern of technical knowledge, by means of a strategically placed—to put it bluntly—bribe? The Poles who, parenthetically speaking, are excellent specialists, are vying to work abroad, where they receive one quarter of the pay given to any British, French, or American engineer, and even then have to return fifteen percent of their pay to their employer, namely *Polservice*, ruin their health in the tropics and, among the uninformed, earn the epithet of Communist agents.

If you are young and have neither health nor constructive talent to offer, with a certain physical effort you can become an athlete. The times when athletes were rather well paid by their clubs and the Central Committee of Physical Culture and Tourism, and held down jobs only to maintain their amateur status, are gone forever. Nevertheless, these advantages have not disappeared altogether; that is because no one in Poland travels abroad so much as the athletes. And trips abroad mean money, even without excessive smuggling. A rather well-known boxer told me at one time how he chose his profession. When he was still in high school, he pondered deep and long what he could do to live well by doing nothing. Because this principle immediately eliminated the idea of further studies, and the physical conditions being favorable, he decided to become an athlete. After a few years, he grew wealthy and had excellent prospects of becoming a trainer, or so-called "official" after he retired from active boxing.

And it is even better to be an official than to run, jump, or swim yourself. An official does not have to go into training, can smoke and drink, and no one will reproach him. And what is most important

—it is not necessary to have knowledge about anything in this post: he must only know as much about the sport as the average spectator. Such an official attends all kinds of congresses, meetings, competitions, matches, collects expense allowances, salaries, and also brings home whatever he can—he knows that he is living, and not at his own expense at that. But it is not easy to find yourself in this group—the way leads mainly through the proper sections of the political secret police and the confidential Party apparatus. If an official has any work to do, it is only to figure out how to get and train the best athletes in their field, as this is what ensures the most frequent and interesting trips. That is why privateering of athletic competitors is so common in Polish sports circles—bribing them with a better job, apartment, greater benefits through belonging to a better "situated" club.

The same goals guide the members or candidates of such folk groups as *Mazowsze* or *Śląsk*. Probably every newly-forming group has visions of New York, Paris, or London—and most often ends up performing in Ostrołęka or Pcim in the backwater provinces. During the Stalinist period a certain writer who was longing for Paris and could not realize his dream by other means, made use of his acquaintance with the director of *Mazowsze* and his ability to play the violin—and consequently spent several weeks in France fiddling away, dressed in a grey russet tunic and striped britches.

People who have no illusions concerning their vocal or choreographic talents must travel abroad at their own expense, on money earned in different ways, for instance through a so-called "cunning in the hands." They can make lamp shades, beads out of cucumber seeds, beans, clay, or pieces of sponge—and sell them to CEPELIA (Center of Folk and Artistic Production) not only as a considerable supplement to their pay, but even as their principal source of income. Even if you haven't the slightest idea about painting, around Christmas or Easter you can get a friendly hand press to print a few thousand gaudy post cards representing the star of Bethlehem or rabbits and colored eggs, and peddle them very profitably in the hinterland. The provinces are also the place to sell wedding pictures, tinted and enlarged from the original, which go for prices approaching those for an oil portrait. The provinces are eager recipients of spectacles written, directed, and played by completely unknown people—this is where a performer can collect a pretty penny, because provincial Poland is starved for entertainment.

We have still far from exhausted the thousands of possibilities open to an enterprising, resourceful man anxious to make money—but it is impossible to list all the methods used; we must leave something to the individual spirit of invention.

Besides honest ways, there are at least as many, if not more, dishonest ways. These are shortcuts which may bring a fortune, but they are threatened by the law and its minions.

Here again the opportunities are limitless, because every occupation (or perhaps it would be better to say almost every occupation) offers its temptations.

Even if you are a minor desk clerk and travel officially or "in delegation," you can save by going second class, listing first class in the expense sheet—which is popularly referred to in Poland as "earning by one's derriere." These few złotys go far to supplement the reducing-diet expense allowance called "miracle allowance"— for county employees 19, provincial employees 21 złotys per day— paid to official travelers.

The higher your position, the greater the access to worldly goods—as witness the meat, flour, leather, salt, customs, and other trials.

A candidate for manager of a shop or restaurant discussing his future employment does not ask about the amount of his salary, but what "allowable shortages" are permitted. This shows how negligeable the salaries are and how knowledgeable the prospective employee is, which is bound to make a good impression on the personnel interviewer; he can see that he is dealing with an expert in the field.

In the Recovered Territories, which at one time were even called unofficially Exploited Territories, the bits of furniture left by the Germans have already fallen to pieces, the radios have gone on the blink and—in a word—there is nothing left to smuggle. Therefore, the ingenuity of a certain rich businessman from Warsaw is to be admired—he dismantled a number of ruined small towns in Lower Silesia for the bricks. The tremendous profit he derived from this venture enabled him to drag his trial through all possible courts and many successive amnesties, until nothing remained of the original eight-year sentence, and the gentleman is again on the lookout for enterprises that no one else has hit upon as yet.

A certain poor laborer who worked in a Radom baby carriage factory decided to smuggle out a carriage, part by part, so that his expecting wife would not have to carry their offspring in her arms. As he put the parts together, no matter how he tried he always ended up with a machine gun, not a baby carriage. And although this factory undoubtedly bears a different name by now, perhaps for instance the "Manufacture Plant of Ideological Equipment," the idea of smuggling out parts produced in your place of work has remained. Thus, everything which might be of any value is carried out. The employees of motor vehicle plants supplying the market with otherwise inaccessible changing parts are in an especially privileged position. Raw materials are removed from other establishments, especially rationed metals such as tin, zinc, lead, and copper; alcohol, cocoa, and coffee are also smuggled, in spite of a personnel check in the guardroom. For the most part, the contraband goods become semi-factures, or raw material for private producers who, in spite of licences, permissions, and blessings received from the State, do not receive the one thing they need most—precisely what they get by way of theft. A duck breeder could not even make a modest living if the employees of a nearby State farm did not supply him with feed at prices lower than official rates. Of course, the feed is stolen. Is it any wonder that private poultry prospers and is sometimes of export quality, while State hens lean on their beaks from hunger?

A suspicion harbored by the Ministry of Foreign Trade that some transactions were backed by foreign merchants with monetary arguments led to the issuance of an internal directive ordering that all gifts, even advertising samples, must be made to the concern, to be divided among the employees. Comrade the minister must therefore have had not only a suspicion but probably certain knowledge of how these things are settled, and not many illusions about the commercial purity of his subordinates.

It is an open secret that employees of embassies, consulates, and commercial councilorships in neighboring countries devote most of their time to trade between the country where they are serving and the land of their fathers.

Therefore, no one is surprised when a minor official with a miserable salary and the burden of six children to boot, after three months abroad buys a Wartburg, Škoda, or Moskvich car of his dreams with money gained by supplementing the diets of the collectivized starvelings in East Germany or Czechoslovakia.

In times when Czech "Jawa" motorcycles were a rarity hard to come by in Poland, the mountaineers from the Tatra Highlands took upon themselves—literally—the task of carrying on their backs the first motorcycles, dismantled into parts, and in a nearby village was formed a workshop engaged in stamping new numbers on the frame and the engine. Besides motorcycles, chemicals needed for the production of mirrors and gold and silver dyes for painting holy pictures on glass were also brought over.

An old saying, dating back from the time of the German occupation, goes that the most difficult thing to carry away or smuggle is a box of something; it is easier to take a boxcar, and a whole train is easiest of all. Certainly in connection with this, there are entrepreneurs in Poland who flood all private, cooperative, and even

State shops (how do they do it?) with, for instance, hundreds of thousands of cans of Kiwi shoe-polish or an equal amount of Swedish or Dutch toothpaste. Sometimes in the private free market there appear ballpoint pens with a painted damsel doing a strip-tease—a well-known Danish product—or thousands of pipes from Czechoslovakia. Sometimes the smuggling is official, as for example the souvenir Soviet Marshal Malinovsky took back home from his visit to Poland: a boxcar of *Carmen* cigarettes, produced in Poland out of American tobacco.

In the resale (Komis) shops one can buy everything that the capitalist world has to offer, from socks to Philips television sets, and from shirts to shavers, gas lighters, and espresso coffee machines. Shopping at a resale shop where, in spite of its name, used goods are seldom to be found, is a proof of the affluence of the buyer and his lack of opportunity to travel himself. In branch stores of this type one can find Bally shoes and Italian and French footwear—often produced locally and only stamped with a cleverly faked brand name by an enterprising manufacturer. The suppliers of models and styles are places some distance from the capital—those that have the greatest amount of contact with abroad (such as, those which receive the largest number of packages from relatives in America or Western Europe). From there, dresses, suits, shoes, and coats bought for next to nothing travel in the suitcases of the big-city traders to bazaars, thrift shops, etc., turning either into ready-made creations for the local elegantes, or into inspiration for the local fashion-setters, along with the easily accessible French, Italian, and American fashion magazines.

The inaccessibility to private manufacturers of various materials produced by the nationalized industry, for instance of chemical products such as nylon, polystyrene, and vinyl, leads to the existence of a huge illegal market for such items. Legally, a producer of ventilators can buy tourist butter containers and alter them by putting motors inside—and in his accounts put down bills for boxes purchased in a sporting-tourist shop. However, illegally he can buy whatever his heart desires and what has appeared on the market either through removal from State enterprises, through the Polish Savings Bank foreign goods exchange, or by way of smuggling from abroad. In fairness it must be said that otherwise neither private craftsmanship nor workshops could exist.

In certain fields private craftsmen have already surpassed State-owned industry; there are some who are able to color optical lenses, while the State has not discovered as yet how this is done.

It is possible to make money on all the ventures mentioned above, and not bad money, and not necessarily go to the pokey for it right away. And the more money you have, the easier it is to come by more or less powerful protectors, even if they can provide only an official seal, letterhead, or consecutive inventory number to prove purchase from official sources. Other illegal profits are difficult to prove because, for instance, a shoemaker who resoles shoes at a cooperative with assigned leather and has to account for every square inch used, stretches the leather while wet so that it is practically transparent, which enables him to resole some third or fourth pair of shoes, already for his own profit, out of material saved in this way. The same method is employed by more or less everyone, from the fruit vendor weighing apples in a thick paper bag to builders who alter the proportions between cement and sand, which lessens the durability of State structures but bolsters private housing in the suburbs.

We can be sure that more than one home-built car was constructed out of parts smuggled out of Zeran, and if it were not for the cumbersomeness of the component parts in the shipyards of Wybrzeże, which weigh many tons, probably more than one ship would sail under the flag of some private amateur sailor.

I have often wondered what Gomułka and his comrades trade in, and it has occurred to me that they are the most clever traders of all, because they manage to peddle for a good price an absolutely unmarketable commodity: a false ideology.

But if you have no commodity of this kind to sell, do not resole shoes or smuggle—and at the same time are conservative, but yet want to have money—only one way is left: to have a career.

Translated by Maria de Gorgey

THE POLITICAL THOUGHT
OF KULTURA

Juliusz Mieroszewski

I. THE EMIGRATION AND POLAND

BECAUSE THE CHANGES taking place in Poland are imposed, we are inclined to consider them to be unimportant, temporary, "occupation" period changes. As a result we pay no attention to the transformation, treating it as *de jure* nonexistant.

If a hurricane levels 60 per cent of the houses in an area, a realistically-thinking man must recognize as an accomplished fact that town X looks different after the hurricane than it did before. If the reconstruction follows a new plan it is necessary to accept as certain that town X has undergone a permanent, irreversible transformation. Accepting this fact in no way changes our attitude toward the hurricane, which we consider a catastrophe.

Anti-communism cannot hide these facts from us. We cannot allow ourselves Senator McCarthy's kind of anti-communist color-blindness. Yet Poles in exile want to be so perfect and blind in their anti-communist attitude that they throw out the baby with the bath.

It is a false view that the present period in Polish history can be described entirely by the term "occupation." It is an occupation, but it is not only an occupation. The Polish nation is engaged in a struggle, but the form, scope, and level of this struggle in no way remind one of the organized resistance against Hitlerism. However, the intensity and depth of the struggle in the present period in all certainty extend beyond the horizons of the battle against primitive Hitlerism. Every struggle means evolution and change. These changes constitute the essence and significance of the struggle, and they will be the content of the victory when the day of liberation comes. For this reason we cannot ignore these changes. It is only we who are not changing—because we are not struggling.

Our relationship to our country is vitiated by these three émigré complexes:

1. *Auto-intoxication through propaganda*, which means that we become stupefied by the propaganda that we ourselves produce. In finding fault with communism from every side, we have created our own, émigré version of Marxism, and believe that it is a program meant for idiots and destined for the sewers. This is not true. Communism is a powerful idea professed by many eminent people on both sides of the "iron curtain." It is an immensely serious problem and underestimating its attractiveness has been and still remains an unexhausted source of catastrophic political errors for the West. By continually ridiculing and jeering at communism we belittle the dimension and scale of the battle being waged in our country. This is all the more true because most of these attempts at "operetta-izing" communism originate with those who are ignorant of the subject.

2. *The secret-service complex*, which makes it possible to write in the émigré press about communism only what it is possible to write about capitalism in the communist press. The dread of being suspected of pro-communist sympathies makes it impossible in practice to explore the changes that are emerging in our country. None of the changes may be termed advantageous. Should someone risk such a view he would immediately be branded and "filed away" as a crypto-communist, an "information channel," or at least as a tool of enemy inspiration. If one does not wish to be a sacrifice of the informers to the English, and particularly to the Americans, one must adapt to the accepted conventions. Certain émigré circles take advantage of demagogic anti-communism in order to underpin their own political authority. If someone dares to charge that one of these circles is, for example, reactionary, the immediate reply is that because the communist press charges that the circle is reactionary, the emigrant who writes that Mr. X or publication Y is reactionary "is cooperating with communist propaganda." According to this logic, if someone in exile asserts that two plus two equals four, "he is cooperating with communist propaganda," because Polish schools to this day teach the unreformed multiplication tables.

3. *The national image problem*. Because most of us associate the word "Poland" with the Poland of 1939, we are subject to the terror of our recollections and think about our country as we do about a photograph which is not subject to the changes of time. Our theory of "representativeness" rests on this static perspective.

The country endures; the nation has not changed; therefore, because we were entitled to representation in 1939, we still have this title today. It seems to me that this is the heart of our problem.

Émigrés always think about recovering the *past*. Those at home, however, never fight for the past, but always for the *future*.

After victory Churchill, at the height of his glory, stepped down, and a socialist government took over in England with a broad program of reform. The war, at a time when conservative Churchill was presiding, gave England not only victory but also a socialist "welfare state." And in Poland the "underground state" with the Council of National Unity in no way reminds one of the inter-war regime.

For Poles at home, pre-September Poland is not a "lost paradise" to which one continually returns in his daydreams. Today this is a closed period, as much a part of history as the epoch of the November [1830] uprising. In Poland no one thinks about legalism or about the Constitution of 1935, but about a future, independent Poland, which will not take the form of a pre-September Atlantis, but will be the sum of the changes and experiences acquired during this most difficult period in our history.

It is very difficult for us to maintain that intimate tie of understanding with our own nation when we must live the history of our country not directly, but second hand, from newspapers and books. But this matter is of such great and fundamental importance that it is necessary to make the maximum effort to maintain these ties. The process of "denationalization" is a two-sided process. It is not only those who soak up foreign culture, language, and society who are denationalized, but also those who lose the feeling of ties with their own nation. At the present time the process of assimilation has not yet overcome us, but the process of estrangement from things Polish is making great progress.

One more and more often hears people say, "we can't imagine ourselves in a liberated Poland," "the changes we will find there can't be undone," "after the return we will be emigrants in our own country."

What do these declarations mean?

They are proof that there is a feeling of foreignness in relation to our own country growing up among us, a growing consciousness that the gulf between the vision of the "lost paradise" and the country as it really is may not turn out to be something which can be waded across. These declarations also mean that many of us will return, but not to just any liberated Poland. If the face of a liberated Poland is too different from the émigré image, a significant percentage of the emigrants will remain abroad.

This is a normal process, and it is immensely difficult to fight against it. But there is not the slightest reason for these processes to be speeded up or for the gulf to be widened. In exile there is a perceptible tendency for "political exile" to be transformed into "exiled nation." "The idea of state in exile" or "exiled nation" is a manifestation of an autonomous movement that is an expression of detachment and distance.

* * *

What conclusions should be drawn from these deliberations?

We should break away from our conception of the national image, from our idea of the national academies and of the national anniversaries. We should study the reality of our country and observe in such a way that the communist trees don't hide the Polish forest from us.

We must muster up the courage and accept the fact that although communism itself is not Polish, it will exert a great formative influence on Poland and the Polish people. Communism, by way of reaction to it, will evoke a set of new values which themselves will be entirely Polish.

We should always remember that the nation in Poland is struggling for the future, and that the starting point of this struggle is the present situation and reality—and not 1939. We should not identify liberation with a restoration of the past. There will be no restoration, and we will return to a different system and to changed conditions.

Finally, the last and most important point: It is high time for those of us in exile to embark upon an objective examination of Polish reality. At present nobody knows what reality really looks like. The face of the country reflected in the mirror of the communist press is entirely false, and the reflection in émigré propaganda is unreal. This is an immensely difficult, but fundamental problem. We will not fulfill our duty to our country if we do not solve this problem.

Although our attempted interpretations of the metamorphosis in Poland will always be imperfect, they will, nevertheless, be nearer the truth than the propaganda images of Poland produced by émigré political circles—if we undertake this task with good will and with the help of patiently gathered supporting information.

2. THE THAW

The Poles living in Poland are witnesses to the profound transformations and shifts of potential power in the east European region.

I watch the process of "thaw" in Poland with concern.

Looking at this phenomenon from a political perspective one must conclude that after ten years Marxism has exerted a minimal influence on the intelligentsia in a positive sense. First of all, it still remains very little known, and is professed by only a small élite. On the other hand, the influence of Marxism is enormous in the negative sense.

An overwhelming percentage of those involved in the thaw are not Marxists. But neither are they liberals, nor Catholics, nor democrats. Therefore, the farther any intellectual stands from Marxism, the less he has to say, because such a person deprives himself of all faith, political convictions, and ideology, and profits nothing in return.

The Marxist critique of the past has had great success, though this was not a difficult task. The entire traditional order of things lay in ruins and the Marxists carried out their autopsy on their own terms.

In exile we repeat many phrases about freedom. Basically, however, people do not want just any freedom. No one wants an empty freedom. Those who are persecuted want freedom from persecution. But no one is persecuting the intellectuals of the thaw in Poland and no one goes hungry. These people can want not freedom "from something," but only "for something"—for introducing a democratic system, for realizing a political idea and system different from communism.

What kind of idea? Do these people have some other idea of Poland than that in which they live?

The negative result of the thaw is in a certain sense a consequence of the political sterility of the Emigration. We *do not know at all* how to oppose the idea of "building socialism" and the "Russian orientation." We do not know how to create a vision of a *different Poland* and focus the attention of our country on it. We are propagandists, but not politicians.

Even those who would like to "reform" Marxism and who are choking with ferment which has not found an outlet for years— even those who with characteristic haste want to take advantage of the "thaw" and throw out everything which ruffles them within the limits of time and what is possible—these people never in any way go beyond the horizon of "People's" Poland. Speaking simply, these people believe that something will come of this. Things are bad, there is a housing shortage and thousands of other short-comings—but something will come of this—of "this," and not from anything else.

"Building socialism," together with the simultaneous stirrings of nationalistic feelings, creates an atmosphere—how nice for a

Pole—that despite everything great things are happening in his country. Not everyone is building socialism, but everyone is speaking and writing about socialism, and that is the most important thing.

Communism is accepted best in countries with a complex of unfulfilled values. We have no refrigerators, automobiles, television sets, or luxuries, but we are building socialism. The high moral order of a political credo cannot compensate for a material deficit, to be sure, but it can justify it. It is a pity to eat potatoes without butter, but it is a great and human comfort to know in the name of what it is so. Western politicians will never understand this and are always concerned about one thing: that the eating of potatoes without butter not be humiliating and not socially degrading.

The Party leaders can say to the workers who spend the night once a week with their wives in the common room of their workers' hotel, "Comrades! Devote your private happiness to the building of socialism, to the revolution!"

*   *   *

The "thaw" brings great disappointment with it, because it is not possible to read anything between the lines. Yet it is my conviction that it is possible to say much between the lines in Poland today.

If we condense the picture, as with a convergent lens, we would get Catholicism at one end and communism at the other. Around these two points the spectrum would break down into a series of shadings. There are Roman Catholics, regime Catholics, faint Catholics, and non-Catholics. There are Party "builders" of socialism, and beside them the "cleanup men" of socialism, and finally the collaborators, the bureaucratic intelligentsia, and those who live by writing and speaking about socialism, but who do not themselves build it.

In "People's" Poland the ruling Party is everywhere, and the problem of "building socialism besieges the individual on every side. If one is not a communist his entire potential for opposition is used up in keeping his head above water—which is by no means an easy task. Everyone is involved in one way or another. It is possible to refuse to discuss the subject of Marx's *Capital*, but it is difficult to refuse to discuss the subject of one's own apartment or the supply of essential goods.

In a communist state it is impossible not to be involved—to turn one's back. This technique—imported live from the Soviet Union—aims at channeling potential opposition. After years of involvement people long for improvements in one area or another, but always in an area of communist reality. They do not run past the horizon beyond which counter-revolution begins.

It is an oversimplification to state that there is no room for opposition in a communist state. In a communist state there is no room only for counter-revolution.

When a patient gets a shot of morphine, following his reaction it is possible to deduce how he would behave after two shots. The "thaw" is a dose of freedom and after the reaction to a minimal dose it is possible to some extent to deduce how the "patient" would behave after receiving a dose three or four times as great.

I do not intend to push this analogy too far. But even if we should imagine a "thaw" three or four times as great, it would still be difficult to see in this picture even the smallest echo of any influence of or connection with the Emigration.

It is horrifying to see the degree to which we are simply not present in Poland.

For the Poles in Poland it is clear that the situation in all of eastern Europe is undergoing a transformation not only in the sense of the political system, but also in the social and economic area. It is also clear to the Poles in Poland that most of these changes are irreversible. Freedom or independence, to the extent that it is to be more than a phrase, must be a conception constituting an attempt to answer a real set of problems.

Besides the communist revolution already mentioned, *another revolution*, to which no one has yet given a name, is taking place in Poland. But both the liberation and the conception of the new Polish politics must come from outside. Never in its history has our country needed a "great Emigration" to such a degree. But there isn't any.

3. BERLIN

That memorable April in 1945 the armies of two extra-European super-powers, the Soviet Union and the United States, met at Torgau, in very middle of Germany and in the center of Europe. There, in the midst of the cheering and general fraternization, the "gordian knot" of the German question was tied. Russia, after years of exile, had returned to the European scene in triumph.

The "German question," from the Russian point of view, can be understood in a few sentences. The Soviet Union aims at the stabilization of its hegemonic position in our eastern Europe. Moscow wants to achieve recognition for the Ulbricht regime, because the recognition of the German Democratic Republic would be tantamount to the legalization of the division of Germany.

East-central Europe may be dominated either by Germany or by Russia. The Red Army, with notable assistance from the West, liquidated the age-old "Drang nach Osten," and a permanent division of Germany in the eyes of Moscow is to secure her victory.

American and British writers often demonstrate a lack of orientation toward Russian continental politics. These politics are always a continuation of a historical drama which is foreign and incomprehensible to the Americans and British.

What the Germans are experiencing today we have had behind us for a long time. Czesław Milosz, in one of his sketches printed in *Kultura*, pointed out that the former Polish Commonwealth, in her post-1772 borders, began to vanish in the feelings of her citizens—like the present state—only after 1863. And equally valid is the fact that the anti-Polish verse of Pushkin was a fragment of the conflict between rivals over the mastery of eastern Europe. The rival was defeated, but not reconciled to his fate. Even the Kiev campaign of Piłsudski belongs in this historical context. It was an act of the "unreconciled."

Taking away East Prussia, Pomerania, and Silesia from Germany was not only an act of revenge. The Russians were concerned above all with tearing away from the Germans once and for all their historical base for beginning their "March to the East."

Does the legalization of the division of Germany lie in our interests? Before we answer this question it is necessary to state calmly that the international legalization of the division of Germany would amount to recognizing the hegemony of Russia in east-central Europe for an indefinite time.

In the Warsaw monthly, *International Affairs*, there once appeared a lengthy discussion entitled, "The Legal Situation of the German Democratic Republic." The author tried to prove that all of the legal reservations put forward in West Germany against the recognition of the GDR are without any foundation.

But the problem lies elsewhere. If the western powers, as heretofore, object to the recognition of the GDR, it is not because the East German government is more of a satellite than the government of Czechoslovakia, but because the Western powers committed themselves to support the German goal of unification by the Paris Pact of October 1954. They also committed themselves in the same treaty to recognize the Bonn government as the only legal German government.

In other words, the Western powers would be breaking their accepted commitments if they offered to recognize the government of the GDR in negotiations with the Soviets behind the back of their German ally.

We are not deciding the heart of the matter at this time, namely, whether the GDR should or should not be recognized. One thing, however, is certain: it is necessary to keep agreements concluded with one's allies. Agreements between allies are not eternal marriages and can be changed. But a basic change in the text of the Paris agreements would require negotiations with the interested party: namely, with the West Germans.

It is my conviction that a revision of the 1954 Paris Treaty is essential. American policy toward Germany is subject to vacillation. This is also clearly related to the existence of important differences in this matter between certain offices of the Department of State and the White House.

One of the major advisors of President Kennedy at the time of the "Berlin crisis" was former Secretary of State, Dean G. Acheson. His secret report—according to J. Alsop of *The New York Herald Tribune*—constitutes the theoretical basis for American policy in relation to the complex set of problems involving Berlin, Germany, and Russia.

Acheson represents the view that Khrushchev accepts every concession offered by the West, but that his main goal is the breakup, or at least the weakening of NATO, and the discrediting of America in the eyes of the world.

If we accept the Acheson evaluation as correct, the problem of NATO and the cohesion of the alliance grows to first-rank importance.

From the point of view of world-wide American policy, an Eastern Europe dominated by a democratic Germany would be infinitely more desirable than an Eastern Europe dominated by Communist Russia.

American policy must be evaluated according to American criteria. Only to émigré politicians does it always seem that it is the obligation of every western statesman to be concerned about Polish interests. An independent Poland is necessary only for us, and not for Europe. In the epoch when a Polish state did not exist, Europe lived through one of the most magnificent periods in its history.

The plan to throw Russia back behind its 1939 borders and replace Russian hegemony over eastern Europe with that of the Germans may be the American doctrine, but it cannot be the doctrine of NATO. Neither England nor France subscribes to this concept.

It is not possible to speak of the cohesiveness of a given alliance if the aims of the allied powers are divergent.

Following the elections in Germany, the American Department

of State published a brochure entitled, "Berlin 1961." Included on the cover of this document was a map of Germany stretching far beyond the Oder. "Under Polish Administration" was written on the Polish western territories. This brochure is an official publication, distributed by American embassies and legations.

In the British press some politicians and members of the House of Commons came out with a series of questions addressed to Washington asking whether belonging to NATO obliges an allied member to support a "provocative German border policy."

The British answer in this affair is decidedly negative.

Looking at Europe from the perspective of Washington, one gets the view that everything is rotten and decadent on the old continent and in the British Isles, with the exception of Germany. Following this line one can come to the conclusion that German revisionism is the only dynamic and offensively oriented form of anti-communism in Europe. Should the Americans ever reach such a conclusion, NATO would have to be replaced by a German–American alliance.

Several weeks ago I had the opportunity to engage in a long talk with one of the American experts on east-central European affairs. In his opinion the Americans carefully distinguish between the postulate of unification and the program of revisionism. The unification postulate is considered morally correct and justified. Moreover, the Americans think that they are obligated to support the German's faith in unification.

The program of revisionism enjoys neither moral nor political support in America, with the exception of certain decidedly pro-German circles.

But the Americans view this set of problems from an entirely different perspective than we do. Once during the course of our conversation the American impatiently brought his fist down on the table and said, "For the first time in the history of Europe a great European city has been cut in two by a wall. They are bringing military transports from the East. There is no telling but what tomorrow the world may begin to hit us over the head—and you keep going round and round about Wrocław."

Whose world? For the first time in history—an American world. The world has already hit us over the head, but then it was our world. In America not even a single brick ever hit anyone on the head. For the Americans Ulbricht's wall is the first in history, but not for us. The same kind of wall cut off the Warsaw ghetto and was, moreover, the work of the Germans.

In conversations with the Americans one immediately feels these differences in perspective. They feel that this is a global war and that everything is good which is anti-communist. Our Polish "provincial" relationship to eastern Europe often irritates them and makes them impatient.

Let us make the assumption that anti-communism should be mobilized on the continent, even at the price of supporting the German territorial claims. But two points should be considered in such a case. A silent, unofficial support will not satisfy the German extremists. And official recognition of those claims—thus identifying them with the goals of American policy—would lead to the disintegration of NATO, because neither England nor France supports such a program. Revisionism, after all, involves not only a Polish Wrocław, but also a *Soviet Königsberg*.

However much one may imagine in theory a peaceful, step by step unification of both German republics as a result of neutralization, to the same extent the recovery of Wrocław or Königsberg is possible only through war.

The stabilization of the situation in Europe, at least for a certain period of time, requires a clarification and more precise definition of the German place in NATO.

It may be that from a purely military point of view a bilateral German–American military alliance would be of greater value than NATO. This would be an offensively-oriented alliance in which the German talents would flare up in full brilliance. But war in Europe would then be inevitable.

Here we inject a note addressed to our friends and the readers of *Kultura* in West Germany: In conversations and in correspondence we are often charged with not wanting to recognize the primacy of anti-communism over nationalism. We admit that we offer no sign of equating anti-communism and freedom, because it is easy to imagine an anti-communist Europe in which there is no place for a free and independent Poland.

From the viewpoint of traditional Polish policy the simultaneous liquidation of both of the "millstones" which have in the past ground our statehood to a pulp constitutes the classic solution.

From the Polish perspective the situation is similar to the arrangement in 1914. Both then and now the Russians and the Germans were found on opposite sides. The Russians slaughtering the Germans, and the Germans slaughtering the Russians—this is a situation "dreamed up" by poets.

The Germans and the Russians must find a way out of the inferno of national imponderables. It would be unreal to demand of the Poles and Germans that they subordinate their basic national interests to the higher rule of anti-communism, and all the more so because anti-communism is an inconsistent and changeable quantity. It stands for freedom for West Berlin but not for East Berlin. It threatens atomic war in the event of an attempt against the freedom of half of a city, while simultaneously agreeing to the enslavement of the other half of the same city.

Anti-communism is supposed to constitute a higher reason of state only for small and medium-sized states. This rule is not obligatory for the great powers, which are farthest from sacrificing their national imponderables on the altar of anti-communism.

Only in time of war—assuming that the war would be waged conventionally and that the German divisions in NATO would be on the winning side—could the Germans give their nationalism wings of anti-communist ideology. But the Polish anti-communists, conditioned by their tradition of Polish national imponderables, see the same war from an entirely different perspective. They count on the bleeding and the fall of both of our historically expansionist enemy powers, that is, Germany and Russia.

Let us not deceive ourselves. Anti-communism does not offer any way out of the inferno of national imponderables. There is no chance that we will reach agreement as anti-communists. If we agree, we must reach agreement as *Germans and Poles.*

A significant percentage of Poles in Poland and in the free world are opposed to the unification of Germany. A divided Germany, belonging to two contending blocs, is naturally weaker than a united Germany. Considering Polish interests, it is necessary to call for a divided Germany.

Loyalty to imponderables, however, cannot be equated with the principle of "my country, right or wrong."

In my opinion those Poles who are opposed to the unification of Germany have no right to require from the West Germans the recognition of the Oder–Neisse border. It is not possible to refuse the Germans a right to Leipzig and Dresden and at the same time demand from them the recognition of the Polish right to Wrocław. It is not possible to fight for the right of self-determination for the Polish nation and simultaneously refuse this right for half of the German nation. In refusing the Germans the right to self-determination and unification, one gives up the possibility of an understanding with the German nation. And our goal should be to search for this understanding.

It is already high time for the Poles and Germans to break away from their traditional understanding of their mutual relationship. Let us stop thinking about war, which the Germans see as a restoration of the *Drang nach Osten,* and the Poles see as a Himmlerite "final solution" to the German problem.

Does it have to be this way? Perhaps it does, but as an independent writer I consider it my duty to say to both interested parties that it could be entirely different and with great profit.

The German Federal Republic should not only recognize the Oder–Neisse border, but also renounce in a ceremonial act all of its territorial claims in relation to Poland, Czechoslovakia, and Russia. A free and voluntary recognition of the Oder–Neisse border would be seen in eastern Europe as a sincere and authentic change in traditional German policy. This reorientation in thousand-year-old German policy toward eastern Europe would in time bring about a reorientiation of the eastern European nations *vis-à-vis* Germany. This process of change would take a long time, but it would crystallize in time.

The problem of a united Germany—a peaceful Germany not making any territorial claims against anyone—would then be our common problem.

Only an insane German revisionism is responsible for the fact that the clear mutual nature of our interests has not been given an opportunity to make itself heard (and may never be given that chance). The East Germans are a satellite state—just as the Poles, Czechs, and Hungarians are satellites. The desire for unification—separated from revisionism—is morally and politically nothing to quarrel about. Undertaken in such a way, a unification movement would create sympathy among the eastern European nations, who realize that as long as a united Germany is not buried their fate is not clinched.

In my opinion, the Germans have never had such an opportunity in their relations with Eastern Europe as they have today. Their only rival has been and is Russia. The Germans cannot threaten the Russians either with their divisions or with their American ally, who will not devote a single soldier to bring the Germans any closer to Königsberg. The Germans could threaten Russia if they would set freedom and self-determination in opposition to being a satellite. But simply setting forth these words would appear comical to readers in Eastern Europe, because for a hundred years we have automatically associated the word of the Germans with annexation, occupation, and slavery.

And this is the central mistake of German political thought. In spite of Clausewitz, Bismarck, and the General Staff, in spite of the dazzling "economic miracle," the Germans are a *failure*: they are a nation which, despite a thousand virtues, never succeeds at all.

The international recognition of the GDR, which I fear is only a question of time, will constitute the official seal on the drive for recognition by the West of the Soviet satellite empire. But reporters and photographers will be able to visit West Berlin from time to time. Freedom without a future for two million West Berliners will soothe the conscience of the West. It was not capitulation. We have capitulated in the matter of a hundred million Eastern Europeans, but two million West Berliners can read the *New York Times* from dawn to dusk.

The Eastern Europeans could be the allies of the Germans in their struggle for freedom and unification. But freedom doesn't interest the Germans. They are interested in Wrocław and Königsberg. Königsberg!

4. THE ABC'S OF POLISH POLITICS

I am aware that the view which I intend to formulate goes against the grain of the traditional opinion of most Poles. But the majority never has a monopoly on what is correct.

All of our political conceptions have lost their points of reference and have become unusable. In the present world system, which is radically different from the pre-1939 system, Polish independence policy must be redefined.

The "power" scheme—that is, neither with Russia nor with Germany—is unrealistic both at present and for the foreseeable future. The last echo of this idea of "between Russia and Germany but neither with Russia nor with Germany" was *disengagement* and the project for a neutral belt in east-central Europe. We supported this project as long as there was even a one in a thousand chance of its realization.

The idea of a federation of Poland, Czechoslovakia, and Hungary, which *Kultura* always supported and still supports, is becoming less and less realistic as a result of German policy. Neither Czechoslovakia nor Hungary wants to tie itself up with Poland, which has a quarrel with the Germans. The German Federal Republic would have to recognize officially the Oder–Neisse boundary and renounce all revisionist claims in order for the idea of a Polish-Czech-Hungarian federation to be transformed into a realistic project.

In the next few years I expect there to be an increase in American military and economic involvement in Asia regardless of the outcome of the Vietnam campaign. The division of the world into the poor and the rich determines the policies not only of the poor but also of the rich. Soviet Russia and the United States, as highly industrialized superpowers, possess a common factor determining their policies—and this factor is a more powerful one than ideological divisions. In their confrontation with the poor and the weak, the powerful always have a common line of action in certain areas, regardless of their flag or ideology. The Chinese understand this perfectly.

In a world ruled by a rich and powerful United States there would be a place for a rich and powerful Soviet Russia. In a world ruled by the Chinese, Soviet Russia would fall to a subordinate position in the table of powers, and the Russian fate would not be enviable.

It is difficult to demand evolution, liberalization, and democratization of the Russians if we, their nearest neighbors, do not show even the slightest desire to abandon our prejudices and change our traditional attitude. John Grigg, one of the most intelligent writers for *The Guardian*, speaking not long ago about British–American relations, wrote the following: "The size of the United States and the psychology of the Americans makes it possible for the so-called 'special relationship' to be no more than the relationship of a master to his servant."

Grigg's statement is full of bitterness and is not objective. I think, however, that although the Polish geopolitical situation is one of the most difficult in the world, Poland has many concrete arguments for building its *special relationship* with Russia on a different basis than that of servant to master. We are the largest Slavic nation of Latin and western culture. To some extent we potentially represent—in an edition of the least foreign of kin— what will never reach the Russians.

We have not known how to build a *special relationship* with either Russia or the West. The relationship of People's Poland to Russia is the typical relationship of a servant to his master. The relationship between People's Poland and the West simply does not exist.

We could end our immensely difficult geopolitical situation only if we in the future could persuade the Russians that we know how to be the major mediator between Moscow and the West. At the same time we would have to convince the West that Poland is the key to Russia.

Sinyavsky, Daniel, and many others whom it is not yet time to mention by name have turned to us by choice and not by accident. These people are true Russians and do not wish to commit treason. They have not committed any. In turning to us they knew well that they were not turning to an enemy of Russia and the Russian nation, but on the contrary were certain that they were establishing contact with a free Polish institution which propagates the idea of closer relations and mutual understanding between Poland and Russia. This mutual understanding will become a realistic proposition when a significant percentage of Poles recognize the correctness of *Kultura's* position in this matter, and when a majority of Russians recognize the correctness of the attitude of their anti-Stalinist writers and underground activists.

I am deeply a pragmatist and therefore maintain that these are not "pious wishes." Even in the second half of the twentieth century, with all of the sputniks and atomic bombs, the main instrument of political action is still the *word*. In printing Sinyavsky and Daniel, and making their writings available to the entire world, we accomplished more in the pure political sense than all the Polish émigré institutions in the course of the past twenty-five years.

The word is the main instrument of political action because, in the final accounting, to be victorious does not mean to beat up but to win over. It is possible only to win someone over to true cooperation, not to force him into it.

We must always remember that Russian communism is a special problem. The Russian intelligentsia, even those most critically disposed toward communism, accept "capitalist encirclement" as axiomatic and are convinced that all attacks on Russia have come from the West.

Walter Laquer, in his excellent book entitled *Russia and Germany, a Century of Conflict*, writes that one day during his stay in the Soviet Union, when he was traveling through one of the Moscow suburbs, he noticed a small column. Curious, he asked one of his fellow passengers what the monument signified. He was told that the column marked the farthest point reached by the Germans in November, 1941.

The Germans were also anti-communists and still are today, asserting revisionist claims. Anti-communism, which is synonymous with a program of parceling out Russia and conspicuously weakening her *vis-à-vis* Germany, not only does not deepen the ferment in the Soviet Union, but significantly dampens it. It is not possible to be an anti-communist if anti-communism is synonymous with treason against not ideological but national interests. This is the line followed by Soviet propaganda—and those of us who voice the necessity of crushing the Soviet Union play into the hands not of Sinyavsky and Daniel, but into those of their judges and prosecutors. Soviet Russia must be reconstructed into a true federation or a looser commonwealth—but this will not be accomplished by Kosygin's generation. At present, the struggle is not about the reconstruction of the Soviet Union, but about the reconstruction of communism, that is, full destalinization.

Communism will undoubtedly evolve, but, as heretofore, within the framework of the doctrine. In the time of Stalin, Sinyavsky and Daniel would have been shot and the western communist parties

would have vied with each other in throwing mud at both unfortunate writers. Much has changed and it is important to
appreciate this, because these are changes of great importance for
the people living in the eastern bloc. But it will be possible to give
an authoritative answer to the question of whether communism is
capable of evolution only when the presuppositions of the doctrine
become subject to revision. Today, criticism—even of the most
anachronistic Marxist presuppositions—is considered counter-
revolutionary propaganda.

We are advancing an evolutionary program for two reasons. First,
the situation in the Eastern European bloc favors evolution. In this
struggle between the forces of social pressure and the Party political
apparatus, the chances of success undoubtedly favor the side of the
opponents; for it is possible to broaden and deepen the extent
of the ferment and possible to strengthen the social pressure, but it
would be immensely difficult for the Party to answer this increased
pressure with a return to Stalinist methods. If the pressure were to
increase, the Party would retreat. If someone begins to retreat,
sooner or later he comes to the point from which there is no return.

A peaceful and evolutionary solution also seems to us to be most
in accord with Polish interests. The disintegration of the Soviet
Union and chaos in Eastern Europe in all certainty do not lie in
these interests.

Eastern Europeans, and above all the Poles, could play an important role in the process of "Europeanizing" Russia. But the initial
condition in this matter is to convince and insure the Russians, and
especially the Russian intelligentsia, that by Europeanization we
understand exclusively the liquidation of totalitarianism and not
the liquidation of Russia as a power.

*   *   *

The word "Russia" invariably comes up in conversations with
Poles from Poland. *Kultura* is in a certain sense pro-Russian,
though not pro-communist. Poles from Poland will acknowledge in
serious conversations—over black coffee only, with no whisky—
that Poland in her relations with Russia must arrive at some sort of
settlement on reasonable terms. At the same time, the slightest
sign not of pro-Russianism but of objectivity in relation to Russia
and the Russians inevitably gets on the nerves of a Pole from Poland.
It is necessary to come to terms sometime, but about Russia and
the Russians it is possible to say only bad things.

A certain young historian from Warsaw once asked me if our
attitude toward Russia is dictated by cool political pragmatism or
if it derives from other premises as well. He was very surprised

when I told him that those "other premises" have to be sought in Japan.

The Japanese attempt to put their enemy in an advantageous light where possible. This is a wise philosophy, which saves face in case of disaster and increases the dimensions of the laurel wreaths in the event of victory. Poles, on the other hand, not only try to belittle their enemy, but also to jeer and scoff at him. If someone were to collect and prepare an anthology of Polish anecdotes, jokes, and sayings about the Russians, it would show that it is a nation of boors, brutes, drunks, incompetents, illiterates, and slaves—and moreover, dirty and louse-infested.

What is most astounding in all of this is the fact that what would seem to be normal thought and logical reflection never seems to enter the minds of any of the representatives of this anti-Russian *vox populi*: namely, if the Russians are lice-infested nonentities, what then are we Poles, who allowed this band of illiterates to push forward from Smolensk to the gates of Przemysl.

We are not a tiny little nation of a few million people who can always justify itself by its own martyrdom and the superior power of others. Historically we constitute a nation of 30 million which thinks enormously well of itself. We cannot forever recall the Molotov–Ribbentrop pact and the Russo-German agreement to explain the division of Poland.

On July 31, 1449, Poland concluded a pact with the prince of Moscow which marked the boundaries of Russian territory along the zone of influence. The Lithuanian border ran scarcely 150 kilometers from Moscow. On January 30, 1667, in the Truce of Andruszow, Poland gave Moscow back Smolensk, Czernichów, Siewierszczyzna, Siebież, and Kiev. And later came the Gryzmułtów peace (May 1, 1686) which laid the foundation for Poland's future dependence on Russia. It was not Kościuszko in a Cracow coat, or the officer cadets or the insurgents, but Polish politics which lost the three-century ascendancy over the east.

Personally, I am anti-Soviet. But national pride does not permit me to join the numerous chorus of those Poles who scoff at and belittle the Russians.

5. THE POLITICS OF RENUNCIATION

In a memorandum which was widely distributed the government of the German Federal Republic proposed the following sequence for a final solution of the "German question": First, the unification of Germany; second, free elections in a united Germany; third, the creation of a government of a united Germany; fourth, a peace conference which would establish the final western borders of Poland.

Clearly the sequence of the entire program should be turned around. With whom does Germany wish to unite? With the German Democratic Republic, whose border runs along the Oder and Neisse Rivers? The recognition of this border by the Bonn government, then, must be the initial step on the road toward unification. The Germans do not understand that readiness to put forward a sacrifice is often the basic condition for an effective policy.

An experienced politician agrees to make an essential sacrifice early, because in this way he avoids delay in achieving his main goal and saves his state endless complications and often the spilling of blood.

France, after losing Morocco, Tunisia, Indochina, and so forth, continued to treat Algeria as a French *Département*. How much blood and money would have been saved if the solution to the Algerian problem had been decided early.

Kultura is the only émigré political center which has taken a clear position in the matter of Lwów and Wilmo. We consider—as opposed to the theses of the political émigrés—that the acceptance of this sacrifice is essential if we wish to normalize our relations with the Ukrainians and with the Lithuanians. The acceptance of this sacrifice is also essential if we wish to defend effectively and logically the Polish western territories.

The Soviet Union does not understand the politics of renunciation. The renunciation of mistaken ideas is sometimes the only method for saving the work accomplished by generations.

Communism in general and Soviet communism in particular heretofore has not managed to create a sphere of coexistence with religion or with nationalism. We understand nationalism in this context to mean the natural feelings of a nation. Similarly, religion, also a national feeling, cannot be exterminated, because man for a thousand years has been genetically conditioned in this direction.

The Russians constitute scarcely 54 per cent of the population of the Soviet Union, but 82 per cent of the newspapers and periodicals printed in the Soviet Union are in the Russian language. Everything is in accord with the thesis of Zasławski, that Russian is the language of socialism, just as French was the language of feudalism, and English the language of imperialism.

The social order doesn't have anything in common with language; nevertheless, it is a fact that 75 per cent of the "heroes of the Soviet Union" are born Russians. Examples of this type can be added up by the hundreds. In the Soviet Union—even though the Russians constitute only half of the inhabitants—one nationalism is cultivated: namely, the Great Russian.

Poland is a communist country and the Ukraine is a communist country, yet the differences between these two countries are enormous. Cardinal Wyszyński is a conservative patriot and Gomułka is a communist nationalist. In People's Poland one does not suppress nationalism—one suppresses only the achievement of independence. As long as the Party does not set up a government which would be pleased with the support of the society, the communist government must solicit the support of Moscow; otherwise it would be carried away in wheelbarrows.

It should be stated objectively that the Party, trying to represent itself to the people in the role of the most nationalistic institution that ever existed in Poland, basically weakens its own position. Achieving independence is the major element of national feeling. The competing celebrations of the Millenium organized by the Church and by the Party enhance Polish nationalism and at the same time potentially strengthen the tendencies toward independence. The Party is concerned that nationalism be not extinguished and competes with the Church in this area. In the Ukraine the Party suppresses nationalism and the Church plays no role at all.

Among Poles a knowledge of Russian is (unfortunately) minimal; in the Ukraine a knowledge of the Russian language is both a necessity of life and a condition of success in every area of professional activity.

What is this discussion aiming at? It seems to me that in the long run it will not be possible to cultivate national communism in one state and Soviet communism in another. This one communism cannot be super-nationalistic in Warsaw and anti-nationalistic in Kiev. It is not possible to liquidate religion in one communist state and in another communist state to recognize a Cardinal of the Roman Church as the *de facto* chief-of-state. It is not possible to carry out intensive Russification in one communist country, and in a second, no less communist country, to give up teaching people even the Russian alphabet.

The Russians must count on the fact that the satellite countries in the course of time will become more and more independent, and will work out institutional models in which the relationship to religion and nationalism will be entirely different from the Soviet pattern. (The Church in Poland is not only struggling, but triumphant, and Gomułka has delayed the laicization of the country by ten years.)

After some years, when a generation of educated people comes to power in Poland, a generation to which Stalin and Stalinism will be known only from history books, great changes will appear as a result. The satellite states—and especially Poland—will create a great problem for Russia in the near future. The problem rests on the fact that even today "liberal"-thinking Russians are prepared to applaud the signs of "liberalization" in Poland or in Czechoslovakia, but not in the Ukraine. In Moscow one can find a place for a bold Ukrainian poet—or for a brave literary critic—under the condition that they write in Russian. Even educated and truly liberal Russians, like the late Professor Karpovich, who was on friendly terms with us, at the very bottom of his soul did not recognize the Ukrainians as a separate nation.

Stalin was opposed to the incorporation of Poland as a Soviet Republic, for then the Russians would constitute a minority in the Soviet Union. If the Russians were determined not to allow any reforms or changes in the Soviet Union, they were guilty of giving up the imposition of communism on the satellite countries. Pro-Russian bourgeois governments in Warsaw, Prague, and Budapest would in the long run represent much less of a danger.

Judging by the response of the Central Committee members of the Italian Communist Party in the matter of the sentencing of Sinyavsky and Daniel—and by the analogical commentary by the organs of the French Communist Party, not to mention the other western communist parties—it is possible to risk the assertion that there exists, if not an open alliance, at least a quiet understanding between anti-Stalinists in the Soviet Union and in the West. This is a fact of great significance.

In Poland when the present leaders vanish from the scene it will turn out that the Stalinists and the neo-Stalinists have no successors. The young Polish or Czech Communists are significantly closer to the Italian or French Communists than to the Polish or Soviet Stalinists.

One can thus make the assertion that unless completely unpredicted circumstances appear, it will be more and more difficult for Russia to seal herself off from Europe—both East and West. The Soviet leaders would save themselves many crises if they could just realize today that in the epoch toward which we are heading, it will be possible to maintain the Russian position only at the price of concessions and renunciations.

In its present form the Soviet Union is a Tsarist-Imperialist-Stalinist conception. It is not a federation, only a totally unified Russian state.

The Americans are a synthetic nation of emigrants. Ukrainians, Englishmen, or Lithuanians, upon landing in America, give up their fatherland and after a certain time receive American citizenship. But who, and in the name of what, has the right to demand from a Ukrainian, born and raised on Ukrainian soil, that he take a fictitious Soviet nationality? If someone wants to start a new nation—such as the Americans—one has first to discover a new continent.

The Czechs number only 13.6 million. The Ukrainians number over 40 million. Communist Czechoslovakia is either Czech or Slovak, while a Ukrainian living on his own soil must be a "Soviet man." Czechoslovakian legations and consulates exist in many countries, but nowhere is there a Ukrainian legation or consulate.

Historical experience teaches us that no power is ever strong enough to insure the continuance of a system which wrongs and degrades tens of millions of people. So far history has not perpetuated on its maps an empire which resisted the dynamics of nationalism. Such was the end of the British and the French empires. The same end inevitably awaits the Soviet empire.

As I have stressed many times, a violent weakening of Russia as a result of nationality conflicts and crises does not lie in Polish interests, because every weakening of Russia constitutes an automatic strengthening of Germany. The evolutionary reconstruction of the Soviet Union into a modern federal state is what is in the interests of Poland and of all Europe. To begin with, it would be necessary to liquidate the gap that exists between the actual state of affairs and Soviet constitutional law. Article 13 of the Soviet Constitution, for example, guarantees every Republic the right to secede from the Union. After February 1, 1944, in accordance with the change in the Constitution, all Soviet republics were to have ministers of foreign affairs and ministers of national defense. The ministers of national defense remained paper creations and the ministers of foreign affairs hold office only in the Ukrainian and Byelorussian Republics, because both the Ukraine and Byelorussia are represented in the UN, UNESCO, and several other international organizations.

The constitutions of the individual Soviet republics empower the highest authorities of the individual republics to "name and recall diplomatic representatives accredited to the capitals of foreign states, and to receive and return the letters of accreditation of the diplomatic representatives of foreign states."

Contrary to constitutional law, the central Soviet (Russian) authorities have monopolies over all diplomatic powers, depriving the federal republics of all attributes of sovereignty.

As the late noted Sovietologist, Walter Kolarz, has already pointed out, the decolonization of the Soviet Union can be carried out both peacefully and legally. We would add ourselves that this is basically a question of further de-Stalinization and burying Stalin's insane theory: "One world, one nation, one language." Full de-Stalinization would imply decolonization, and decolonization would simply be a return to legalism.

Nationality problems, and particularly the Ukrainian problem, constitute a "taboo" in Soviet politics. For this reason the Americans never raise this matter. The Americans will not Europeanize Russia. Only the Europeans can Europeanize Russia.

The liquidation of the "cold war" on our continent, including Russia in a broader European system, normalizing Polish–Russian relations—all of this depends on the decolonization of the Soviet Union. In Europe, colonial powers no longer exist, and Russia—if she wishes to take her due place in the concert of European powers—must go through the same process of decolonization that France and England already have behind them.

Russia is in a significantly better situation than France and England, because she has greater possibilities for making partners out of her satellites. As a consequence, decolonization would make Russia stronger and not weaker, because a solution to the nationality problem would mean disarming the "mines" that threaten to explode at the most dangerous moment for Moscow: namely, in periods of great crisis or war.

6. GEO-IDEOLOGY

We will not normalize our relations with Russia as long as we fail to extricate ourselves from our isolation, because the difference in potential power condemns an isolated Poland to a position of satellite in her relationship with any Russia—either red or white.

We should hold as our ideal the "Europeanization" of Russia, that is, including her as an active partner in the European system. Only the "Europeanization" of Russia secures us both against being a satellite and against a Rapallo.

Those of us who dream about displacing Russia from Europe—or of building a new "bulwark"—are thinking in terms of half a century ago. Russia, by another road, aims at the same goal as all the other European states: namely, at the construction of a modern, classless, industrial society.

Never in history has Russia been so near to Europe and at the same time so far away. A belated industrial revolution and technological progress are Europeanizing the Soviet Union. The over-all differences between the western European societies and industrial Russia decrease each year. The "inferiority complex" toward the West, which has colored (and still colors) the entirety of the complex of relationships connecting Russia with Western Europe, is also slowly being corrected.

Ilya Ehrenburg, in the last volume of his memoirs (*The War*, 1941–1945) literally describes the absurd working conditions of Soviet writers and journalists during the last war. Not only foreign correspondents, but also members of the allied military missions were immobilized in their quarters and cut off from all information. In addition to the chaos and errors, of course, many great things happened which can and should be praised. In the battle near Kurski, the Germans brought 2000 tanks into action. In the course of three days of murderous fighting they lost 1500 tanks, and the Russians took the offensive.

Ehrenburg cites the characteristic answer of the Soviet diplomat, Umansky: "We do not understand what we can be proud of. We hide and make secrets of all the best things. We act like a band of arrogant, awkward striplings and quake with fear that some foreigner will discover that there aren't any washing machines in Mirogradz."

One irrefutably concludes from Ehrenburg's book that the Russian distrust of foreigners is dictated both by espionage-mania and by the fear of losing face. This is a typically eastern trait. The Russian will give up showing a foreigner a marvelous factory if there is any chance that the foreign observer could notice some elementary shortcoming in the sanitary facilities on the neighboring kolkhoz.

When their standard of living approaches the western European level, the inferiority complex will begin to fade. Distrust and arrogance always characterize a consciousness of deficits and the fear of losing face. But these are marginal considerations.

Both Dmowski and Piłsudski viewed Polish–Russian relations in an entirely different historical context which cannot be compared with that of the present day. Today there is no territorial dispute between us and Russia (in contrast to Germany). The Polish–Russian conflict today is exclusively an ideological and political matter. Our conflict constitutes a portion of the world-wide conflict between East and West. In an epoch of technological revolution, in an epoch of the atomic bomb and space ships, there is no room either for "local" incidents or for national history.

This has its good side and its bad side. Before the war no Rumanian Premier had a chance to affect world politics. Today every move of the Rumanian government is commented upon by the leading periodicals of the western capitals. Why? Because the politics of Bucharest constitutes a portion of the conflict of the epoch and at the same time constitutes a portion not of local Rumanian history but of our common history of the twentieth century.

The Polish situation is different from the situation of the western European states because the Poles do not limit their aims to the discharging of conflict exclusively in the political sphere.

Strictly political solutions are many. Both NATO and the communist states are losing their cohesiveness. The uneasiness of Moscow in relation to Rumania—similar to the uneasiness of Washington in relation to France—results from the fact that neither of the bloc leaders wants his bloc to collapse first.

If the German problem were solved and the Oder–Neisse border internationally recognized, the blocs in Europe would to a significant degree lose their reason for being. Then it would be very difficult for the bloc leaders to oppose the neutralist tendency. A neutralist state has its own system of government, frees itself from servile alliances, trades with everyone, and takes money from everyone. This is a very inviting prospect. Then groupings of "uncommitted states" could be formed: for instance, Rumania–Yugoslavia, Poland–Czechoslovakia–Hungary, and so forth. Although these groupings would be neither formal alliances nor federations, they would facilitate resistance and the common defense of interests *vis-à-vis* the Soviet Union.

Development along these lines would undoubtedly constitute progress. It would be a departure from satellite communism to independent communism, from aggressive communism to neutralist communism adapted to the European political system. But in the "uncommitted" states, trading with the East and the West, the communist parties, perhaps, would be seated more firmly in the saddle than they are today. The Communist leaders of these states would emphasize their "ideological community" in relation to Russia and their "uncommittedness" in relation to America. This is undoubtedly the shortest possible road to economic well-being available in the future for the East-Central European states.

But though the development of the situation in the direction mentioned would be advantageous, it would not guarantee a solution to the central problem.

We write a lot about the Millenium—about the 1000th anniversary of our history—but the balance sheet of the Millenium closes in the red. We have returned to the Oder, to be sure, but we have lost our independence.

Most Poles ultimately accept the priority of the "national interest" over any ideology. By "national interests" Poles now, as in the past, mean independence. Our ideal was ideological isolationism: proper relations at the Soviet border, proper relations at the German border, and in the middle a Polish island with peace in her countryside . . .

We consider the ideological conflict between East and West not as our conflict, but only as a clash between the great powers of the world. This clash takes place at our expense, but above our heads.

There exists the concept and term "geopolitics." I have ventured to coin a new term, "geo-ideology."

No Italian politician, irregardless of his convictions or views, can turn his back on Christianity, because the Italian capital is the geo-ideological seat of this great religion. The national interests of Italy are directly connected with this geo-ideological disposition.

For hundreds of millions of people in the world, Rome is the Pope and the Vatican. Without the Pope, Rome would fall to the position of a provincial European capital.

An analogical geo-ideological disposition determines our relationship to communism. Poland's most powerful neighbor is not only a communist power, but Moscow still continues to be the main seat of the world communist movement. Everything which happens in Moscow affects us directly, and for this reason the East-West conflict is to a larger degree our problem than it is the problem of any other state in Europe, or beyond Europe.

For France, England, or the United States, this conflict has an ideological character and not a geo-ideological one, and consequently only indirectly influences the calculations of their "national interests."

The term "geo-ideology" embraces the relationship connecting ideology and geographical location. Church and intellectual circles all over the world exert an influence on Catholicism, but any change in doctrine can be made only in Rome. All communist parties exert an influence on the evolution of communism, but nonetheless, fundamental doctrinal changes in European Marxism can be effected only in Moscow. Communism is not a voluntarily accepted Polish ideology, but it is our geo-ideology because the problematics of European communism are connected genetically and through evolution with the geographical zone that encompasses Poland.

It is possible to ignore ideology, but it is not possible to ignore geo-ideology. If a man from Naples, living in New York or Paris, says Vesuvius does not concern him because he lives beyond its reach he has ceased being a Neapolitan.

Poles both in Poland and in exile demonstrate an astounding talent for uniting sentimental patriotism with a complete disdain for geopolitics and geo-ideology. We love Poland, but the facts that make up Polish reality act on our nerves.

If Poles were fully conscious of their geo-political and geo-ideological situation they would take into account the fact that the evolution of communism is a problem affecting us all, irregardless of our individual political views and opinions.

* * *

The following point in the development of the conflict between East and West seems to me to be the most important:

We write about the universal technological revolution, about the communications media, about the shrinking of the world, and as a result Soviet Russia each month becomes more and more similar to us and more and more different from us. These similarities, which increase every day, not only emphasize, but also deepen the differences dividing us. These disproportions are ominous and menacing.

Soviet technology, space ships, atomic-powered ships, intercontinental missiles—these constitute the triumph of rationalism. The Communists are rationalists as long as they manipulate material things—from steel mills to the atom. They cease to be rationalists when they begin to manipulate people, sociology, religion, and philosophy.

The conviction that rationalism is indivisible has prevailed in the West for a long time. The western theory of evolution today still derives from the premise that the rising and overpowering influence of the exact sciences—which constitute the intellectual base of technology—will in time effect a rationalization of that doctrine. Many Sovietologists believe that the generalization of rationalism through technology will in the end lead to the fall of dogmatism and mythology within the framework of communist doctrine.

I do not share this optimism. If it were so it would be necessary to give the Soviets the most advantageous conditions for enormous loans so that their level of technology and standard of living could equal that of the West. Everything else would follow automatically and inevitably.

It is my belief that rationalism is basically indivisible. The definition of rationalism as understood by western evolutionists, however, is completely mistaken.

Technology is "know-how." The exact science can be linked with Buddhism or with Catholicism, with communism or with fascism. Rationalism is neither technology nor exact science. Rationalism is a philosophical view of the world and the cultural attitude that is the consequence of that view.

In the West there is a division between the state and religion, between the state and philosophy. If the state is subordinated to a single official religion, or a single official philosophy, then rationalism becomes heresy.

There is a great danger in this schizophrenic dualism of rationalism in relation to matter and dogmatism in relation to people. The closer the rationalization of the technological processes comes to perfection, the greater the risk that this potential will be used in support of irrational decisions. Decisions are not made by scientists and technologists, but by *aparatchiks* and doctrinarians. One cannot have confidence in people who are rationalists with only half of their brains. This is all the more true of those people who are prepared to realize their "historical mandate" with the most modern technological means—atomic weapons not excluded. Then scientific civilization would be subordinated to barbarism, which is everything that rationalism is not.

Only experts and technocrats can make the communist economy efficient. And only humanists can rationalize the approach to man. A rationalization of views on philosophy, sociology, history, and literature would be equivalent to a Europeanization of the communist movement.

The old guard Bolsheviks both in Russia and in the satellite countries are in no position to escape from the grim circle of Stalinism.

Note well the following: In town X in Siberia the concentration camp was liquidated after the death of Stalin. The police dogs were given away to the people. The dogs had been trained to keep a column of prisoners marching to work in an orderly formation. One step to the left or right and the fangs of a wolf dog would rip into the leg of the careless prisoner.

A year after the liquidation of the camp the May Day parade marched through the village. Suddenly the dogs appeared and as if by command took up their former duties. The years of training did not go to waste. After a short deliberation an old ex-prisoner led the terrorized column of people into the courtyard of a factory. He remembered that the dogs had been taught to stay at the gate leading to the camp. The strategy worked, and the dogs stopped at the gate to the factory yard.

I have summarized a story which aroused an understandable commotion in Moscow.

Everyone in Russia knows about Pavlov's dogs and about "conditioned reflexes." The ex-Stalinists have been converted into neo-Stalinists. Not to diminish his service in the struggle with the ghost of the satrap, it is necessary to emphasize that to the very end of his career Khrushchev had no idea of what he should use to replace Stalinism.

Lenin said that as long as there is a class struggle it is not possible to speak of objective social sciences. In the communist way of thinking, the social sciences include all of the humanities. Only when the stage of full communism has been achieved will the elimination of class conflict make possible the repropagandizing of the humanities.

Here is the source of the complete basic a-rationalism of the communist doctrine. It appears to the *aparatchik* that it is possible to achieve a rational objective with a-rational methods.

Let us sort out our discussion up to this point:

I. In order to normalize our relations with Russia we must adopt the view that comprises the following sequence of points:

a. We cannot even potentially be in a state of war with both Germany and Russia. A potential state of war with Germany excludes a potential state of war with Russia.

b. If we hold the present borders of Poland to be inviolate, we should see that Russia makes no territorial claims against us, which is extremely important.

c. Even a decolonized Russia will be, if not the second, then the third power in the world, and will certainly become the most powerful state of continental Europe. There is a great probability that certain emergent nations in the fold of the Soviet Union will choose a true and not a fictitious federation with the new Russia rather than a belated start toward independence on their own.

d. We have neither the possibility of removing Russia from her dominant position in Eastern Europe nor any chance of building an anti-Russian "bulwark of defense" out of the nations that were formerly in the fold of the first Republic. These nations have learned by our example that they would be nations full of folly were they to undertake the role of a bulwark against Russia.

We did not succeed as a multi-national state, and we will not find willing partners to repeat that experiment. We did not know how to be imperialists in an imperial epoch, and it would be strange for us to undertake an imperial experiment in an anti-imperial era.

e. Neither were we successful at bilateralism, that is, a policy of balancing between Germany and Russia. In the future we should create a Polish-Hungarian-Czechoslovakian grouping which would strengthen the position of the cooperating partners *vis-à-vis* Moscow. This would not, however, be an anti-Russian formation.

II. We are geo-politically and geo-ideologically connected with Russia. Even if we assume that communism will not evolve but will collapse, Poland and Russia would then be ex-communist states with decades of common history and experiences. If communism does evolve—which I personally do not doubt—our sacrifices will not be wasted, because it will turn out that one can restore Russia to Europe only through the rationalization of communism by the eastern European states and particularly by Poland.

III. The cardinal problem in the evolution of communism is pushing through the full rationalization of the system. The rationalization of thought must be the right and privilege not only of physicists, chemists, mathematicians, and technologists, but also of sociologists, philosophers, historians, and writers.

The inhumanity of Stalinism and neo-Stalinism rests on the fact that the rationalization of the technological base is occupied with the dogmatization of the superstructure, that is, the humanities in the broadest sense of the word. Both older and newer style Stalinists consider that a condition of rationalizing the base, and at the same time hastening technological progress, is the dogmatization of the superstructure, or all of the humanities. They fear that if the humanists are granted the right to rationalism (or to freedom), the superstructure would turn against the base, slowing technological progress and production. The Party leaders, instead of concentrating all their energy and attention on economic matters, would then have to struggle with the sociologists, writers, and philosophers who, themselves producing no material goods, would criticize the directors of the production of material goods, namely the Central Committee of the Party.

IV. It is the conviction of the Stalinists and neo-Stalinists that the superstructure has been condemned to extermination. In the period of full communism rationalism will be the privilege of every citizen, because there will be no other rationalism than technological rationalism. Then that fatal dichotomy of today will give way to universal unity and everyone will be free in his own narrow-mindedness.

V. The Intelligentsia in the Eastern European countries has never had as important a task nor as historical a role to play as at present. The rationalization of the system and the restoration of freedom for the humanities can be secured only by the humanist-intelligentsia. They will never obtain their goal if freedom is identified with the liquidation of communism. They must, however, fight for an evolutionary reconstruction of the system, granting the creators of cultural goods the same independent status the physicists, mathematicians, and technologists have.

The difference between East and West does not rest on the nationalized economy or central planning. The difference rests exclusively and solely on the fact that neo-Stalinism constitutes the "blueprint" of the new, wonderful world in which technological perfection and productive efficiency are occupied with the extinction of the humanities. In that world there is a place for a Schaff but not for a Sartre. The neo-Stalinists require of the humanistic intelligentsia that they prepare the ground of their own cemetery with their own hands.

VI. The humanistic intelligentsia must convince the *aparatchiks* and technocrats that rationalism is basically indivisible and that therefore the communistic "brave new world" is a utopia. Crushing the anti-conformity of the humanistic intellectuals may in a given period make an economic "great leap" more efficient and subordinate potential social power to a single goal, but when the first stage of industrialization has been achieved, freedom for the humanities should be completely restored.

Hundreds of years of the history of Western civilization teach us that a wonderful humanistic culture can exist without technology. These same experiences also teach us that technology without the humanities does not lead to the "brave new world"—but only to creations *à la* Hitler's Third Reich.

Personally, I am absolutely certain that the decay of freely-pursued humanities would be equivalent to the decay of rationalist thought—which in consequence would have to bring about the fall of technology. Half-educated people like Gomułka or Kliszko cannot grasp that in historical perspective the humanities are the base of the technological superstructure. Marx, in this light, was a humanist who, had he lived in Stalinist Russia, would have been put to death, and in Gomułka's Poland would have a choice either of being a second Schaff or of going abroad. I have no doubt but what he would have chosen the second alternative.

In other words there is no rational technology without rational humanities. There are no rational humanities where one is not allowed to reason freely.

VII. These are the problems of our geo-ideology, because the fate of the state, the nation, and Polish culture depend directly on the solution of these problems.

7. A MODEL FOR THE YEAR 19??

Would there be anything left of communism if the de-Stalinization process were carried out to the end?

With the example of Rumania we see that de-satellitization is more easily achieved than de-Stalinization. It also appears that there is potentially a greater possibility of de-Stalinization in Russia than in the satellite states.

Western Sovietologists write in circles about liberalization, polycentrism, evolutionism, and the like. I. Deutscher, in a conversation with a correspondent for *The Review*, even observed that the one-party system was never a Marxist ideal before Stalin. Everyone expresses his wishful thinking, but nobody outlines, even roughly, the model toward which evolution should aim.

Neither do orthodox Communists have a clear conception of the future. Stalin in *Foundations of Leninism* (Vol. VI, p. 181), risked the following view: "With the decay of social classes and with the withering away of the dictatorship of the proletariat, the Party will also have to disappear."

Today it is not allowed even to recall this Stalinist theory of the withering away not only of the state but also of the Party. Khrushchev emphasized many times that the Party, as the highest form of social organization, will exist and blossom even in the period of full communism. In a speech at the 21st Congress of the CPSU in February, 1959, Khrushchev stated that the problem of the withering away of the state has to be understood dialectically. The essence of this process is the evolutionary shaping of the socialist state into communistic community self-government.

Stalinism, as Joseph Gabel rightly observed, was the antithesis of all dialectics. For the Stalinist all opponents of the Soviet Union were identical and nothing differentiated between them. Truman was Hitler's successor, and such absurd linguistic monstrosities as "Hitler-Trotskyism" did not sound strange in the Stalinist vocabulary.

F. Fejto wrote in 1962: "The split vision of the world which is characteristic for orthodox communism seems to replace the vision which is at the same time unitary and pluralistic, i.e. dialectical."

Is it really so? Communism exists without Stalin, but can the communist system exist without Stalinism? There is still no convincing answer to this question.

When Khrushchev states that he would put abstractionist painters naked in the nettles so that they could see their errors, he is absolutely sincere in his pious indignation. In this case it is not a question of wounded asthetic feelings, but of wounded feelings of dogma. Abstract painting is bad because it deviates from Marxist dogma. In *Foundation of Democracy* Hans Kelsen properly emphasizes that the adherents to political dogma consider that those who represent a deviant opinion commit not only an error but a crime. Only the Party's version of Marxism-Leninism is true. Truth is the highest good. Everything which is opposed to the good is by definition bad or criminal.

Full de-Stalinization of communism must mean the secularization of doctrine. Neo-Stalinists realize that a significant percentage of the Marxist "axioms" would not survive in the daylight of free, rational criticism.

It is true that today no one speaks about "Hitler-Trotskyism," but isn't the term "socialist realism" equally nonsense?

One can agree with Lukacs that every great literature is realistic, because it reflects reality. This concerns both Homer and Kafka. "Soc-realism" is a dud not because it is socialistic, but because it is not realism. Socialist realism was to fulfill in literature the identical role that so-called "lip service" fulfills in journalism. The aim of "lip service" is not a reflection of reality but, on the contrary, an accommodation of reality to myth. Realistic literature would have to be a complete reflection of a country's reality, and not of neo-Stalinist mythology. For these reasons realistic literature is unthinkable in the present situation in Poland.

Entangling ourselves in contradictions constitutes part of our "human condition," but without a doubt progress must mean a reduction in these contradictions and not their continual growth.

Let us take one more characteristic example. In People's Poland people speak and write endlessly about "commitment." At the heart of the matter, however, is the fact that in Poland today it is possible to be a pro-Party writer but not a committed writer. It is also possible to be a neutral writer operating on the safe periphery.

Commitment—as Silone once rightly stressed—is uncompromising service to a higher cause, and not being a lackey for the *establishment*. A writer for whom commitment is defined in every concrete case by a Party directive is not a committed writer, but only a literary *apparatchik*. Gomułka, trained and shaped in the Stalinist school, does not want either committed writers or a committed literature, just as he does not want a realistic literature. It is sufficient for him to have a completely pro-government blotter.

Comrade Gomułka has innoculated Poles with a love of the classics. He revived Kraszewski, Sienkiewicz, and Zeromski—all our literature of the past. Because the press of People's Poland is deathly boring, people reach out for books a hundred years old. But what does a contemporary man look for in these archaic novels? He looks for the humanism which Gomułkaism has completely sterilized in Poland. People satisfy their hunger for humanism with the classics and religion. Roman Catholicism is like Homer in the feelings of the social mass in Poland. It represents a century of western humanistic culture. People read Kafka for Kafka, but they reach for the classics to satisfy their needs for continuity. The poorer the building the more carefully we look at the foundations. The foundation gives one a feeling of security and faith in the possibility of reconstruction.

The tactics of revolution in a capitalist system have been worked out with precision. But how is revolution to look in a neo-Stalinist system?

From history we know that no period lasts long. In this sense the days of neo-Stalinism in Gomułka's edition are numbered. History also teaches us that evolution takes place in leaps. Sometimes the leap is so violent that it takes the form of a revolution.

If we assemble the intellectual achievements of the Polish and Hungarian revisionists of 1956, it is necessary to repeat after Peter Dumitri that this was the only original revolutionary movement that has so far occurred in the second half of the twentieth century.

In the West revisionism arouses sympathy as a freedom movement and not as a revolutionary movement. Western workers have long since passed into the post-Marxist epoch, and the Western European bourgeois have grown accustomed to considering Soviet Russia as the same kind of a great power as all the others. No one is interested in revolution in the West.

The Russians look at these matters differently. For them communism is both an international movement and a Russian national movement. The Party and the communist government receive no support from the outside. Calling Russia "the greatest subjugated country," as do certain American Sovietologists, is complete nonsense. The achievements of the communist governments are enormous by the standards of Russian power politics. In a period of not quite 50 years Russia has transformed herself from a "military camp" into the second power in the world. Russia owes this phenomenal success to the *failure* of communism on the international plane. Had the German Weimar Republic fallen not to Hitler but to the Communists, the Soviets in all certainty today would not be the second power in the world. Not Moscow but Berlin would be the capital of the international communist movement. The Germans had more outstanding philosophers and excelled the Russians in organizational genius and in technological and industrial achievements. Communism in Russia developed into a Russian national ideology thanks to isolation. In my opinion Ulbricht fulfills a useful role in this regard, for he diminishes the German potential, blocks the road to revisionism, and frightens the West Germans away from the idea of communism. The satellite states are useful, but there are only problems with great communist powers, as one can see in the example of China.

For the reasons outlined above, it is not possible to compare the "thaw" or liberalization in Russia with the analogical phenomena in Poland. Communism in Poland is not a national ideology but, on the contrary, represents the conquerer. Every "thaw" carries with it the risk of an anti-Russian national insurrection.

A liberation movement can have a national or an ideological character. All the uprisings had a national independence character. "October," however, had the character of a revolutionary ideological movement on the intellectual plane. Poles value independence more than freedom. It is necessary to break with this tradition. Independence and freedom are not synonyms. Stalinist Russia was undoubtedly independent, but in reality it was an independent prison. In Austria or in Finland people are immeasurably freer than in the Soviet Union, despite the fact that the sovereignty of these states is very limited in comparison with Russia.

The traditional Polish national philosophy states: "First independence, then freedom." It is important to reverse this order of things, which is politically fatal and socially futile.

The fact that most Poles feel that freedom and independence are synonyms shows that we have neither a tradition nor an idea of freedom. Freedom is a form of social structure and the sum of the socio-cultural maturity of the citizen. Freedom must be worked out and safeguarded from within, because the enemies from within threaten it no less than the enemies from without.

It is not true that we are prepared to fight for freedom. We are always prepared to fight for independence. Those same people who showed astounding courage during the occupation and the Warsaw Uprising refuse to support the 34 today out of civil cowardice.

Where does this come from? We do not have behind us either a revolutionary tradition or a democratic tradition. And for this reason we do not believe in the political power of human conviction. As a result a group with definite convictions—whether this be Piłsudskiites or Communists—can easily impose their government on us because a distinct majority of Poles are independence patriots without any political convictions. An independence-patriot is prepared to fight against every foreign occupier, but he becomes a naive and defenseless child on the day of demobilization. He wins at every Monte Cassino but loses every election. His philosophy is simple. Courage is an uprising; power is a rifle. When he has no barricade and no rifle, a humiliating and futile passivity sets in. Yesterday's hero changes into a cheap Positivist and sounds the slogan, "Death to the Sucker." But the poor devil does not realize that there is no greater sucker than he himself.

For clarity let us put our analysis into the following series of points:

I. Part of the Poles in Poland and nearly all Poles in exile consider that we are choosing between communism and democracy. Neither Russia nor Poland has a tradition of parliamentary democracy. The fall of communism by counter-revolution would result in an explosion of nationalism, bonapartism, and an extreme rightist dictatorship.

II. A right-wing nationalist government in Russia in all certainty does not lie in the Polish interest. The only hope both for Russia and all of Eastern Europe is complete de-Stalinization and a slow development toward a new form of socialism.

III. The decolonization of the Soviet Union depends on the developments outlined above. A nationalistic, right-wing counter-revolution would be more imperialistic than Stalinism. The Soviet Ambassador has much to say in Warsaw, but an ambassador representing a chauvinistic Russian military dictatorship would have immeasurably more to say in Warsaw.

IV. To those who say that complete de-Stalinization in Russia is fantasy it is necessary to reply that the democratization of the Soviet Union on the western European model is not even a fantasy, but nonsense.

V. The collapse of communism is not in any way the equivalent of freedom—and less of Polish independence. We would not find allies against a right-wing Russian government in Paris, in London, or in Washington. Even following a war, a Russian "Adenauer" would after several years be a more valuable and immeasurably more influential ally of Washington than of Poland.

VI. It is easier to improve and rebuild an existing structure even after half a century than to import a form of social system which has no historical roots in Russia. It would be in the interests of all Eastern Europe for Russia to change from a neo-Stalinist state to a genuine socialist state, because socialism brakes the drive toward imperialism with significantly more effectiveness than does the Western European type of democratism.

It is necessary to emphasize once more that the decolonization of the Soviet Union is possible only through socialization. Even after a victorious war the Russian government created with the support of the Americans would immediately announce a declaration stating that it takes the position of the inviolability of the 1939 borders. The chances for Ukrainian independence would then be the same as for the Bavarians if they wanted to leave the German Federal Republic.

*   *   *

In considering the prospects and possibilities of the evolution of communism one must remember that neo-Stalinism may lead either to an ideological thaw or to a renaissance of nationalism—in other words, either to socialism or to red fascism.

The Stalinists [in eastern Europe] will defend their positions to the end. If ideological evolution takes place faster in Russia than in the satellite countries, the Stalinists will take up the slogan of independence from the Soviet Union, counting on China or on the support of the mass of society, who identify freedom with independence. But independence in the Stalinist form—even though it provided a maximum of state independence—would be independence without freedom.

What should one understand by the term ideological "thaw"? First of all, one should understand the democratization of communism or the linking of socialism with freedom. Polycentrism should be obligatory not only in the relations between communist parties but also within those parties. It means freedom of discussion and freedom of criticism.

In a socialist state the majority of the society should be convinced of the correctness of the basic principles of socialism. But it does not mean that the majority of society must be atheists. It is my belief that it is possible to realize democracy within the framework of a single party system under the condition that the party of which we speak recognizes the principle of multiple world views. And vice-versa—a party recognizing ideological monism constitutes a potential danger for democracy, even in a parliamentary system.

A democratic system does not rest on contention between several or many political parties where each one dreams of a *coup d'état* and dictatorship. Democracy rests on the emergence of even one party that combines a progressive program with respect for the principle of many world views. Poles do not understand that democracy is a clash of convictions and opinions, and not a life and death struggle of dogmatists. Every second Pole is a dogmatist; there are very few Poles with pluralistic world views.

Democracy does not mean multiple parties, but a pluralistic world-view, even if within the framework of a single party. Socialism has great possibilities for becoming such a party in Poland.

It would be better to have clubs in the Party operating openly, rather than as they do today, with unofficial factions mutually struggling against one another. If the unity of the socialist movement is to be more than a fiction, it must be understood dialectically: this means that it should be unitary on the outside and pluralistic on the inside. If, however, pluralism is sacrificed for dogmatic unitarianism, the result is neither unitarianism nor pluralism. We observe such a state of affairs in the Polish United Workers' Party.

The model outlined above would make possible a legal opposition within the Party. The dogma of the infallibility of the first secretary and of his politburo would be replaced by the play of democratic forces. The most powerful club possessing the broadest support of society would hold power. At the same time the club or clubs constituting a minority at a given time would have an open, legal road to becoming a majority at the next election.

In this way we could have the beginning of an evolution from imposed socialism to accepted socialism.

The purpose of this chapter is not to work out some sort of "recipe" for a new system, but to encourage Poles at home and abroad to consider the subject of a gradual remodeling of the system. After being in the West for twenty-five years I am convinced that the importation or imitation of the western European system in Poland, or in Russia, is impossible. We are differently conditioned, historically, politically, and geographically. The Anglo-Saxon democracies are the product of a long development which has no analogy in our history. The French model which we adopted after the First World War did not succeed either in Poland or in France.

Evolution and progress are not caused by the resistance of the discouraged—only by the pressure of the convinced. Poles idolize freedom, but they consider the independence-patriot without any crystallized socio-political convictions as to the ideal.

A nation of 30 million is to a greater or lesser degree dependent on someone in every situation and in every geo-political situation. The freedom of an average-sized nation is the sum of the full exploitation of the opportunities in any given situation. In my evaluation the Poles have not taken advantage of even 25 or 30 per cent of their existing opportunities. Were the international situation to change significantly to our advantage, there is no guarantee that freedom would be attained in Poland. Different people would do the censoring and imprisoning of someone else—that is all. If the communists were treated like the anti-communists are treated today in People's Poland, most Poles would consider this type of behavior as freedom plus democracy. In Poland the "democrats" and defenders of freedom are always those who exercise the dictatorship, and the anti-democrats are invariably those who oppose the dictatorship. Comrade Gomułka has not deviated one milimeter from this national tradition. Gomułka is a Stalinist and at the same time a classic product of the second Republic.

These are problems affecting everyone, both socialists and non-socialists. If we are to work out socialism in time in Poland, that socialism must be acceptable to everyone. The Social Democratic Party has ruled in Sweden for 28 years. Does this mean that all Swedes are Social Democrats? By no means. This does mean, however, that the model worked out by the Social Democrats has been accepted by the overwhelming majority of the people.

Polish socialism will be very different from Swedish socialism, but the degree of its universality must be identical. That universality can be achieved only by evolving ways of democratizating the present system.

8. THE MYTH OF COMMUNIST UNIVERSALISM

Well-informed diplomatic correspondents for American newspapers maintain that Kosygin earnestly advised Dr. Castro to stop his revolutionary activities in the Latin American countries and focus his influence on agricultural reform programs. Kosygin also advised a policy which would be capable of shaping the local communist parties in the South American countries into socio-political organizations accepted by their respective societies.

Dr. Castro obstinately proclaims that the first duty of a revolutionary is to "make revolution." It would seem doubtful, then, that Kosygin's advice managed to convince him.

But how does Moscow behave in relation to Egypt? Despite the advice given Dr. Castro, classic Soviet policy has always tended toward discounting economic and military assistance on the ideological plane. According to this schema, the crowning Egyptian operation should be the molding of the United Arab Republic into the "Arab People's Republic." In such a situation, of course, Nasser would have to disappear from the scene and be replaced by an orthodox communist.

It is characteristic that to the same degree that Russian foreign policy becomes more pragmatic, the policies of the satellite states, and Poland in particular, become violently more ideological. At the VIII Plenum of the Central Committee of the Polish United Workers' Party, it was repeated over and over again that "there is no coexistence of ideologies." On the recommendation of the Central Committee the entire press concentrated on that theme.

The ruling communist parties (with the exception of Rumania, which has ceased to be a satellite state) read great danger into Soviet pragmatism—and rightly so! If in the future one could demonstrate that it is possible to have Soviet bases on one's territory, take advantage of economic and military aid, play host to hundreds of Soviet advisors, and simultaneously escape communism, then dangerous thoughts could occur to the Poles or Hungarians. If close cooperation with Moscow does not mean communism in Egypt, why should it be different in Poland?

It is necessary for Gomułka to make politics more ideological because he and the "new class" he represents owe their positions and privileges exclusively to ideology. Coexistence terrifies Gomułka because every form of coexistence is a compromise achieved at the expense of ideology in favor of pragmatism.

Were Kosygin to adopt Dr. Castro's maxim that the first duty of a revolutionary is to "make revolution," then the Soviet Union would have to choose between returning to the isolation of the pre-war period or accepting the inevitability of armed conflict with the United States. Gomułka believes that Soviet financial, economic, or military assistance for some country in the "third world" should mean a communist revolution and the establishment of a local "Gomułka" in the driver's seat. If the Russians continued to behave according to the above "recipe" they would supply ammunition to those circles in Washington that proclaim that communism is a world-wide conspiracy with which coexistence is impossible.

Accepting the principle that arms and economic aid should be supplied only to potential revolutionaries would on the one hand limit the Soviet Union's worldwide political opportunities and on the other hand mean the undertaking of a "holy war" against American capitalism. Anti-Anglo-Saxon feelings are strong and widespread in the "third world," but it would be a mistake, however, to offer any sign of equating anti-colonialism and pro-communism. Everyone in the Afro-Asian societies is an anti-colonialist, but there are only a handful of authentic communists. Molding Egypt or some other distant country into a communist state does not now guarantee a pro-Soviet attitude. There always exists the possibility that a pro-Chinese faction will come to power.

Where are these considerations leading? I want to show that if Moscow wants to maintain its position vis-à-vis the United States, the Kremlin leaders will have to learn not only to live together with states with a different social system, but also to recognize that being a communist regime is not an essential qualification for a potential Soviet ally.

One of the basic elements of the great crisis in the Soviet Union can lead to the following proposition: Internally, the ideology serves to justify the dictatorship of the "new class." Externally, that same ideology constitutes a ball and chain around the leg. Soviet world politics are a betrayal of the ideology because it is impossible to be faithful to the ideology and avoid world war.

In my opinion politicians like Kosygin recognize the fact that the world will never be Communist. On the other hand politicians like Brezhnev must realize that an official departure from the universal theory of revolutionary communism opens the way for a basic revision of the Marxism-Leninism that constitutes the foundation of the rule of the "new class." This fundamental contradiction between the interests of Russia as a world power and the interests of the "new class" that rules Russia stands out more and more clearly.

The reader will consider here that this contradiction does not exist in practice because externally Russia cultivates a pragmatic and not an ideological policy. This is basically so, but nevertheless that doctrinal obligation to propagate communism on a global scale mobilizes anti-communists all over the world, equips the most powerful state, the United States, with an anti-communist ideology, and last but not least makes it impossible for Russia to construct an alliance on which it can depend.

As a result of polycentrism, the communist bloc has lost its cohesion, and the common ideology does not guarantee allied solidarity with Russia. At the same time, however, an alliance with Russia for states with a non-communist government always carries with it the threat of a revolution, which makes Moscow a dangerous ally. As a result, the Soviet Union depends only on the satellite states. The satellite states are not in an alliance with Moscow in the real sense of the word, for they are not alliances of states and nations, but only inter-party understandings.

The major thesis of the present note is the following view: If in the future Russia wants to have the status of a world power she will have to (a) renounce the dogma of communist universalism and (b) make an attempt at organizing "a-ideological" agreements and alliances.

If the ruling class in the Soviet Union comes to the conclusion that an evolution in this direction is incompatible with dictatorship and totalitarianism, Russia will develop into a regional power without any important world-wide ties. Deepening polycentrism will in time lead to a complete disintegration of the so-called camp of socialist states. China is communist and Yugoslavia is communist, but what are the advantages of this for Russia? If China were ruled by a right-wing general, perhaps the relations between Peking and Moscow would not be as tense as they are now.

It is not Russia which is losing in the world political arena, but communist ideology. It is the evolution inside the Soviet Union which will decide whether Russia as a world power will share the world-wide loss of communism. The evolution of doctrine is not keeping up with evolution of the political situation. Let us consider an example. Polycentrism today is a historical fact, but nevertheless to this day Moscow has not worked out any theoretical form with which to define this phenomenon.

Someone will say that there is nothing to worry about, because practice and life are always more important than theory and ideology. It is not always so. The Catholic Church does not submit for revision those dogmas that would deprive the Vatican of its reason for existence. The ruling communist parties object to the revision of the dogmas that constitute the foundation of their power, because there is nothing with which to replace those dogmas contradicted by life and practice. Ideological motivation can be replaced only by the support of the people, which in turn can be won only by a program of fundamental reforms of the system.

Communist universalism is suspended in the framework of the communist camp, which is evolving in the direction of poly-centrism and not universalism. On the other hand, the ideological obligation of Moscow to communize the world has equipped America with an anti-communist ideology which, practically speaking, is the global policy of the United States. In other words, communist universalism far more effectively mobilizes anti-communists than communists.

The myth of communist universalism often paralyzes the most pragmatically thought out policy of the Soviet Union. Nasser announced clearly and positively that *he wants no Soviet armies* on Egyptian territory. The Egyptian president fears—and rightly so—the political and ideological consequences of such an operation. Communist universalism makes it impossible for the Soviet Union to construct an alliance system, and there are fewer and fewer candidates for satellites, even in the camp of the "socialist states."

But the liquidation of the myth of the communization of the world is an internal problem for the Soviet Union. At the heart of the matter Russia has no other problems than internal problems.

9. THE TITLE REMAINS THE SAME

Thirty years have passed since the appearance in Warsaw of Adolf Bocheński's book, *Between Germany and Russia*, published by *Polityka* [a weekly published in Warsaw before the war by the editor of *Kultura*]. The problem embraced by the title is as real today as ever. The contents of our historical scenario have undergone radical changes, but the title remains the same.

We repeat over and over again to the point of boredom that Poland lies between Russia and Germany, but what does this really mean? Is this an unchanging geographical fact which undergoes no change or evolution? Unfortunately this is a dynamic and not a static problem and, consequently—if we can express it this way—Poland is more and more between Russia and Germany and not less and less. The proportions of this problem continually grow, and not to our advantage.

Olgierd Górka, in his work about the causes of the collapse and rebirth of the Republic, cites the following figures from the period of the First Partition: The Prussia of Frederic II had about 4 million inhabitants, the Russia of Catherine II about 20 million, and the Polish Republic 12 million. In other words, Prussia and Russia together had at their disposition twice as much potential power and possibilities as Poland. The relationship of the Republic to both of her neighbors can be expressed by the ratio of 1:2.

At the time of the Second Partition this ratio was already 1:3.5.

In 1937, when Bocheński wrote his book, the ratio had assumed the proportions of 1:8.

And today in 1967? According to recently announced data, Poland numbers 32 million inhabitants. According to the last edition of the *Dictionary of Politics*, Soviet Russia numbers 226,253,000 inhabitants. (An American source gives the figure of 235 million.) The German Federal Republic numbers 58,587,000, and the GDR, 16,116,000 inhabitants. Rounding out the above figures we may assume that the combined potential of Soviet Russia and (a united) Germany amounts to more than 302 million inhabitants. It follows from the above data that while the relationships of Poland to both her neighbors at the time of the First Partition was expressed by the ratio of 1:2, today the ratio is nearly 1:10.

In maintaining that we are more and more and not less and less between Russia and Germany I had in mind the continual increase in this ratio to our disadvantage.

Adolf Bocheński was neither the first nor the last to analyze this problem. The political problematics of Germany and Russia have in the course of the past thirty years undergone change and reorientation, but Poland is still between Russia and Germany, and Bocheński's study had not lost any of its contemporary significance—though the development of events has underscored several of his ideas and conclusions.

We should learn from the mistakes of distinguished politicians and journalists, because the errors of average politicians and journalists show only that they did not understand the problems with which they were occupied.

Bocheński, thirty years ago—to a certain extent like us today— saw the greatest danger for Poland in an understanding between our neighbors. The Ribbentrop-Molotov Pact, which Bocheński did not foresee, was the *de facto* beginning of the Fourth Partition of Poland.

Antagonism between Germany and Russia lies in our interest. Experience teaches that in every situation of this type one of the sides always shows a greater tendency toward an understanding. Bocheński voiced the view that we should support the neighbor that demonstrated the most intransigent position and not the neighbor ready to sign an agreement. Thirty years ago Soviet Russia showed a tendency toward understandings and agreements, while Germany took an implacably anti-Soviet position.

The author of the book discussed concluded the following: The most dangerous of all possible combinations is a Russian-German agreement. German-Russian antagonism is advantageous for us, but it never lasts long. Only the liquidation of one of our neighbors could permanently protect us from the specter of an understanding between Russia and Germany. The Germans, according to Bocheński's theory, aimed at the dismemberment not of Poland but of Soviet Russia. Here is a characteristic quote: "Today from the time of Ludendorf and his 'Balticum,' the great, powerful aspirations that have been aroused for German expansion deep into Russia have indisputably moved ahead of the little imperialistic plan for conquering the sandy districts of Pomerania in an agreement with Russia."

The adherents of these views have simultaneously underestimated and overestimated the Germans. They underestimated their territorial acquisitiveness which made them look greedily even at those sandy Pomeranian districts. On the other hand they overestimated the German political genius. The Germans are not and never were imperialists. The English and the French were the imperialists. The Russians are imperialists. The Germans are invaders, and up until the fall of the Third Reich believed that foreign policy is a byproduct of military action. The Germans betrayed Clausewitz because they reversed his thesis. They considered to the end that military operations solve all political problems. The Germans had no plans and no political program in relation to Soviet Russia, and suffered disaster because they had nothing to offer the Soviet nation except slavery.

The leading idea in Bocheński's solution is always the specter of a German-Russian understanding, which should be avoided at all costs. It is clear and logical that the liquidation of Russia or Germany would exclude for all time the possibility of a German-Russian understanding. For years we have repeated the saying about the two millstones which have ground us down. Breaking one of the two stones would, of course, free Poland from catastrophe.

The theoretically logical thesis that the liquidation of one of our neighbors bars a German-Russian understanding and thus strengthens and safeguards our independence has been shown to be completely erroneous. This is a logical thesis on condition that the liquidator of Germany is not Russia or, vice-versa, that the liquidator of Russia is not Germany. At the end of the Second World War Germany underwent liquidation, but Poland did not obtain independence. Had Germany won the war and defeated Russia, Poland would not have obtained her freedom either.

It has been shown, then, that breaking one of the "millstones" does not in the least automatically bring an improvement in Poland's situation.

Bocheński underestimated the significance of the peculiar balance of power between our two neighbors. Thirty years ago, as today, the rebuilding of the Soviet Union lay in Polish interests, but on condition that the reconstruction did not mean a significant strengthening of Germany. The Germans today are concerned not about the "sandy districts of Pomerania" but about the land beyond the Oder and Neisse rivers. For these reasons to the same degree that an independent Ukraine would decrease our dependence on Russia, which would be desirable, an independent Ukraine allied with Germany would clearly make our situation worse.

Is it realistic in practice to evaluate every political project according to the criteria of the German-Russian balance of power, and at the same time aspire to make ourselves independent of both Germany and Russia? This is basically a situation from which there is no exit, because our natural ally against Germany is Russia and our natural ally against Russia must be Germany. The victory of one side or the other—whether it be Russia or Germany—destroys the balance between our neighbors which constitutes the condition of our independence. Entering into an alliance with Russia against Germany makes us dependent on Russia, and entering into an alliance with Germany against Russia makes us dependent on Germany.

Anyone trying to solve the above matters after three decades must conclude that the problem of Polish independence in its 1939 borders was a square circle. Bocheński was right when he asserted that Poland (then) must be a revisionist country, aspiring toward a change in the *status quo*. He was also right in maintaining that German-Russian antagonism is a passing phase.

A state that can exist only as long as both its neighbors disagree in reality is not an independent state. Independence for such a state is clearly circumstantial and automatically comes to an end when understanding appears between its neighbors.

Joseph Piłsudski was a man who was fully aware of this problem.

His conception of an eastern policy aimed at leading Poland out of the German-Russian vicious circle. In January 1920, Piłsudski proposed an alliance of all of the nations of Russia's former empire with Poland and with a democratic Russia, and made it clear that Ukrainian independence must be recognized.

Unfortunately, there was no democratic Russia then, and Piłsudski's proposition was considered impossible to accept by either the Bolsheviks or the White Russians.

The battle of Warsaw has been proclaimed to be one of the most important battles of modern European history. From the Polish point of view this only delayed disaster for nineteen years. We won the battle but lost the eastern program. We won the battle, but we lost the war.

It seems that all too small a percentage of Polish society fully understood what the struggle was all about. It is always possible to mobilize Poles with some locally patriotic slogan such as the "Defense of Lwów." If Poles have to choose between Zaolzie or a Polish-Czechoslovakian Federation," they choose Zaolzie. If they have to choose between Lvov or an alliance with an independent Ukraine, they choose Lvov. There are always some inflexible people who cover up their stupidity and shortsightedness with a gesture of Reytan.

Historians cite dozens of reasons for the disaster of Piłsudski's eastern program. It is a fact, however, that then we still had a chance of taking up the eastern idea independently, in our own name. The Russian peace constitutes a slab placed on the grave of an independent Polish eastern policy.

Bocheński concluded that we can undertake a new eastern experiment only with Germany as a partner.

It is easy to criticize today and even easier to condemn. Bocheński was searching in the conditions of his time for a way out of the historical trap in which the Second Republic found itself. It is possible to criticize Beck and the camp of Piłsudski's followers, but it should be stated objectively that there was no way out of the trap. If Piłsudski's eastern program—even in its basic points— had been realized, and if an independent Ukrainian state had been created and united with Poland by an alliance and economic agreements, then it could be conceded that the Second Republic would have extricated itself from the German-Russian trap and obtained the basic right of independence.

The "Miracle on the Vistula" constituted a repulsion of the enemy from the gates of the capital, but it was not a victory which made it possible to impose Polish conditions on Russia. Nonetheless the legend of the "Miracle on the Vistula" gave rise to a false theory of power politics which made it difficult to assess reality objectively, even with a sober head, during the interwar period.

If someone in 1937 had written that Poland is a seasonal state, he would have been accused of treason and cooperation with German propaganda. In reality we were a seasonal state, because our independent existence depended entirely on German-Russian relations, over which we had no influence. We were in a significantly worse situation than in the period of the First Partition. At that time Poland had three times as many people as Prussia and had diplomatic and political possibilities. I personally think that the anti-Russian policy of the Four-year Sejm was erroneous, but nonetheless there were then still various solutions which offered the possibility of choice. In the final years of interwar independence Polish policy had no choice and every solution led straight down the path to catastrophe. The German-Russian understanding meant a new partition. A German-Russian war had to bring victory to either Russia or Germany, and consequently complete dependence of Poland on its victorious neighbor. Complete disaster for both Germany and Russia was a one-in-a-million chance.

Not only did we have no possibilities for extricating ourselves from this fatal circle, but the rim of the circle became more and more difficult to break with every year. I mean by this that our neighbors became more and more powerful neighbors in proportion to both their population potential and industrial power. It was not within our power to change the fact that the ratio of potential power (population plus industry) of our neighbors was growing more rapidly than the Polish potential, with the result that Poland became relatively weaker and weaker *vis-à-vis* Germany and Russia and not stronger and stronger.

Had the Second World War not occurred and had atomic energy not been discovered, the super-powers of Russia and the United States would not have come into being. I will risk the view that Poland had no possibility of enduring in a Europe of the old style as an independent state. Even if there had been no Hitler, German-Russian antagonism sooner or later would have been transformed into a coincidental understanding at Poland's expense. Were the historical epoch of sovereign states to have lasted unbroken until the end of this century, Poland would have to have fallen, because she would not have been capable of defending her sovereignty.

Had there been no Second World War in which 20 million Soviet citizens perished, Russia and Germany would have overwhelmed us with their population potential. Piłsudski was right in appreciating that only a world power could endure between Russia and Germany, but not a middle-sized state. That great power super-patriotism which reached its peak after Piłsudski's death was not only an amusing manifestation of megalomania but also a sign of an unconscious instinct which told us that Poland should be great in order to survive. Those same people who swore at Piłsudski for his Kiev campaign, eighteen years later gave voice to the slogans of a great power. But then it was already too late to think about being a great power.

The English and the French can mourn to the depths of their souls the passing of pre-war Europe with its "concert" of sovereign powers which looked neither to Moscow nor to Washington, but decided the fate of its own continent. But the Poles have no reason to share these sentiments, because there was no room for an independent Poland in a Europe of sovereign powers.

We lost our chance in 1920 because we were not able to reconstruct a great-power Poland. We were not yet a great power nation and therefore Piłsudski's idea did not meet with the solid mass support of the society, which was an indispensible condition of success. Piłsudski had thousands of brave Kmicices and Wołodyjowskis[1] behind him but he did not have any empire builders around him, nor did he have a society behind him, which thought in great-power terms.

Historically we are an old nation—significantly older than the Russians. We already have our imperialistic great-power phase behind us and no one will make the Poles into an imperialist nation, just as no one will make an imperialist nation out of the Spaniards. Both the Spaniards and we had our great days centuries ago.

Though we are today a satellite nation, our prospects for the distant future are better than in the years preceding the Second World War. We are still between Russia and Germany and, as before, we cannot bar a German-Russian understanding. Germany, however, is divided and not fully sovereign. An American army is stationed on West German territory. A Europe of sovereign powers, whose grandeur and full bloom falls in the nineteenth century when Poland did not exist even in the form of a satellite state—that Europe belongs to the past.

Personally, I do not believe in the restoration of Europe as an independent "third force." I tend toward the view of many American economists that by the end of this century Japan will secure the position of the world's third super-power.

I am convinced that the role of the United States in Europe will increase and not decrease. From the moment when the Russians

1 Brave Polish soldiers in Henryk Sienkiewicz's *Trilogy* of historical novels about seventeenth-century Poland. [ed.]

undertake construction of an anti-missile defense system (ABM), the European atomic mini-potential will be reduced to almost zero. It is possible that the Soviet ABM system will not fully protect Russia against a massive American atomic attack, but I believe we can assume as certain that it would fully protect the Soviet Union against an attack by a miniaturized French or British atomic force.

The Russians will have their ABM system. On the other hand, it does not appear that Europe will ever have its own ABM system. In sum, it must be maintained that the security of western Europe will depend on the United States to an even greater extent than heretofore. The idea of sovereignty based on an atomic mini-potential has in Europe proven to be a costly dud.

From time to time there appears in the world press a small bit of news which throws a ray of light on an immeasurably important problem.

Arnaud de Borchgrave in one of his articles (*Newsweek*, October 16, 1967) cites the characteristic results of a study done by one of the public opinion polling offices. According to the data cited, it appears that only one Frenchman in five fully trusts Germany. In Germany the situation turns out to be almost identical. At the same time this study shows that the Germans trust the Americans significantly more than they do the French, and the French trust the Americans significantly more than they do the Germans.

The Americans will not leave Europe because the European nations trust the United States more than they do each other. And this factor is perhaps more important than the continually widening gulf between the technological power of the United States and of Europe.

All this means that while Poland is still clearly between Russia and Germany, this fact has a different meaning than it did thirty years ago. Our fate has ceased to be a function of Russia's relationship to Germany and is today to a certain extent a function of Russia's relationship to the United States. Any changes in eastern and central Europe can appear only as a consequence of an understanding between Washington and Moscow. No European power, individually or collectively, can change the *status quo* on the continent.

In speaking about the *status quo* we always have in mind the "Iron Curtain." At the heart of the matter the *status quo* embraces both eastern and western Europe. In the same way that the Poles cannot change the Polish-Czechoslovakian border, the Germans cannot move their border with France by a single milimeter. Not all European states are satellites, but no European state either individually or collectively can negotiate with Russia or with the United States as an equal with an equal.

In recent years the Soviets have significantly expanded their conventional armed forces and would probably be capable of seizing all of western Europe without using atomic weapons. Correspondents for American papers in the Soviet Union emphasize in their political evaluations the paranoid Russian fear of closer American-Chinese relations. Many Russians suspect that the Americans have secretly helped the Chinese in their construction of atomic weapons. Soviet specialists have a very bad opinion of Chinese technology and it is difficult for them to believe that Peking has produced atomic weapons without any help from the outside.

If the Russians should conquer Europe with conventional forces, the Americans would not risk an atomic bombardment of the Soviet Union. But then Washington would have to undertake a very unorthodox policy in order to restore the swaying world balance of power. Closer relations with the Chinese, though at the price of significant concessions, would then be an obvious move because of its immediate suitability.

The security of Europe depends to a great extent on the situation in Asia. If a normalization of Soviet-Chinese relations occurred after the death of Mao Tse-Tung, Moscow's policy in Europe would take on an aggressive character. This does not mean that the Russians would move to conquer France, but I believe that they would try to impose a one-sided solution to the Berlin problem.

For hundreds of years the Polish question has been a strictly and exclusively European question. Both for Prince Adam Czartoryski and for Adolf Bocheński, the Polish question began and ended in Europe. Both for Czartoryski and for Bocheński Europe was not only a concert of sovereign states but the continent that created History and led the world.

Certain historians maintain that ancient Rome fell because 60 per cent of its budget was devoted to paying for pageantry. Europe fell not as a result of decadence nor as a result of military disaster. The Europeans produced the twilight of their continent in their laboratories. The inventions and scientific discoveries which constitute the foundation of contemporary technology came into being in Europe. It has developed, however, that technology requires gigantic financial resources and a spacious economic base. We raised the magical plants, but Europe is too small a "flowerpot" to insure the proper conditions for the development of those plants. Contemporary technology—90 per cent of it of European origin—

has molded two continental states beyond Europe into super-powers, whose appearance on the historical scene has brought about the twilight of Europe.

The Polish question has ceased to be a strictly European problem, because today there are no strictly European problems. Is this a turn for the better or for the worse?

Despite the fact that ten centuries of our history links us with the Europe of the leading sovereign powers of the world, and despite the fact that the Poles have always been European patriots, it is my conviction that we have no reason to shed tears at the funeral of old-style Europe.

If the Polish question were still a strictly European question this would mean driving Poland back into a situation with no way out. There would be no room for us between Russia and a powerful, united Germany without an American controller. Those who answer with a program of federation for eastern Europe forget that in such a system the Germans simply would not agree to any federation. It would be sufficient for Berlin to lead the Czechs and Hungarians to understand that it considered a federation with Poland an unfriendly act in relation to Germany.

A powerful Germany controlled by no one would make never-ending territorial claims against us. An alliance with Russia against Germany, or an alliance with Germany against Russia, or an alliance with neither Russia nor Germany in passive anticipation of a German-Russian understanding—each of these variants spells disaster.

The historical lesson of the twenty-year inter-war period can be conceived of as follows: In an independent Europe of sovereign states Poland can be either a great power, or a Congress Kingdom, or a General Government. In our geographical position only a great power, and not a middle-sized state such as the Second Republic, can survive in an old-style Europe.

A skeptical reader will consider here that it is more and more difficult for the super-powers to control smaller states. Rumania has—to a certain degree—broken away from the Soviet line, so where is the guarantee that Germany will not one day break away from American care and control?

The emancipation of the small and medium-sized European states in both spheres of influence will certainly go forward, which is certainly very much in the Polish interest. The super-powers, however, will not give up their exclusiveness in deciding matters of war and peace. Germany can be more or less sovereign, but Moscow and Washington will not agree to a system which makes it possible for Germany to decide unilaterally the detonation of World War

III. Should the German Federal Republic choose to liberate East Germany, the Americans would use the sharpest means to liquidate this "liberation" from the start. And vice-versa, should Communist East Germany choose to "liberate" the Federal Republic, it would be brutally called back into order by the Soviet authorities.

Young people raised in post-war Europe are not surprised at anything. For me, however, raised in a Europe of sovereign powers, the bisecting of Berlin is a more astounding phenomenon than a flight to the moon. In old-style Europe a state only half the size of Germany would never agree to the bisection of its own capital. But today Berlin is first of all a Soviet-American problem and only secondarily a European and German problem. For the Germans Berlin is a fundamental and urgent problem. For the Russians and Americans Berlin is neither a fundamental nor an urgent problem— only one of many.

A neutralist frame of mind is very slowly crystallizing in Europe. Such a frame of mind is being nurtured among the population and will in time find expression in government policies. People are questioning the size of the military budgets even in Germany, and even in Germany people are speaking about a reduction in military forces. Both NATO and the Warsaw Pact are clearly losing their impetus and dynamism.

It is difficult to be surprised at this reaction. The "man on the street" concludes that if someone were deprived of his driver's license for life he would be furious if he were taxed for the purchase of an expensive car. Why should we spend billions for defense, if the right to decide about war and peace has been taken from us. Regardless of whether we are armed or unarmed, Washington and Moscow will decide about war and peace, not the European capitals.

Of course governments and the *Establishment* still think in the traditional way and the evolution in the direction of neutralism will move forward slowly.

Military forces make sense if it is possible to change or defend the *status quo* with them. None of the European armed forces meets the above criteria. The armed forces of the German Federal Republic exist to *guard the status quo*, because this is what Washington wants. At the same time the government of the Federal Republic proclaims a program of *revising the status quo*.

There are no policies free of contradictions, but progress and evolution always aim in the direction of eliminating contradictions. A neutral Germany within the framework of a neutral Europe would seem to be a far more probable solution than a fully sovereign Germany with its own atomic weapons.

Europeans, both east and west, no longer have any reason "to play Indian," because though they are allowed to produce expensive equipment, they are not allowed to use it. "Playing Indian" on our continent has become completely monopolized by the Russians and the Americans. It is possible to take as a given that there will be no European war. Only a Soviet-American war can explode on European territory—no other kind can.

Despite the fact that we are today a satellite state, I consider Poland to be in a better position between Russia and America than it was between Russia and a sovereign Germany. Poland is a satellite state, but it exists on the map of Europe and it will not disappear from the map of Europe. The United States and not Germany is Russia's contracting party on the continent, and the chances of a reversal of the alliances and a German-Russian understanding are smaller than ever in the past. The elimination of Germany as the dominant power on the continent creates for Poland the possibility of being transformed into the leading eastern European state and gaining the position of Russia's major partner. The condition for an evolution along these lines is not only the gradual conciliation of the continent and a solution to the German question, but also the discovery of a historical significance for Poland in a new Europe, which is in no way similar to the old.

10. FOOD FOR THOUGHT

The policy of containment has degenerated into the policy of being a "policeman." In other words, America intervenes militarily in the belief that a small war protects her against a large war. The basic argument in the Vietnam debate goes like this: if we do not offer military resistance to the Viet Cong today, tomorrow we will have to fight hundreds of millions of Chinese.

Generally in the West we do not realize the dimensions of this "policeman" policy. I have taken the following data from Ronald Steel's book, *Pax Americana* (NY: The Viking Press): In 1967 the United States had 700,000 troops in 30 countries of the world. America is a member of four regional defense alliances, is linked by mutual aid agreements with 42 nations, belongs to 53 international organizations, and permanently provides economic and military assistance to more than 100 nations in different parts of the world.

Obligations of this scale, and especially the war in Vietnam, to a greater and greater degree condition the internal socio-economic structure of the United States. Senator Fulbright in a speech given on December 13 of last year expressed the view that America is adapting its economy for permanent war. According to the data cited by the Senator, industries and trade corporations working for the military employ 10 per cent of the total working force of the United States. The "military-industrial complex" is becoming an important factor directly influencing both the politics and the economy of America.

A power that is linked by pacts of mutual assistance with 42 nations of the world must undertake "small wars" as a permanent phenomenon. Each "little war" of course can turn into a medium-sized war, bloody and expensive like Vietnam.

At *Kultura* we are also very far from affirming the politics of force as a universal ideal. Personally, I am furthest from endorsing the theories of Machiavelli, but in describing and analyzing the course of a chess game one cannot depend on the rules binding in tennis. Pragmatic politics can be understood and evaluated only within the framework of the categories of pragmatism.

A world government, the liquidation of national armies, universal disarmament, and the abolition of all boundaries would be to my liking. Perhaps it will be this way someday. One may regret that the lion murders innocent gazelles and does not live on spinach, but nevertheless an objective scientist analyzing the lion's habits must accept the fact that he is a flesh-eating animal. In the epoch in which we happen to live, there is, unfortunately, no world government, only powers who carry out the politics of force. One can regret this, but a scientist cannot replace factual analysis with lamentations and moral preachments.

I have put my entire life's work into the study of political problems and in a modest way I feel professionally qualified for analysis and criticism in this area. On the other hand, I do not feel qualified to anathematize or morally condemn.

In Vietnam people die not only as a result of the American bombardments. For many years the Viet Cong have carried out assassinations, bestial murders, and liquidations of villages with women and children included. The anti-communists in Vietnam certainly have the moral right to defend their lives and their convictions.

In my estimation, there is nothing more immoral than to reduce a complicated moral problem to a few campaign slogans. This is the method which the communists have used for fifty years. The Soviets fight Israel not only politically but also condemn her morally. In totalitarian states morality, like everything else, is subordinated to current political tactics.

One should always openly condemn what is obviously evil, such as the sentencing of Daniel and Sinyavsky, for example. In complex matters, however, where the right if often fighting against the right and the bad against the bad and barbarianism against barbarianism, it is necessary to avoid oversimplification. In such a situation putting off judgment is not moral indifference, only honest caution.

Let us return to the main course of our discussion. We were speaking about the "policeman" policy of the United States. Every policy is evaluated by its actual achievements. In Asia the results are positive, because China has not been able to expand her sphere of influence. There is also some data which permits one to nourish the hope that Japan in time will be won over to an active policy of containment, which would significantly lighten the Americans' burden.

At the same time a "Napoleonic" situation looms in Europe. In the past the English considered the main dictate of their policies to oppose effectively all attempts at domination of the continent by one power. The Americans took over this postulate from the British and took part in two world wars only for the purpose of not allowing German hegemony over the European continent.

Soviet Russia in recent years has exploited the three following elements of the international situation:

I. The war in Vietnam and the commitment in Asia has brought about not only an atrophy of interest in Europe, but has also created in Washington the supposition bordering on certainty that nothing threatens them from the Russian side. China, and not Russia, represents militant revolution. Personally, I also tend toward the supposition that war does not threaten us from the Russian side, but if it is possible to realize an imperialistic policy successfully without war, only a madman would detonate a war.

II. President Roosevelt admittedly was an opponent of all imperialism and colonialism and in particular had no love for British imperialism. There are many kinds of imperialism. It is possible to administer and prepare people for autonomy according to the British tradition; it is possible to try to mold Negroes into black Frenchmen; and, finally, it is possible to limit oneself to supplying arms and technical assistance in exchange for bases in strategically key locations. This last and least troublesome and most effective kind of imperialism is cultivated by the Russians.

III. No democratic state can declare that it reserves for itself the right of a preventative atomic strike. The person who strikes first is not always the aggressor. If the Polish air force had bombed Berlin on August 31, 1939, Poland would not have been the aggressor with this attack because the German campaign against the Republic was already set to go and had been put into effect. Similarly last year, though Israel struck first, the aggressor was not Israel, but Egypt.

Democratic states, and above all the United States, are limited to a so-called "second strike" strategy, because all others could be termed aggression, and this word is anathema in the democratic vocabulary.

Two points should be emphasized in connection with the above. It is easy to imagine a situation in which a preventive strike could be the only and unrepeatable strategic course guaranteeing not only victory but also rescuing the world from catastrophe. And the second point: Who can guarantee that in ten years' time Russia will not have such a gigantic atomic potential at its disposition that a country attacked by Russian nuclear forces will be incapable of retaliation?

Let us consider the points cited in greater detail. Hitler imagined that the conquest of the continent must mean putting a German governor in every European capital. The model of Russian imperialism is not the "general province," but Finland.

Europe is bordered by three great bodies of water: the Baltic, the Atlantic, and the Mediterranean. The Mediterranean has played the key role in this geographical disposition for a thousand years. The firepower of the American Sixth Fleet still surpasses the firepower of the Soviet Mediterranean units. But numerically, according to British estimates, the Soviets have outdistanced the Americans because the Soviet Mediterranean fleet numbers fifty-five ships and the Sixth Fleet only fifty. The Soviets have the use of bases not only in Egypt and in Syria, but are also negotiating for a former French base in North Africa and for the former British base in Aden. The French are leaving Mers-el-Kebir in Algeria, in spite of the fact that they could hold this base for another ten years according to treaty. Mers-el-Kebir is one of the most modern naval bases. The Russian dream of a "warm water sea" is being realized before our eyes.

Parallel to the strengthening of the Soviets in the Mediterranean basin, a systematic demobilization of NATO is taking place on the continent. The withdrawal of sixteen French air squadrons and six army brigades was a blow to NATO strength. These reductions are also foreseen: the British Army of the Rhine by 5,000 men and the American Seventh Army by 35,000 men.

I have never found any mention of reductions in the Soviet army stationed in East Germany (twenty-two divisions). But why should Russia withdraw from the GDR? No one has demanded this of them and no one is demanding it now. NATO is reducing its forces without setting any conditions for doing so.

Some military and political commentators conclude from the state of affairs outlined above that the weakening of NATO potentially strengthens Germany. If the Americans and the English withdraw from the continent, it follows that the Germans must play an increasingly important role in NATO. In such a situation it will be more and more difficult to refuse the Germans atomic weapons, because the defense of western Europe will to a large extent fall on their shoulders.

The above reasoning is, in my estimation, entirely erroneous. Endowing Germany with atomic weapons would be the most anti-Soviet move which could be imagined in Europe. Only a very powerful NATO and a very powerful western Europe could permit an anti-Soviet provocation on this scale. In reality the Soviet fleet in the Mediterranean Sea, bases in Egypt and Syria—and to-morrow in Algeria, in Aden, and in the Persian Gulf—all seal the division of Germany and completely exclude the possibility of conceding atomic weapons to Germany. The eventuality of negotiations over Berlin and the German question have also been put off into indefinity, because the Russians are in such a favorable position that negotiating the smallest concession from them must be done in one's daydreams.

A Soviet fleet in the Mediterranean, thousands of Soviet specialists in Egypt and in other Middle-Eastern countries—in my opinion, all of this constitutes a part of the Soviet European policy. It is not possible to dominate Europe from the Baltic. It is not possible to dominate Europe with atomic missiles, because Europeans do not believe in the possibility of atomic war on their continent. What would be the advantage to the Russians of the radioactive ruins of the cities of Europe? Europe can be dominated only by conventional means and with an orthodox strategy. Neither Napoleon nor Hitler dominated the seas. The Russians have decided to add a preponderance in naval forces to their preponderance in land forces. According to American sources, Russia is changing herself from a typical land power into a first-rate military power. In the ensuing decades Russia will have not only a chain of bases but also the largest fleet in the Mediterranean Sea. Then the operation to outflank Europe entirely will be completed. What Napoleon and Hitler could not achieve will come true for the Russians. I am not saying that it will happen this way, but I do maintain that the Russians are aiming at this goal with full determination, and I also maintain that no one is hindering them in this operation.

I am certain that the Russians, in contrast to Napoleon and Hitler, do not intend to seize Europe with armed force. They do not foresee war on the continent either. If they succeed in fully out-flanking Europe, it will not be necessary for them to occupy Europe, just as it is not necessary to occupy Finland.

The terms, "threat," "domination," and the like require new definitions today. Western Europe may bloom economically, but nevertheless it is more difficult each month to translate that wealth into political-military strength. If by "threat" we understand an armed invasion, it seems to me that western Europe is not threatened. If by "domination" we understand the creation of a system which makes it impossible to effect any changes on the continent without the agreement of Russia, then domination is increasingly an accomplished fact.

The reader will observe that it has not been possible to change anything in Europe without Russia's consent since the war. This is true, of course, but it is also necessary to consider the chances of obtaining that consent. These chances are a function of the balance of power. Only the side that negotiates from a position of strength can count on success at the bargaining table. From the moment when the Russians have expanded and secured their potential in the Mediterranean Sea and in the Middle East, not only will it be impossible to change anything on the continent with Russia's consent, but no one will have any chance of obtaining that consent through bargaining.

I have emphasized many times in previous articles that the goal of Russia's European policy is security. The Kremlin considers that it is not possible to do too much in this matter. The Russians want to create a situation in which even thinking about a change in the *status quo* would seem comic in its surrealism to a European. In other words, they want to outflank Europe and create a power structure which would make the acceptance of the continental *status quo* an obvious matter which is not subject to discussion.

A rich, technologically advanced western Europe is as necessary to Russia as Hong Kong is necessary to China. But the fundamental problem is to disable Europe without resorting to war. The probability of war recedes with every passing month.

In maintaining this, I have in mind the continually advancing Soviet military potential around western Europe.

Because Moscow does not meet any resistance in its plans, it is necessary to conclude that in the near future the Soviet preponderance in the European sphere will be so enormous that war in this area will not be a realistic proposition in the purely strategic sense.

Europeans on the whole think in an old-fashioned and conservative way. By conquest they understand invasion. If Soviet tanks were moving on the continent, there would be panic and chaos. But a Soviet fleet in the Mediterranean Sea does not even make anyone blink. Winning a dominant position need not mean invasion.

The Russians are too realistic to dream about Soviet *Gauleiters* in every European capital. Their goal is to secure the *status quo* on the continent and to make impossible its revision.

Although neither the Americans nor even the Germans have ever proposed a revision of the *status quo* by force, it should be stated as a matter of fact that *there does not in fact exist any other method than force to change the status quo.* I do not have in mind military action. But in negotiations of this kind the leading role is not played by legalism or by the logic of argumentation, but only by the potential power at the disposition of the negotiators.

As soon as Europe has been outflanked and the *status quo* secured, the Russians will turn to the solution of the German question. Of course only speculation is possible in this area. I believe that Moscow will lean on the GDR, which it will try to make more attractive. Joining Berlin and Szczecin would significantly strengthen the position and status of the GDR. Berlin is the historical capital of Germany, and Szczecin is a great port, which the German Democratic Republic lacks. The purpose of this operation would be to demonstrate to the world that the GDR and not the Federal Republic, is the real German state. A second purpose would be to emphasize the thesis that for all Germans, Bonn included, the road to Moscow leads through the GDR and only through the GDR.

Of course, the Russians are in an immeasurably favorable position in Europe compared to the Americans. The Atlantic does not separate them from Europe, and they are not carrying on an expensive and bloody war at the other end of the world. Absolutely nothing threatens Russia from the side of western Europe. There is not a single battalion on the entire continent which would be prepared to march against Moscow. Then what are the Russians afraid of? The staged trial and sentence of Ginsburg and his associates can be explained only by panic. The communist press in England condemned that trial as beyond comprehension. No one in the West—communist or anti-communist—understands this panic.

I think, however, that I would also fear the West if I were a member of the ruling class in the USSR. Is it really possible to democratize Russia and maintain, unimpaired, her *status quo* as the second power in the world?

The paranoid Russian dread of the West—not militarily, but in the sense of cultural and social influence—rests on the fact that there exists in Russia a hunger for freedom which cannot be satisfied by the local Russian product. As a result, young people are inclined to read looking for a foreign freedom, imbedded in the context of foreign culture and foreign social and political influences.

In the European West we observe the internationalization of culture, especially in the expanding field of mass culture. But this same phenomenon means something completely different in Russia. This is an import from a different world—from the enemy camp.

* * *

There is chaos in our concepts and definitions. As an example let us take the policy of containment. From the American point of view the policy of containment has fulfilled its purpose in Europe. The march of communism has been stopped. But the problem of western Europe today is not the march of communism, nor communist aggression, nor revolution. The problem of Europe is the dislocation of the balance of power, and the policy of containment has no answer to this problem.

On January 16 of this year the last period of the British Empire came to an end. On this day Premier Wilson presented the House of Commons with a government austerity program. England ceased to be an active ally of America in Asia and the Far East. The cuts in the budget of the Ministry of Defense, and particularly the canceling of the order for fifty F-11 fighters had a great influence on the further worsening of the European balance of power. But why should we spend 400 million on modern planes capable of bombing Moscow and Leningrad when there will be no war in Europe? The success of the policy of containment has turned against us, leading to a dangerous erosion of the balance of power between western Europe and the Soviet Union. Neither does it seem possible to rebuild the balance of power in Europe. It would be necessary to counter the Soviet atomic missile capability with an analogical American capability based on Western European territory. No one in western Europe would agree to such a project. To sum up, it must be stated that we are accepting not only the *status quo*, but also a *Pax Sovietica*, of which the *status quo* is the symbol.

In the long run, however, I am not a pessimist. There is a fundamental contradiction in Soviet policy. The Russians want to outflank Europe and dominate the continent in order to insure security for themselves from the West once and for all. They want to be in Europe and want to play the leading role in Europe, but at the same time they want to maintain the "Soviet man" in complete isolation and in untainted ideological purity.

The Russians dominate Europe, but inside Russia Europe dominates Soviet society. A European generation of Russians, who do not want to share responsibility with the older generation for the crimes of the past, is growing up.

The Russians have come to Europe—and, in my opinion, for good. Russian military force would crush Europe more quickly than Hitler's did. In accepting peace the Russians are *de facto* agreeing to slow defeat. There is not the slightest doubt that western cultural influences are incomparably more powerful than Soviet cultural influences. It is possible to state objectively that the liberal press in the West has become a spokesman for the Russian intelligentsia. It not only supports, protests, and defends, but also in full measure provides protection. A courageous fighter like Dr. Pavel Litvinov has become a well known personality in the West and should he disappear one day in Moscow, this would be noticed in a few hours. Of course the Soviet authorities could arrest him and send him to a concentration camp, but they could not do this secretly and without paying a penalty. The arrest of Litvinov would bring about a new wave of protest in the western press. A front of solidarity of intellectuals and western intelligentsia with the Russian intelligentsia is slowly beginning to loom up. This is a phenomenon of great political significance, because to a great extent it makes it impossible for the Soviet secret police to commit an illegal act secretly. Thanks to contacts with the West, important documents have gotten through to the outside, and consequently Soviet society has asked about the trial of Vladimir Bukovsky and Ginsburg and associates. In this way the deceptive reports of this trial in the Soviet press have been demasked and the ferment in Russian intellectual circles has deepened even further.

Without boasting it should be stated that this front of solidarity with the Russian intelligentsia was begun by *Kultura*, which first presented the world with the writings of Daniel and Sinyavsky.

And how does the cultural counter-offensive of the official Soviet agents look? A Soviet *Digest* is being published in London. The intellectual level of this richly bound monthly is unbelievable. One must read several issues to believe this with one's own eyes. It is possible to maintain that *the Soviets in giving up the use of force have given up everything, because they have nothing else*. The further evolutionary development of the situation will follow from the above simple fact.

In the sphere of political power it seems to me that the European *balance of power* can be rebuilt only outside of Europe. The American involvement in southeastern Asia suits the Russians fine, and a Chinese-American war would suit Moscow's wishes even better.

From the point of view of the global policy of the United States, there is no German problem, only a European problem. Similarly, there is no Vietnam problem, only a problem of southeast Asia, and especially of China.

The Americans will be able to undertake talks with Moscow about European affairs when they have some chance of negotiating some concessions. They will have these chances in Asia when—with the help of Japan, and perhaps of Japan and India—they build a new security system which can endure for a long time.

Only one danger threatens Europe in this critical period, namely, a false conception of "Europeism," proclaiming that Europe is a problem exclusively of the Europeans. Then we would be returning to a "Munich situation," with the difference that this time the role of the Third Reich would be played by the Soviet Union.

11. THE PASSIVE PARTY

I have emphasized many times in my articles that only communists can reform communism. But only social pressure can change communists in a given country.

It is possible to outline models and project reforms, but it is most difficult to show the way. In other words, what should be done, practically speaking, in answer to the basic question?

A writer in Poland—even if he differs only in part from our views—is restrained by censorship. Émigré writers (in certain cases) take advantage of their complete freedom, but the estrangement of many years of separation is a burden to them.

Kultura is in an exceptional situation. We receive letters from Poland through various means and talk with dozens of Poles visiting the West. How do Poles from Poland evaluate the situation at home? I will try to answer this question on the basis of authentic and carefully gathered materials.

The majority accept uncritically the official arguments that the Polish People's Republic has made "enormous" economic progress in its twenty year history. Polish society is characterized not only by a low standard of living but also by small demands. A large part of the society has made real social and economic advances. These people evaluate their situation as significantly more advantageous than before the war.

At the same time Polish society tolerates bad organization, waste, low productivity, and low efficiency in work, and difficulties and inconveniences in arranging the simplest matters in offices and institutions. Everyone grumbles and remains satisfied with grumbling. This chronic grumbling makes no impression on anyone.

Individuals absolve themselves with the statement: "What can I do in a matter in which the entire nation is powerless?" After the fiascos of collective armed action a lack of faith in the purposefulness and effectiveness of any collective action has taken root. I quote verbatim: "The people complain, criticize and even condemn, but always as a passive party."

Polish patriotism has lost its activism. One of our correspondents puts forward the view that in the present situation, passivity and apathy are the unpatriotic if universal base.

The tradition of collective action and manifestations has been broken. Collective action—undertaken in an absolutely proper matter—would renew society's faith in its own power, even if it would bring certain sacrifices (arrest, loss of position). This type of action, undertaken spontaneously in 1956, brought about important gains.

War, occupation, the uprising, the period of Stalinism—one can count many causes of exhaustion and discouragement. But in the eyes of our correspondents and those with whom we have talked, the causes cited above do not explain the phenomenon of social passivity. At best they explain it only in part.

The people are aware of their economic impotence. A good and efficient economy constitutes the base of all demands, from increases in pay to greater political independence. "A producer of a good product," to quote an opinion from Poland, "is always more independent than a bungler."

The Finns owe their political status in large measure to the remarkable organization of their economy, which arouses the admiration of the Soviets. It is sufficient to cite the opinion of Zhdanov (Djilas, *Conversations with Stalin*) about Finnish goods: "Everything is always delivered punctually, perfectly packaged, and is of first-rate quality." High quality products impress not only the Russians, but all customers, both East and West.

In summary:

I. High quality goods give the producer an objective basis for demanding a high price for the articles produced and gives the worker a basis for demanding a high salary.

II. High quality goods create possibilities for economic maneuvering. They are more sought after, and it is easier to sell them with the advantageous conditions of a greater number of buyers. Only first-rate goods win permanent foreign markets.

III. High quality impresses Russia. If Polish production were on a high level, it might be possible to exploit this in negotiations with the Soviets.

IV. Increasing the standard of living of a society is possible only through making the economy more efficient and making labor more productive.

The above theses, which could be multiplied endlessly, do not exhaust the problem.

From the socio-political point of view, most important are the damages of a higher order caused by a bad economy. Inefficient work, and the like—the entire nightmarish climate—demoralize and weaken the society. Dogmatic anti-communists, who can be compared only to the Stalinists, and vice versa, pay homage to the principle of "the worse the better."

Dogmatic anti-communists count on the bankruptcy and fall of communism. Dogmatic communists count on the bankruptcy and fall of capitalism. In reality, however, it does not look like either the bankruptcy of communism or the bankruptcy of capitalism. On the other hand, the bankruptcy of dogmatism on both sides of the Iron Curtain should be speeded up, because dogmatists, regardless of their political color, retard progress and evolution in the desired direction.

Many of our correspondents put forward the thesis that it is impossible to organize an efficient economic system in the existing system of the Polish People's Republic. Hundreds of examples are cited in support of this assertion. The evidence in this matter is so enormous that it is impossible to doubt the correctness of the opinion. But what is the way out? A significant percentage of the people in the country show passivity, apathy, and cynicism toward the above state of affairs. And this is why the perimeter of the vicious circle remains closed.

"The worse, the better." This is worse for the society and better for the ruling class. The society becomes emaciated, undynamic, and subjugated. This means security for the ruling class, and not less but more stabilization. The dictatorship of the ruling class can be maintained and secured only at the price of Sovietization of the society.

What is the essence of Sovietization? The Soviet man, as a result of long-lasting conditioning, accepts the view that society by definition is a passive mass ruled by an active Party élite. This is that eastern "father" complex. The Tsar is father of the nation, Stalin is father of the nation, Khrushchev is father of the nation. In this system, society is a perpetual child which must suffer the consequences of its father's faults. But one does not choose his father nor make him responsible. He is the father and that is enough.

Polish society, conditioned by western culture, does not demonstrate a tsar-father complex. Nonetheless the Sovietization of the psyche of the society has made significant progress. The cardinal sign of Sovietization is the passivity flowing from the acceptance, not of the system but of one's own impotence. An analysis of jokes from Poland throws interesting light on this problem. The joke fulfills the role of a "substitute reaction." One laughs at those whom one cannot fight. One makes a clown out of Gomułka, whom no one dares oppose. One jeers at a system which everyone humbly endures. But the basic social meaning of the Warsaw jokes rests on the fact that it is not the *mocker*, but the *jeered at* who *laughs last*.

If it is true—which I personally do not doubt—that the present socio-economic model makes it impossible to introduce a rational economy, it is also true that the Polish system will not be cured by the Americans, nor by the French, nor by the Eskimos; only the Poles can make it healthy.

In the estimation of our correspondents, incompetence constitutes one of the fundamental plagues of Poland's economic life. In industry the administrative positions are teeming with dilettantes whose only qualifications are a Party card and a diploma from the E U M L. The E U M L or Evening University of Marxism-Leninism is a popular version of the Higher School of the Social Sciences of the Central Committee. In Silesia and in Poznań well-trained personnel in several cases have carried out a successful boycott of the E U M L graduates. The engineers and skilled workers are aware that the top positions would be filled by E U M L graduates even if the higher technical institutes graduated an army of experts for whom there was no work. But Gomułka does not want experts. The First Secretary values only docile Party men.

Only genuine experts can improve economic life. In Hungary remarkable improvements appeared after the principle was adopted that not Party qualifications, but professional qualifications should determine who occupies a position in industry.

Why are organization and the level of economic life so important?

Hungry people driven to extremes organize riots. People who earn well and who live in regularized economic and social conditions are sure of themselves and conscious of their rights. Neither of these two types of "social masses" is ideal for a dictatorship. The ideal for a dictator are the socio-economic conditions obtaining in the Polish People's Republic. No one is dying of hunger, but on the other hand no one is certain any day or any hour. The daily routine—public transportation, arranging things in public offices, buying food and clothing, chasing additional sources of income—everything, in sum, makes one become exhausted, lose hope, and become passive. If one adds to this the daily battling with the bureaucracy, incompetence, and negligence, the picture is complete. All this constitutes one of the methods of the Sovietization of society. The goal is acceptance—not of the system (the Party does not depend on this), but of one's own impotence. The goal is the recognition of the passivity of society as normal. The goal is to convince everyone and each person individually that any collective action is unrealistic madness. The goal is to beat into people's heads that any form of democracy is neither good nor bad, but simply absurd. The essence of Sovietization is to create in people—after long conditioning—the certainty that the system in which they live, irregardless of how we classify it, constitutes a situation with no exit with which they must come to terms in order to live.

Personally, I do not agree with all the points of our correspondents' evaluations. Many of them put all their hopes in forms of pressure from outside. There are even those who consider that the ideal in our situation would be the Anglo-Saxon model which "has passed its examination in Western Germany remarkably well."

These are all dreams characterizing the degree of Sovietization of the society. Because politics in the Soviet system is an area reserved for the ruling élite, the general level of political thought declines each year and loses its connection with reality. Independent political thought has collapsed completely under present conditions.

I would propose that our analysis include the following points:

I. Industry is being built in the Polish People's Republic, but there has been no industrial revolution. An industrial revolution is not a high standard of living, and not even the advance of the working class to the status of a partner with full rights, but above all it is a change in the social mentality. We are characterized by a feudal mentality, anti-economic and anti-mercantile. An efficiently operating industry does not automatically bring freedom. Even with favorable international circumstances, freedom is accessible only to those countries at a certain economic level.

II. Only experts can make the communist economic system healthy. Individual actions are important, but creative changes require collective action. Under Polish conditions collective action must have a professional and not an ideological character. The solidarity and consciousness of the experts should be the point of exit. The protest of the thirty-four writers is a good example of collective action with the support of professional ties. Why should the engineers, chemists, or electrical technicians be worse than the writers?

III. One of the main conquests of the industrial revolution is fixing in the mass of workers the conviction that industrial action leads to its goal. In our tradition the strike is treated on a level with Somosierra.[2] It is a mad act ending in hopeless struggle with the

2 A defile leading to Madrid which Polish cavalry opened up in an almost suicidal charge during Napoleon's campaign in Spain. [ed.]

police and with the military. It would not occur to anyone in Poland to apply the term industrial action to these Somosierras. This is why I maintain that industry is being built in the Polish People's Republic, but that the industrial revolution has been strangled. Consequently, we have industry, but we are not an industrial nation. Because we are not an industrial nation our economy is bad and inefficient.

The indicator of steel production is a magical formula only for the Stalinists. Industrial mentality is in fact a much more important factor. Switzerland does not have a Nowa Huta,[3] but thanks to the economic mentality of its citizens, it will be a model which we could not imitate for the next hundred years.

IV. A fundamental condition for Poland's beginning its evolution toward the model of industrial democracy, is for society to regain a feeling of dynamic initiative. Society must cease to be a passive commandeered mass; it must cease to be a grumbling infant and an object in the contest for power between factions of the ruling class.

Under Polish conditions it is necessary to begin everything from "A." Every collective action, even if on a small scale and even if it does not bring immediate results, rebuilds in a society the sense of initiative and faith in one's own strength.

V. We are not encouraging ill-considered action, but bald nonsense and bald injustice should not be acquitted with passive grumbling.

Collective action should always concern indisputably correct matters. It should avoid a "general showdown." Collective action should always concern a concrete matter. The solution proposed must always be realistic and possible to adopt.

VI. The experience not of twenty years as in Poland, not of fifty years as in the Soviet Union, but the experience of hundreds of years embracing the brightest period of industrial development in history shows that industrial action always pays and that nothing can replace it as an instrument of emancipation for the working world. Industrial action takes the form of a strike only in a crisis situation. At the heart of the matter the right to strike means the right to criticize and the right of a given group of workers to collective defense of its socio-economic interests.

People in power—whether it be Gomułka or the director of a super industrial firm—are liberal and conciliatory only in proportion to the pressure of those whom they rule. If there is no pressure from the ruled, the "liberalism" of the rulers is at an end.

VII. Neither a new constitution nor free elections will create democracy in Poland. The actual form of democracy must be

3 A huge steel-producing complex near Cracow. [ed.]

fought for and evolved. A change in international political circumstances may improve or worsen our chances, but no one will offer
us democracy as a present. It is a kind of socio-political culture
which must grow out of us alone.

Communism is totalitarianized socialism. All of us agree with
the basic postulates of socialism, but only power can force
acceptance of totalism. Totalitarianism, like every kind of force,
can be fought only by never-ceasing pressure. We are not struggling
against Marxism, only against the ways in which it has been
interpreted. Socially it is not important whether someone is a
Catholic or a Marxist. What is important is how one understands
Marxism and how one understands Catholicism. A Torquemada-
Marxist and a Torquemada-Catholic are equally dangerous for
society.

In writing his testament Togliatti considered that communism
had changed from an ideology to an instrument of power policy
in the contest between the two great communist powers. He did
not want to allow the excommunication of the Chinese so that this
degradation of communism into the role of a tool of imperialist
politics would not appear evident and obvious to everyone.

It follows from his critical observations addressed to the Soviet
Union that Togliatti considered that the process of de-Stalinization
in Russia had been stopped half-way down the road.

The position of the Soviet Union *vis-à-vis* Peking would have
been immeasurably stronger if Russia had been able to contrast the
full Stalinization of China with the full de-Stalinization of the
European communist bloc.

Within the framework of Stalinism it is not possible to resolve
nationality problems or problems of independence, nor to democratize the system, nor to convince the Poles, Rumanians, or
Czechs that a lasting understanding with Russia need not be the
equivalent of annexation.

De-colonization is always a two-sided process. The pressure and
progress of the colonial peoples must bring about changes in the
political thinking of the colonizers. The Indians had no chance to
defeat England and win independence with weapons in their hands.
Through long-lasting pressure the colonial peoples in time convinced the enlightened strata of Great Britain that imperialism does
not return those profits it once did either in the economic or political
sense.

It is my conviction that Russia will sometime have to choose
between old-fashioned, imperialistic Stalinism, or the loss of eastern
Europe; but only the satellite nations can set in motion the process
leading to the crystallization of that decision.

12. THE RUSSIAN COMMONWEALTH

How will all this end? If it is by war, there are certain premises which make possible a reconstruction of the end. But if there is no atomic war, what awaits us?

An attempt to answer this question can be made from two perspectives: from the perspective of Moscow or from the perspective of Washington.

For a communist in the Soviet Union there is an obligatory dogma which proclaims that the present crisis and rivalry will end with the world-wide triumph of communism. Let us try to imagine such a situation. Let us assume theoretically that communist governments have been established all over the world by peaceful means—accompanied only by conventional local wars. How does the position of Moscow look in this kind of system?

First of all, "capitalist encirclement" would have disappeared from the historical scene. There would not be any imperialists, nor any capitalists, nor any monopolists, nor any Wall Street.

In Soviet and Chinese eyes "capitalist encirclement" has played a most decisive role. The feeling of ideological solidarity in the face of a powerful enemy is more powerful than the sum of the differences separating Peking and Moscow. But if the common enemy were to disappear, only the differences would remain, with nothing with which to smooth them over.

If we want to give an approximate answer to the question of how the communist world would look we must consider the evolution in the eastern bloc.

During the Stalinist period matters were clear and transparent. Only he who (according to Stalin's words) was ready to serve the Soviet Union blindly and without discussion served in the name of the communists and the revolutionaries. For the Stalinists the "world triumph of communism" meant the expansion of the Soviet Union over the entire earth.

The Stalinist myth above has collapsed not only around the world, but also in Moscow. There will never be a world-wide communist union ruled centrally from the Kremlin. It has not been possible to build this type of union on a significantly smaller scale even today when there exists a capitalist encirclement in whose name it is possible to call out for unity and solidarity.

In spite of the fact that everything in the Soviet Union is "Soviet," the Russians have never been as nationalistic as they are today. The enthusiastic crowd that greeted Gagarin in Moscow was not a crowd of international communists; nor was it a crowd of

"Soviet people"—only a mass of people drunk with the success of a Russian. The force that thrust Gagarin into space was neither a desire to serve a humanitarian ideal nor a thirst for knowledge, but rather the dynamic Russian nationalism associated with this long-standing inferiority complex in relation to the West. In other words, communism, instead of making the Russians more cosmopolitan, has made them more nationalistic.

The political expression of nationalism is always and invariably imperialism. If the Russians were internationalists and unselfish apostles of the communist idea, their policies would not have met with such resistance and distrust within the eastern bloc. But the Russians do not practice ideological apostleship, only propaganda and ordinary power politics. Nationalistic power politics always arouses a nationalistic reaction. The answer to nationalism is nationalism. We observe this kind of reaction in Poland and in all subjugated countries. The popularity of Gomułka is not measured by the criteria of "proletarian internationalism," but on the contrary, by the elbow room for nationalism, that is, the degree of independence from Moscow.

During the Stalinist period Russian nationalism was identified with "proletarian internationalism." By this operation the Russians guaranteed themselves the right to their own nationalism while simultaneously depriving all other nations of the same right. If the nations had accepted the uncomplicated Stalinist philosophy, theoretically nothing would have stood in the way of organizing in time a world-wide Soviet Union with its capital in Moscow.

The Russians did not know how to surmount their own nationalism. It was naive on their part to expect that other nations, on whom communism had been imposed by force, would uproot their own nationalism at home. If the Russians have a right to national communism, why should others not have that same right?

But in the world of power politics, irregardless of ideology, practice decides everything. The Chinese are not Soviet satellites, not thanks to Russian generosity, but simply because they are too big. The Russians have no practical possibilities for controlling Chinese politics. Consequently, they can have China in the eastern bloc only on Chinese terms.

The patient reader will consider here that although all of this is true, the system nevertheless functions. True, but there is only one, isolated China. How would the system function if there were several "Chinas," that is, several great powers which Moscow would have no practical possibilities for controlling.

If India should become a communist power, it would probably be oriented toward Peking and not Moscow. Does it lie in Soviet interests to communize India at the price of turning it into a Chinese satellite?

When the Laotian crisis exploded people wondered why the intervention in support of the communists was undertaken by Moscow, thousands of miles away, and not by China, which borders on Laos. Several American experts have put forward the hypothesis that Moscow wanted to beat the Chinese to the punch, fearing that Chinese intervention would not end in Laos and would include India, which could lead to a serious conflict.

It is difficult to answer the question of whether the above hypothesis is correct. It can be taken as given, however, that it is not in Moscow's interests for Chinese political influence to include India and south-east Asia. China might then come to the conclusion that it could organize its own bloc of communist states under the leadership of Peking.

Communism has not known how to solve the problem of nationalism. The nationalization of the means of production and distribution has not changed national feelings in the least. Nationalists need not live in private homes. They can live and successfully propagate themselves in state-owned apartment buildings. Socialism *per se* does not solve nationality problems. The slogan of culture which is national in form and socialist in content will remain an empty phrase until Soviet foreign policy becomes socialist in spirit and in substance. Today Soviet policy is socialist in form and imperialist in substance, and this constitutes the crux of the entire problem.

Communism has brought about a revolution in every field except foreign policy. No changes have appeared on the plane of international relations. And if they have appeared it has been for the worse and not for the better. The charge of the Cossacks in Grzybowski Square in Warsaw seems like a romantic idyll compared with Soviet tanks on the streets of Budapest.

Russian imperialism determines the steady rise of Polish, Hungarian, and Rumanian nationalism, just as British imperialism was the real father of Indian nationalism.

A young Polish communist with whom I talked about Russia some years ago put the problem this way: "So-called Soviet imperialism is revolutionary in content and consequently is not imperialism."

If this were so there would not have arisen the objective causes within the Eastern bloc that have brought about the evolution from the "Soviet bloc" to the "bloc of communist states," from the Comintern and Cominform to a loose conference of the leaders of the communist parties, from the red pope, Stalin, to Khrushchev, who at a conference of eighty-one communist parties gave up the title of leader.

In observing the evolution in the eastern bloc one may take as given that communism in the Soviet edition will not unite the world even if most of the states of our globe adopt communism. I tend to assume that a red premier of India, dependent on Peking, would have significantly worse relations with Khrushchev than did Premier Nehru.

Let us assume that America adopted communism through either evolution or revolution. It is obvious that a communist United States would not be anyone's satellite. Washington would gather the states of both American continents around it, and Marxism-Leninism in its Anglo-Saxon form would certainly differ from the interpretation of both Moscow and Peking. If Albania today can be more pro-Chinese than pro-Soviet, then Warsaw could be more pro-American than pro-Russian. Today it is easy to fight American influence in Poland in the name of the struggle against capitalism, imperialism, and reaction. But it would be very difficult to fight the influence of a red America in Poland, even if that influence meant heresy in Moscow's eyes. It would lead to complications with a powerful communist bloc of North and South American states.

A world triumph of communism achieved—as Premier Khrushchev recites on every occasion—by peaceful means, would inevitably lead to the degradation of the Soviet Union. Today the Soviet Union is state number one in the bloc of communist states and with the support of this bloc is the second power in the world. But in a communist world there would exist powerful blocs other than the Soviet bloc: the Chinese-Asian bloc with India and Japan, the bloc of both Americas, the Western European bloc with Germany and Great Britain, and a series of smaller blocs. In such a configuration the Soviet Union would not be the second power in the world. It would fall to third, and perhaps even fourth place.

After some time we would have old wine in new bottles. If communism in the Soviet Union—the fatherland of revolution—has become a dynamo of political force and conquest, there is no reason to assume that this same communism would change the Chinese, Japanese, or Germans into pacifistic, cosmopolitan apostles. It should rather be considered certain that newly es-tablished blocs of communist states would practice power politics, struggling over countries and continents.

In observing the development of the situation in the present bloc of communist states, one must conclude that agreement and unity in a communist world would be immeasurably more difficult than in today's world. Today agreement between Moscow and Peking is conditioned, among other things, by the existence of a powerful capitalist encirclement. In addition, the Soviets economically and militarily dominate all of the states of the Eastern bloc, including the Chinese. There is only one atomic power in the bloc. In other words, the Soviet Union has the possibility of control and intervention. It can hold up aid and the delivery of raw materials and freeze credit. In extreme cases it can send tanks and planes.

In a communist world all of these would come to an end. If the Soviet Union remained an atomic power, a communist America would be an atomic power. And if general disarmament were carried out, Moscow would have no possibilities for control, let alone intervention, in either the American or the Chinese-Asian blocs.

The historical experience of centuries teaches us that the unity of doctrine can be maintained only as long as heretics can be burned at the stake. Stalin understood this perfectly. And Khrushchev understood this—with Budapest being the best proof. The difference between Tito and Imre Nagy in the world of realistic power politics is found at only one point: Hungary has a common border with Russia, and Yugoslavia has no common border with Russia.

The history of the evolution of the communist states supplies irrefutable proof that the chance of heresy increases in a relationship proportional to the distance from Moscow. Heretics, if they have any possibilities of this, do not hesitate to seek support from those of "another faith" to secure their independence. In 1954 Tito signed the Balkan Pact with Greece and Turkey. Aid for Tito from the United States so far amounts to the respectable sum of 940 million dollars.

All this is understandable. In the epoch of ideological imperialism one's independence within the framework of the communist world could be noted only on the ideological plane. The GDR is a satellite compared with Yugoslavia not because there are Soviet divisions stationed in East Germany, but because Ulbricht is an ideological yes-man for Khrushchev, and Tito is not. Ulbricht is a conformist because conformism can be imposed on him by force. And this is the essence of his satellite nature.

People in the West cannot comprehend the purpose of these "theological" discussions between the Soviet and Yugoslav communists. We published the Soviet-Yugoslav discussion concerning the program of the Union of Yugoslav Communists in the *Kultura* "Biblioteka" series. It is necessary to understand that in the communist world, to which Yugoslavia belongs, there is no other road to winning independence—independence and one's own national identity. Someone will say, why communism for them at all? This is not an answer, because here it is not a question of the problem of communism *versus* democracy, only of the cardinal problem of the communist world. The Yugoslav communists want to be communists, but they want to be adult communists who have the right to their own opinions, who have a right to self-determination both for Yugoslavia and for Yugoslavian communism. Both Polish and Yugoslav revisionists understand that the orthodoxy of Moscow is not only ideological conformism, but an *expression of political servitude*. The Marxist version of socialism will survive only if it is not necessary to identify it with ideological conformism imposed by force.

Conformism robs the communist movement of its most valuable individuals. Everything is a matter of indifference only to opportunistic communists. No problems exist only for careerists with no convictions of their own. A communist with ideas and convictions wants to share in the creation of and in the responsibility for the movement which he serves and, therefore, will not give up his own convictions on a matter of decreed conformism from Moscow. In other words, what the Soviets brand as revisionism is an independence movement in the ideological sphere. If communism is to survive it must be reconciled with independence—independence with the right to the autonomy of national interpretation. There never has been and never will be an ideology in the name of which people and nations are prepared to give up the right to their own convictions, even within the framework of a doctrine, and their right to independence, even within the framework of a bloc or alliance.

In summing up our discussion so far, it must be stated that the Soviet version of communism can be imposed on the world only by force. The Soviets would have to have the possibility of direct intervention in every case of deviation from decreed conformity. Every capital in the world would have to be reduced to the status of Budapest. Even if the Soviet Union were the only power with atomic weapons, the satellization of the world would exceed their practical possibilities. The existing bloc of communist states does not consist only of satellites, despite the fact that Russia is the only atomic power in the communist orbit. Atomic bombs can be used in a world war, but not as an instrument of intervention. Columns of tanks were sufficient to crush the Hungarian uprising, but intervention in China would mean war with all of its unforeseen internal and external consequences. And for this reason there has not been and will not be any Soviet intervention in China. Only total war between the USSR and China is possible.

If I were a Soviet communist, I would understand the following: Satellization is possible only at arm's length. The Soviet arm reaches to Warsaw, Prague, and Bucharest, but does not extend to Belgrade. The experience of the last dozen or so years teaches us that wherever the Soviet arm does not reach, a national, independent communism is born. Hence the conclusion that there will be an increase of new Yugoslavias and Chinas, and not of new Hungaries or East Germanies. Today, in a conference of Communist Party leaders, Khrushchev can mobilize a front of his people, but if the communization of the world should go forward the Soviets could find themselves in the situation of the United States in the UN: namely, that of losing its automatic majority.

I am inclined to assume that the Soviet leaders are prisoners not only of their own doctrine, but also of their own nationalism. It seems to them that their national communism is the purest Marxism-Leninism and Russian imperialism the most authentic "proletarian internationalism." The fact is, however, that the copyright on ideology ends the moment when one begins to export it. Doctrinal conformity can be maintained in one state or in one empire, but it is naive to suppose that it is possible to impose it on the entire world.

Despite our sympathy for America, it should be said that the United States, like the Soviet Union, often erroneously reads the sense of contemporary historical changes. It is sometimes difficult for a great power preoccupied with global politics to understand the revolution of the medium-sized and smaller nations.

If a revolt breaks out in state X, Khrushchev considers it to be an "inevitable historical process," leading straight to communism. The fact is, however, that the nations in Asia, Africa, and Latin America do not long for communism, but only for freedom and independence. In attempting to crush these aspirations for freedom, one pushes them into the Soviet political orbit.

We nourish no sympathy for Dr. Fidel Castro, whose regime has nothing in common with democracy. Nonetheless it should be said that independence for Cuba means independence from the United States, just as Polish independence has to mean independence from Russia. Geo-political arguments cannot question the right of any nation to independence. On the other hand, the United States is entitled to expect a friendly attitude from an independent and democratically governed Cuba. In the Russian number of *Kultura* we also stated that Russia would be entitled to expect a friendly attitude from a democratic government of an independent Poland.

If the Soviet leaders would come out of their ideological cage they would understand that the historical process does not in the least correspond to the Marxist-Leninist prophecy. The two great colonial empires of Britain and France have been overwhelmed by revolution—not of communism, but of freedom and independence. In the period of a single generation, 40 million people gained their independence in the French Empire and 600 million in the British Empire.

If it is possible to speak of some authentic historical force, it is not communism, but freedom. History is not on the side of either the Marxists or the capitalists, but on the side of those who know how to read the currents of history in time. It seems to the Soviet leaders that communism is a magical formula which allows one to be simultaneously "independent" and a satellite of Moscow. This formula, which constitutes the content of "proletarian internationalism," has already failed in the bloc of communist states (China, Yugoslavia). What, then, can one expect of it on a world-wide scale?

The facts, if one is prepared to analyze them objectively, say something quite different. The communist method of industrialization, if it is successful in a given country (in comparison with the past), strengthens nationalism and aspirations for independence. Every new factory and every new industrial plant make China more independent of Russia, not only economically, but politically and ideologically.

Not all communists give up independence in favor of "proletarian internationalism" or the status of a satellite. Only those—and exclusively those—who have Soviet divisions on their territory and who must consequently count on intervention. There is no "proletarian internationalism," only Soviet interventionism, period. Wherever the Soviet military arm reaches, "internationalism" also ends.

Those people always win who manage to read the meaning of historical processes and move ahead of history in their planning. The communist camp cannot be divided into satellite states and independent states. Why? Because if we assume, as does Premier Khrushchev, that communism will expand, there will be an increase of independent communist states, and not of satellites. There may be more satellites, but they will be Peking's, not Moscow's.

The revolution that has embraced the continents of Africa, Asia, and Latin America will in time create a much more threatening environment around the Soviet empire than the present "capitalist environment." Hundreds of small and medium-sized states which have gained their freedom are emerging. These states will create regional federations or loose organizational unions like the "British" Commonwealth, which officially is not even called British.

I repeat: Neither Soviet communism nor the most liberal and enlightened colonial policy of the western states will manage to solve the nationality problem; they will not manage to persuade the people on five continents that only certain nations have the right to independence and that other nations, "not worth a few kopecks" (to use one of Premier Khrushchev's phrases), do not have this right. It is also necessary to emphasize once again that communism has not proven to be an effective substitute for freedom. Only those communists who must agree do agree to being satellites, and Soviet conformity is accepted only by those communist parties who can be called to order by the threat of armed intervention.

Walter Lippman not long ago compared Khrushchev to Metternich. The comparison is very apt, though Lippman interpreted the analogy differently. Metternich was an enemy of freedom and a defender of the "old order," and the specter of the "Spring of Nations" terrified him all his life.

We do not realize the scale of the changes. This time it is not a matter of a handful of revolutionaries in Geneva coffee houses or of street riots in a few European capitals. Today not only nations, but entire continents are in ferment and revolt.

Historical experience teaches us that regimes never reform themselves, but only collapse. But there are exceptions. The future of Russia as a world power will depend on whether it constitutes a new exception to the rule cited above.

It is not possible to support freedom for Cuba when one crushes it in Hungary. It is not possible to be anti-colonial in Africa and pro-colonial in Eastern Europe. The Russians think that Soviet colonialism is not colonialism only because it is Soviet. Who is going to believe this outside of the chosen Russian nation? Do the Russians think that thanks to this semantic formulation only they will hold onto their colonial empire in a changing world?

The semantic possibilities in this area have been both exhausted and discredited. We have already had black Portuguese and coffee-colored Frenchmen, but it did not prolong the life of colonial rule. Colonialism is colonialism, regardless of terminology. If Poland and Hungary were black, the world would quake with indignation and thunderbolts of condemnation would be hurled at the Soviet colonizers from all sides. But undoubtedly the turn of the white Negro will come.

The present Soviet empire would have a chance of enduring in the world of Metternich. If governments rested in the hands of the great powers whose only problem was to maintain the *status quo*, then nothing would threaten the Soviet empire. But since the time of Stalin and Roosevelt an enormous decentralization of authority has taken place in the world. This decentralization of authority has appeared in the bloc of communist states as well. This process will go on.

In the post-colonial epoch toward which we are tending, the Russians can maintain their great power status only at the price of transforming their empire into a Commonwealth, into a free community of independent nations. There is no other way to unload the nationality problem, which is the cardinal problem, and ultimately the tombstone, of every empire.

The Russians think that this does not concern them, because history is on their side. But the nations whom Russia subjugates are not on her side, and in the last analysis only this will count.

In this article we want to outline only generally this problem, to which we will return again. I want to close this discussion with the observation that in speaking about the transformation of the Soviet empire into a Commonwealth, we do not have in mind counter-revolution, but evolution—slow, gradual, unyielding pressure. There is no other road before the "white Negroes" in eastern Europe than the one taken by 600 million former subjects of the British Empire. Empires do not reform themselves voluntarily. They are reformed through concessions which in turn must be secured through struggle.

13. EVOLUTION OR REVOLUTION?

We have put forward many contradictory political ideas in the columns of *Kultura*, but in a historical perspective these contradictions are only apparent. During the Warsaw Uprising the Poles fought like lions. In 1956, unlike the Hungarians, they showed surprising restraint. These positions can appear to be contradictory, though the second is conditioned by the first. At the heart of the matter there is no contradiction in these such different positions of the Poles, but on the contrary, there is a close causal connection.

All year we have tried to clarify Polish-German relations. I published a book in German devoted exclusively to this goal. The book's title summarized its contents: *Kehrt Deutschland in den Osten zurück?* (Will the Germans Return to the East?) I answered the question contained in the title affirmatively. The Germans can return to the East, but only in a different character.

Almost from the very beginning we realized that the Germans are in a favorable situation in relation to Eastern Europe. The hatred of the Germans in Poland was and still is authentic, but it above all concerns the followers of Hitler. In the period of the October thaw, there appeared in the Polish press many objective and even friendly reports from West Germany. The Poles have always differentiated between good and bad Germans. Even in the literature of the occupation period one finds characters who are good Germans. On the other hand it was an act of great courage to depict a good Bolshevik in one's recollections of a stay in the Soviet Union. In pre-war Poland the word "Bolshevik" was a curse. By definition a Bolshevik cannot be good. Thirty years ago Bocheński, in his book *Between Germany and Russia*, proposed cooperation with Hitler's Germany. An author who had written a similar book before the war, but proposing instead an alliance with Soviet Russia, would have been stoned. The following judgment would, of course, be an exaggeration: Good Russians were to be found in Tsarist Russia and went to the grave with her. There is much less exaggeration in the exaggerated opinion above than we would tend to suppose. After years of work trying to straighten out the "Russian complex," I came to the conclusion that it is unfortunately very difficult to exaggerate in speaking about the hatred of the Poles for the Russians.

The Poles hate both of their neighbors, but there is a great difference in these hatreds. There is no contempt in the hatred of the Germans. On the contrary, the Poles, like all Slavs, are impressed by the Germans. The Germans represent qualities which the Slavs lack—above all economic and organizational genius. The Russians, on the other hand, with all their sputniks and atomic bombs, in the opinion of the Poles symbolize chaos and disorder. When the Russians launched the first sputnik into orbit, the presumption presented in one of the Polish weeklies in London was that the signals being sent from the spaceship were being sent from earth. The Poles cannot get it through their heads that this contemptible land of the Bolsheviks, where periodically one cannot get a razor blade, could produce the first spaceship in the world.

The differences that emerge in our hatreds of the Germans and of the Russians create a situation where the Poles are potentially better able and more ready to normalize their relations with the Germans than with Russia. It is easier to come to terms with an enemy for whom one has no contempt. It is easier to come to terms with an enemy who has certain qualities which impress and arouse respect.

The memory of German atrocities in Poland is alive and will live for a long time yet. But the hatred of Russia in Poland is also alive, and the Germans could politically discount this hatred to their advantage. The opinion of Polish society could be won over in the course of a few years if the Bonn government would recognize the Oder–Neisse boundary without delay, if as a conciliatory gesture it would establish several new scientific laboratory-institutes in Poland, if it offered long-term loans on favorable terms to Warsaw, if it declared its desire to invest significant sums in the reconstruction of Polish industry, and if it undertook a policy of reconciliation and friendship. Then the anti-Russian feeling in Poland would act as a dynamo of pro-German sympathy. Then the Poles would more easily forgive the Germans for Auschwitz than the Russians for Katyń.

Germany was the only state on the European continent that had concrete and practical resources for building "bridges" between Western and Eastern Europe. Germany was also the only state on the continent that was capable of convincing the Poles tangibly and with their own eyes that a Polish-Russian alliance is an inevitable necessity for us. The Bonn government has had its own way in this matter. Though the Poles are still anti-Soviet, the majority favor an alliance with Russia, and the majority distrust the great chance for a return to the East which was wasted by the Germans.

After many years of fruitless attempts to work out even a provisional form of Polish-German understanding, I have come to the conclusion that greater changes are taking place in the Soviet Union than in Germany. The Germans have not changed a bit in their relations with Poland.

All of this promised to be different. The Common Market and NATO promised integration and a politically unified Europe. But Europe betrayed its own goal. This goal was the unification of all of Europe and not the integration of her western portion. In writing off the loss of the Eastern European states, Western Europe wrote herself off as a loss. Unfortunately, there is not an ounce of exaggeration in this assertion.

Western Europe is today outflanked by Soviet Russia and finds herself in the field of fire of a variety of Soviet atomic missiles, for which there is no strategic answer.

Every strategic situation has its own meaning and political expression. John J. McCloy, the former military governor and American High Commissioner in Germany, put the above situation as follows: "The Soviets hold Europe as a hostage in their relationship with the United States" (*Interplay*, Feb. 1968).

It seems to me that everything is said in this one sentence. In a critical moment the Russians can always threaten the Americans with, "One missile on Moscow or Leningrad and we will wipe Western Europe off the face of the earth." In reality it is not Western Europe which profits from the American "atomic umbrella." It is the Russians who have, themselves, made Europe an "umbrella" protecting them against American atomic bombardment. This is how the naked truth really looks.

One should consider the policy of *Kultura* toward Russia against the background outlined above. Our relationship with Russia is dictated by common sense. A certain American diplomat rightly observed that nations acquire common sense only when they have no other alternatives. The Poles have no alternative and therefore must be sensible.

I repeat that the development of events could turn out differently, but in the period when the Russians were building underground shelters for their atomic missile launchers—shelters which, in the opinion of American experts, can be harmed only by direct hits with atomic rockets—mass demonstrations against American bases were taking place in England and on the continent.

A confrontation of power always brings a certain risk with it. Europeans do not want to undergo any risk. All anti-bombing philosophy leads to the assertion that a small force provokes and does not at the same time insure security. The conception of security held by President de Gaulle is based on similar assumptions. The presence of American bases and armies can provoke a Soviet attack in time of conflict, and at the same time foreign bases do not guarantee security and neither are they capable of protecting France from destruction.

After two world wars Western Europeans do not want their continent in time of conflict to become one of the theaters of a third world war. All Western Europeans, including the English, are Gaullists to a greater or lesser degree. No one in Europe wants to be an active participant in any eventual Soviet-American conflict. One does not speak or write about this publicly, but the facts noted above are the main cause for the atrophy of NATO and of the reduction of defense budgets. Western Europe seeks not confrontation, but only accommodation with the Soviet Union. Can a "hostage" behave differently?

We must win peace with Russia, because we will not win a war with her. We will not win a war if only for the reason that a war with Russia on European soil should be considered as almost excluded. As everyone knows, it takes two to make war. It is difficult to get a glimpse of that "second" person in western Europe.

In reviewing the annals of *Kultura* one must come to the conclusion that October 1956 divided the history of our monthly into two separate periods. The collapse of the Polish October and the Hungarian revolution forced us to undertake a review of the assumptions of our policy up until that time.

In that period, thanks to innumerable meetings with Poles from Poland, we became aware of the changes in the attitudes of Polish society. Before October, *Kultura* had run a survey on the subject, "Which of the changes in Poland are irreversible?" Agricultural reform, the rapid expansion of industry, urbanization, and the maritime economy—in conjunction with the changes in the population structure—had caused changes to take place in many aspects of the traditional attitudes of Polish society.

It is obvious that the process of molding an agricultural country into an industrial-agricultural country—irregardless of ideology and politics—must cause numerous changes in people's attitudes. Because the Poles in exile have not taken part in this process, their attitudes have not undergone change. Thus the slogan that is obligatory to this day: "The Poles have not changed." The Poles as a nation and as a society have changed very significantly—in some areas for the better and in some areas for the worse.

The lonely defeat of the Hungarian uprising convinced us that the leading postulate both in Washington and in Moscow is not to tolerate an armed conflict between America and the Soviet Union. If the price of maintaining such a peace in Europe is the maintenance of the *status quo*, the Americans are prepared to pay that price. In such a perspective the division of Europe has changed from a hasty, temporary post-war state of affairs into a pillar of coexistence crowned with the higher goal of maintaining peace.

And what is defeat? Defeat is the *lack of an answer*. The [Polish World War II] Home Army and the resistance movement was the answer to the Nazi terror and occupation. The Hungarians replied to Stalinist oppression and Soviet imperialism with the uprising. And what is our answer to communism?

"Evolutionism" is an attempt at a peaceful answer. There can be various answers, of course. We have never maintained that "evolutionism" is the only possible answer. A revolutionary solution is also possible and worth examining somewhat more closely.

It is possible to improve every system. Radical reforms can make the economy healthy, can significantly raise the standard of living, can expand and improve social services, and can even reduce exploitation to a significant extent, if not liquidate it entirely.

"Evolutionism" is a *de facto* revolution on the instalment plan. The reforms initially undertaken, in the name of making the communist system more efficient and not to overthrow it, are always achieved at the expense of the central authorities. One can observe this process in Yugoslavia.

No one in Poland is satisfied with the present system, most of the communists included. Communism is considered to be a calamity by 80 per cent of the population, but this calamity differs from all other calamities in that no one in Poland has an answer to it.

The revisionists—even the revolutionary kind—have not crossed the Rubicon which separates communism from democratic socialism. On the other hand, the non-Marxist opposition has in general produced nothing. It is possible to criticize the program of the revisionists, but it must be said that the non-Marxists have not found anything that can be compared to the program of two young Marxists [Kuron and Modzelewski].

Evolutionary changes that are achieved through social pressure are in the last analysis an improvement in the system and not an improvement of communism. The essence of communism is total centralization of authority. The fact that things are happening in Moscow today that would have been unthinkable in Stalin's time proves that no one in the Soviet Union has authority as total as Stalin's. All concessions and reforms take place at the cost of curtailing totalistic central authority, and their basic value rests on this fact.

Certain conclusions should be drawn from the situation which is looming up in the Eastern European bloc.

More than eleven years have passed since the Hungarian revolution and the Polish October. Evolutionary changes that should not be treated lightly have appeared, but today there is no doubt but what we have overrated the Polish Marxist revisionists.

During the period of October we wrote in these columns that only Marxists could reform and revise communism. If the Marxists do not do this, then communism will fall, because an ideology and system incapable of development sooner or later lands in the junkpile of history.

The danger of the situation in Poland rests on the fact that ferment and pressure grow in Poland without a program. Freedom is not the equivalent of carrying several men out on a wheelbarrow. Freedom is a definite program. Freedom reigned for a brief time during the October period. I know from journalists from Poland that the censorship did not operate and that everyone could write what he wanted. But neither the revisionists nor the non-Marxist opposition had any program. Only Gomułka and his people had a program.

Someone will say that it is first necessary to overthrow communism and then work out a program. This is a naive idea which has never and never will bring any results. In reality only a definite program could mold the atomized centers of resistance and ferment into a conscious potential of revolutionary force.

There is no program shouting that communism should be replaced by democracy. Should England—God forbid—be occupied by the Soviet Union and the British Communist Party rule in London, the English in such a situation would not need an alternate program. It would be enough to say that democracy should be restored.

But what should be restored in Poland? The people who re-member another system from personal experience are over sixty years old. Over 50 per cent of the people in general know no other system than communism. In a geographical, economic, population-structural, and governmental sense, Poland is today a completely different country than it was thirty years ago. Poland has 1000 years of history, but it does not have a "yesterday" to which it is possible to refer.

Despite the obvious difficulties, it is astounding that in the course of the past twenty years the non-Marxist opposition, in the face of the helplessness of the revisionists, has not made an attempt to work out an alternative program—a program which would keep what is worth keeping and boldly throw out what should be thrown out. We have published several books written in Poland which contain shattering critiques of communism, but they do not constitute an answer to communism. This is anti-communist, but not revolutionary literature.

I know that many anti-communists in Poland throw out "evolutionism," arguing that communism cannot be corrected. If one throws out communism and "evolutionism," one must formu-late, even if only in a general outline, a program for a new system which, cutting itself off from the evolutionary method, would by definition be a revolutionary program.

I personally tend to the view that there is no general prescription for a solution to the above problem. It is not out of the question that the Russians and Poles will someday choose the revolutionary method.

It is necessary to conclude from a series of articles by Victor Zorza in *The Guardian* that the liberalization in Czechoslovakia and the victory of the Union of Czechoslovak Writers are creating real anxiety in Moscow and Warsaw. The reform movement has been taken up by the youth. *Mlada Fronta*, the organ of the Union of Communist Youth, until recently the most orthodox periodical in Eastern Europe, has put forward the thesis that "the Union need not automatically identify itself with the policy of the Party."

Mlada Fronta proclaims that a union of youth should be an independent and truly representative organization. At the same time, the chairman of the Union of Czechoslovak Writers, Goldstuecker, presented the position of the Czechoslovak writers openly and uncompromisingly in a television interview in Prague. The writers expelled from the Party last fall, with Ludwig Vaculik at the head, were given back their top positions in the resurrected *Literarni Listy*. In the first number of the periodical, which appeared on the first of March of this year, the prominent writer, Aleksander Kliment, declared himself in favor of free elections, a parliamentary opposition, and the recognition of a social role for public opinion.

It appears that Czechoslovakia is evolving ("evolutionism"!) along the lines of the Yugoslavian model and it is not out of the question that the process of democratization will progress more rapidly in Prague than in Belgrade. At the moment I write these words I still cannot pronounce a final judgment about the events in Czechoslovakia. I can, however, state the following: (1) The supporters of liberalization, and especially the writers, had a *definite program*. (2) The Czechoslovaks profited from the experiences of both the Poles and the Hungarians. (3) The situation in Russia, in the international communist movement, and in the world arena, from the point of view of reformers, is significantly more advantageous than in 1956. (4) The Czechs have no Oder–Neisse boundary, and are not paralyzed by the problem of a guarantee, which in Poland gives rise to the principle of "don't annoy the Russians."

The Czechs have a democratic "yesterday" which we lack. The Rumanians also lack a democratic "yesterday," and it is more important to them to have state independence from Russia than to have democracy.

Only one mortal danger threatens a Polish revolution: namely, degeneration into a national anti-Russian uprising. Only a Polish-Russian revolution would have a chance of victory. In other words, the Polish revolutionaries would have to act in close alliance with the Russian revolutionaries.

The chances of an overthrow on a smaller, purely Polish scale, would also depend on the attitude of society toward Russia and Poland's other neighbors. If the Poles put the major emphasis on the democratization of the system—restraining themselves from escalation to state and national goals—the Russians, in the present situation, would not risk armed intervention. Of course, if a new government in Warsaw declared a withdrawal from the Warsaw Pact, proclaimed neutrality, and directed an ultimatum at the Soviet army stationed in Poland, the matter would take a different turn.

There are millions of anti-communists in Poland, but how many of them understand revolution to mean an alliance with Russian revolutionaries and not a national uprising against Russia? How many of these millions of Polish anti-communists understand revolution to mean revolution and not counter-revolution?

15. A DISCUSSION OF METHOD

How should one approach Russia?

If a great American firm wants to export its washing machines to country X, it carries out an extensive, expensive, and thorough study of the new market, the local customs, social conventions, and so on. It is completely out of the question for a representative of the American firm to "drop a brick," as the English expression goes, that is, to offend local social "taboos" or to make a fundamental *faux pas* arising from lack of familiarity with the area.

Political negotiations are not even in part as carefully prepared as great trade operations. It has occurred to me more than once that it would probably be advantageous to entrust the negotiation of a given treaty with Russia (or with another state, depending on the situation) to a great private firm or corporation—for a high fee, of course. Then the terrain would be examined thoroughly and the negotiations carried out by skilled masters, in comparison with which the foreign service officers of the great powers must seem like a set of amateurs and bureaucrats.

Thomas Barman, a diplomatic correspondent for the BBC for many years, describes the following episode in one of his auto-biographical sketches: Immediately after the war the British Ambassador in Moscow ran into unexpected difficulties in getting supplies of food for himself and the embassy personnel through the Soviet customs office. Not finding any other way out he finally turned for help to Vyshinsky, who was then the Soviet Minister of Foreign Affairs. During the conversation the Ambassador said, "If you can expedite a quick settlement of this matter, I am pre-pared to offer half of this transport of food to the hungry people of the city of Moscow." Vyshinsky turned purple and replied, "There are no hungry people in Moscow." The audience was at an end.

The British Ambassador dropped a classic brick in this case. As is generally understood, neither in Moscow nor in any other Soviet city is there officially hunger. This was the year 1947, and in this case thousands of people in Moscow were literally starving. But elementary tactical principles require that one does not "drop a brick" in negotiations if one wants to get results. In the above case the British Ambassador demonstrated good will and ignorance. It is highly improbable that a representative of a large British concern negotiating a large contract in Moscow for the delivery of a nylon factory would drop even the tiniest brick in a conversation with Soviet dignitaries. Where millions of pounds are at stake it pays to undertake a careful study of the terrain and acquaint oneself with all the "taboos" and conventions of the market. The customs and conventions of the contracting parties should always be respected, even when they seem funny and hypocritical. It is possible that our customs and conventions also appear funny and hypocritical to foreigners.

In negotiations with Russia it is necessary to be hard within the limits of realistic possibilities. It is necessary to be hard, not because Russia is Russia, or because of the Bolsheviks, Katyń, the labor camps, and the like. It is necessary to be hard because Russia is a great power. Leaders, diplomats, and representatives of great powers from habit expect concessions, if not full capitulation. In negotiations with great powers like Russia it is necessary to be hard, because the margin of permissible errors for small or medium-sized states is immeasurably smaller than the analogical margin for super-powers. The United States can end the war in Vietnam through a disadvantageous compromise and can sink millions of dollars into the Indochinese jungles, and still remain a super-power. Neither England nor France have such a broad margin of permissible error.

The policies of medium-sized states must be extremely carefully and painstakingly formulated, but at the same time they must be hard and unyielding, because medium-sized states cannot afford the luxury of errors.

A chaos of ideas prevails in this matter both in Poland and among Polish émigrés. Poles are sometimes inflexible, but seldom hard and unyielding. Among Polish émigrés "inflexibility" is the equivalent of trying to sell unrealistic maximalist slogans. Hardness and an unyielding position always characterize realists, never romantics or super-powers. A realistic politician formulates his program within a framework of concrete possibilities and defends it without yielding. Only in a realistic program is it possible to determine clearly the limits of admissible compromise.

In a very significant percentage of cases medium-sized states are led to catastrophe by "inflexibility," because maximalists always play into the hands of their enemies, making it easy for a powerful neighbor to replace negotiations with armed intervention.

Let us imagine that an uprising should break out in Warsaw on the model of the Hungarian uprising of 1956. The Russians at first would take a "wait and see" position. The greatest danger threatening an uprising is always from the side of inflexible and superpatriotic leaders. In an atmosphere of struggle and patriotic inebriation, the maximalists put forward increasingly more unrealistic demands. Sober politicians are in such a situation pushed aside as capitulationists and compromisers. And, of course, it is clear and obvious that the uprising cannot succeed. An uprising is a dramatic instrument of pressure with which it is possible to win certain concessions. Patriotic maximalists ruin these chances by putting forward demands that cannot be accepted by the other side.

The classic pattern for an uprising is as follows: The "inflexibles" take power, putting forward an unreasonable program and demands that scorn all realism. Then follows the armed intervention that crushes the uprising. The capitulationists then come forward and organize a "new order." The sober politicians do not have a chance to make themselves heard for a second. The whole affair is played entirely by the "inflexibles" and the "capitulationists." One initiates it; the other ends it. (The above observations do not concern the Warsaw Uprising, which was basically not an uprising but only one of the battles of the Second World War. The Poles were continuing their military action against the Germans, which had gone on without interruption since September, 1939.)

It is always very difficult to see what and how much it is possible to win through such an unpredictable form of pressure as a revolt or uprising. On the other hand, it is possible to determine with a great probability of success the things an uprising cannot achieve. The Russians might agree to the overthrow of the Gomułka administration, and would probably also accept liberalization and certain economic and political reforms. On the other hand, they would certainly not accept Poland's withdrawal from the Warsaw Pact or the restoration of a democratic system in the western sense.

We do not recommend an uprising, but it should be objectively stated that revolts and uprisings are traditional forms of struggle and pressure. The success of such an operation depends almost entirely on the political doings of the leaders. In the period of the October upheaval in Poland, the entire nation stood behind Gomułka, and for this reason *Kultura* gave him conditional support. I have never regretted this. Those who were outside Poland during those critical days are the ones who should be sorry. The October upheaval accomplished a great deal. The gains of October were not liquidated by the Russians, but only by Gomułka. If there had been a real statesman in Gomułka's place, October would have been a revolt crowned with considerable success.

An uprising is an operation with limited goals and scope. An uprising is not a war, but like a strike constitutes a demonstration of solidarity and force whose goal is the achievement of postulates which fit into the framework of realistic possibilities. A Poland with Wilno and Lwów, independent, democratic, deserting the Warsaw Pact—this is a program cut out for World War III, but not for any uprising.

Where is this discussion leading? I want to show that it is necessary to be hard and unyielding in relationship to a powerful neighbor. By being hard and unyielding it is possible to defend only realistic postulates. Risk is inseparable from political activity. Political genius rests on a skilled evaluation of what is realistic and what is unrealistic. There is no encyclopedic definition of realism. The same plan or postulate which is unachievable today, in two years, under changed conditions, may become a realistic proposition. Realism basically depends on an accurate evaluation of reality— on an error-free feeling for the actual political situation.

The policy of medium-sized states is always a policy of compromise. We will never be in a situation in which we can dictate our conditions to Russia. Even if there should be a war and the Soviet Union should be defeated, it would not be we who would dictate the terms of capitulation.

The "inflexibles" formulate their postulates as if we should expect the capitulation of Russia from month to month: Lwów, Wilno, general elections, the liquidation of communism, and the like. The "inflexibles" always answer their critics by saying that their demands are justifiable and morally correct.

Unfortunately, not everything which is correct is realistic. Perhaps the election of a Negro to the office of President of the United States would be a morally justifiable act. Nonetheless, it is an unrealistic proposition in the present historical situation. The American Negroes would be mad to throw away the possibilities for equality of rights, which are today realistic, by demanding the presidency of the United States. One of the causes of Polish political incompetence is the fatal tendency to sacrifice achievable programs on the altar of correct and lofty, but unrealistic slogans. This typical Polish distaste, if not contempt, for a policy of compromise, has its source here: If a given policy involves moral or ethical canons, no compromise is possible. This is why the positive term "agreement" has negative overtones in the Polish vocabulary. We agree to nothing, because agreement, if it does not mean capitulation to an opponent, must necessarily be based on compromise. Because we have no possibility of forcing Moscow to capitulate, we give up any policy in relation to Russia. If we were to win certain important concessions from Moscow through a hard and patient policy, this would be agreement. And agreement is a "rotten compromise," unworthy of those who represent absolute moral correctness.

We will not improve our situation until we accept the idea that a middle-sized state cannot carry out any policy other than a policy of compromise. We must also accept the idea that greatness does not depend on the proclamation of great programs, but on the realization of achievable goals.

Dictation is one-sided politics, with the conditioned capitulation of the opponent. The politics of compromise, on the other hand, is two-sided politics. This means that a realistic conception of compromise must be based both on an evaluation of one's own situation and on an evaluation of the bargaining possibilities of the opposite side. A policy of compromise requires great skill in accurately balancing both of the above elements. An indispensable condition for carrying out this kind of policy is perfect knowledge of one's opponent or partner. This is why no other nation in the world so much needs to know about Russia as Poland.

Personally, I do not consider myself to be a Russian expert, but in observing the international scene professionally since I was thirty-six, I have come to certain conclusions. I would formulate my general conclusion in regard to Russia as follows: Because of the fact that knowledge of Russia is so terribly scant in the West, including Poland, we put forward in relation to Moscow propositions which have no chance of success, while we give in on matters where decided pressure would bring success.

Let us illustrate this point with an example.

There appeared in *Pravda* on October 31, 1956, an official announcement, in which we read, among other things, "Because the presence of Soviet troops in Hungary could lead to a further deterioration of the situation in that country, the Soviet government has directed the commandant to withdraw the Soviet Army divisions from Budapest. The Soviet government is also prepared to open negotiations with the government of the Hungarian People's Republic and with other states of the Warsaw Pact in the matter of stationing Soviet troops on Hungarian territory."

The previous day (October 30, 1956) Nagy had called for elections with the participation of all parties existing in 1945. He also announced publicly that he had not called for the intervention of Soviet troops, but on the contrary had demanded the immediate evacuation of the Soviet units from Budapest. That afternoon the Soviet troops began to leave Budapest. Drunk with victory, the leadership of the Hungarian Air Force announced an "ultimatum," giving the Soviet troops twelve hours to evacuate

Budapest, threatening to fight them after that time. That afternoon the fighting came to an end everywhere.

On October 31, which was the following day, a secret conference took place in Budapest, with Mikoyan and Suslov and Nagy and Tildy taking part. At the very beginning Mikoyan declared a readiness to withdraw immediately from Hungarian territory all those Soviet divisions which were not stationed in Hungary under the authority of the Warsaw Pact. Mikoyan also announced that those Soviet divisions stationed in Hungary on the basis of the provisions of the Warsaw Pact could be withdrawn after consultation with the member states of the Warsaw Pact.

Tildy rejected Mikoyan's offer and demanded the immediate evacuation of all Soviet troops. He also declared that Hungary in any case was withdrawing from the Warsaw Pact.

Early in the morning of the following day (November 1, 1956), Mikoyan and Suslov had an intimate meeting with Kadar. In the course of this conversation, the decision was made to summon a new government, which would call for Soviet military assistance.[4]

The Russians, as we know, crushed the Hungarian uprising with unparalleled brutality according to the classic imperialist models. But stating this fact does not answer the very important question of whether the Hungarians themselves did not commit some errors.

It is my belief that Tildy committed a fundamental error in announcing to the Soviet delegates that "Hungary would definitely repudiate the Warsaw Pact."[5]

It must be clear to every sober thinking person that Hungary cannot count on total victory crowned by the capitulation of Russia. Achievable was a compromise which could have meant a very significant improvement in the Hungarian situation.

An opponent who is not defeated on the field of battle, like Russia in this case, cannot be treated as defeated and powerless at the conference table. The withdrawal of Hungary from the Warsaw Pact threatened the disintegration of the entire system. If Moscow had agreed to the withdrawal of Hungary, she would also have had to agree to the withdrawal of Poland or Czechoslovakia from the Pact. Someone will say that Hungary had a right to withdraw from the Warsaw Pact, and similarly had the right to declare Hungary a neutral state.

4 The Hungarian uprising is an historical event of equally great importance to both Poles and Hungarians. A rich literature on this subject exists today. I have drawn the facts cited above from the excellent recently-published work of Raymond L. Garthoff, *Soviet Military Policy—A Historical Analysis* (New York: F. A. Praeger). The facts and chronology are according to Garthoff; the analysis and conclusions are mine.

5 Garthoff puts the above sentence of Tildy in quotation marks.

I will repeat once more—the Negroes have the right to a Negro in the chair of the President of the United States, but at this moment this is not a realistic proposition. Émigré writers and journalists should logically, tirelessly, and uncompromisingly demand the restoration of all rights to the nations of eastern Europe, but politicians and statesmen in these countries must be guided by other criteria. It is one thing to have a declaration of goals and rights, and another thing to have a practical policy. In the real world, he who aims too high, misses; he who demands everything, achieves nothing. Everyone in private life is free to apply the principle of all or nothing, but it is not permissible to apply this maxim at the expense of others—or contrary to the interests of the entire nation.

It is possible to take the view that if Tildy and Nagy had put forward a compromise formula in their discussions with Mikoyan and Suslov, Soviet intervention would still have followed. This possibility cannot be excluded, but it should be said that the sources that are available today do not confirm this theory.

Imperialist states do not willingly intervene militarily, because intervention always compromises oneself. Bloc cohesion and the policy of coexistence are compromised, progressive and liberal circles all over the world are antagonized, and above all the ideology is discredited by intervention. The Red Army, "the mainstay of the world proletariat," crushes the resistance of the workers of a small state. When the tanks roll, ideological phrases fall like leaves from a tree and only naked, horrifying imperialism remains. In October, 1966—the tenth anniversary of the Hungarian uprising —radio stations in the free world broadcast special programs. Once again we heard the clatter of Soviet tanks, the report of shots, and the strangled voice of Premier Nagy. One of the myths broadcast by émigré Sovietologists says that Moscow does not care about world opinion. It would be difficult to find a more false view. The Soviet Union spends millions to buy and win the favor of world opinion. The Russians are extremely sensitive to criticism and equally sensitive to praise. Soviet arrogance masks their persistent inferiority complex toward the West. People who are sure of themselves are never arrogant.

To return to the main course of our discussion, it is necessary to emphasize that the major political "wares" insurgents have to sell is intervention. In the face of crisis, Russia agreed to significant concessions in order to avoid armed intervention, but then the demands of the insurgents must be formulated in such a way that intervention is rendered politically unprofitable.

An insurrectionist policy is immeasurably difficult because the leaders find themselves under the pressure of the revolutionary mood of society and of the "inflexible" politicians who bob on the surface. Moderation and common sense are considered treason, and compromise a disgrace. These often heroic people do not consider that they are in fact playing into the hands of the enemy. After their death, the capitulationists come to power and sign, not agreements of compromise, but one-sided, imposed dictations.

In sum, uprisings or revolts are powerful instruments of a policy of pressure and protest, but only when they are under full control. The moment they turn into a spontaneous phenomenon, they lose all connection with policy.

It is not enough to have the nation behind you; it is also necessary to be in full control of the situation. To be in control of the situation means to know how to silence and, if necessary, to lock up extremist agitators, enthusiasts, and candidates for heroism at the expense of the nation. That is why in analyzing the situation I have held back from criticism of the leaders of the Hungarian Revolution in order to learn from the experience of these events. Nagy had the nation behind him, because every hour he put forward bolder and increasingly extreme demands. In my opinion, if Nagy and Tildy had on October 31, 1956, presented the Soviet delegation with a reasonable and moderate compromise agreement, they would have had rebellion in their own ranks that same day.

The tragedy of leaders of uprisings rests on the fact that if they put forward extreme demands, they provoke armed intervention in the end, and if they put forward compromise solutions, they cause rebellion or a split in their own camp.

In the last analysis, everything leads to the problem of popular support. Only those Eastern European leaders who enjoy the solid support of their societies can negotiate with Russia. The essence of being a satellite rests on the fact that the ruling party in a given country substitutes Soviet support for the support of their own people. A satellite arrangement, as opposed to a feeling of national dignity, makes the national mood antagonistic toward the hegemonic power—in our case, toward Moscow. In such an atmosphere, in a crisis situation, the leadership, in wanting to gain mass popular support, is in some measure forced to put forward extreme slogans and demands.

We are excluding world war or the disintegration of the Soviet Union as a result of internal difficulties from our solutions in this sketch. This does not mean that we are deleting revolution and war from the table of possible occurrences, only that these problems are not now the subject of our analysis.

The politics of the medium-sized states neighboring Russia require not only mature leaders but, above all, great maturity on the part of the individual societies. Society must be mature enough to lend solid support to leaders who do not operate with extreme nationalistic slogans, but on the contrary put forward a modest and realistic program, and who are at the same time prepared to be hard and unyielding in the defense of those postulates. Demanding what is not achievable in a given historical situation is not proof of unshakability, just plain stupidity.

If in a given situation demanding free and general elections has to be considered unrealistic, this does not mean in the least that the Polish nation is giving up this postulate. It means only that putting forward this kind of demand has to await a more favorable moment.

A historical nation of 30 million has no reason to give up on anything. It is a great error, however, to put forward inappropriate postulates at an inappropriate time. A wise French proverb says that "better" is the enemy of "good." The fact that we cannot realize a maximum program in the present situation causes apathy and inertia, which makes it impossible to realize a middle program in the sphere of politics or economics.

Above all there exists the great problem of humanizing socialism. Here it is a question of giving the word socialism a human and humanitarian meaning. Personally, I am convinced that there exists in Poland a margin of significant possibilities for reform and development in this area. We should explain to the Russians that Stalinism both in Russia and in Poland is nationalistic—which is fully in accord with the truth. In the context of the Polish situation every nationalism is not only anti-Soviet but also anti-Russian. It is sufficient to glance at a map of Poland distributed by the illegal Polish Communist Party. A modernized, humanized Polish socialism by definition and in fact would not be nationalistic and, consequently, would have some possibility for working toward improved Polish–Russian relations.

It seems to me that in Poland today the majority of young and middle-aged people are aware of the fact that the reform and reconstruction of socialism in Poland are paralyzed not so much by the Russians as by Gomułka and his faction. Of course, the Russians would look with great distrust on any process of reform and modernization of the Polish model of socialism. Yet if free speech did not lead to an outbreak of hatred for Russia, but on the contrary emphasized the necessity of cooperation with our eastern neighbor, Moscow, in time, would accept the Polish model of socialism.

By the humanization of socialism I do not have in mind either a "second stage" or a western type of social-democracy. I am convinced that the Poles are capable of working out a new model adapted to and growing up from Polish soil, experience, and conditions.

One point is particularly important in this matter. Humanization of a Polish model of socialism must mean a conspicuous broadening of the area of freedom. Yet if the Poles use any broadened margin of freedom for giving full play to their hatred for Russia and for formulating maximalist national postulates, they will achieve neither the reconstruction of the socialist model nor independence for the state.

We will neither defeat Russia nor force her to capitulate. On the other hand we could directly influence the changes in the Soviet Union if the Polish model of socialism were economically more efficient, socially more just, and in general respects more humanistic than the Soviet model.

I repeat once again: Having had the experience of Budapest, the Russians, to avoid intervention, would accept, though unwillingly and with distrust, the reconstruction of the Polish model of socialism on the condition that in the course of this process there would not be any outbreak of nationalism in Poland or any escalation of demands injurious to the structure of the existing alliance system. In other words, only a controlled revolution, carried out by sensible people, has any chance of success. This revolution should express itself by the use of pressure and, if necessary, by mass protests. The Russians, in all certainty, will not retire Gomułka for us, will not endow Poland with a more enlightened leadership, and will not liquidate the "Small Penal Code" for us.

Technological equipment and scientific apparatus can be brought from outside the country, but social progress and humanization of life have to be produced on location.

I would like to conclude this discussion with the following general observation. I do not belong to those writers who expect an upheaval or revolution in the Soviet Union in the next few weeks or months. Yet it is appropriate to state objectively the following: In the United States every tenth citizen is a Negro. In the Soviet Union nearly 50 per cent of the citizens are of a nationality other than Russian. The decolonization and independence of the African and Asian peoples has influenced the crystalization of national feeling and racial dignity of the American Negroes. This same set of factors has affected the arousal of nationalism among the emerging peoples within the framework of the Soviet Union. I believe that in the next few decades the Americans will have to solve their Negro problem, and the Soviets the super-problem of their national minorities.

The danger rests on the fact that difficulties and key problems are evolving in the Soviet Union *more rapidly* than the political system. In a normal, democratic state the political system evolves *together* with the society. Even the nature of conservative England has undergone an enormous transformation in the last ten years.

Returning to the problem of nationality, it seems to me that this matter is ripening toward a solution which the doctrinal Soviet system is not in a position to supply. And here is where the threat of crisis is.

If in the next few years the Poles manage to work out a model of a socialist system which is closer to the requirements of the twentieth century than the Soviet model, it is possible that the Russians, in a period of growing crisis, would adopt some of the institutions and devices of the Polish model.

Translated by James F. Morrison

About
the
Authors

JÓZEF CZAPSKI was born in 1896 in eastern Poland. He was educated in St. Petersburg, where he witnessed the Russian Revolution of 1917. He took part in the Polish-Soviet war of 1920, after which he returned to his art studies at the Cracow Academy of Art, and then in Paris. As a successful *avant-garde* painter, he exhibited in Paris, Geneva, New York, and in Poland, collecting many prizes and awards. He published essays and articles on art theory and was highly noted as an art critic.

In 1939, he fought against both the Germans and the Russians who invaded eastern Poland. Subsequent to his capture by the Russians, he was one of the 79 survivors of the massacre of 4,000 Polish officers in the Katyn Forest. After escaping from the Soviet Union, he served with the Polish forces in Egypt and Italy. His book, *Memoirs from Starobielsk,* a detailed description of his imprisonment in Russia before the notorious slaughter, was published in Italy in 1945. It has since been translated into many languages, including English. His second book, *The Inhuman Earth,* which appeared in Paris in 1948, was also widely translated.

Mr. Czapski, who presently lives in France, is a contributor to French journals and magazines, and is considered an outstanding expert on Russian culture and literature. He is one of the leading figures among the Polish intellectuals gathered around *Kultura.*

GEORGE J. FLEMMING is the pseudonym of *Jerzy Jan Dzialak,* born in Warsaw in 1921. He spent his early years in the Polish underground resistance movement against the German occupation. After the war he completed his studies of law and history in Belgium. A journalist and writer, he worked for a time with the Polish State Radio, but was forced to leave because of his political past. He left Poland in 1964, and since then has been freelancing for the Danish, French, and West German press.

GEORGE GÖMÖRI was born in 1934 in Budapest, Hungary. He studied Polish and Hungarian literature at Eotvos Lorand University, Budapest, leaving his native country in 1956. In 1963–1964 he taught Polish and Hungarian at the University of California at Berkeley, and the following year he was a Research Fellow in the Harvard Russian Research Center. He is presently Senior Research Associate at the Centre for Russian and East European Studies at Birmingham University, England. His publications include two books of poetry, translations, numerous essays in Hungarian, Polish, and English, and a study of the post-war poetry in Eastern Europe, *Polish and Hungarian Poetry 1945 to 1956* (Oxford University Press, 1966).

GUSTAW HERLING-GRUDZIŃSKI was born in Kielce, Poland in 1919. The war interrupted his university studies in Warsaw, and after the fall of Poland, in 1939, he and his friends founded one of the first Polish underground anti-Nazi organizations in Warsaw. After fleeing to the Russian-occupied sector of Poland, he was captured by the NKVD in 1940 and spent two years in a Soviet slave labor camp on the White Sea. His experiences there are described in his book *A World Apart* (with a preface by Bertrand Russell), which was translated into many languages, and included two American editions in 1952.

After his release by the Russians, in 1942, he joined the Polish Army organized in Russia, and went to the Middle East and then to Italy, where at the battle of Monte Cassino he was awarded the highest Polish military honor. After the war, he lived in London and Munich and finally settled in Naples. His new book, *The Island: Three Tales*, has been published recently in America (The World Publishing Company), and also in Italian and German translations. He contributes regularly to *Kultura* in Paris, and to *Tempo Presente*, *La Fiera Letteraria*, and *Il Mondo* in Italy. Some of his articles have been reprinted in America by *The New Leader*, *Atlas*, and *Dissent*.

ALEKSANDER HERTZ was born in Warsaw on December 3, 1895. He studied at the Universities of Warsaw and Vienna (Austria), and received the Ph.D. from Warsaw University in 1923. As a university student he was active in the Socialist youth movement and the Polish Socialist Party. He held teaching positions with the Institute of Eastern Europe (Wilno) and the State Institute of Theatrical Arts (Warsaw), and for a time he was a member of the editorial boards of several Polish monthlies. Since 1940 he has been living in the United States. He has published ten books in Polish on social, cultural, and educational matters, and has contributed to various periodicals, in Poland and elsewhere, including a number of articles to *Kultura*, and various articles in English.

PAWEŁ HOSTOWIEC (see Jerzy Stempowski).

KONSTANTY A. JELEŃSKI was born in Warsaw in 1922. He studied in Austria, Switzerland, and Great Britain (Saint Andrew's University and Oxford). During World War II he fought in Normandy in the Polish Armored Division. A noted publicist and art critic, he lives in Paris, contributes frequently to *Kultura*, is a staff writer of the French monthly *Preuves*, and is an active member of the Congress of Cultural Freedom.

ZBIGNIEW A. JORDAN was born in Poland in 1911 and studied in Poznan, Bonn, and Paris. He fought in World War II with the First Polish Armoured Division. He is now Professor of the Philosophy of the Social Sciences at Carleton University, Canada. His works, published in Polish and English, include *The Development of Mathematical Logic and of Logical Positivism in Poland between Two Wars* (Oxford University Press, 1945), *Philosophy and Ideology* (Dordrecht, 1963), and *The Evolution of Dialectical Materialism* (London, 1967).

JURIJ ŁAWRYNENKO was born as a son of a peasant family in the area of Kiev, Ukraine, in 1905, and studied history and linguistics at the University of Kharkov. He was arrested in 1929 and deported to a Siberian concentration camp. He later returned illegally to Kiev during World War II and, after Hitler's army invaded the Soviet Union, he was arrested by the Germans and sent as a forced laborer to Germany. Liberated by the Allies in 1945, he remained in Western Europe, editing and contributing to various Ukrainian emigré publications.

Since 1950, he has been in the United States, where he published a major work entitled *Ukrainian Communism and Russian Policy toward the Ukraine.* He was founder of the Ukrainian Writers Union in New York, and is a member of the PEN-Club in Exile.

BOGUSŁAW MIEDZIŃSKI was born in southern Poland in 1891. He studied at the Lwow Politechnic, and the Jagellonian University in Cracow.

From high school days on, he maintained contact with the PPS (Polish Socialist Party) and was used for auxiliary service in the Combat Organization of the PPS. As one of five officers of the POW (Polish Military Organization) at the rear of the Russian Army, he was appointed Second Lieutenant of the First Brigade by Piłsudski. In 1918, he was Supreme Commander of the POW in Kiev. In 1921, he joined the adjutancy of the Chief of State. After the May, 1926 *coup d'état*, he became Minister of Posts and Telegraphs. In 1929 he assumed the editorship of *Gazeta Polska* (The Polish Gazette), the official paper of Marshall Piłsudski's political group. After the September campaign of 1939, he escaped via Rumania and Italy to France. At the beginning of 1941, he entered the army. Since 1947 he has lived in England.

JULIUSZ MIEROSZEWSKI was born in Cracow, Poland in 1906. He studied law at Cracow University and graduated at the Higher School of Trade and Commerce. Until 1939, he was on the editorial staff of *Ilustrowany Kurier Codzienny*, one of the major newspapers of Eastern Europe. He specialized in German affairs.

Mieroszewski was in Bucharest in September, 1939. For a year, he worked there in the office of the Polish Military Attaché. He then joined the Polish Independent Carpathian Brigade, fighting in Africa, and subsequently the 2nd Polish Corps, with which he served until the end of the Italian Campaign. After the war, he joined the Polish exile community in London. Since 1949, he has been the London editor and chief political publicist of *Kultura*, and has published several books in Polish and German. In English he has published *What Europe Thinks of America* (with others) (New York: John Day Company, 1953). He has translated into Polish the works of Arnold Toynbee, George Orwell, Bertrand Russell, and Lionel Trilling.

VLASTA ŠLIKOVA is a pseudonym of a Czechoslovakian female writer whose moral and ideological ponderings have reached the West after the recent tragic events in Czechoslovakia.

ANDRZEJ STAWAR was born in 1900 as a son of poor Polish peasants. He joined the Polish Communist Party in the early 'twenties, and published many articles and brochures, in which he fought for Marxist ideas in the field of art and culture. After the Stalinist purges and the Moscow trials of the late 'thirties, he left the party and published periodicals considered as schismatic by faithful Stalinists. During the war he was a refugee in Hungary. After the war he came back to Poland, became a high-ranking official in the communist Ministry of Culture, and achieved a remarkable position as a Marxist literary critic. In 1961, during a trip to France, he refused to return and offered his writings, which were censored and prohibited in Communist Poland, to the *Institut Littéraire* for publication. Mr. Stawar died in 1961.

JERZY STEMPOWSKI (*Paweł Hostowiec*) was born in Cracow in 1894. He was educated in Warsaw, and studied history and medicine in Cracow, Munich, Geneva, and Zurich. After World War II he worked in the Polish Foreign Ministry and as a representative of the official Polish news agency in France, Switzerland, and Germany. After a short period of public service, he devoted himself to writing, chiefly to historical and philosophical essays. He is well-known as a cultural critic and contributor to intellectual journals in pre-war Poland. Since World War II, he has lived in Switzerland and is one of the closest *Kultura* associates.

ALEKSANDER WAT was born in Poland in 1900, and studied philosophy at Warsaw University. In 1919 he made his debut with a volume of *avant-garde* poetical prose. He was an author of poetry, short stories, and essays, and was publishing literary periodicals of the Polish intellectual Left of the 'twenties and 'thirties. After the outbreak of World War II, he was arrested by the Soviet secret police and imprisoned in Russia. He was repatriated after the war to Poland, where he refused to publish anything except translations from foreign languages. After 1956 his poetry reappeared in the Polish literary press. Mr. Wat spent the last years of his life living in Paris, contributing to *Kultura*. He died in 1967.